PARTNERSHIP AND CHANGE

Partnership and Change
Toward School Development

Edited by

John Chi-kin Lee, Leslie Nai-kwai Lo
and Allan Walker

The Chinese University Press

**Hong Kong Institute of
Educational Research**

This is a collection of selected articles from the international conference "Rejuvenating Schools through Partnership," which is part of the Accelerated Schools for Quality Education Project sponsored by the Quality Education Fund.

Partnership and Change: Toward School Development
  Edited by John Chi-kin Lee, Leslie Nai-kwai Lo and
  Allan Walker

© **The Chinese University of Hong Kong**, 2004

ISBN 962–996–113–X

THE CHINESE UNIVERSITY PRESS
The Chinese University of Hong Kong
SHA TIN, N.T., HONG KONG
Fax: +852 2603 6692
    +852 2603 7355
E-mail: cup@cuhk.edu.hk
Web-site: www.chineseupress.com

**HONG KONG INSTITUTE OF
EDUCATIONAL RESEARCH**
The Chinese University of Hong Kong
SHA TIN, N.T., HONG KONG
Fax: +852 2603 6850
E-mail: hkier@cuhk.edu.hk
Web-site: www.fed.cuhk.edu.hk/~hkier

Printed in Hong Kong

Hong Kong Institute of Educational Research

The Hong Kong Institute of Educational Research (HKIER) was inaugurated in September 1993. Its founding was made possible by the fervent support of the Tin Ka Ping Foundation with a generous donation designated as the setting-up costs and operating capital. The Institute helps to strengthen the roles of The Chinese University of Hong Kong as a leading centre of educational research, as a responsible institution that addresses the needs of the teaching profession, and as an active consulting agent for international organisations, public agencies, and local education bodies. It also helps to strengthen the University's ties with local schools and overseas institutions. Projects initiated by the Institute are to facilitate educational planning, produce policy alternatives, and enlighten policy makers and members of the educational profession.

The objectives of the Institute are to conduct strategic research with strong policy implications for educational developments in China and Hong Kong; to effectively deploy resources for educational research; to disseminate research ideas and findings in publications of journals and books; to promote the role of the Institute as a consultant and a development agent; and to win international recognition of its work.

Director	Professor Leslie Lo Nai-kwai, Faculty of Education The Chinese University of Hong Kong
Associate Directors	Professor Hau Kit-tai, Faculty of Education The Chinese University of Hong Kong
	Professor Tsang Wing-kwong, Faculty of Education The Chinese University of Hong Kong
	Professor Wong Hin-wah, Faculty of Education The Chinese University of Hong Kong

Contents

Part Two: Changes in School Development

Conclusion

Acknowledgments

The Editors would like to thank the Quality Education Fund for sponsoring the Accelerated Schools for Quality Education Project and the associated international conference "Rejuvenating Schools through Partnership" held in May 2001 at The Chinese University of Hong Kong. For the conference, we would like to thank other members of the organizing committee who include Professors Stephen Yue-ping Chung, David Wai-ock Chan, Derek Sin-pui Cheung, Fan-sing Hung, Ling-po Siu, Hin-wah Wong and Mr. Yee-wang Fung. Thanks are extended to the HKSAR Education Department, Caput Schools Council, Grant Schools Council, Hong Kong Prevocational Schools Council, Hong Kong Private Schools Association, Hong Kong Special Schools Council, Hong Kong Subsidized Secondary Schools Council, and Subsidized Primary Schools Council as collaborators for the conference. Moreover, we would like to thank Ms. Erica Ho for supporting the conference organization and Professor Tsang Wing-kwong for supporting the publication of this book. The Editors would like to thank the reviewers for their useful comments for improving the manuscript as well as Mr. Fung Wai-kit of the Hong Kong Institute of Educational Research and colleagues at The Chinese University Press for their technical help in copyediting. Thanks are extended to the Centre for University and School Partnership, the Hong Kong Institute of Educational Research, and The Chinese University Press for making this publication possible.

Contributors

Gunnar F. Berg is Professor in Education at Uppsala University and University of Dalarna, Sweden and Visiting Professor at Universy of Tromsö, Norway. His research areas cover such topics as the school as an state and societal institution and schools as organizations, teacher professionalism, implementation of educational reforms, school development and school leadership and management.

Bill Boyle is Director of CFAS, University of Manchester, U.K. CFAS is the largest independent education and social science research group in the U.K. Currently he directs the Monitoring of Curriculum and Assessment Project (QCA), a longitudinal study of professional development models for teachers and their impact on school effectiveness and a number of short-term research projects for QCA and TTA. He is also lead consultant in CFAS's curriculum and assessment work with the Gulf Arab States Education Research Council.

Nicole Breeze has been a key agent for social justice through her work at the Edmund Rice Centre for Justice and Community Education in New South Wales (NSW). She has had responsibility for the carriage of the Community Outreach Program at the School of Education in NSW at the Australian Catholic University. Her work for social justice has involved her working around the globe including Brazil, England, Ireland and various parts of Australia.

Jude Butcher is the Head of School Education, New South Wales, and is Chair of the Management Committee of the Edmund Rice Centre for Justice and Community Education. Jude's research has been in the areas of professional development, partnerships between different organizations and sectors, benchmarking community service in teacher education, student community service learning, and social responsibility indicators for policy, practice and performance.

Chan Hung-ki, Thomas is Lecturer in the Department of Educational Psychology, Counselling and Learning Needs at The Hong Kong Institute of Education. He is specialized in the education of the mentally disabled children. Having a strong interest to develop relationship with China's special schools, he also provides consultancy to special schools in Shanghai.

Mary Cheung is Headteacher of T.W.G.Hs. Ko Ho Ning Memorial Primary School, Hong Kong. Her research interests include learning organization and action research in curriculum.

Cheung Siu-ming joined the English Schools Foundation (ESF) from the U.K., where he was an Education Department Adviser in the London Borough of Lambeth. He was Deputy Principal at West Island School and a member of the ESF's Ensuring Excellence Project team, funded by the Hong Kong Quality Education Fund. He was later a project director planning the curriculum of new ESF private independent schools. He is now Principal of Phoenix International School, a private independent school operated by ESF Educational Services Ltd.

Per Dalin created the "IMTEC Foundation" in 1972, with the purpose of being an active partner in school development and research in the process of educational change worldwide. He is Professor of Pedagogy at the University of Oslo. He has published some 20 books, and has worked with educational development projects in 30 countries, both in industrialized as well as in developing countries.

Sue Dockett was Head of Early Childhood Teacher Education, School of Education and Early Childhood Studies, University of Western Sydney, Australia in 2002. She is currently co-director of the Starting School Research Project at the university, and specializes in early childhood education, especially in the areas of play, children's thinking and transition to school.

Richard Dyer is currently Deputy Principal at West Island School in Hong Kong. He is responsible for the development of school self-evaluation at the school and was a member of the Quality Education Fund Ensuring Excellence Project from 1998 to 2002. He is also involved in running a course on school self-evaluation for serving teachers at the University of

Hong Kong. He is engaged in doctoral research into teacher professionalism and cultures in primary schools.

Christine Ebert is Professor in Instruction and Teacher Education and Associate Dean of the The Graduate School at the University of South Carolina (USC), Columbia. Her areas of expertise are elementary science and teacher education. She has worked in the development of USC's Professional Development School Network for over 10 years and authored four books. *Changing the Classroom from Within* is based on her work at Pontiac Elementary, one of USC's Professional Development Schools.

Ho Fuk-chuen is Lecturer in the Department of Educational Psychology, Counselling and Learning Needs at The Hong Kong Institute of Education. He was previously an inspector in the Special Education Inspectorate at the Education Department. He has also been engaged in two research projects on autism and dyslexia.

David Hopkins is Head of the Standards and Effectiveness Unit at the Department for Education and Skills, and in that position is the Chief Adviser to Ministers on Standards issues. Between 1999 and 2002 he was Chair of the Leicester City Partnership Board and a member of the Governing Council of the National Colleges for School Leadership. Previously, between 1996 and 2002, David was Professor of Education at the University of Nottingham where he served as both Head of the School, Dean of the Faculty of Education and now as Professor Emeritus. His professional interests are in the areas of teacher and school development, teaching and learning, educational change, teacher education, and policy implementation. He has published over 30 books on these themes.

Peter Howard is Senior Lecturer in the Faculty of Education NSW of the Australian Catholic University. He has a particular interest in the human quality dimensions of the teacher educator as it applies to social justice awareness and equity-based issues. In his administrative role as Coordinator-Community Outreach he has been responsible for the implementation of a program that supports teacher education students in their personal growth and efficacy in learning through community service and identifying the implications for classroom teaching. He has published papers and conference presentations in the areas of mathematics education, community service learning and early childhood education.

Hui Leng-han, Martha is Senior Lecturer in the Department of Educational Psychology, Counselling and Learning Needs at The Hong Kong Institute of Education. She has rich experiences in teaching children with special educational needs and is also an experienced teacher trainer in that area. She is actively involved in a number of research projects in special needs education and in Quality Education Fund (QEF) projects. She was previously a member of the QEF Assessment Sub-Committee and Working Group on QEF Dissemination Work.

Elizabeth Labone is Lecturer in the School of Education at the Australian Catholic University. Her interest is particularly in the development and enhancement of efficacy beliefs. She is currently involved in researching the outcomes of the Community Outreach Program within the School of Education, with particular emphasis on the development of efficacy beliefs through this type of social engagement.

Edith Lai is Assistant Professor in the School of Education and Languages, The Open University of Hong Kong (OUHK). Before joining OUHK, she was Teaching Consultant and Project Manager of the Unified Professional Development Project in the Department of Curriculum Studies, The University of Hong Kong.

Iasonas Lamprianou joined the Centre for Formative Assessment Studies (CFAS) in 1999 as an analyst. He is currently working as a Research Fellow on projects involving educational assessment, measurement, test equating and Item Banking. His research interests include psychometrics and specially test-equating, Item Response Models and person-fit statistics. Currently, he is mainly involved as an analyst contributing to the Standards and Evaluation Reports for the National Curriculum (NC) tests. He is also generating diagnostic feedback for schools based on scrutinized NC test results.

John Chi-kin Lee is Dean of Faculty of Education, The Chinese University of Hong Kong (CUHK) and Professor in the Department of Curriculum and Instruction. He is also Director of the Centre for University and School Partnership at the CUHK.

Henry M. Levin is the William Heard Kilpatrick Professor of Economics and Education and Director of the National Center for the Study of Privatization in Education at Teachers College, Columbia University. He is the David Jacks Professor of Higher Education and Economics, *Emeritus*, at Stanford University. Levin is the founder of the Accelerated Schools Project and an author or co-author of 16 books and about 300 academic articles. He has also been an advisor to the Hong Kong Accelerated Schools Quality Education Project in Hong Kong.

Bernard V. Lim is Professor in the Department of Architecture, The Chinese University of Hong Kong. He has established professional specialization/research in areas of (1) educational, elderly and institutional buildings, (2) energy efficiency designs, and (3) community participatory planning and workshops. He has been actively leading a research in "Developing Innovative School Design Parameters for Hong Kong" supported by the Quality Education Fund in collaboration with the Education Department and The Hong Kong Institute of Architects (HKIA). Since 1996, he has been a Council Member of the HKIA contributing particularly in new initiatives for community development and partnership with schools.

Leslie Nai-kwai Lo is Chair Professor of Educational Administration and Policy, Faculty of Education, The Chinese University of Hong Kong. He is also Director of the Hong Kong Institute of Educational Research.

Lo Mun-ling is Principal Lecturer and Head of the Centre for the Development of School Partnership and Field Experience of The Hong Kong Institute of Education (HKIED). Before joining the HKIED in October 2001, she was Associate Professor and Project Director of the Unified Professional Development Project at the Department of Curriculum Studies, the University of Hong Kong.

Pang Sun-keung, Nicholas is Associate Professor in the Department of Educational Administration and Policy, The Chinese University of Hong Kong. His research interests include administrative and organizational theories, organizational culture and climate, school effectiveness and excellence, school-based management, school self-evaluation and performance indicators, quality of school life, as well as educational research methodology and applied statistics.

William H. Parrett is Director of the Center for School Improvement and Professor of Education at Boise State University. He has received international recognition for his work in school improvement, small schools, alternative education, and for his efforts to help youth at-risk. His professional contributions include public school and university teaching, curriculum design, principalships and college leadership, media production, research and publication.

Bob Perry was Head of Primary Teacher Education, School of Education and Early Childhood Studies, University of Western Sydney, Australia in 2002. He is currently co-director of the Starting School Research Project at the university, and specializes in mathematics education and early childhood education, particularly transition to school.

Sin Kuen-fung, Kenneth is Senior Lecturer in the Department of Educational Psychology, Counselling and Learning Needs at The Hong Kong Institute of Education. He was previously a teacher of children with special educational needs. His expertise lies in the area of emotional disorders, learning difficulties and information technology in special education.

Irma J. Van Scoy is Associate Professor in Instruction and Teacher Education and Associate Dean of the College of Education at the University of South Carolina (USC), Columbia. She is a Leadership Associate with Goodlad's National Network for Educational Renewal and has worked in the development of USC's Professional Development School Network for over 10 years. Her areas of expertise are early childhood development and curriculum and teacher education.

Allan Walker is professor and Chair of the Department of Educational Administration and Policy at the Chinese University of Hong Kong. He is also Associate Director of the Hong Kong Centre for the Development of Educational Leadership. He has been a teacher and principal and worked in universities in Australia and Hong Kong. His research interests include principalship preparation and development, cultural influence on school leadership and leadership needs analysis.

Scott Willison is Director of the Center for Multicultural and Educational

Opportunities and Associate Professor of Education at Boise State University. He was a high school administrator and directed the development of alternative school programs. He has published and presented on topics related to alternative education, multicultural education and innovative teaching strategies including the use of portfolios as an assessment tool for teacher education graduates.

1

Partnership and Change for School Development

John Chi-kin Lee, Leslie Nai-kwai Lo & Allan Walker

Introduction

School restructuring is very much on everyone's agenda in the new millennium. There is a growing movement for schools to become involved in partnerships with key players in the educational system to enhance the quality of school education and make them maximally relevant in the 21st century. There is also a call for national decisions to reflect on purposes of schooling such as "to learn to know, to learn to do, to learn to live together, to learn to be" (Hughes, 1999, p. 27) which have implications for curriculum, organization and connections as well as teaching staff and students. A wave of major reforms in school administration, curriculum, teaching and learning began in some countries in the late 1980s. In England and Wales, for example, the introduction of a national curriculum in 1988 was followed by school-site management known as the Local Management of Schools (LMS) (O'Donoghue & Dimmock, 1998). In Australia, a National Project on the Quality of Teaching and Learning started in 1991, and in the late 1990s, there was a trend toward standardizing assessments at key stages of the curriculum (Dimmock & Lee, 2000). In Chinese Mainland and Taiwan, curriculum and school reforms as well as issues on teacher development receive strong attention in the education arena (Lo, 2000; Ou, 1999, 2000). One of the proposed strategies adopted by the Education Commission's (2000) educational blueprint *Learning for Life, Learning through Life* for reforming the educational system in Hong Kong is to forge partnerships between schools and different sectors of society to provide students with diversified learning activities and to make better use of the support that these bodies can offer. The recently released document by Curriculum Development Council (2001) endorses "the emphasis on partnership/ collaboration with different parties, with the whole of society contributing, instead of a top-down approach to development" (p. 4).

Over the last decade, educational policy-makers, principals, and teachers alike in many diverse countries strive to devise ways of changing schools to meet changing needs. Various commentators have described educational reform from the mid-1980s as moving through at least three waves (Murphy, 1990). First-wave reforms targeted school and student achievement through course and testing mandates; second-wave reforms concentrated on teaching and teacher education; and third-wave reforms emphasize defining more challenging standards for learning while restructuring schools so that they can produce dramatically better outcomes (Darling-Hammond, 1997, p. 5; Walker & Dimmock, 2000, p. 5). According to Elmore (1990), there are three main approaches to school restructuring: reforming the core technology of schools, reforming the occupational conditions of teaching, and reforming the relationship between schools and their clients. In a similar vein, Murphy (1991) suggests three major components of restructuring, namely revisions to the core technology, changes in the design of work, and alterations in organization and governance structure. There are also prevalent strategies for reframing education such as choice and voice, school-based management, teacher empowerment, and teaching for understanding. Ou (1999, p. 58; 2000, p. 228) and others (e.g., Lee, 2002) suggest restructuring, re-schooling, reculturing and reconceptualizing as approaches for reforming schools and curriculum.

All these restructuring efforts lead to the emergence of two major themes of school restructuring, as Murphy (1993) concludes: the mercerization of education and the redefinition of the roles of educational stakeholders. One of the issues related to the mercerization of education is to expand the availability of alternative schools such as the charter school movement in the United States. With regard to the roles of educational stakeholders, students are expected to become active constructors of their own understanding. Teachers in turn act as facilitators and employ teaching methods that are "designed to give students the opportunity to observe, engage in, and invent or discover expert strategies in context" (Collins,

Hawkins, & Carver, 1991, p. 178; Murphy, 1993, p. 14). The redefinition of the role of teachers also calls for more control over their profession and the routines of the workplace. Teaching is seen as a collaborative activity and at a micro level, new organizational structures are created to allow teachers to plan and teach together. New conception of teaching also expands teacher roles to become mentor teacher, master teacher, and even teacher-director (Murphy, 1991). Principal's role is reframed toward transformational leadership, which encourages teacher empowerment and shared decision-making. Parents become partners in the school restructuring movement and they are solicited to work with the school to help create a healthy and caring learning environment conducive to students' success — an environment in which home and community are emphasized. In essence, key players in the school system needs to act in a consistent, concerted, and coherent way for successful implementation of the new curriculum and school restructuring (Dimmock & Lee, 2000). Schools, historically perceived as sheltered monopolies, or delivery systems, become more accountable to the public, and relationship between schools and the public is reworked toward partnerships (Murphy, 1991, p. 17).

Because of the changing context of school reform, various national governments, school improvement projects, and school development consultants have come up with various strategies for school improvement. Dalin (1998), based on an extensive review, concludes that there are individual, organizational, and system strategies. Individual strategies tend to view the teacher and principal (headteacher) as change agents and involve initiatives in forms of pre-service, in-service, and management training that might influence attitudes, knowledge, or skills. In addition, pupils and parents can play an active part in school development (e.g., Epstein, 1994; Rudduck, Chaplain, & Wallace, 1996). Organizational strategies tend to focus on school as the unit of change and a learning organization. Often internal and/or external organizational development consultants are recruited to help build school's internal capacity for change. In addition, internal school evaluation, which is widespread in the Anglo-American community, is seen as a strategy for change. MacBeath (1999) further remarks that school self-evaluation may serve such purposes as accountability, professional development, organizational development, improvement of teaching, and improvement of learning. System strategies tend to emphasize the state having a development rather than a maintenance function for the quality of schooling as a consequence of decentralized management. MacBeath (1999) and others (e.g., Barber & Phillips, 2000; Lee, 1999) suggest an optimum blend/fusion of support and pressure, bottom-up and top-down change, as well as internal and external evaluation. With respect to change forces, Fullan (1993) strongly argues for the construction of alliances and partnerships as major vehicles for learning. He states that "school systems and universities — two learning organizations working at internal development, and external collaboration with each other. This is what will be required for the future" (p. 120).

University-School Partnerships: From Teacher Development to School Development

There have been enduring practices of partnerships between individual university tutors and schoolteachers, particularly in terms of supervisory/ mentoring or "provider-led" relationships between tutors and teachers in the teacher training/development programs, as well as research and development relationships between university tutors and the education community. Nonetheless, the nature of these "partnerships" has evolved over the last decade partly because of the impact of educational reforms. As Day (1998) remarks succinctly, "the usefulness, rigor and relevance of university research has been called into question and universities have been forced to compete for custom as their own standards of research and teaching have come under close finance led, ideologically determined public scrutiny" (p. 807).

Professional Development Schools: University-School Partnership for Developing a Profession and School Renewal

With regard to teacher education in the United States for example, there have been concerns about the preparation of teachers as follows (Clark, 1999, pp. 5–8):

1. Teachers do not know enough to teach about the responsibilities of living in a democracy.
2. Colleges and universities provide little sustained commitment to teacher education.
3. Because of teacher shortage, some states allow teacher certification through questionable shortcut programs.

4. The undergraduate curriculum is inadequate for prospective teachers.
5. The socialization of new teachers tends to reinforce the status quo.

The emergence of the Holmes Group, a national reform-minded consortium of research universities committed to excellence in the preparation of teachers, had led to the establishment of Professional Development Schools (PDSs). According to the Holmes Group's (1986) report, PDSs

> provide superior opportunities for teachers and administrators to influence the development of their profession, and for university faculty to increase the professional relevance of their work, through (1) mutual deliberation on problems with student learning, and their possible solutions; (2) shared teaching in the university and schools; (3) collaborative research on the problems of educational practice; and (4) cooperative supervision of prospective teachers and administrators. (p. 56)

Nonetheless, there are some variations in practices of PDS. In the case of PDS organized by the Ohio States University, there are PDSs situated in one school, networks bringing specialist teachers from many schools together, and consortium of groups of teachers and their administrator from several schools. There are also diversity in subject matter focus, subject focus, and teaching approaches (Johnston, 2000). For the partner schools or PDSs in John Goodlad's National Network for Educational Renewal (NNER) serve four main purposes (Clark, 1999): (1) pre-service teacher preparation through components of admission, team building, curriculum and instruction, and portfolio evaluation process; (2) professional development through networking within and across schools in the school-university partnership; (3) inquiry efforts providing answers or solutions to questions raised by schoolteachers, university faculty, local school/district board, and individuals seeking professional growth; and (4) school renewal related to learner-centered practice through school quality review process and school renewal activities such as special courses and seminars.

Nature of, Benefits and Barriers for Developing University-School Partnerships

Day (1999, p. 154) reviews on issues related to learning through partnerships and he gives examples of partnerships between higher education tutors and school practitioners including:

1. Limited term development consultancies related to preparation for external inspection, areas of curriculum, teaching and assessment, team building or appraisal;
2. External audit support related to auditing of an aspect of school policy, evaluation of the effectiveness of school programs, strategies for supporting teachers' professional development, etc.;
3. Producing and disseminating research knowledge about education;
4. Generating education knowledge, for example, through collaborative action research work; and
5. Building communities of intelligent practice in which teachers from different schools or groups work together with education personnel over a period of years on a project related to school development.

In addition, there have been various interpretations of partnerships (e.g., Wang & Wong, 2001). With regard to the relationships between advisory teacher and schoolteachers, Biott (1992, p. 11) makes distinctions between implementation partnerships and development partnerships. The former refers to being imposed, formal/planned, brief events, mechanistic, discharging of specified duties, and having high prediction. Being voluntary, informal/spontaneous, sustained/evolving, organic, responsive, and having low prediction characterize the latter. Goodlad (1988) instead suggests the concept of "symbiosis" in university-school partnership by stating:

> For there to be a symbiotic partnership, presumably three minimum conditions must prevail: dissimilarity between or among the partners; mutual satisfaction of self-interests; and sufficient selflessness on the part of each member to assure the satisfaction of self-interests on the part of all members. (p. 14)

In essence, it is imperative to make use of win-win strategies for fostering university-school partnerships (Tang & Lee, 1999). Clark (1988) suggests that there are possible gains from collaboration in school-university partnerships. Firstly, schools and universities both can develop a stronger position and promote change by collaboration. Secondly, they can acquire additional resources. Schools can benefit from obtaining training, curriculum development and evaluation services while universities can enhance status, research and development opportunities.

While there are perceived benefits of school-university partnerships, there exist prevailing barriers. With regard to PDS as a form of school-university partnerships, Berry and Catoe (1994, pp. 192–197) identify six categories of barriers:

1. Miscommunication and a lack of education — lack of communication within the College of Education and across the departments;
2. The limits of time and rewards — lacking time for team planning and university faculty expecting rewards associated with PDS work;
3. Territorial imperatives — a divisive public funding structure, institutional mistrust, and partisan politics which may not be conducive to creating PDSs which demands diverse leadership and connected influence;
4. Overstuffed agenda and curricular disconnections — lacking regular communication among teachers, university faculty and district administrators;
5. Policy disconnections — competing policy initiatives between emphasis on inventive teaching for understanding by College of Education faculty and emphasis on teaching isolated skills by school may deter building up a shared view of teaching; and
6. The press for equality among K-12 schools — a tension between building resource-enriched PDSs by the university and maintaining equality among schools by school district administrators and school board members.

Other than PDSs, Kersh and Masztal (1998), on the basis of an analysis of studies of collaboration between universities and K-12 schools conclude that the following essential components are needed for fostering successful partnerships:

1. The nature of reform
   • Various parties such as parents, teachers, administrators, and other school personnel need to be involved in the discussion, planning, and implementation of reform, which should reflect the genuine problem the school has encountered.
   • Time commitment to, understanding of, and involvement in the reform efforts is a critical element.
   • Patience, long-term planning, and establishment of attainable goals are essential.
   • Workshops alone do not transform schools. Active participation in the creation, development, and reflection in evaluating the

effectiveness of the materials is more useful to help teachers embrace the changes as their own.

2. The nature of partnership
   - Partnership necessitates commitment, respect, trust, equity, cooperation, flexibility, dialogue as well as shared leadership.
   - Communication and building shared vision can help reduce ambiguity, uncertainty, conflict, and confusion.
   - Funding is necessary for compensating and releasing both parties' time.
3. The school
   - Collaborations involving teachers as project leaders are valuable. Leadership training and empowerment (e.g., through site-based management), however, need to be provided to teachers acting as leaders and trainers.
   - Successful collaborations need to reach out to parents and community members.
4. The university
   - University faculty needs to act as inquirers rather than experts in leading reforms.
   - University personnel may take part in the evaluative aspect of the partnership but it is better to conduct evaluation "with" than "to" the school participants.

University-School Partnerships for Large-Scale Change Initiatives

With regard to projects related to school development, some universities in the United States and the United Kingdom, for example, have been involved in launching large-scale change initiatives based on particular programs or models. In the United States, such programs are basically divided into two categories, namely comprehensive reform and curricular reform (Wang, Haertel, & Walberg, 1998). The former is exemplified by the *Accelerated Schools Project* founded by Henry Levin (1998) at Stanford University (now at Teachers College, Columbia University) (Chapter 2 in this book; Finnan, St. John, McCarthy, & Slovacek, 1996), *Community for Learning* developed by Margaret Wang (1992) at Temple University, *Coalition of Essential Schools* founded by Theodore Sizer (1986) at Brown University, *School Development Project/Program* developed by James Comer (1996) at the Yale University and *ATLAS* (Authentic Teaching, Learning, and Assessment for all Students) communities initially developed through a collaborative effort among Coalition of Essential Schools, School Development Program, Project Zero (founded by Howard Gardner and David Perkins at Harvard University), and Education Development Center as well as three school districts. The latter is represented by *Success for All* developed by Robert Slavin at the Johns Hopkins University, and *Paideia program* founded by Mortimer Adler (now based at the National Paideia Center at the University of North Carolina, Chapel Hill) (McChesney & Hertling, 2000; Protheroe & Perkins-Gough, 1998).[1] According to Education Research Service, a comprehensive school reform program encompasses all the following components (Protheroe & Perkins-Gough, 1998, pp. 10–11):

1. Effective, research-based methods and strategies;
2. Comprehensive design with aligned components;
3. Professional development;
4. Measurable goals and benchmarks;
5. Support within the school by school faculty, administrators and staff;
6. Parental and community involvement;
7. External technical support and assistance;
8. Evaluation strategies; and
9. Coordination of resources.

In the United Kingdom, some universities have also engaged in school reform initiatives since the early 1990s. One of the well-known projects is the *Improving the Quality of Education for All* (IQEA) originally led by David Hopkins, Mel Ainscow, Mel West and other colleagues at the University of Cambridge Institute of Education. It is now based both in Cambridge and at the University of Nottingham involving over 100 schools in the network (Hopkins, Ainscow, & West, 1994; Hopkins, West, & Ainscow, 1996; West, 1998; West, Jackson, Harris, & Hopkins, 2000). As early as the 1980s, some scholars such as Brian Caldwell and Jim Spinks tried the Collaborative School Management (CSM) Model in Tasmanian schools, later applied to schools in Victoria and Western Australia. The CSM approach, for example, involved Victorian schools in "drawing up their own School Improvement Plan, whereby each council, through a collaborative process of planning between parents, students and teachers, submits a plan for a cyclical evaluation of their school activities with the ultimate goal of improving learning experiences for all students" (Marsh, 1988, p. 184). Action Research approach to school improvement has also developed in Australia through the initiation and development by, for example, Stephen Kemmis and Robin McTaggart (1982) at Deakin University, Shirley Grundy (1987) at the University of New England, as well as David Tripp at Murdoch University.

Changes in School Development: Toward New Professionalism and Visions of Future Schooling

As discussed in the previous section, there have been attempts in restructuring schools and university-school partnerships for enhancing quality education in schools. While there are success stories of school reform, there are also deep-seated problems and limitations in school and society that have not made these reform efforts work effectively. Our times are situated in an age of paradoxes and there have been concerns about the dilemma of educational purpose schools face, such as the tension between serving the needs of the market place and the requirements of democratic living (Stoll & Fink, 1996). Andy Hargreaves (1995) comments on the paradoxes affecting education and he asserts that the paradox influences "stronger orientation to the future and create[s] greater nostalgia for the past" (p. 15). Stoll and Fink (1996) further remark that "this is the paradox of change *and* continuity, and this is the fundamental paradox for schools" (p. 4).

Not only are schools facing paradoxes of change, but also teaching is a "paradoxical profession" (Hargreaves & Lo, 2000). While there are calls for teacher's new professionalism, the forces of deprofessionalization such as declining support, intensification of work, standardization, and restricted opportunities of professional learning has affected the progress of school development in many countries. In some societies such as Hong Kong, the increase in control over teachers stems from dissatisfaction with certain aspects of schooling that may be linked with the teachers. The assumption is that poor learning outcomes are associated with certain deficiencies in the knowledge, skills, or qualities of teachers. This "deficit" view about teachers and teaching does not help teachers work effectively in school systems that are burdened by ability segregation. On the contrary, it exerts more pressure on teachers who are struggling to find an appropriate pedagogical approach for the compulsory education. To help overcome these constraints and establish the new professionalism, there is a need to encourage a sense of purpose, collegiality, room for professional growth through strategies of teacher empowerment and support (Lo, 2000, pp. 248–249). In addition, Morris, Lo, and Adamson (2000) echo that the deficit models of teachers and pedagogy have been paradoxically central to the development of educational reform in Hong Kong. They argue that we should learn from good practices in the past just as

> we do not expect pupils to learn and improve if their performance is constantly critiqued, if their prior learning is ignored, if good practices are not recognized, and if overall they are treated as empty vessels or blank sheets of paper with no prior history or achievements. The same applies to teachers and schools. (p. 262)

From the research perspective, there has been a significant development in the knowledge base of school effectiveness research (e.g., Teddlie & Reynolds, 2000) and linking school effectiveness and school improvement (e.g., Gray et al., 1999; MacBeath & Mortimore, 2001). Many theoretical and practical models of schooling have been suggested but before deciding which model for implementation, we need to ponder and answer the following questions (Dalin, in press):

1. Who is a student?
2. Who is a teacher?
3. What is the curriculum?
4. What is a textbook?
5. What/where is the classroom?
6. What is a productive use of the learning resources?
7. Who pays?
8. Who owns and who controls?
9. Can schools learn?
10. What do we want the school to be in Year 2020?

Townsend, Clarke, and Ainscow (1999, p. 363) propose that future schools, known as Third Millennium Schools, require some underlying "Third Millennium Thinking" or "integrative thinking about learning" (Clarke, 2000, p. 28) as follows:

1. People can learn things from many sources.
2. Everyone must understand the learning process and have basic learning skills.

3. The learning process is controlled by the learner.
4. Education and learning are highly interactive activities. Success is based on how well learners work together as a team.
5. Formal education is the basis for lifelong learning.
6. "School" is only one of a multitude of steps in the education journey.
7. Formal education provides a range of interactions between learners and the world of business, commerce and politics.
8. The more capability and adaptability you have, the more successful you will be.
9. Basic education is funded by both government and private sources.

To meet future demands from the information society and reflect on purposes of schooling, different scholars have offered visions of future schooling. Caldwell (1999) proposes a gestalt (vision) for schooling in the knowledge society, which consists of the following components:

1. Connectedness in curriculum — cutting across the subject boundaries and changing emphasis on excited lived exploration;
2. Workplace transformation — scheduling of time for learning and approaches to human resource management;
3. School fabric and globalization — everything from building design to the size, shape, alignment, and furnishing of space for the "knowledge worker" in the school needs transformation (schools having no walls);
4. Professionalism and great teaching — a wide range of professionals and paraprofessionals support learning in an education parallel to the diversity of support found in the health care profession;
5. Teams and pastoral care — emphasis on team and pastoral care of students;
6. Cyber-policy, access, and equity — common use of electronic networks for communication; and
7. Virtual schools — learning, networked electronically, occurs in various modes and from various sources.

Moreover, Stoll, MacBeath, and Mortimore (2001) look forward to the possibilities of school effectiveness and improvement beyond 2000 and suggest the following 10 imperatives:

1. Develop a wider range of skills and qualities for a fast-changing world.

2. Emphasize learners and learning and consider implications for teaching.
3. Listen to the pupil's voice.
4. Facilitate "deep" learning of teachers.
5. Promote self-evaluation.
6. Emphasize leadership and management.
7. Ensure high-quality critical friendship.
8. Build communities, networks and partnerships.
9. Take a "connected" approach to improvement.
10. Strive for sustainability of improvement.

All these suggestions seem to point to the importance of the following trends in future schooling:

1. Adopting student-centered learning, which emphasizes basic and generic skills such as working in teams, as the core for school development;
2. Viewing learning as interactive and lifelong activities with connections to the outside world;
3. Emphasizing teacher's professionalism and professional development;
4. Encouraging partnership and networking development, and involving professionals, paraprofessionals and stakeholders to work collaboratively in school development;
5. Stressing connectivity among leadership and management, curriculum, teaching, learning and assessment as well as provision of workplace for teachers and learning environments for students;
6. Using school self-evaluation for improvement; and
7. Providing basic education by public and private bodies.

Synopsis of the Book

When planning for this book, the Editors find that there has been a dearth of books covering themes and issues related to university-school partnerships and school development from an international perspective, particularly providing examples on university-school partnerships in the Asia-Pacific region. As Patterson, Michelli, and Pacheco (1999) comment on challenges of collaboration, "although hundreds of school-university partnerships exist, little has been written describing effective operation. New partnerships find little to inform their establishment and function" (p. 31). Most of the books in this area published to date tend to focus on certain projects or experiences from partner schools in the network (e.g., Clark, 1999). It is hoped that the book will fill this gap and enrich the discourses of rejuvenating schools through partnerships.

The book is broadly divided into two parts. Part One focuses on university-school partnership while Part Two highlights changes in school development. Contributors to this book are world-renowned scholars, school reformers, and experienced practitioners from the United States, Norway, Sweden, the United Kingdom, Australia, and Hong Kong. For the first part, Henry Levin in Chapter 2 emphasizes that schools tend to resist changes and school reform have not been highly successful around the world educational systems. He argues that schools need an internal transformation of culture, the empowerment of school participants to change their practices, expectations, and attitudes through an Accelerated Schools Project (ASP) process. The ASP process encompasses three principles (namely unity of purpose, empowerment coupled with responsibility, and building on strengths) and five steps (known as stock-taking, forging a vision, setting priorities, governance, and inquiry decision-making). In ASP in the United States, an external ASP coach, the principal, and an internal school facilitator work together as a team in transforming the school. While all of them take part in formal training workshops to learn the knowledge and skills required for setting up Accelerated Schools, coaches mentored by staff from ASP regional centers work at the school site on a weekly basis to build school's capacity and trouble-shoot challenges. For the implementation of ASP in Hong Kong through the Accelerated Schools for Quality Education Project (ASQEP), Levin presumes there have been differences in progress. Based on the U.S. experience, three hypotheses related to leadership, time, and examination pressures are put forward to explain the causes of differential progress. The first element depends on the leadership at the level of coaches (or School Development Officers in the Hong Kong model) and principals who have enthusiasm, commitment, skills as well as open attitudes toward change. The second element is related to the time committed to formal training for each phase of the ASP process as well as for internalizing inquiry process and implementing powerful learning. The last element is related to the view of examination results as the only recognized indicator of school quality.

In Chapter 3, John Lee discusses the initial experiences of the pioneering

Accelerated Schools for Quality Education Project (ASQEP) as a school reform laboratory in Hong Kong, which is a university-school partnership project serving 50 primary and secondary schools through a comprehensive approach to school change. ASQEP is adapted from ASP originated by Henry Levin in the United States, which has had about 16 years of success in several countries. ASQEP differs slightly from the U.S. model in the following three aspects: the buying-in process, the involvement of School Development Officers (coaches in the ASP model in the U.S.), and the stocktaking process. John Lee uses Larry Cuban's (1998) two major criteria for defining the success or failure of ASQEP. The first set of standards is related to effectiveness, popularity, and fidelity while the second set of standards is related to adaptiveness and survival (or longevity). With regard to the effectiveness standard, there seems to be significant improvements in teacher empowerment particularly in primary ASQEP schools and some gains in the quality of school life at Primary 6 as experienced by students. With regard to the popularity standard, there have been a lot of positive remarks made by the schools. On the fidelity standard, the project would have only partial success. With regard to the adaptiveness standard, schools have progressed closer to the ideals of ASQEP in varying aspects, in varying manners, and at varying speeds. The longevity (survival) standard is not yet applicable to the initiative. Some early lessons were learnt from ASQEP. One of them is that partnership development is context-specific and pivotal to the success of the project. This is to some extent affected by the role of the School Development Officers and the continuity of their work as well as the existence of a shared meaning of ASQEP among principals and teachers. Another lesson is that change takes time and that more time seems to be needed for change in secondary schools than in primary schools.

In Chapter 4, David Hopkins laments that although there has been a rhetoric of a principled and strategic approach to school improvement, there is in reality often a quick fix and pragmatic response to educational change. In addition, the short-term remedies focusing on bureaucratic interventions are not often conducive to enhancing student achievements and learning. Hopkins advocates authentic school improvement which has the following principles: achievement-focused, empowerment in aspiration, research-based and theory-rich, context-specific, capacity building in nature, inquiry-driven, implementation-oriented, interventionist and strategic, externally supported, and systemic. He went on to describe the "Improving the Quality of Education for All" (IQEA) project, an authentic school improvement program, which has been implemented in hundreds of schools in England and recently in Hong Kong and elsewhere. The IQEA program is conducted through a contract between the school and its teacher, and in some cases, the Local Education Authority (LEA) or sponsoring agency, and the IQEA team. The IQEA team provides training for the school coordinators and representatives, makes regular school visits, provides staff development materials, and monitors the implementation and progress of each school's project. The IQEA program has a clear focus on enhancing the learning experiences, achievement, and progress of pupils, which is supported by images of powerful learning, powerful teaching, and powerful school. It is further underpinned by three phases of school improvement: (1) establishing the process which involves commitment to the school improvement approach, selection of school improvement group or cadre, enquiring into the strengths and weaknesses of the school, designing the whole school program, seeking partners (e.g., university, LEA or commercial provider), and seeding the whole school approach; (2) going whole school which may include organizing the initial whole school INSET days, sharpening the curriculum and teaching focus, setting up the learning teams, undertaking the initial cycle of enquiry, and sharing initial success and impact on student learning on the curriculum tour; and (3) sustaining momentum which entails establishing further cycles of enquiry, building teacher learning into the process, sharpening the focus on student learning, finding ways of sharing success and building networks, and reflecting on the culture of the school and department.

Chapter 5, by Mun-ling Lo and Edith Lai, describes a university-school project known as the Unified Professional Development Project for Teachers and Student Teachers (UPDP), which aims at linking teacher education with school improvement on the one hand, and enhancing the professional development of teachers on the other. UPDP, to some extent resembling the Professional Development Schools movement in the United States, emerges because of the need to re-conceptualize the teaching practicum component in the initial teacher education programs at the University of Hong Kong. The project consists of three major components, namely the School-University Partnership Scheme, the Unified Professional Development Fellowship, and the School-based Development Consultancy. In the School-University Partnership Scheme, the whole school is involved in providing support to student teachers during teaching practicum. In addition, a formal induction program, mentoring, pre- and post-lesson tripartite conferences are provided to them. In the Unified Professional Development Fellowship, teachers from the partner schools are released from their teaching duties for a period of 3 to 5 months to engage in projects ranging from curriculum development, use of information technology in teaching and learning, teacher development to students' academic and social development. With regard to the School-based Development Consultancy, consultancy in such areas as the development of higher-order thinking skills, invitational education, the use of information technology in teaching and learning, and curriculum integration is offered to school. In Phase I of UPDP, Mun-ling and Edith remarked that matching school needs with the range of expertise available in the University was perceived to be the major challenge. In Phase II of the project, a focus is placed on the creation of a mentoring force for school improvement. More emphasis is given to collaborative studies between teachers and the university staff as well as grouping schools into clusters for collaboration and dissemination of good practice.

Chapter 6, by Irma Van Scoy and Christine Ebert, focuses on teacher development and empowerment through the Professional Development Schools (PDS) at the University of South Carolina (USC) of the United States. The USC PDS holds key assumptions such as building a community of learning, appreciating diversity and promoting social competence and justice, creating flexible and innovative organizational structures that support shared decision making, demonstrating essential good practice based on professional knowledge including teaching for understanding, engaging in inquiry and reflection about teaching and learning, and providing high-quality clinical experiences. The university-school partnership operates in areas including shared supervision of pre-service teachers, school-university action research, on-site university courses for pre- and in-service teachers, as well as collaboration through organizational structure and committees. The authors discuss the effects of PDS and it is found that there have been changes in teaching practices for university-based professors, school-based teachers, and pre-service teachers. Through pursuing further studies and undertaking action research projects, teachers generate and share their knowledge and experiences of teaching and learning. In addition, the PDS has provided opportunities for teachers to assume leadership roles of a coaching teacher, a clinical adjunct, a practicum instructor, a school-based supervisor, and even a national consultant to schools and universities that are developing PDS in other parts of the state and country.

Chapter 7 describes and analyzes a partnership between the Australian Catholic University and nationally based community agencies. The chapter also reports on a number of student outcomes from the partnership and shows how these vary from a richer and more personal understanding and appreciation of the world of the disadvantaged to a preparedness to address the sources of disadvantage. The partnership targeted the development of a community outreach program that included the integration of social analysis theory with the practical application of a social justice community placement. The partnership was grounded in a commitment to enhance the learning of all students, regardless of background or social status. This commitment recognized that the increasing diversity of student backgrounds and the number of students from low socio-economic areas requires teachers to develop an understanding of students' worlds and to be dedicated to social justice in all aspects of school and community life. In the chapter, the authors, Jude Butcher, Peter Howard, Elizabeth Labone and Nicole Breeze, suggest that school communities give priority to citizenship values and practices, become advocates for marginalized groups, and work with these groups to address the inequities they commonly experience. The authors challenge teachers to listen to the voices of their communities, particularly those of marginalized groups, and to ensure that they and their schools become engaged citizens who are committed to justice and equity.

Chapter 8, by William Parrett and Scott Willison, discusses different approaches to school restructuring focusing on the establishment of alternative, magnet and charter schools, now often referring to public schools of choice in the United States. These schools share some similar characteristics such as voluntary participation, small school size, caring teachers with high expectations, customized curriculum/personalized instruction, and safe learning environment. Nonetheless, alternative or optional schools are characterized by offering programs for students ranging from at-risk, expelled and violent ones to those exceptionally gifted and talented. In addition, many alternative schools serve students with average achievement. With regard to technical magnet or career-theme schools, students focus on and apply curriculum to a career theme as well as participate in internship and service experiences. For charter schools, they refer to public schools for exchanging state and district mandated rules, regulations, and requirements for contractually specified student performance outcomes. In addition, charter schools usually provide comprehensive site-based management and local governing boards. It is noteworthy that there are alternative and magnet school models focusing on such aspects as specific curricular and instructional approaches, the needs and interests of students, career-themes and professional relevance, experiential learning as well as organization, administration, governance and funding. Parrett and Willison also refer to the ANSER Charter School, which emphasizes a collaborative environment of partnership for educating the whole child. The design of the school is based on Expeditionary Learning, a U.S. school reform model and part of the curriculum is labeled Enrichment in which parents and community groups are involved in its module development. The school has also established partnership with the university in which pre-service teachers are engaged in various teaching and learning experiences and graduate students undertake school-based studies.

Chapter 9 in Part Two, by Iasonas Lamprianou and Bill Boyle, discusses a collaboration program entitled "School Sampling Project (SSP)" between the University of Manchester and schools for the enhancement of enriched curriculum delivery strategies based on the interpretation of National Curriculum (NC) test results. The project is a longitudinal study, which the university has run for the government's Qualifications and Curriculum Authority (QCA) that monitors and analyzes the NC test results across a nationally representative sample of primary and secondary schools in England. It aims at empowering teachers through group discussions about the content, the style, and the conceptualization of the tests and providing technical support for preparing students for the tests. In addition, the project provides feedback related to the overall achievement levels of the students by subject and the comparison between the school and the national results. Item-level analysis feedback from each year's results is also offered, hoping that such repetition of errors in national tests could be prevented. The initial experiences reveal that the percentages of schools that used analysis of previous years' NC tests performance on a question-to-question basis and analysis of returned marked scripts to prepare students for their examinations has increased respectively. The same trend is evident for schools to employ test-preparation strategies. However, students tend to repeat the same errors year after year while teachers tend to adopt "revise question types which appear to reoccur" strategy, which might have the effect of narrowing the curriculum. An analysis of the Head of Department questionnaire data shows that the lack of time is a major constraint for schools to employ a formative use of the NC test results for the enhancement of learning.

In Chapter 10, Sue Dockett, Bob Perry and Peter Howard discuss an example of home-school partnership entitled the Starting School Research Project in Australia. The project emerges because of the emphasis on starting school as a key experience not only for the children but also for the educators and the families. It also represents a partnership between university researchers, educational practitioners in school and prior-to-school settings, parents, and other interested parties. The chapter reports on the data in response to the question, which asks about who should be involved in the transition to school and how much involvement those people should have. "Transition" programs refer to those programs which have a longer term and more catered for individual needs of children and families than "orientation" programs which focus on helping children and parents to become familiar with the school setting. Views of four types of respondents (namely parents or guardians, prior-to-school educators, school teachers, and representatives of the Advisory Committee for the project) are obtained. The results reveal that each type of respondent opines similar findings for each group of possible participants in the child's transition to school. In general, parents/guardians, the child, the school, and prior-to-school educators are rated as having "a lot of involvement" through to almost "total involvement." On the other hand, the child's siblings, friends, grandparents, other members of the child's extended family, and school staff other than teachers are rated as having at least "some involvement." In addition, government bodies, doctors, and religious groups are rated as having less than "a little involvement." Interviews with children of varying schooling experiences are also conducted and children have views on how parents, educators, and teachers can help them start school. For example, parents should wash clothes and get them ready as well as wake children up in the morning. Educators ought to teach children some letters and teach them to say "thank you" and "goodbye." In addition, teachers in schools should tell children what to bring in their lunch box, to eat breakfast every morning so that they have enough energy to play.

In Chapter 11, Hui Leng-han, Sin Kuen-fung, Ho Fuk-chuen, and Chan Hung-ki offer insights into a partnership between a tertiary institution for teacher education and a special school for the visually impaired. The uniqueness of this partnership is in geography — teachers of a higher institution in Hong Kong working with teachers of a special school in Shanghai. The partners initiated contact in 1998 and developed a staff development program at the Shanghai School for the Blind. Activities that emerged from the partnership eventually transcended the boundary of one school to include interests in special needs education in some of Shanghai's mainstream schools. Societal differences notwithstanding, the partners managed to solve professional problems by working together and relying on "mutuality" (sense of ownership), trust, and reciprocal benefits. To the authors, the manner in which partners work out collaborative arrangements to advance self-interests and solve common problems has a lot to do with the outcome of the project. In adhering to what Goodlad (1988) called "symbiotic relationship," the partners had made their own objectives clearly known to one another at the outset of the project. The special school in Shanghai sought professional support for the development of her staff. The higher institution in Hong Kong aimed to establish linkage with special schools in Shanghai and to launch projects in the Chinese Mainland. The partners agreed to these objectives and worked to ensure desirable outcome.

Chapter 12, by Gunnar Berg, differentiates the concepts of "uni-professionalism" and "multiprofessionalism" with respect to the teaching profession and the school organization. He first refers to a matrix of four types of professional, occupational practice based on qualitative or quantitative approach on the one hand, and on occupational groups outside or within their organizational context on the other. Gunnar then analyzes actors in the school organization through lenses of autonomy, corps spirit, and knowledge base. For example, he views school leaders as having autonomy in the work organization, having administrative "back-up" esprit de corps, and as an "autodidact" in terms of knowledge base. He then refers to teachers in the uniprofessional organizations as having autonomy in the classroom, having solitary esprit de corps and specialist knowledge base. All these characteristics imply a relatively strict division of labor among school leaders, teachers and others each of which have their own well-defined "invisible contracts." For the school's occupational groups in the multiprofessional perspective, there exists a relative integration of labor among different occupational groups of teachers, school leaders, student care personnel, student health personnel, and so forth. This suggests in the ideal condition that while the respective occupational groups maintain their specialist knowledge and remain loyal to colleagues in the same occupation, each of them share the same attitude toward the school's basic mission and fulfill operative tasks in line with the mission. In addition, each occupational group in the school broadens its occupational roles both as specialists and generalists and possesses some "knowledge of the surrounding world" directly related to the collective mission. By viewing the teaching profession from a multiprofessional perspective, teachers would need to address professional issues such as the content and work method/form being consistent with the school mission as well as teacher's practice being related to and coordinated with other teacher colleagues' and other school personnels' practice.

In Chapter 13, Nicholas Pang and Mary Cheung report on and discuss an empirical study of school's learning capacity in Hong Kong. Their research framework draws on Peter Senge's five disciplines (namely Personal Mastery, Mental Models, Shared Vision, Team Learning, and Systems Thinking), Getzels-Guba's model of social behavior, and Pang's framework of a learning organization. According to Peter Senge's five disciplines in the school context, Personal Mastery refers to teachers' mastery of their subject and other knowledge. Mental Models refer to teachers' personal paradigm in the views of school organization structures, processes, and power patterns. Shared Vision refers to the conditions that enable teachers to pursue a clear, shared purpose for all. Team Learning is related to a successful learning relationship with others and a climate of trust for open dialogues among teachers. Systems Thinking is concerned with the ability to understand the complex causal relationships among a set of organizational factors including things and operations. Pang and Cheung have developed a 78-item questionnaire based on Peter Senge's five disciplines and 25 primary schools' learning capacity at both the teacher and organizational levels in Hong Kong were assessed accordingly. The results revealed that all schools had teachers' Personal Mastery comparatively higher than other disciplines but schools appeared to be weak in Mental Models. With regard to the effects of the five disciplines on school's learning capacity, the effect of Systems Thinking on learning capacity ranked the highest with the effects of Personal Mastery lowest. In addition, whole-day primary schools were found to have higher learning capacity than bi-sessional schools. It implies that the infrastructure of whole-day schools tend to allow greater flexibility in allocating time and place for teachers to develop deep group interactions than bi-sessional schools. Moreover, it is postulated that schools that provide more opportunities for teachers to examine their own beliefs and assumptions might encounter great leap in school improvement. School leaders are also encouraged to inspire their teachers to think in a system perspective.

In Chapter 14, Richard Dyer and Siu-ming Cheung discuss the case history of West Island School, an international school in Hong Kong involved in developing self-evaluation methods for school improvement. The case was originated from a pilot project on self-evaluation called the Ensuring Excellence project. According to the case study, the project has embraced the concept of "evaluation as development" and consists of different phases of development, namely piloting the initiative, moving toward whole school implementation, and moving toward embedding and consolidation. The process of self-evaluation comprises several key stages: (1) initial choice of an aspect of teaching and learning to focus on, (2) the use of existing professional expertise to draft statements which attempt to capture the essence of excellent practice in the area, (3) an extended cycle of lesson observations using the draft Indicators of Excellence and Observable Features, (4) an evaluation of one aspect of the area of teaching and learning because of time limitation, (5) an analysis of the evidence gained from the evaluation and the setting of development targets and strategies, and (6) the whole set of Indicators of Excellence and Observable Features becoming a policy document. During the process of self-evaluation, the school encounters a dilemma between accountability and development, and faces questions like: "Is the purpose of its self-evaluation activity to prove or improve quality?", "Who are the audiences of the school's self-evaluation activity?" and "To what extent should teachers be professionally involved?" When reflecting on the West Island experience, Dyer and Cheung felt that little turbulence or destabilization had occurred probably because the philosophical assumptions of the project were not incongruent with the prevailing school culture. In addition, they remarked that involvement in self-evaluation could enhance professionalization of teachers and that the strong involvement of teachers in teams was the impetus for exploring and enhancing teaching and learning approaches in the classrooms.

Chapter 15 outlines an innovative project "Exploring Architecture and Designing the Built Environment Programmes" led by Bernard Lim at The Chinese University of Hong Kong and organized by the Community Development Committee of the Hong Kong Institute of Architects (HKIA). Through a partnership among voluntary architects, university undergraduates of architecture, university professors, school teachers, students and parents, the project aims at inspiring primary and secondary students from over 120 schools to take a closer look at the people, processes, and materials that create buildings and places. In addition, the project hopes to help students appreciate the built environment and architecture, and understand that they can have a positive impact on the built environment through their design creativity and decision-making. The project adopted a discovery process and several types of activities were organized. Firstly, a 3-day discovery camp was arranged to stimulate secondary school students to explore and discover the built environment and the architecture. They are asked, for example, to imitate as a group an object or a building in a game called "The human LEGO." In a theme known as "Discovering Hong Kong culture," students were asked to visit and examine the heritage of an old urban area as well as to explore possibilities in integrating old and new architecture. Secondly, creative workshops were arranged for primary school students. In the workshops, students were stimulated to observe textures of different materials and then engage in creating a dream school. Thirdly, design competitions were organized to provide opportunities for students to exercise their imaginative thinking and visionary perspectives in designing built environment. Alongside the competitions, a School Design Charette, where teams of "potential users" and "architects" discussed ideas of creating a combined primary and secondary school and presented ideas and conceptual models, was set up. Finally, a public exhibition was opened for sharing the fruitful experiences, ideas, and creations.

In Chapter 16, Per Dalin refers to an international project "School Year 2020" in 1987, which aims at creating a holistic view of the world in change and providing a picture of what a "good school" would be for children in this new century. In the project, 10 revolutions with a major impact on the future of schooling are identified. They are the knowledge and information revolution, the population revolution, globalization, the economic revolution, the technological revolution, the ecological revolution, the social and cultural revolution, the aesthetics revolution, the political revolution, and the values revolution. In addition to the macro forces, major changes have taken place at the home, the peer group, the religious institutions, the media, and the workplace. Per Dalin based on the "School Year 2020" project suggests the following visions for the future of society: (1) an ecological vision: life in harmony with nature; (2) a vision of a fair, democratic society; (3) from dominance to partnership in social relations; (4) from a war to a peace economy; (5) a worthwhile life for the world's poor; (6) from mono-culturalism to multi-culturalism; (7) the vision of work for all; (8) technology in the service of human growth; (9) life skills in the service of health; and (10) from standardization to creativity. He further highlights the learning needs of children and youth as follows: (1)

students need to learn basic knowledge and skills; (2) the basic is also learn to learn; (3) students need to acquire problem-solving, communication, knowledge and understanding; (4) students learn about closeness and belonging; and (5) students learn how to be consumers and producers.

Concluding Note

Many chapters in this book illustrate the nature of different partnerships as well as experiences of and research on school development in connection with individual strategies and organizational strategies (Dalin, 1998). Moreover, many of these partnerships are project-based initiatives, which on the one hand may not be able to sustain without ongoing external funding support, and on the other may need to experiment in different settings to provide more generalizable experiences for large-scale educational change. Fullan (2000) highlights three stories of school reform: (1) *the inside story* — there is no substitute for internal school development; (2) *the inside-out story* — schools need the outside (for example, through partnerships with universities or members of other reform networks); (3) *the outside-in story* — establishment of external reform infrastructure of large districts through policies focusing on decentralization, local capacity building (investments of training, professional development and ongoing support), rigorous external accountability (intervening in persistently failing schools), and stimulation of innovation (investments in research, development, and innovative networks). Many stories in this book reveal the "inside" and the "inside-out" perspectives, which share similar issues of concern in school reform. Hughes (1999, p. 53) advocates that some of the major directions to be pursued in future educational reforms need to address international, regional, national, local, and individual levels. More sharing of international experiences on partnerships and change with a focus on school development is timely. We need to have a drive to reflect on our valuable past knowledge and imagination to develop our present ideals as well as our collaborative commitment to launch new possibilities into the future.

Note

1. All the programs cited in this section are seen as comprehensive models for school improvement or comprehensive reform programs (McChesney & Hertling, 2000; Protheroe & Perkins-Gough, 1998).

References

Barber, M., & Phillips, V. (2000). *Fusion: How to unleash irreversible change — Lessons for the future of system-wide school reform* (Education Policy Studies Series No. 32). Hong Kong: Faculty of Education & Hong Kong Institute of Educational Research, The Chinese University of Hong Kong.

Berry, B., & Catoe, S. (1994). Creating professional development schools: Policy and practice in South Carolina's PDS initiatives. In L. Darling-Hammond (Ed.), *Professional development schools: Schools for developing a profession* (pp. 176–202). New York: Teachers College Press.

Biott, C. (1992). Imposed support for teachers' learning: Implementation or development partnerships? In C. Biott & J. Nias (Eds.), *Working and learning together for change* (pp. 3–18). Buckingham, England; Philadelphia, PA: Open University Press.

Caldwell, B. (1999). Education for the public good: Strategic intentions for the 21st century. In D. D. Marsh (Ed.), *Preparing our schools for the 21st century* (pp. 45–64). Alexandria, VA: Association for Supervision and Curriculum Development (ASCD).

Clark, R. W. (1988). School-university partnerships: An interpretive view. In K. A. Sirotnik & J. I. Goodlad (Eds.), *School-university partnerships in action: Concepts, cases, and concerns* (pp. 32–65). New York: Teachers College Press.

Clark, R. W. (1999). *Effective professional development schools.* San Francisco: Jossey-Bass.

Clarke, P. (2000). *Learning schools, learning systems.* London: Continuum.

Collins, A., Hawkins, J., & Carver, S. M. (1991). A cognitive apprenticeship for disadvantaged students. In U.S. Department of Education (Ed.), *Teaching advanced skills to educationally disadvantaged students* (pp. 173–194). Washington, DC: U.S. Department of Education.

Comer, J. (Ed.). (1996). *Rallying the whole village: The Comer process for reforming education.* New York: Teachers College Press.

Cuban, L. (1998). How schools change reforms: Redefining reform success and failure. *Teachers College Record, 99*(3), 453–477.

Curriculum Development Council. (2001). *Learning to learn: Life-long learning and whole-person development.* Hong Kong: Author.

Dalin, P. (1998). *School development: Theories and strategies.* London; New York: Cassell.

Dalin, P. (in press). Toward schooling for the Twenty-first century. In J. C. K. Lee, L. N. K. Lo, & A. Walker (Eds.), *Partnership and change: Toward school development.* Hong Kong: The Chinese University Press; Hong Kong Institute of Educational Research.

Darling-Hammond, L. (1997). *The right to learn: A blueprint for creating schools that work*. San Francisco: Jossey-Bass.

Day, C. (1998). Re-thinking school-university partnerships: A Swedish case study. *Teaching and Teacher Education, 14*(8), 807–819.

Day, C. (1999). *Developing teachers: The challenges of lifelong learning*. London; Philadelphia, PA: Falmer Press.

Dimmock, C., & Lee, J. C. K. (2000). Redesigning school-based curriculum leadership: A cross-cultural perspective. *Journal of Curriculum and Supervision, 15*(4), 332–358.

Education Commission. (2000). *Learning for life, learning through life: Reform proposals for the education system in Hong Kong*. Hong Kong: Author.

Elmore, R. F. (1990). *Restructuring schools: The next generation of educational reform*. San Francisco: Jossey-Bass.

Epstein, J. L. (1994). Theory to practice: School and family partnerships lead to school improvement and student success. In C. L. Fagnano & B. Z. Werber (Eds.), *School, family, and community interaction: A view from the firing lines* (pp. 39–60). Boulder, CO: Westview Press.

Finnan, C., St. John, E. P., McCarthy, J., & Slovacek, S. P. (Eds.). (1996). *Accelerated schools in action: Lessons from the field*. Thousand Oaks, CA: Corwin Press.

Fullan, M. (1993). *Change forces: Probing the depths of educational reform*. London; New York: Falmer Press.

Fullan, M. (2000). The three stories of education reform. *Phi Delta Kappan, 81*(8), 581–584.

Goodlad, J. I. (1988). School-university partnerships for educational renewal: Rationale and concepts. In K. A. Sirotnik & J. I. Goodlad (Eds.), *School-university partnerships in action: Concepts, cases, and concerns* (pp. 3–31). New York: Teachers College Press.

Gray, J., Hopkins, D., Reynolds, D., Wilcox, B., Farrell, S., & Jesson, D. (1999). *Improving schools: Performance and potential*. Buckingham, England; Philadelphia, PA: Open University Press.

Grundy, S. (1987). *Curriculum: Product or praxis*. London: Falmer Press.

Hargreaves, A. (1995). Renewal in the age of paradox. *Educational Leadership, 52* (7), 14–19.

Hargreaves, A., & Lo, L. N. K. (2000). The paradoxical profession: Teaching at the turn of the century. *Prospects: Quarterly Review of Comparative Education, 30* (2), 167–180.

Holmes Group. (1986). *Tomorrow's teachers: A report of the Holmes Group*. East Lansing, MI: Author.

Hopkins, D., Ainscow, M., & West, M. (1994). *School improvement in an era of change*. London: Cassell.

Hopkins, D., West, M., & Ainscow, M. (1996). *Improving the quality of education for all.* London: David Fulton.

Hughes, P. (1999). *Where is the focal point for reform? Secondary education as the key to change* (Education Policy Studies Series No. 18). Hong Kong: Faculty of Education & Hong Kong Institute of Educational Research, The Chinese University of Hong Kong.

Johnston, M. (2000). Context, challenges, and consequences: PDSs in the making. In M. Johnston, P. Brosnan, D. Cramer, & T. Dove (Eds.), *Collaborative reform and other improbable dreams: The challenges of professional development schools* (pp. 1–17). Albany, NY: State University of New York Press.

Kemmis, S., & McTaggart, R. (1982). *The action research planner* (2nd ed.). Waurn Ponds, Australia: Deakin University.

Kersh, M. E., & Masztal, N. B. (1998). An analysis of studies of collaboration between universities and K-12 schools. *The Educational Forum, 62*(3), 218–225.

Lee, C. K. (1999). *School reform and education in Hong Kong SAR for the 21st century* [in Chinese] (Education Policy Studies Series No. 20). Hong Kong: Faculty of Education & Hong Kong Institute of Educational Research, The Chinese University of Hong Kong.

Lee, C. K. J. (2002). *Curriculum, teaching and school reforms: Educational development in a new century* [in Chinese]. Hong Kong: The Chinese University Press.

Levin, H. (1998). Accelerated schools: A decade of evolution. In A. Hargreaves, A. Lieberman, M. Fullan, & D. Hopkins (Eds.), *International handbook of educational change* (pp. 807–830). Dordrecht, Netherlands; Boston, MA: Kluwer Academic Publishers.

Lo, L. N. K. (2000). Educational reform and teacher development in Hong Kong and on the Chinese Mainland. *Prospects: Quarterly Review of Comparative Education, 30*(2), 237–253.

MacBeath, J. (1999). *Schools must speak for themselves: The case for school self-evaluation.* London; New York: Routledge.

MacBeath, J., & Mortimore, P. (Eds.). (2001). *Improving school effectiveness.* Buckingham, England; Philadelphia, PA: Open University Press.

Marsh, C. (1988). *Spotlight on school improvement.* Sydney; London: Allen & Unwin.

McChesney, J., & Hertling, E. (2000). The path to comprehensive school reform. *Educational Leadership, 57*(7), 10–15.

Morris, P., Lo, M. L., & Adamson, B. (2000). Improving schools in Hong Kong — Lessons from the past. In B. Adamson, T. Kwan, & K. K. Chan (Eds.), *Changing the curriculum: The impact of reform on primary schooling in Hong Kong* (pp. 245–262). Hong Kong: Hong Kong University Press.

Murphy, J. (Ed.). (1990). *The educational reform movement of the 1980s: Perspectives and cases.* Berkeley, CA: McCutchan.

Murphy, J. (1991). *Restructuring schools: Capturing and assessing the phenomena.* New York: Teachers College Press.

Murphy, J. (1993). Restructuring: In search of a movement. In J. Murphy & P. Hallinger (Eds.), *Restructuring schooling: Learning from ongoing efforts* (pp. 1–31). Newbury Park, CA: Corwin Press.

O'Donoghue, T., & Dimmock, D. (1998). *School restructuring: International perspectives.* London: Kogan Page.

Ou, Y.-S. (1999). *School in the new century* [in Chinese]. Taipei: Taiwan Book Company.

Ou, Y.-S. (2000). *Curriculum reform* [in Chinese]. Taipei: Taiwan Normal University Book Company.

Patterson, R. S., Michelli, N. M., & Pacheco, A. (1999). *Centers of pedagogy: New structures for educational renewal.* San Francisco: Jossey-Bass.

Protheroe, N. J., & Perkins-Gough, D. (1998). *Comprehensive models for school improvement: Finding the right match and making it work.* Arlington, VA: Educational Research Service.

Rudduck, J., Chaplain, R., & Wallace, G. (1996). *School improvement: What can pupils tell us?* London: David Fulton.

Sizer, T. (1986). Rebuilding: First steps by the coalition of essential schools. *Phi Delta Kappan, 68,* 38–42.

Stoll, L., & Fink, D. (1996). *Changing our schools: Linking school effectiveness and school improvement.* Buckingham, England; Philadelphia, PA: Open University Press.

Stoll, L., MacBeath, J., & Mortimore, P. (2001). Beyond 2000: Where next for effectiveness and improvement. In J. MacBeath & P. Mortimore (Eds.), *Improving school effectiveness* (pp. 191–207). Buckingham, England; Philadelphia, PA: Open University Press.

Tang, M. S., & Lee, J. C. K. (1999). Curriculum change through university and school partnership — The case study of whole language writing in Hong Kong primary school. *Curriculum Forum, 9*(1), 96–113.

Teddlie, C., & Reynolds, D. (2000). *The international handbook of school effectiveness research.* London; New York: Falmer Press.

Townsend, T., Clarke, P., & Ainscow, M. (1999). Third Millennium Schools: Prospects and problems for school effectiveness and school improvement. In T. Townsend, P. Clarke, & M. Ainscow (Eds.), *Third millennium schools: A world of difference in effectiveness and improvement* (pp. 353–366). Lisse, Netherlands; Exton, PA: Swets & Zeitlinger.

Walker, A., & Dimmock, C. (2000). Developing educational administration: The impact of societal culture on theory and practice. In C. Dimmock & A. Walker

(Eds.), *Future school administration: Western and Asian perspectives* (pp. 3–22). Hong Kong: The Chinese University Press; Hong Kong Institute of Educational Research.

Wang, M. C. (1992). *Adaptive education strategies: Building on diversity.* Baltimore, MD: Paul H. Brookes.

Wang, M. C., Haertel, G. D., & Walberg, H. J. (1998). Models of reform: A comparative guide. *Educational Leadership, 55*(7), 66–71.

Wang, J., & Wong, H. W. (2001). *The missing link of educational reform: Theory and practice of school-university collaboration* [in Chinese] (Education Policy Studies Series No. 45). Hong Kong: Faculty of Education & Hong Kong Institute of Educational Research, The Chinese University of Hong Kong.

West, M. (1998). Quality in schools: Developing a model for school improvement. In A. Hargreaves, A. Lieberman, M. Fullan, & D. Hopkins (Eds.), *International handbook of educational change* (pp. 768–789). Dordrecht, Netherlands; Boston, MA: Kluwer Academic Publishers.

West, M., Jackson, D., Harris, A., & Hopkins, D. (2000). Learning through leadership, leadership through learning: Leadership for sustained school improvement. In K. A. Riley & K. S. Louis (Eds.), *Leadership for change and school reform: International perspectives* (pp. 30–49). London; New York: Routledge/Falmer.

2

Learning from School Reform

Henry M. Levin

Abstract

Major school reforms show only rare success throughout the world. Although there are occasional reports of success for individual or small groups of schools, the more typical case is one where the substantial change that was promised does not emerge. This chapter comprises three parts.

First, I discuss the concept of school culture to explain the challenges to school reform. I attempt to show why existing school culture is necessary for a smoothly functioning and stable school, but an obstacle to educational change. Attempts to transform school culture through external means have almost always failed. As an alternative I introduce the concept of internal transformation of culture, the empowerment of school participants to change their practices, expectations, and attitudes through introducing a change process that sets new goals and a set of tools that can be used to reach them.

The second part introduces the Accelerated Schools Project (ASP), a project that was established in 1986 and that presently encompasses over 1,000 schools in 41 states of the United States and 50 schools in Hong Kong. The issue that is raised is whether a reform model developed in one country and premised on very different cultural characteristics can succeed in transforming schools in another entity, Hong Kong. The various parts of the ASP process are introduced and linked to their role in the internal cultural transformation of schools.

The final part asks what has been learned after 3 years of experience in Hong Kong among the 50 schools. Has the process been introduced and implemented effectively? Does it work? The chapter sets out a strategy for ascertaining under what conditions the ASP approach has shown success and how those conditions might be replicated.

Introduction

One of the major challenges to school reform is that most schools are not looking for change. They have settled into a set of standard routines and relationships that are widely accepted by participants. Even when there is concern by some staff about a particular issue, the larger context and operation of schools is rarely challenged. This is understandable. Any institution, including the school, needs to have shared premises on which its continuous functioning depends. This agreement is often tacit in the sense of "this is the way we do things," and new members absorb their roles through experiences within this context. There are strong advantages to schools or other institutions in maintaining and reproducing their operations and culture in this manner. Such functional accord assures stability over time rather than sharp fluctuations or deviations from normalcy. It provides clear roles, expectations and modes of behavior for its participants. And, even as personnel change, the traditions carry on smoothly as new members are initiated into the routines.

But, this arrangement has drawbacks in a changing world. Its very stability creates formidable obstacles to mobilizing for change. Respect for tradition and force of habit can be insurmountable hurdles to modification of practice. Certainly, this has been the overwhelming experience with school reform (Sarason, 1982). Pressures have been placed on schools to modify their operations in response to globalization, information technology, pressures for innovation, and changing views of human development. Although there are popular calls for school reform to create a different system of education and educational outcomes as the world changes, schools tend to resist.

This chapter asks the fundamental question of how one obtains change in a system characterized by conservatism and stability. In the next section, we review some of the reasons that schools are so remarkably resistant to change. We pay specific attention to the difficulties of transferring school practices from one site or locale or country to another. In the following section we will present the strategy of the Accelerated Schools Project (ASP) and its challenges in initiating changes in over 1,000 schools in the United States and 50 schools in Hong Kong. In the final section, we will view the Accelerated Schools Model as the basis for a school reform laboratory from which much can be learned about the possibilities and strategies for school reform in Hong Kong.

Why Do Schools Resist Reform?

Schools resist reform because their operation depends upon a stable and shared understanding or culture that makes it possible to function smoothly. That culture is built on tradition, habit, expectations, and images of what schools should do and be. To suggest that schools should change is to suggest that traditions, habits, expectations, and images be immediately modified, a virtual impossibility. So, school reform tends to focus on the illusion that it is only personnel skills that must be changed. But it is attitudes and modes of operation which are the greatest obstacles to change, not a lack of skills. Skills can be taught to school participants if they are convinced that they need those skills. But, if they are not persuaded that change is needed in the first place or that the school is fundamentally flawed, it is unlikely that they will direct their efforts toward transformation.

So, if existing school culture is the greatest obstacle to reform, is there the possibility of using culture to effect reform? To answer this question, we must attempt to define the components of school culture. School culture refers to widely shared understanding, behavior, and attitudes that characterize a school's participants and operations as reinforced by interactions with others and perceptions of the world.[1] School culture refers to those aspects of schools that we take for granted. That is, we are so immersed in them, and they are so much a part of our lives, that we do not question them. We accept these features as necessary and integral to schools and school operations.

School culture has many dimensions that give meaning to the daily lives of all of the participants including students, staff, parents, and members of the larger community. Some specific features of school culture include: (1) expectations about children in terms of normal behavior and what they should learn, including the possibility of different expectations by race, gender, and social class; (2) expectations by the students themselves about appropriate school experiences and student self-images of their own proficiencies; (3) expectations about the roles of adults in the school in terms of legitimate actions; (4) opinions about acceptable educational practices; and (5) basic beliefs about the desirability for change. It is the tacit agreement around these dimensions that enables schools to function as purposive institutions. If each were a source of conflict, schools would have difficulty in carrying out their missions, for the mission itself would be contested in daily life.

Because schools have their own cultures, they resist changes that are premised on a very different set of beliefs. For example, a school that believes that students must be tracked into ability groups will not be enthusiastic about a reform that is premised on mixed ability grouping. A school that defines mathematics in terms of the memorization of "math facts" and the carrying out of specific mathematical operations will be unlikely to embrace an emphasis on conceptual approaches to mathematics and problem-solving. A school that views writing as highly stylized and evaluates it largely for mechanics of presentation rather than content will resist a new curriculum where writing is viewed primarily as a creative and expressive skill. And, teachers who are used to high degree of structure and authority in the classroom will feel uncomfortable when pressed to consider more participative and democratic forms of pedagogy.

The point is that every school reform that is proposed is embedded in and assumes the existence of a specific constellation of school culture that may not be compatible with the actual school culture that exists in a particular setting. It is this lack of congruence that is primarily responsible for the failure of school reforms to take hold in new settings. This insight provides an explanation of what has typically happened with school reforms. In many cases, school culture was incompatible with the proposed school reform. In those cases, it is rare that the reform is implemented beyond a surface existence. In fact, when reforms are forced on schools that are not receptive, the school often has more influence in modifying the reform than the reform has in modifying the school (McLaughlin, 1990). Schools are not inert entities that can be easily molded in the shape desired by reformers. Schools are active communities of members united by a deeply etched culture that will resist the invasion of alien ideas and practices. This challenge has been too little recognized by educational reformers. Yet, so much of educational reform has failed, both nationally and internationally, because of the ill fit between the reform and the extant culture of the school.[2]

Even when a reform succeeds in one school, it may not succeed in another school in the same neighborhood. Schools are characterized by their own local cultures deriving from their histories and specific populations as well as the more general culture that all schools in a particular society might share. Sarason (1982) is pessimistic that school culture can be changed. Cuban (1990) even suggests that cycles of reform are repeated again and again in futility because the reformers do not seem to recognize that school culture is not compatible with their movements. The result is that the reforms are abandoned and adopted once again, and they continue to fail, even after repeated attempts.

More recent reforms have recognized the resistance of school culture to change. Accordingly, they have responded in two different ways. The first is requiring that any school that is "interested" in adopting a reform needs to demonstrate its "buy-in." Buy-in generally consists of making information on one or more reforms accessible to members of the school community, and ultimately requiring a vote of the school staff. In the United States, a typical requirement of the sponsors of major, national reforms is that 80% of the teachers (in accelerated schools, staff and parent representatives as well as teachers) must support the adoption of a specific reform before the reform organization will agree to collaborate with the school.

Presumably, those schools that buy-in are ones that are prepared to accept change and to examine their practices. But, a substantial number of schools that have indicated buy-in fail to fully implement the reforms. In some cases the so-called "buy-in" was superficial or non-existent (Datnow, 2000). The voting process may have been distorted by pressures from the principal or school district. Or the vote may have been a fair one, but not well-informed because the staff was not provided with time and data to understand the intricacies and demands of the reform model. Even when substantial information is provided, school staff may not be able to envision how the abstractions of a reform translate into concrete changes in the life of the school. They may renege when they realize that the reform will require greater changes in educational practices and attitudes than were anticipated. This becomes apparent only after direct experience with the reform.

Accordingly, some of the reforms use a different approach, even after obtaining buy-in by school staff. Rather than requiring the school to adopt specific instructional practices and curriculum, the school is expected to accept a process of implementation that places the principal responsibilities for these decisions on the actors themselves, staff, parents, and students. These reforms place great emphasis on a process of change that empowers the school community to set goals and use problem-solving processes to reach them. This is the strategy taken by the ASP in conjunction with the 80% buy-in requirement.[3] The assumption underlying the empowerment process is the view that if the school can undertake its own process of democratic decision-making by staff, parents, and students, it will be able to transform its own culture. We will discuss this process at greater length in the next section.

Accelerated Schools Project

ASP was established in 1986 as a way of transforming traditional schools that place heavy reliance on rote learning into schools using the type of instruction for gifted and talented students. Although the project was started initially to provide academic acceleration for educationally at-risk students, it has been extended to schools where students have good results according to traditional academic measures, but lack more enriched strategies and outcomes. The long-term priority is to establish schools in which enrichment replaces memorization, in which student projects replace drill, and in which student assessment is based upon what Sternberg (1997) has called measures of successful intelligence, not inert intelligence. Of course students learn basic skills, but these are integrated into enrichment activities and ones that connect these activities and skills to real-world challenges. Sternberg (1997) has emphasized the integration of the three types of intelligence in the education of every child. The inculcation of "analytic intelligence" would extend far beyond memorization of facts to analysis and problem-solving. "Creative intelligence" would be manifested in the solution of problems in non-ordinary ways, encouraging the viewing of the world from different perspectives and utilizing artistic devices and metaphors to address one's creative instincts. "Practical intelligence" is reflected in applying analytical and creative intelligence to real-world situations.

These approaches can best be satisfied through creating what is normally thought of as gifted and talented instruction within more democratic schools.[4] ASP was established in the United States in 1986 and presently encompasses about 600,000 students in 1,100 schools in 41 states as well as Australia and Hong Kong. In its 16th year, ASP is one of the largest and oldest comprehensive school reforms in the United States, so it draws upon considerable experience at transforming schools.[5] The goal of accelerated schools is to transform schools educating at-risk students from an emphasis on drill to one that embodies the pedagogy for gifted and talented students so that students will meet both their developmental needs and those required for adult life through an integrated system of powerful learning.[6] Powerful learning is embodied in research projects, artistic endeavors, community studies, and a range of applications where knowledge is applied to real-world activities. Many important competencies required for the "new" workplace can be embedded in each activity (e.g., developing initiative, cooperation, group work, peer training, evaluation, communication, reasoning, problem-solving, decision-making information, planning, learning skills, and multicultural skills).[7] And students can generate authentic ideas, products, artistic performances, literary works, and problem solutions that can be assessed directly for quality rather than assuming that examination scores will be adequate assessment instruments.

ASP places great weight on a transformation process at each school site that encourages reflection and ideas by the teachers, students, and parents who must engage in change. The process is neither mechanical nor automatic, but requires the building of school communities dedicated to new goals and transformation. This process is at the heart of initiating an internal transformation of school culture in the new directions that are sought. The process provides guidelines and tools for transformation and benchmarks to be used in assessment. It also requires a trained coach who will work with the school patiently and support the change process and will assist the school to trouble-shoot problems as they arise. Finally, it requires strong leadership on the part of the school principal and others and the time to work together to receive training and to engage in the process.

ASP was established initially to address the needs of students in at-risk situations, those with low levels of family income and parental education as well as marginalized immigrants and racial minorities. Although its success has been extended to schools with students from middle-class families, its predominant commitment is to those who need the most attention, at-risk populations. Recent research on gifted and talented students is highly supportive of the benefits of using academic enrichment for all students.[8] This calls for a dramatic shift in the culture of the school so that it values a wider range of pedagogical activities and goals rather than the more traditional memorization activities. This means creating a school which is much more democratic in character and in which staff (with the participation of parents and students) undertake planning, problem-solving, collaborative endeavors, assessment, and many of the other behaviors required of high-participation and high-productivity workplaces (Levin, 1997b).

The Accelerated Schools Process

Educational reform is often viewed abstractly as a design for change rather than as a complex process of change. But the change process itself is the key to implementation. The accelerated school change strategy represents a philosophy and a process for transforming conventional schools into environments where powerful learning experiences are daily occurrences for all members of a school community. It focuses on changing school culture and school practices simultaneously. The philosophy of the Accelerated Schools Model encompasses an overall goal, three principles, certain values, and a theory about powerful learning. The process of the Accelerated Schools Model is a systematic set of practices for "getting from here to there" — from conventional schools to accelerated ones. A brief discussion will highlight the concrete nature of what is meant.

Living Principles

Accelerated schools build on incorporating continual practices based upon three central principles:

1. "Unity of purpose" refers to an active collaboration among parents, teachers, students, support staff, administrators, and the local community toward setting and achieving a common set of goals and activities for the school. These shared goals and values become the focal point of everyone's efforts.
2. "Empowerment coupled with responsibility" refers to the ability of the participants of a school community in both the school and at home to make important educational decisions and to take responsibility for implementing those decisions and for their outcomes. The purpose of this principle is to replace the present stalemate among administrators, teachers, parents, support staff, and students in which the participants tend to blame each other as well as other factors "beyond their control" (e.g., the government)

for the poor educational outcomes of students. Unless all of the major actors can be empowered to seek a common set of goals and influence the educational and social processes to realize those goals, it is unlikely that the desired improvements will take place or be sustained.

This shift from a central authority to the school requires the establishment of three sets of institutional changes that are usually not present. First, there must be an effective system of school governance that can involve and stimulate participation of all of the pertinent constituencies in an effective way. Second, since good decisions are informed decisions, the school must adopt a method of problem-solving that addresses its challenges and provides appropriate decisions based upon a thorough understanding and a good base of information. Third, the school needs its own system of assessment to ascertain the consequences of its decisions. The development of all three of these is incorporated into the accelerated schools process.

3. "Building on strengths" refers to utilizing all of the learning resources that students, parents, all school staff, and communities bring to the educational endeavor. Accelerated school communities actively look for and build upon the strengths of all students, parents, teachers, support staff, administrators, the district and the local community as they implement the accelerated schools process and develop powerful learning experiences.

Underlying the accelerated principles and practices are a set of central values, beliefs, and attitudes, which are a basis for school development. When shared, they help create the culture for accelerated school change. Equity, participation, communication, collaboration, community, reflection, experimentation, trust, risk-taking, and the school as the center of expertise are among the central values that orient all actions of an accelerated school. Many of these values stem from the philosophy of John Dewey.

But, especially central to building on student strengths is the powerful learning approach, which integrates curriculum, instruction, and school organization rather than viewing each dimension as independent.[9] The conception of powerful learning is based on the premise that the educational approach that we offer to "gifted" children works well for *all* children. Accelerated schools create powerful learning situations that motivate students to grow and succeed. In accelerated schools, students see meaning in their lessons and perceive connections between school activities and experiences outside of the school. They learn actively and in ways that build on their own strengths, develop their natural talents and gifts, apply them in creative ways toward problem-solving and decision-making, two key ingredients of workplaces in the information economy.

These learning experiences require higher-order thinking, complex reasoning, and relevant content. In such situations, children actively discover the curriculum objectives, rather than passively going through textbooks and filling out worksheets. At the same time, this type of learning environment requires organization and support, so that adults are challenged to create a safe environment for learning that extends far beyond the classroom into every aspect of the school, home, and community.

Implementation

In order to function as accelerated schools, school communities need to work toward a unity of purpose, to make responsible decisions, and to build on strengths. For these reasons, ASP has developed a systematic process which is designed to establish for the school a unified purpose, shared decision-making authority and responsibility, and a capacity to build on the many strengths unique to each school site.

A school community can initiate the accelerated schools process in a set of interrelated processes. The following paragraphs provide a brief picture of the steps in the process.

Stock-Taking

First, the school takes stock of the "here," that is, where the school is at the onset of the change process. The entire school gathers quantitative and qualitative information on the history of the school; data on students, staff, and school facilities; information on the community and cultures of students and their parents; a description of curricular and instructional practices; analysis of the quality of students work; information on the attitudes and beliefs of school members; particular strengths of the school; and data on attendance, disaggregated test scores, and other measures of student performance. The process of collecting, analyzing, and discussing baseline information provides a useful record of the school's status at the beginning of the transformation process against which we can measure progress over time. Taking stock fosters a sense of ownership of the process and begins to build unity of purpose in the school a basic requirement for shifting school culture.

Forging a Vision

During the vision process, the school community begins to forge a desired picture of the school that will become the focus for change. Again, the entire school community — including teachers, support staff, principal, vice principals, parents, central office administrators, the community, and, most importantly, students — should engage in creating a vision. In forging a vision, all adult parties think about the kind of school they would want for their own children, and students develop a description of the dream school they want for themselves. The elements of the visions of the different parties are brought together into a comprehensive aspiration. The all-inclusive nature of defining a vision results in ownership of a common set of goals and long-term commitment to achieving them.

Setting Priorities

Next, the school community compares the taking stock information with the vision in order to become aware of the areas in which their current situation falls short of their vision. The school community compiles and synthesizes all of the differences between the present situation and the future vision. This process may identify a very large number of challenges, but together the school community sets three to five initial priorities, which will become the immediate, primary focus of the school.

Governance

After setting priorities, the school establishes its governance structures that focus on participatory decision-making. Each participant selects one of the priority areas on which to work. These priority groups become cadres or small task forces that use the *Inquiry Process* to address their challenges. Representatives from the cadres, administrators, and other representatives from groupings such as departments, grade levels, the student body, parents, and community members form the steering committee which serves as a clearinghouse for decision-making and communication. Decisions are made by the school-as-a-whole, energizing members to take collective action.

Inquiry Decision-Making

The Inquiry Process is the method used by all members of the school community, whether in cadres, departments, or as individuals to move the school toward the vision and accelerated practices throughout the school. Through the Inquiry Process, teachers, administrators, and parents identify and define educational challenges, look for alternative solutions, and implement and evaluate those solutions. One full cycle of the process can take up to a full school year because it entails a wide range of issues which touch upon all facets of the school — on culture as well as pedagogical practices.

The Inquiry Process provides schools with the opportunity to examine challenges in an in-depth manner in contrast to the traditional superficial search for solutions. Inquiry also encourages the school community to produce knowledge for its own use, thus building on the many strengths at the school site. In addition, Inquiry empowers those at the school site to make the changes they know are best for students. It is important to note that Inquiry may lead different schools in very different directions since each school has different challenges, strengths, and visions.

Assessing Progress

On a regular basis, the accelerated schools communities examine their practices, student experiences, and school climate to see if they meet the standards that they would set for their own children. The overall philosophy of assessment is based upon the premise that if the school is not good enough for the children of staff, it is not good enough for any child. This means that the staff must work together to create for all children in the school the experiences that they desire for their own children.

Progress is assessed in accelerated schools by a system that focuses on both school and student development. Schools work to align their assessment practices with goals of the accelerated schools philosophy and process. School communities also review their action plans and the implementation process to make sure that decisions make their way into school practices.

ASP has developed an Internal Assessment Toolkit. This Toolkit provides guidance to school communities for assessing their implementation of an accelerated school with particular emphasis on measuring that progress against established benchmarks. In addition, accelerated schools evaluate such school outcomes as levels of student and family participation in school activities. Accelerated schools also assess student performance to assure that students are successful in their learning and are leaving the school with the necessary skills and accomplishments reflected in the school vision. Periodic evaluation on wide-spectrum, standardized achievement tests as well as on tailored assessments created by school staff for each curriculum strand are essential ingredients as well as assessments of the students' acquisition of higher-order thinking and reasoning skills in core curricular areas.[10]

Capacity Building

Although we have used different training models, we have concluded that one is superior for our purposes (Levin, 1998). ASP prepares an external coach (at least 25% time), the principal, and an internal facilitator (at least 25% time) to work together as a team in transforming the school. Accordingly, we have established formal training workshops for accelerated school coaches, principals, and school facilitators at regional centers that can be used to provide the knowledge and skills required for establishing accelerated schools. These workshops emphasize an understanding of accelerated practices that will be implemented at designated pilot school sites following the training.

In addition to the more formal training requirements, coaches are at the school site on a weekly basis to build capacity and trouble-shoot. All coaches are mentored by staff from regional centers with regular communications, monthly meetings, and mentorship visits to school sites. Through this model, we are attempting to ensure that all schools have accessibility to trained coaches and facilitators who can provide the training, follow-up, and guidance at the school site that we have found necessary. There is also a National Conference for ASP that draws participants, both nationally and internationally, for sharing experiences and ideas at workshops and through major presentations and informal discussions.

Accelerated Schools in Hong Kong

The rationale for establishing accelerated schools in Hong Kong was to find a way to move from a traditional educational approach to a more active strategy that would prepare the young for major changes in the workplace (Levin, 1997a, 2001). Initially the plan was to select just three schools as pilot schools. Staff from The Chinese University of Hong Kong (CUHK) would receive training from ASP in the United States, and they would get hands-on experience in transforming the three schools during the next few years. There was particular concern with the issue of taking a reform from one culture and applying it to another. So, at the heart of the Hong Kong project was a focus on institutional learning prior to any scale-up.

During the 1997–1998 academic year, the Hong Kong government issued a tender for educational reform projects. The CUHK applied for funding for a substantial scaling-up of ASP, a 3-year project to launch 50 accelerated schools. This funding was awarded, and the expansion began in the Fall of 1998. Professor John Lee was appointed by Dean Chung to direct the project. He assembled a staff with an assistant, Mr. Chiu, and 11 School Development Officers (SDOs) who were expected to receive training. Each would work with about 5 schools. Lee has written descriptions of the project in Chapter 3, so this should be referred to for details. Pilar Soler of ASP in the United States was asked to provide training, three sessions in the first year and two sessions in each subsequent year, to the CUHK training teams. Having been the Assistant Director for Training Development at the National Center for the Accelerated Schools Project, Soler had designed basic parts of the ASP process, and was the founder and director of the New York Accelerated Schools Center at Columbia University.

The Hong Kong component was called the Accelerated Schools for Quality Education Project (ASQEP), and its several reports discuss some of the details of the activities. The purpose of this part of the chapter is to suggest methods of analysis that can reveal useful information about changing school culture in Hong Kong, especially the shift from schools based upon memorization to powerful learning strategies based upon constructivist approaches. These lessons are complicated by two cultural shifts. The first is that of a cultural change in school pedagogy. This is similar to what ASP has faced in the United States. But, the second is a cultural shift in schools from one society to another. Beyond the pedagogy, there are differences from country-to-country in the larger culture of schooling or what has been referred to as "Societal Assumptions Influencing School and Classroom Culture" (Finnan & Swanson, 2000, pp. 68–72). It is likely that the societal perspectives and individual school perspectives are closely aligned. When a school change model is introduced into one country from another, both types of cultural change must be confronted.

What Was the Intervention?

In analyzing school change, it is important to first be clear about the intervention. In the previous sections we referred to the challenge of changing school culture and the development of ASP as a strategy for internal transformation of school culture. But, the actual intervention depends upon how the ASP model was implemented in the Hong Kong project. How was the model introduced to the participating schools? Why did they select it? How much did they know about it? What incentives beyond its intrinsic features were present? How did the project build its capacity to work with schools on the ASP? What kind of training and how much training were received by the school development officers and school staff both prior to and during the conduct of ASQEP? How did the training activity of SDOs translate into training and other activities at school sites? How often did SDOs visit the sites, and what did they do on these visits? How much time was devoted to ASP activities at school sites? How strong was the emphasis on inquiry and powerful learning? These are examples of the types of documentation that are needed to know what the actual intervention was as opposed to the features of the ASP model as described above.

Implementation of ASQEP

Obviously, the purpose of all of this activity is to obtain change in the schools that participated, especially shifts from regulated and centrally administered approaches of school operations to inquiry-based empowerment and from rote learning to powerful learning. The study of implementation requires a focus on the activities of stock-taking, vision, setting priorities, governance, and adoption of inquiry-based solutions to challenges and powerful learning. How was each stage addressed and connected with the previous stages, and what were the implementation outcomes? SDOs maintained records on activities at school sites. Moreover, ASP provides an assessment toolkit consisting of a rubric of benchmarks, ratings, and suggested evidence. ASQEP has applied these benchmarks to ascertain levels of implementation of ASP at each school. It is our understanding that these assessment criteria are being applied to the 50 schools, so that ASQEP will have data on implementation at each site.

Ideally, it would have been useful to collect baseline data on school operations at the outset to see where schools were starting from. However, the timing of the funding cycle and the need to begin immediately in the Fall of 1998 precluded this possibility. Nevertheless, the fact that so much of the ASP process was new to all schools meant that almost all were starting from a baseline that looked very different than the ASP model. In the future, new ASP interventions in Hong Kong ought to collect baseline data and view implementation in terms of change from baseline.

Explaining Differences in Progress

Presumably there have been differences in progress. Some schools have transformed their cultures and operations significantly and have made considerable inroads into inquiry and powerful learning. Others have made some progress, often uneven in pattern, meaning that they have made greater progress on some aspects of implementation than on others. Other schools are likely to look not very different than at the outset. To maximize overall learning on this school reform, it is important to understand why some schools made considerably more progress than others. Moreover, it is important to consider whether the conditions that make for greater progress can be replicated at other sites to raise the probability of success as the model expands to additional schools.

Based upon what we have learned in the United States, there are at least three initial hypotheses that might be used to explore the causes of differential progress: leadership, time and examination pressures.

Leadership

Leadership at the level of the coach (or SDO in the Hong Kong model) and principal can account for large differences in implementation. Some leaders have enthusiasm, commitment, and skills to support a move to inquiry and powerful learning. Others are less open to change and embrace the existing school culture so completely that they will not make much effort to engage and lead the process. Good leadership must be continuous in supporting day-to-day application of the ASP process, inquiry and powerful learning. It must be active and passionate. It must be obvious to the school community that ASP success is deeply desired by the coach and principal. Simply paying lip service to the words of ASP without appropriate actions will give a message of superficiality and commitment to the status quo. Finally, leaders need skills to demonstrate change and to protect the school from outside influences that stand in the way of transformation (Christensen, 1996). It is our belief that most of the skills can be taught, but not the commitment, passion, and interpersonal support that are needed. We have found that differences in leadership are primary causes of differences in school success.

Time

Changes in school culture and in individual behavior take time. Most teachers have spent at least 4 years in post-secondary education training to be teachers. In addition, they have gone to workshops and have been conditioned by many years of teaching experience. This means that their attitudes, expectations, and practices are likely to be deeply rooted and impervious to brief training experiences. One cannot offset years of traditional training and experience with a few hours of in-service work. For this reason ASP has provided a continuous process that requires mutual support and interaction and extends into daily school activities. This process necessitates a substantial and deep time-commitment to formal training for each phase of the ASP process as well as for practicing inquiry and powerful learning during the work regimen of school staff. If that time allotment is not provided, it is unlikely that there will be much change. Schools need to find adequate time for training, planning and decision-making, and the application of powerful learning. In our experience, inadequate time allocations are also a major reason for a lack of school progress.

Examination Pressures

A third hypothesis derives from the perceived pressures that school staff feel to obtain high marks on student examinations as the only measure of success for the school. Accelerated schools aim for a much wider variety of competencies as reflected in the work of Sternberg (1997) on successful intelligence. In a changing society that is increasingly challenged by globalization and technology, the traditional measures of school success that are measured by traditional examinations are no longer good measures of human development nor predictors of economic success for individuals and society (Levin, 1997a, 2001). If a school feels pressured to view the examination results as the only recognized measure of school quality, it is unlikely to deviate from putting pressures on students to memorize material as the main pedagogy. Such preparation for existing examinations will take precedence over consideration of the other learning goals and alternatives which are inherent in powerful learning and accelerated schools. Perhaps the most important cultural factor operating against change and risk-taking at the school site is the importance that Hong Kong authorities and parents place on the examination rankings. Even if the Hong Kong government broadens its own assessment of schools, the memorization-examination process is so deeply embedded in Hong Kong education and Chinese history that school culture may be unwilling to yield its importance, even it is modified by official policy.

Although these are three of the leading hypotheses for explaining differences in school progress, they are not the only ones. One approach to uncover the importance of these and other influences on progress is to use the assessment tools to classify schools according to three levels of implementation: high, medium, and low. An attempt can be made to explain progress among the three groups by studying if there were systematic differences in characteristics of schools and their engagement in ASQEP. Clearly, three of the variables that need to be examined are the amount of time devoted to ASP, quality of leadership, and perceived pressures of the examination system which undermine other potential goals. However, other dimensions may also be important including characteristics of the teaching force, parental pressures, formal organization of the school, extent of school autonomy, history of centralized versus decentralized decision-making at the school site, and previous experience with constructivist approaches to teaching and learning. All of these and others may account for the differences.

Such differences in factors that predict success in cultural transformation of schools and accelerated schools practices can be used to both improve implementation in the initial schools and to help plan for greater success in subsequent efforts at new schools. Improving our record at school reform requires continuous learning from previous reforms that can only be derived from deliberate and systematic study of them. If we fail to learn from school reform, we will continue to be frustrated in our quest to make major educational changes. At the heart of effective school reform is the successful transformation of school culture. Only with such transformation can new curriculum and instructional strategies be fully embedded in school life.

Notes

1. Finnan and Levin (2000) address this topic in greater detail, and the challenges of change are covered more generally in Altrichter and Elliott (2000) and in

Hargreaves, Lieberman, Fullan, and Hopkins (1998). For a more extensive version, see Finnan and Swanson (2000).

2. Hargreaves et al. (1998) provide a rich source of studies that illustrate these challenges.

3. Details on the process are found in Levin (1998) and Hopfenberg et al. (1993). The cultivation of change in a school is found in Finnan and Swanson (2000).

4. A good source on educational change and school reform is Hargreaves et al. (1998). In the United States, two models with overlapping democratic and human development objectives with Accelerated Schools are the Coalition of Essential Schools and the League of Professional Schools. The Coalition model is discussed by its founder in Sizer (1996). The League model is found in Glickman (1998).

5. The evolution of the project is documented in Levin (1998). Evaluation results have been strong in terms of increased student achievement, parental participation, student attendance, and the establishment of gifted and talented approaches. A recent evaluation of six schools in Memphis, Tennessee found that over 3 years, students had progressed from about the bottom third of the distribution in reading achievement to the top third (see Ross, Sanders, Stringfield, Wang, & Wright, 1999). A national evaluation of results for the 5-year period following adoption of the model in a national sample of schools found that Accelerated Schools had improved student performance on standardized test scores by about one-fourth of a standard deviation, despite the fact that the intervention was designed to focus primarily on outcomes not measured by examination scores (see Doolittle, 2001). The full report is available from the Manpower Development Research Corporation in New York City.

6. Powerful learning refers to a pedagogical strategy in which curriculum, instructional approaches, and school context (organization, climate, and resources) are integrated around academic enrichment approaches (see Hopfenberg et al., 1993, pp. 159–280; also see the analysis of the components of powerful learning on http://www.acceleratedschools.net).

7. The connection between these workplace requirements and Accelerated Schools is discussed in Levin (2001).

8. See, for example, the information available at http://www.gifted.uconn.edu which provides studies and content from the National Research Center on the Gifted and Talented at the University of Connecticut. Also, see Finnan and Swanson (2000).

9. Powerful learning also embraces five components of learning: authenticity, continuity, child-focus, inclusion, and interaction. For details on these and other aspects of the powerful learning model, see http://www. acceleratedschools.net.

10. A good source on performance assessment is Wiggins (1993).

References

Altrichter, H., & Elliott, J. (Eds.). (2000). *Images of educational change.* Buckingham, England; Philadelphia, PA: Open University Press.

Christensen, G. (1996). Toward a new leadership paradigm: Behaviors of accelerated school principals. In C. Finnan, E. St. John, J. McCarthy, & S. Slovacek (Eds.), *Accelerated schools in action: Lessons from the field* (pp. 185–207). Thousand Oaks, CA: Corwin Press.

Cuban, L. (1990). Reforming again, again, and again. *Educational Researcher, 19* (1), 3–13.

Datnow, A. (2000). Power and politics in the adoption of school reform models. *Educational Evaluation and Policy Analysis, 22*(4), 357–374.

Doolittle, F. (2001, April). *Using interrupted time-series analysis to measure the impacts of accelerated schools on the performance of elementary school students.* Paper presented at the Annual Meeting of the American Educational Research Association, Seattle, WA.

Finnan, C., & Levin, H. M. (2000). Changing school cultures. In H. Altrichter & J. Elliott (Eds.), *Images of educational change* (pp. 87–98). Buckingham, England; Philadelphia, PA: Open University Press.

Finnan, C., & Swanson, J. D. (2000). *Accelerating the learning of all students: Cultivating culture change in schools, classrooms, and individuals.* Boulder, CO: Westview Press.

Glickman, C. D. (1998). *Revolutionizing America's schools.* San Francisco: Jossey-Bass.

Hargreaves, A., Lieberman, A., Fullan, M., & Hopkins, D. (Eds.). (1998). *International handbook of educational change* (Part One and Part Two). Dordrecht, Netherlands; Boston: Kluwer Academic Publishers.

Hopfenberg, W. S., Levin, H. M., Chase, C., Christensen, S. G., Moore, M., Soler, P., Brunner, I., Keller, B., & Rodriguez, G. (1993). *The accelerated schools resource guide.* San Francisco: Jossey-Bass.

Levin, H. M. (1997a). *Accelerated education for an accelerating economy* [Education Policy Studies Series No. 9]. Hong Kong: Hong Kong Institute of Educational Research, The Chinese University of Hong Kong.

Levin, H. M. (1997b). Raising school productivity: An X-efficiency approach. *Economics of Education Review, 16*(3), 303–311.

Levin, H. M. (1998). Accelerated schools: A decade of evolution. In A. Hargreaves, A. Lieberman, M. Fullan, & D. Hopkins (Eds.), *International handbook of educational change* (Part Two, pp. 807–830). Dordrecht, Netherlands; Boston: Kluwer Academic Publishers.

Levin, H. M. (2001). Pedagogical challenges for educational futures in industrializing countries. *Comparative Education Review, 45*(4), 537–560.

McLaughlin, M. W. (1990). The RAND change agent study revisited: Macro-perspective and micro realities. *Educational Researcher, 19*(9), 11–16.

Ross, S. M., Sanders, W. L., Stringfield, S., Wang, L. W., & Wright S. P. (1999). *Two year and three year achievement results on the Tennessee value-added assessment system for restructuring schools in Memphis.* Memphis, TN: Center for Research in Educational Policy, University of Memphis.

Sarason, S. B. (1982). *The culture of the school and the problem of change* (2nd ed.). Boston: Allyn & Bacon.

Sizer, T. R. (1996). *Horace's hope: What works for the American high school.* Boston: Houghton Mifflin.

Sternberg, R. J. (1997). *Successful intelligence: How practical and creative intelligence determine success in life.* New York: Plume.

Wiggins, G. P. (1993). *Assessing student performance: Exploring the purpose and limits of testing.* San Francisco: Jossey-Bass.

3

Accelerated Schools for Quality Education: Initial Experiences of School Change

John Chi-kin Lee

Abstract

In autumn 1998, the Faculty of Education and the Hong Kong Institute of Educational Research of The Chinese University of Hong Kong (CUHK) launched the Accelerated Schools for Quality Education Project (ASQEP) under the auspices of the Quality Education Fund. ASQEP is adapted from the Accelerated Schools Project (ASP) originated by Professor Henry Levin in the United States (Levin, 1998a). The pioneering ASQEP school-university partnership project serves 50 primary and secondary schools through adopting a comprehensive approach to school change where the whole school community works together toward quality education.

Using evidence collected to date, this chapter attempts to track the progress of ASQEP during its first years of implementation. The chapter has three major sections. The first section outlines the cardinal principles of the project, namely "Unity of Purpose," "Empowerment with Responsibility" and "Building on Strengths." It also summarizes the five core processes that guide the school change initiative. The second section explains how the original ASP principles and processes have been adapted to "fit" the culture and context of Hong Kong. For example, in Hong Kong, ASQEP members rather than the entire school community conduct the "stocktaking" stage. The final section addresses the vital question of whether the project has been successful. In order to construct a comprehensive picture of progress to date, the project is examined using

Cuban's (1998) major criteria for defining school reform success. Cuban's first set of criteria, which are often used by public officials, policymakers and researchers to judge success, is based on standards related to effectiveness, popularity, and fidelity. In contrast, a second set of criteria, often used by practitioners, is based on standards related to adaptiveness and survival (or longevity).

This chapter uses Cuban's various perspectives to address the initial experiences of school change in ASQEP schools and attempts to identify any early lessons to be learned. It is hoped that a deeper understanding of both the process and outcomes of change can inform further school-level reform efforts in Hong Kong and contribute to building stronger school-university partnerships.

Introduction and Context of ASQEP in Hong Kong

In autumn 1998, the Faculty of Education and the Hong Kong Institute of Educational Research of The Chinese University of Hong Kong (CUHK) launched the Accelerated Schools for Quality Education Project (ASQEP) under the auspices of the Quality Education Fund. ASQEP is adapted from the Accelerated Schools Project (ASP) originated by Professor Henry Levin in the United States, which has had about 16 years of success in several countries (Levin, 1998a). ASQEP, a pioneering school-university partnership project, is seen as a laboratory for school reform in Hong Kong, serving 50 primary and secondary schools over an initial period of 3 years. The project adopts a comprehensive approach to school change in which the whole school community works together toward quality education.

This chapter attempts to track the progress of ASQEP during its first years of implementation. It has three major sections. The first section outlines the features of ASP. The second section describes the design and adaptation of ASQEP before its implementation in the context of Hong Kong. The final section discusses the initial experiences of ASQEP according to the standards of school reform suggested by Cuban (1998).

The project took place at a time when education reform was a key agenda item in Hong Kong. During the 1990s, the Education Commission (1997) issued its Report No. 7, which set the scene for enhancing community appreciation of the need for quality school education. In the report, the Education Commission recommended that a Quality Education Development Fund should be set up to encourage school-based initiatives. This was put into effect in early 1998 as the Quality Education Fund (QEF). At approximately the same time, the Faculty of Education of CUHK launched the Problem-based Partnership Project (Lee, 1997) and the pilot Hong Kong Accelerated Schools Project, which was later expanded to become ASQEP under the auspices of the QEF. The call for quality education in Hong Kong continued, and at the beginning of the new century, the Education Commission (2000) and the Curriculum Development Council (2000) issued two important blueprints. The former published an educational plan for the 21st century entitled *"Learning for Life, Learning through Life."* This states that a priority should be placed on enabling students to "enjoy learning, enhance their effectiveness in communication and develop their creativity and sense of commitment" (Education Commission, 2000, p. 4). The latter is a consultation document entitled *"Learning to Learn,"* emphasizing the promotion of moral and civic education and a reading culture in schools, as well as encouraging schools to make effective use of project learning and information technology to enhance student learning. In the same year, a consultation document on school-based management was also issued. All these call for unprecedented changes in school leadership and management, in curriculum, and in teaching and learning practices in school. How ASQEP may echo some of these reform proposals will be discussed in the following sections.

Features of ASQEP

ASP rests upon three cardinal principles, namely "Unity of Purpose," "Empowerment with Responsibility," and "Building on Strengths." The first principle maintains that all members of the school community should share a vision for the school, and work together toward a consensual set of goals that will be conducive to powerful learning for students. The second principle suggests that every member of the school community should be empowered to participate in the decision-making process, to share in the responsibility for implementing the decisions, and be held accountable for their outcomes. The third principle asserts that in creating an accelerated school, the school community should recognize and utilize the knowledge, talents, and resources of every member of the school community (Levin, 1998a). In addition to the three principles, the Accelerated Schools process comprises five steps: taking stock, forging a vision, setting priorities, generating a governance structure, and engaging in the inquiry process

(Hopfenberg, Levin, & Associates, 1993; Levin, 1996a). Furthermore, ASP has a set of underlying and interrelated values, attitudes and beliefs, that is, equity, communication and collaboration, participation, community spirit, school as center of expertise, risk-taking, reflection, experimentation and discovery, and trust. The ASP philosophy and process including the five steps are known as the "big wheels." At the same time, there are "small wheels," informal innovations initiated by individuals or small groups, which interact with the "big wheels" (Brunner & Hopfenberg, 1996).

ASP in Hong Kong: ASQEP

As Levin suggests (1998b), "the Accelerated Schools process must be adapted to the culture of Hong Kong schools. This means that although its overall structure should probably remain intact ... it must incorporate and build upon Hong Kong ideals and perspectives" (p. 22). Much of the adaptation of ASP in Hong Kong was in recognition of the quite different cultural context within which schools operate (Walker & Dimmock, 2000). To some extent, Hong Kong displays a shared East Asian culture of schooling characterized by student preparedness to conform to requirements, particularly examination ideologies, in their pursuit of excellence, and their belief in perseverance (Lee & Dimmock, 1998). Li, Yu, Lam, and Fok (1999) analyzed the cultural heritage of Hong Kong and concluded that the following phenomena at the policy-making level were counter-productive to school reforms: a bureaucratic establishment constraining teachers' effectiveness and their participation in curriculum development, the administrators' "we-know-what's-best-for-teachers" attitude, and the close supervision of teachers to ensure a standardized method of operation. Morris, Lo, and Adamson (2000) further commented that recent education reform initiatives had been constructed upon a deficit model of schooling and pedagogy. At the school level, Walker and Cheng (1996) found that Hong Kong primary school administrators tended to emphasize the need for hardware and technical support, and to downplay the importance of professional development in school improvement. Lo (2000) echoed that teacher development was not the central concern in reform efforts in Hong Kong and teachers in general lacked the much-needed professional space for reflecting on their work and effecting change.

While ASQEP in Hong Kong adopts the philosophy and basic principles of ASP in the United States, it differs slightly from the U.S. model in the following three aspects, namely the "buying-in" process, the involvement of School Development Officers, and the "stocktaking" process.

"Buying-in" Process

In the United States, a school will not be permitted to join ASP formally, unless at least 80 to 90% of its full-time staff and school community representatives agree to do so. The "buying-in" process for ASQEP in Hong Kong did not involve securing the support of the majority of the school community. This was because when the project was launched, little was known in schools about school restructuring models or ASP. In addition, in Hong Kong, many teachers were skeptical of the worth of such projects. They were more concerned about matters such as workload, especially the paper work that would fall on them from participating in such projects, and they were anxious to know what kind and how much of support the project would offer them.

Involvement of School Development Officers

Based on the experience in the United States which revealed that schools achieve greater success implementing the model with the support of "coaches" outside the school site, School Development Officers (SDOs) were recruited as coaches to facilitate the implementation of ASQEP. An intensive 5-day (instead of 8-day) train-the-trainers workshop was provided for the SDOs. This was activity-based and embodied a constructivist approach to learning. In addition, unlike in the United States, in ASQEP there are no highly trained internal coaches in the participating schools who work with the SDOs on a regular basis (Levin, 1998a, p. 820). This is partly because the project has not secured enough funds for internal coaches to be released to work with the SDOs. It was planned, however, that the SDOs would have regular meetings with a core group of teachers and cadres to help each school build the capacity for change. They also supported and encouraged principals and teachers to develop powerful learning approaches and activities to realize the principles and values of ASP.

"Stocktaking" Process

In ASQEP, the "stocktaking" process is undertaken by ASQEP team members rather than involving everyone in the school community (Hopfenberg, Levin, & Associates, 1993; Lee, Chiu, Poon, Tang, & Tam, 1999). This represents a point of departure from the original design. In ASP, "stocktaking" provides an opportunity for school community members to begin to take responsibility for school challenges and to learn about all facets of the school. This process usually takes about 4 months (Hopfenberg, Levin, & Associates, 1993). We suspect that the involvement of the whole school community in stocktaking might not work in the current context of constraints in Hong Kong. Teachers in Hong Kong tend to have a greater teaching workload than their Western counterparts. A primary or secondary school teacher in Hong Kong would normally have 30 to 32 teaching periods (35 to 40 minutes each) per week cycle. In order to establish trust between the project team and the school staff and to provide a baseline for monitoring the performance of all schools in the project, a number of well-validated instruments were administered, and a 2-day stocktaking exercise was conducted in all project schools. SDOs were then requested to write reports and present the findings in a form that could be understood by the staff in the schools. These were to form the basis for the next two steps, namely vision-building and priority-setting. Responses from the schools were almost unanimously positive about the value and professional standard of the stocktaking exercise (Caldwell, 1999).

Having described how ASP was adapted to the Hong Kong context, in the next section we turn to the implementation and outcomes of ASQEP. The project experience is described from various perspectives, including that of judging the extent of the success of the reform initiative.

Criteria for Understanding School Reform: Towards a Multiple Approach

"Is it successful?" is a question frequently asked about reform initiatives. Cuban (1998) suggests that there are two major sets of criteria for defining the success or failure of school reforms. The first set of criteria which is often used by public officials, policymakers and researchers to judge success is based on standards related to "effectiveness," "popularity" and "fidelity." In contrast, the second set of criteria used by practitioners and social scientists is based on standards related to "adaptiveness" and "survival" (or "longevity").

While different scholars, for example, Connelly and Clandinin (2000), have other lenses through which school reform initiatives can be analyzed, this chapter attempts to address the initial experiences of school change and the lessons to be learned from ASQEP primarily using Cuban's (1998) perspectives.

The information for this chapter was derived from initial statistical analyses of first two years' data, case studies of selected schools, documents, observations and personal experiences of working with schools in ASQEP. It must be stressed, however, that at the time of writing, complete data is still unavailable. For example, the first two years' quantitative data have been partially analyzed. The final round of data collection will only be conducted at the end of the project. The results and lessons set out here should therefore be viewed as preliminary.

ASQEP: The Initial Experiences

The Effectiveness Standard

The effectiveness standard usually refers to what students have learned in school by using proxy measures such as students' test scores and other measures to determine the success of change outcomes. The effectiveness of ASQEP, however, can be assessed in a range of different ways. At the outset of the project, it was hypothesized that schools undergoing the ASQEP transformational process would exhibit the following changes:

1. Improved participation and collaboration, communication and consensus (these relate to the first principle of "unity of purpose" and to the ASP values of participation, communication and collaboration);
2. Improved collegiality and teacher autonomy as well as increased teacher empowerment (these relate to the second principle of "empowerment coupled with responsibility");
3. Improved ratings by students on powerful learning activities (this refers to activity-based, interesting learning experiences for students); and
4. Improved ratings by students on the quality of school life and their own self-concept, and improved academic test scores.

In an attempt to gauge the effectiveness, a quantitative "pre-post" and "treatment-control" comparative design was adopted for ASQEP. This involved 50 ASQEP schools and another 50 control schools conveniently sampled and with no involvement in the project. A number of quantitative measures were employed. These included: teacher empowerment (Klecker & Loadman, 1996; Rinehart, Short, Short, & Eckley, 1998), teachers' sense of organizational commitment (Cheng, 1990; Mowday, Steers, & Porter, 1979), teachers' perceptions of school organizational values (Pang, 1998a, 1998b), students' perceptions of the degree to which the classroom environment is effective and the teaching and learning activities powerful (Lee, Chiu, Wong, et al., 1999), as well as students' perceptions of the quality of school life (Pang, 1997; Ramsay & Clark, 1990), students' self-concept (Marsh, 1990, n.d.) and academic achievement (in terms of Hong Kong Aptitude Test [HKAT] scores) (Lee, 1999).

Initial cross-sectional statistical analyses of the data collected from teachers in 1998–1999 (first-year survey undertaken in November, 1998) and in 1999–2000 (second-year survey undertaken in November, 1999) revealed the following (Table 1):

1. In ASQEP secondary schools, teacher autonomy was perceived to be significantly higher in mean value in the second year than in the first year. There was no such significant mean difference in this factor in the case of control schools.

2. In ASQEP primary schools, factors of professional growth, decision-making, self-efficacy, impact and autonomy associated with teacher empowerment were perceived to be significantly higher in mean values in the second year than in the first year. There were no such significant mean differences in these factors in the case of control schools.

3. In ASQEP secondary schools, factors of professional growth, decision-making, self-efficacy and autonomy associated with teacher empowerment were perceived to be significantly higher in mean values in the second year than in the first year. However, there were also significant differences in the factors of professional growth, decision-making and autonomy in the case of control schools. Nonetheless, the increase in mean values between the 2 years for the factors of professional growth and decision-making appeared to be slightly greater in ASQEP schools than in their counterparts.

4. In ASQEP primary schools, the mean values of teachers' sense of organizational commitment appeared to be significantly lower in the second year than in the first year. There are no such significant mean differences in these factors in the case of control schools.

Table 1   *Change in Teachers' Perception at ASP Schools on Factors in Major Domains Across Two Years (1998–1999 to 1999–2000)*

	Major domain		
School level	Teacher's personal values inventory	Teacher empowerment	Job satisfaction
Primary school	• Not significant	• Professional growth • Decision making • Self-efficacy • Autonomy • Impact	• Teacher commitment*
Secondary school	• Teacher autonomy	• Professional growth • Decision making • Self-efficacy • Autonomy • Impact	• Not significant

* The factor is decreasing statistically.
$p < .05$.

5. In control primary schools, teacher participation in school decision-making and collaboration with each other were perceived to be significantly lower in mean value in the second year than in the first year. No such significant mean difference in this factor emerged in the case of ASQEP schools.

All these mean values, unless otherwise stated, had significant differences at the .05 confidence level.

A comparison of the data collected from teachers in 1998–1999 and in 1999–2000 between ASQEP and control schools by MANOVA revealed that (Table 2):

1. Change in the mean values for professional growth, decision-making and autonomy, associated with teacher empowerment, were significantly higher in ASQEP primary schools from the first year to the second year than in control schools. There were no significant differences in the change of mean values in schools' espoused values and teachers' personal values as well as teachers' sense of organizational commitment between ASQEP and control primary schools.

Table 2 *Difference Between ASP and Control Schools in Teachers' Perception on Factors in Major Domains Across Two Years (1998–1999 to 1999–2000)*

School level	Major domain	
	Teacher's personal values inventory	Teacher empowerment
Primary school	• Not significant	• Professional growth
		• Decision making
		• Autonomy
Secondary school	• Teacher autonomy	• Not significant

$p < .05.$

2. Change in the mean values for teacher autonomy, associated with teachers' personal values, were significantly higher in ASQEP secondary schools from the first year to the second year than in control schools. There were, however, no significant differences in the change of mean values in schools' espoused values, teachers' perception of empowerment as well as teachers' sense of organizational commitment between ASQEP and control secondary schools.

With regard to the data collected from students in 1998–1999 (the first year) and in 1999–2000 (the second year), the cross-sectional statistical analyses revealed the following (Table 3):

1. There were significant increases in primary school students' ratings given to active learning (P.4, P.5, & P.6), adventure (P.4, P.5, & P.6), achievement (P.5 & P.6) and social integration (P.5 & P.6) in

Table 3 *Change in Students' Perception at ASP Schools on Factors in Domains Across Two Years (1998–1999 to 1999–2000)*

School level	Domain		
	Classroom environment	Self-concept	Quality at school life
Primary school	• Active learning	• General self-concept	• Adventure
		• Honesty	• Achievement
			• Social integration
Secondary school	• Active learning	• Honesty	• Achievement
			• Social integration

connection with the quality of school life, and to general self-concept (P.4, P.5, & P.6) and honesty (P.4 & P.5) in the second year compared with the first year. Similarly, there were significant increases in secondary school students' ratings given to active learning (S.1 & S.2), achievement and social integration (S.1 & S.3) in connection with the quality of school life, and to honesty (S.1, S.2, & S.3) in the second year compared with the first year.

While it is too early to establish causality at this stage, the initial results suggest that after 16 months, there seem to have been more significant changes in variables associated with teacher empowerment in ASQEP schools than in the control schools. Moreover, the impact of ASQEP seems to have been greater on primary schools than on secondary schools. In general, when judged against Cuban's effectiveness standard, while ASQEP can claim some successes, it must also be admitted that a number of areas require further work.

The Popularity Standard

The popularity standard refers to the extent of the spread of an innovation and/or to the extent of public attention attracted to the innovation. With regard to popularity, there has been a persistent demand from schools to join ASQEP. It has also attracted a great deal of public interest. During April, 1998, a total of 88 primary schools and 97 secondary schools expressed a strong interest in ASQEP. ASQEP was launched in September, and throughout its first two years it has attracted substantial positive media coverage, such as an appearance in a program filmed by the Hong Kong Television Broadcast Company and another by the Educational Television (ETV) of Radio Television Hong Kong for teachers. Because of the early success of ASQEP, a localized model for school improvement was established to work with another 40 primary schools and 10 secondary and special schools. This project, entitled "University and School Partnership for Quality Education" (USPQE), was supported by the Quality Education Fund, and was launched in 2000. On October 23, 2000, over 300 school principals and teachers from over 90 secondary schools and 150 primary schools attended a seminar on successful experiences in ASQEP and requested support from the Centre for University and School Partnership. Thus, against the criterion of popularity, ASQEP can be deemed a success.

The Fidelity Standard

The fidelity standard refers to the match between the initial design, the formal policy, the subsequent program(s) it generates, and its implementation. The initial design of the ASP model emphasizes a deep commitment to professional development both at the school site and with the school team (school principal and both internal and external coaches). In the United States, the most basic training agreement involves 19 days of training for coaches and school principals in the 1st year (Levin, 1999). However, most schools in Hong Kong have only 3 full days in an academic year for staff development and this has inevitably constrained the amount of teacher development undertaken at the school site.

There are some subtle differences in the way ASQEP has had to be implemented. These can be examined through Fullan's (2000) four elements underpinning structural reform at district level, namely policies focusing on decentralization, local capacity building, rigorous external accountability, and stimulation of innovation. With regard to decentralization, the governance structure of ASP in the United States usually encompasses three levels: the School as a Whole (SAW), the Cadre, and the Steering Committee. It is worth noting that the SAW consists of teachers' aides, instructional and non-instructional staff, and parent and student representatives, while the Steering Committee consists of teachers' representatives, aides, other school staff and parents. Parent and student representatives in Hong Kong, however, do not normally participate in school decision-making. Thus in ASQEP, parent and student representatives are not involved in major decisions that affect the entire school.

With regard to local capacity building, school districts in the United States provide support services to help accelerated schools fulfill their mission, and central office staff assist the cadres and steering committee in identifying challenges, implementation, staff development, and evaluation as well as help to obtain staff release time for meetings, staff development, discussion, reflection and planning of change alternatives (Levin, 1996b). In Hong Kong, the Regional Education Offices (REOs) of the Education Department (similar to School Districts in the United States) have only just begun to play a role in school reform through their support services starting from 1999 to 2000, but officers of the Education Department have not been directly involved in supporting the implementation of ASQEP. With regard to staff release time for professional activities, a capacity enhancement grant from the government was allocated to primary and secondary schools starting from 2000 to 2001 to employ extra staff or hire services to alleviate the workload of teachers. In addition, to obtain extra resources for school development, schools can submit proposals to the Quality Education Fund on a competitive basis.

The implementation of ASQEP in general follows the suggested procedures of ASP, namely taking stock, forging a vision, setting priorities, creating a governance structure and engaging in an ongoing inquiry and improvement process. With regard to the inquiry process, not many schools have found it easy to adopt and apply a disciplined approach to problem-solving. Rather, school members tend to skip parts of the process, limit the inquiry to the working group (cadres), or undertake the process inadequately (Soler & Levin, 1997). This is similar to a certain extent to what happened in the United States, in that "the little wheels of inquiry were evident in many of the schools, but the big wheels of inquiry had not yet emerged by the second semester in the Accelerated Schools Project" (St. John, Meza, Jr., Allen-Haynes, & Davidson, 1996, p. 135). Overall, ASQEP can claim substantial success against the fidelity standard but has some distance to go before total success can be claimed. The successes were associated with the implementation of the five steps, but work is needed in terms of support of ASQEP at the district level and the implementation of the inquiry process at the school level.

The Adaptiveness Standard

The adaptiveness standard refers to the way in which teachers adapt and make an innovation work with respect to their own school context. Teachers tend to judge the success of their work in terms of students' attitudes, values, and actual behavior in academic and non-academic tasks in and out of the classroom, rather than simply on test scores (Cuban, 1998). To the practitioner, the process is as important as the product. To study this, six ASQEP schools (three primary and three secondary) were selected based on the initial patterns of teachers' and students' scores in 1998–1999. They were not intended to be representative of all schools in ASQEP, but rather to serve as illustrations of ASQEP activities and changes in particular school settings.

In one of the primary schools, in which teachers' and students' scores were average in 1998–1999, initial teacher resistance toward the project was prevalent, again because it was the principal's decision to join the project rather than theirs. One of the focuses of development in this school in the first year was the enhancement of teaching and learning. Through the intensive efforts of the ASQEP development team, a series of workshops was organized to help teachers internalize the principles of powerful learning and liberate themselves from the paradigm of traditional teaching. The feedback toward the workshops was positive and included comments such as "extending my horizons and stimulating my thinking," "powerful learning gave me a dream of teaching and direction," and "a joyful way of learning, making teaching and learning happen in an interactive situation" (school development coach journal). In addition, a 2-day "powerful learning" event was co-organized between the school and our team. The powerful learning days provided an authentic and attractive environment for P.2 students to explore ideas and engage in learning activities. The event involved the participation of parents and was well received. While some teachers had reservations about the amount of manpower and resources given to this event, the observations and interview findings revealed that some teachers had displayed changes in their attitudes and commitment toward their work and the project. Following this event, the principal decided that similar activities should be extended to other year levels in the second year of the project. In the third year, while the SDO went on providing professional advice on design and implementation, teachers organized powerful learning activities mainly on their own.

In another primary school in which teachers' scores were relatively high in 1998–1999, the progress of the project was quite slow, partly because the principal was on leave and the acting principal did not feel that it was his role to introduce major changes into the school. The leading SDO attached to that school also left, further retarding the pace of development. The school had substantial experience in curriculum innovation and teachers were generally committed to change, but they felt overloaded with work. When the principal returned in the second year of the project, he wanted the teaching staff to reflect on their teaching and to undertake some action research. With the support of the university team and the principal, two action research projects were undertaken by a few teachers to explore reading in Chinese and in English respectively. The teachers felt that the extra workload was considerable and that the tasks were demanding, but most of them found the action research experience rewarding and insightful for their future teaching. In the third year, action research projects continued and were extended to Mathematics.

In one of the secondary schools with moderate teacher ratings in the 1998–1999 survey, the principal had initially proposed that the school join ASQEP, but the majority of staff had voted against it. The final decision, however, taken by the principal and vice-principal, was that the school should join. On the one hand, there was an initial expectation among some of the staff that ASQEP would "change the principal and the senior management." On the other hand, the principal and vice-principal hoped that the project would extend the horizons of the staff and bring about change with the support of outside forces such as the university team (interview notes). There was a general mistrust and lack of communication between the management and teaching staff. In the first two years, a number of workshops were arranged for the staff but the responses were quite negative. A substantial number of teachers simply "watched" the activities somewhat passively, feeling that they were not useful for their work. While the stocktaking process and subsequent discussion brought opportunities for staff to voice their grievances and concerns, the management only paid lip service to their views. Teachers' frustrations grew and it was generally reckoned that the project had failed. At the end of the second year, it was decided that the SDOs should only work with some enthusiastic Social Studies and History teachers to design and implement an integrated curriculum project. Teachers' and students' responses were quite positive. This helped to restore the partnership between the university team and the core members of the school.

In another school in which teachers' scores were relatively high in 1998–1999, the principal and most staff supported participation in ASQEP. The first year's work involved stocktaking, vision-building and enhancement of team spirit. Workshops on powerful learning, curriculum integration and multiple intelligences were also arranged to provide a theoretical foundation for "small wheels" development such as small-scale curriculum change within the school. In the second year, the SDOs helped the staff focus on issues of concern and set priorities for school development. In addition, the SDOs helped teachers map teaching objectives and approaches against the cultivation of students' competencies. Moreover, some S.1 teachers of Economics and Public Affairs, History and Geography attempted to integrate subject content through the theme of "Food" and to incorporate some powerful learning activities within this. The school also invited parents to observe a "powerful learning" event. Overall, the students appeared to engage very actively in interesting activities. Despite the heavy workload and inadequate logistic arrangements, many teachers felt that the activities were useful for student learning and that the event had stimulated their reflection on school-based curriculum change. A new curriculum integration project for S.1 and the introduction of project work have been planned for implementation in the third year.

In terms of "adaptiveness," from the above discussion it can be seen that each of the six schools chose to pursue particular aspects of the ASQEP project in line with particular features of its context in the early years. With regard to teaching and learning activities, one primary school chose to focus on powerful learning and peer observation, another on powerful learning, and another on action research. One secondary school chose to work on project work and two on integrating the curriculum. In terms of school change, there were some successful stories of extending teachers' horizons and enhancing teacher development through participation in the design and implementation of powerful learning activities. However, it seems that some of these schools are still struggling with issues of improving staff communication and collaboration and with trying to increase teacher participation in school-based curriculum development. In general, against the adaptiveness standard, ASQEP can claim considerable successes but must still face a number of issues to further improve its performance.

The Survival (or Longevity) Standard

The survival standard refers to the extent to which an innovation lasts and becomes widespread. According to the ASP model in the United States, the school transformation process takes about 5 to 6 years for completion (Brunner & Hopfenberg, 1996, p. 45; Dalin, 1998, p. 203; Levin, 1996b, p. 344; St. John et al., 1996, p. 135). Under the auspices of the Quality Education Fund, the development work of ASQEP in schools will formally cease to operate in August 2001. Unless other sources of external funding are secured, it is unlikely that ASQEP can continue to operate under the present conditions or in the current format. It is therefore not possible to make a judgment of ASQEP against the survival standard at this stage.

In summary, it is apparent that ASQEP has experienced some success as well as some difficulties when judged against the different standards proposed by Cuban. We turn now to an attempt to identify early lessons obtained from the ASQEP experience, since these may have implications for future school improvement in Hong Kong.

ASQEP: Lessons Learned

Partnership Development Is Context-Specific and Pivotal to the Success of the Project

ASQEP adopts a school-based strategy for improvement that allows each school to have considerable autonomy in determining its own priorities for development and in constructing its own methods for achieving these priorities. Thus, while the university and school partners are all involved in one project (ASQEP), there is considerable scope for each school to take its own developmental pathway. Kushman and Chenoweth (1996) suggest that there are four non-linear phases for successful implementation of the ASP model in the United States: courtship, training and development, changing school structure and culture, and changing classroom practices. In the case of ASQEP, most schools followed these phases but a few of them concentrated on changing curriculum and classroom practices rather than on changing school structure and culture. In addition, the experience of both school and university partners highlights the fact that it is the development of an effective partnership between the SDOs of the university team and school staff that is crucial to the success and progress of the project. It also indicates that there are two major strands affecting such partnership development:

1. The role of the SDOs and the continuity of their work; and
2. A shared meaning of what ASQEP entails among principals and teachers, and the need for leadership and participation in school development.

Our experience indicates that partnership development is inevitably affected by politics and personalities as well as other contextual factors.

The Role of the SDOs and the Continuity of Their Work

From our experience of early encounters with teachers, we found that teachers treated the SDOs as "experts" and "consultants" rather than as facilitators. Teachers expected the SDOs to provide information on successful educational practices and advice on the design of innovative school programs. Some principals and teachers also liked to ask the SDOs for feedback on their own ideas as to how to go about marking assignments and setting examination questions. This seems rather similar to the overseas experience of faculty in school reform ventures (Goodman, 1995):

> In these situations, we often found ourselves in the role of "legitimizing" the teachers' and the principals' views.... By being placed in the position of "experts," in most situations we were able to furnish these teachers with "authoritative endorsement" for educational practices, curricular content and/ or social visions which they intuitively believed were good but which had never been "sanctioned" by anyone "in power".... (p. 72)

It was also the case that some SDOs presented themselves as "experts" so as to gain confidence and trust from school community members. Some of them gave demonstrations of teaching practice. Others provided ideas for stimulating teachers' professional work. For schools with greater readiness and a capacity for change at the start, the SDOs tried to play the role of facilitator rather than expert or consultant. In general, our approach was to attempt to progress gradually from an expert-led to a more participative mode of operation, so as to strike a good balance between providing educational consultancy and empowering teachers (Lee, Wong, Chiu, Chung, & Lo, 1999).

By way of summary, the contribution of the SDOs to the early success of ASQEP is described by two vice-principals in one of the secondary schools as follows (document, March, 2000):

> (1) good relationships with the school; (2) willing to offer help with regard to the school's needs; (3) able to make recommendations for improvement and offer assistance according to the school's problems; (4) a good balance between theory and practice as manifested through well-organized seminars and activities; (5) members are responsible persons and good partners; and (6) assistance to school is supported by substantial manpower and resources.

It was found that staff turnover in either the university team or the ASQEP schools affected progress in individual schools. For example, it was unfortunate that in some ASQEP schools the partnership development was slow partly because of the resignation of a few SDOs during the first two years of the project. It took a few months or even longer for newly assigned SDOs to establish good working relationships with school staff. In cases where the principal had left or a key teacher leader such as a vice-principal had been promoted to another non-ASQEP school, SDOs had to secure other core group members within the school as key change agents to keep the momentum of the project going.

Shared Meaning of ASQEP Among Principals and Teachers and Their Leadership and Participation in School Development

The importance of shared meaning or vision is well documented in the literature of educational change (e.g., Hargreaves, 1997; Sammons, Hillman, & Mortimore, 1997). In any change effort, it is essential that principals, teachers and schools agree on the direction they are heading in. As Fink (2000) states: "Teachers cannot be given a purpose. Purposes must come from within. Pursuing their own inspiring mission together is what can most help teachers turn their schools around" (p. 8). ASQEP, based on ASP of the United States, can best be understood as an organizational strategy for change in which "while the schools, on their part, must commit themselves to the broad vision, in the process they will further develop it …" (Dalin, 1998, p. 204).

In the implementation of ASQEP, there are clearly variations in commitment among the staff in individual schools, and between one school and another. In some schools, for example, ASQEP is seen as a symbolic means of showing that they are doing something significant for their students or as a means for acquiring much needed resources (Chenoweth & Kushman, 1996). In other schools, ASQEP may simply be seen as an "add-on" program. For teachers, there are a number of concerns — whether ASQEP will bring extra workload for them, whether it will directly address school problems, whether it will have an immediate effect on their working lives, or whether it will introduce strategies that produce positive and immediate effects on student learning, etc.

In the literature of school reform initiatives, leadership has been shown to be a critical factor for success (e.g., Smith, Ross et al., 1998). In the traditional school, administrators tend to view themselves as the source of all decisions and activities. In accelerated schools, it is expected that principals adopt a more transformational style and move towards empowering their teachers to share responsibilities with them (Mims, 1996). As one of the ASQEP primary school principals said when reflecting on change in her own school:

> Initially the power was very centralized. Colleagues were instructed to implement measures in many occasions only after decision by the principal. This gradually led to one person's [the principal's sole] decision. They [the staff] have a different view. They only implemented your ideas, which then made the working atmosphere less harmonious among the staff. I then gradually introduced the division of labor. At the start, the vice-principal and the senior

teachers (were empowered). Later I invited the senior teachers to form a group themselves. This became [a] better decision-making process.

Another secondary school principal remarked that:

I think I would let a lot of colleagues help shoulder the authority. So I would not chair the staff meeting.... I would let my colleagues offer more participation and autonomy in decision-making. This is related to what the ASP gives us the point on empowerment.

Inevitably not all principals see empowerment in a favorable light. A few tend to see shared decision-making as an erosion of their power base, and a few tend to have very low expectations of their staff and their students and so do not want to involve them in decision-making. Others realize that having strong supporters of change or core group members in the school makes implementation of change easier (Lam, 1991).

Change Takes Time, and More Time Seems to be Needed for Change in Secondary Schools Than in Primary Schools

The initial quantitative results of ASQEP over a 16-month period reveal that changes take place in ways and speeds that are associated with teacher empowerment, particularly in primary schools. This is to some extent congruent with the U.S. first-year evaluation outcomes of three primary (elementary) accelerated schools, which demonstrated most progress in team-building and goal-setting rather than in teaching and learning (Ross et al., 1997). Smith, Maxwell et al. (1997) further comment that school restructuring models such as ATLAS, Modern Red Schoolhouse and ASP tend to emphasize the development of school vision and organization in the first year and "take a slower approach to starting-up, based on the belief that more up-front preparation is required by their models" (p. 149). More analysis of longitudinal data is needed to ascertain the long-term sustainability and effects of ASQEP.

In summing up overseas school reform experience in various parts of the world, Fullan (2000) remarks that it takes at least 3 years for a small number of primary (elementary) schools to achieve a successful change in student performance, and 6 years for a small number of secondary schools to achieve the same. In this project, the initial quantitative results also suggest that the impact of ASQEP seems to be greater in primary schools than in their secondary counterparts. There may be several reasons for such a difference. The first is related to the size of school staff (over 50 teaching staff in a secondary school compared with about 30 colleagues in a primary school). The second reason arises from the way in which secondary schools are organized into separate departments. This makes it more difficult to implement an integrated approach to curriculum or powerful cross-curricular learning activities on the one hand or improve inter-departmental staff communication and collaboration on the other. A further reason stems from the relatively low parental involvement in secondary schools compared with their primary counterparts (Finnan, 1992).

Constraints Affecting the Implementation and Effectiveness of ASQEP in the Local Context

ASP in Hong Kong has undergone adaptation in its implementation due to contextual differences with the United States, in particular with regard to training, stocktaking and governance structure. Other local factors include the fact that most classrooms in ASQEP schools were designed in the traditional manner in which seats are arranged in fixed rows. There is thus a limit to the extent to which it is possible to organize powerful learning activities in such a space. In addition, in school's staff-rooms, teachers are crammed into a very small space on desks overflowing with books, papers and other resources. The conditions in which staff and students work are thus not very conducive to developing and sustaining the kind of changes envisaged by ASQEP (Caldwell, 1999, 2000).

As mentioned in the introduction, ASQEP was launched and implemented at a time of considerable educational rethinking in Hong Kong. During the last 2 to 3 years, there have been a number of different reform initiatives and measures such as school-based management, benchmarking of language teachers, medium of instruction policy, and training for information technology in education. Many principals and teachers were burdened with extra tasks and responsibilities. Schools have often felt that they were responding to multiple but seemingly unrelated initiatives and innovative programs. While ASQEP provides an umbrella for integrating school-based changes, it can also appear to be just another separate initiative, unrelated to the others, to some teachers. When this happens they lose sight of the grand picture and lose direction. As one senior teacher in a primary school said:

> There seem to be many directions.... Many reforms are good but the
> consultation is inadequate and they do not match the reality in school operation.
> Nor do they meet the schools' and students' needs.

Another secondary principal echoed that:

> We [some principals] feel that if individual parts of recent reforms are
> mentioned, all of them are good.... However, the pace and strategies (of
> reform) have a lot of problems.... In the last few years when I look at our
> cooperation with ASQEP, in certain aspects I think it is a very good mechanism.
> I think if the road can go ahead, meaning that if there is a collaborative
> relationship between a group of university colleagues who have a mission
> and wish to reform education and those from primary and secondary
> schools, particularly for primary schools, this will be a good direction for
> development.

Conclusion

This chapter attempted to examine the success or failure of ASQEP from
various perspectives using various criteria. While the initial results and
experiences of the first two years of implementation provide only tentative
observations, the findings seem to suggest a mixed picture of partial
success and areas of weakness. With regard to the effectiveness standard,
there seem to be significant improvements in teacher empowerment,
particularly in ASQEP primary schools and some gains in the quality of
school life at primary six as experienced by students. However, there
seems to be a decline in the quality of school life and in self-concept as
perceived by secondary school students in ASQEP schools. With regard to
the popularity standard, there would seem to have been some success, as
there have been a lot of positive remarks made by the schools. On the
fidelity standard, ASQEP would have only partial success. With regard to
the adaptiveness standard, schools have moved closer to the ideals of
ASQEP in varying aspects, in varying ways and at varying speeds — some
very slowly. The survival (or longevity) standard is not yet applicable to the
initiative, as it has only been going for three years.

The success or failure of any school reform project, whether deriving
from the ASQEP model or not, depends on many factors. School
development is about changing the attitudes and actions of staff. It is about
transforming their beliefs and their behaviors as well as improving student
learning. One of the lessons from ASQEP, however, is that reforms may

change schools, but schools also adapt and change reforms (Cuban, 1998). As Finnan (1996) succinctly points out:

> The participants are creating change; they are not *being* changed ... people do not mind being changed (that is what learning is about) if they *choose* to be changed and are able to create the change [original emphasis]. (p. 120)

In retrospect, it would have been desirable to accept only those schools in which a majority of staff supported change in the "buying-in" process. It would also have been desirable to have insisted that principals and senior teachers involved in the project participate in a pre-training session designed to provide an overview of the ASQEP model and to explain what was expected of them (Mims, 1996). This would have helped to build their understanding of the meaning of change in ASQEP and might have enhanced their initial commitment to the project.

My own initial reflections on ASQEP as a pioneering school-based school improvement project in Hong Kong can be briefly summarized as follows. School development is a difficult endeavor, full of excitement and uncertainties. It involves rational planning, resolution of internal conflicts in school, as well as demand for perseverance and commitment on the part of both school and university partners. This echoes Ainscow and Southworth's (1996) comment that "school development is not easy or straightforward ... it is personal, idiosyncratic and micropolitical" (p. 250). Educational change is not just a rational endeavor involving careful design, rigorous planning and systematic training, but also a process involving deep emotions, dependent on trust, collaboration, shared meaning and even conflict (Hargreaves, 1997). Involvement in projects such as ASQEP is best seen as an ongoing journey of risk-taking, reflecting, acting and rethinking.

Acknowledgments

I would like to thank Professor Henry Levin and Ms. Pilar Soler for their guidance on the training and development of ASP in Hong Kong. Sincere thanks are extended to the Management and Advisory Committee members, Consultants, Co-investigators, Development, Research and Administration team members, Honorary SDOs and participating schools in ASQEP. Gratitude is also extended to Professor Allan Walker and Dr. John Clark for their valuable comments on this article.

References

Ainscow, M., & Southworth, G. (1996). School improvement: A study of the roles of leaders and external consultants. *School Effectiveness and School Improvement*, 7(3), 229–251.

Brunner, I., & Hopfenberg, W. (1996). Growth and learning: Big wheels and little wheels interacting. In C. Finnan, E. P. St. John, J. McCarthy, & S. P. Slovacek (Eds.), *Accelerated schools in action: Lessons from the field* (pp. 24–46). Thousand Oaks, CA: Corwin Press.

Caldwell, B. J. (1999, June 25). *Accelerated schools for quality education*. First report of the external reviewer.

Caldwell, B. J. (2000, September 12). *Accelerated schools for quality education*. Second report of the external reviewer.

Cheng, Y. C. (1990). An investigation of antecedents of organizational commitment. *Educational Research Journal*, 5, 29–42.

Chenoweth, T. G., & Kushman, J. W. (1996). Building initial commitment to accelerate. In C. Finnan, E. P. St. John, J. McCarthy, & S. P. Slovacek (Eds.), *Accelerated schools in action: Lessons from the field* (pp. 145–168). Thousand Oaks, CA: Corwin Press.

Connelly, F. M., & Clandinin, D. J. (2000). Bringing narrative inquiry to school reform. *Educational Research Journal*, 15(1), 167–183.

Cuban, L. (1998). How schools change reforms: Redefining reform success and failure. *Teachers College Record*, 99(3), 453–477.

Curriculum Development Council. (2000). *Learning to learn: The way forward in curriculum development*. Hong Kong: Author.

Dalin, P. (1998). *School development: Theories and strategies*. London; New York: Cassell.

Education Commission. (1997). *Education Commission report no. 7: Quality school education*. Hong Kong: Printing Department.

Education Commission. (2000). *Learning for life, learning through life: Reform proposals for the education system in Hong Kong*. Hong Kong: Author.

Fink, D. (2000). *Good schools/real schools: Why school reform doesn't last*. New York: Teachers College Press.

Finnan, C. (1992). *Becoming an accelerated middle school: Initiating school culture change*. Report prepared for the National Center for the Accelerated Schools Project.

Finnan, C. (1996). Making change our friend. In C. Finnan, E. P. St. John, J. McCarthy, & S. P. Slovacek (Eds.), *Accelerated schools in action: Lessons from the field* (pp. 104–123). Thousand Oaks, CA: Corwin Press.

Fullan, M. (2000). The three stories of education reform. *Phi Delta Kappan*, 81(8), 581–584.

Goodman, J. (1995). Working with teachers to reform schools: Issues of power, expertise and commitment. In J. Smyth (Ed.), *Critical discourses on teacher development* (pp. 65–79). London; New York: Cassell.

Hargreaves, A. (1997). Rethinking educational change: Going deeper and wider in the quest of success. In A. Hargreaves (Ed.), *Rethinking educational change with heart and mind: The 1997 ASCD yearbook* (pp. 1–26). Alexandria, VA: Association for Supervision and Curriculum Development.

Hopfenberg, W. S., Levin, H. M., & Associates (1993). *The Accelerated schools resource guide.* San Francisco: Jossey-Bass.

Klecker, B., & Loadman, W. E. (1996, April). *An analysis of the School Participant Empowerment Scale (Short & Rinehart, 1992) based on data from 4091 teachers in 183 restructuring schools.* Paper presented at the Annual Meeting of the American Educational Research Association, New York.

Kushman, J. W., & Chenoweth, T. G. (1996). Building shared meaning and commitment during the courtship phase. In C. Finnan, E. P. St. John, J. McCarthy, & S. P. Slovacek (Eds.), *Accelerated schools in action: Lessons from the field* (pp. 82–103). Thousand Oaks, CA: Corwin Press.

Lam, C. C. (1991). *The implementation of curriculum change in moral education in secondary schools in Hong Kong.* Unpublished doctoral dissertation, University of London, England.

Lee, J. C. K. (1997). The challenges and choices of education in the future: The role of school-university partnerships [in Chinese]. *Education Journal, 25*(2), 99–116.

Lee, J. C. K. (1999, October). *Theoretical background and related literature of the quantitative survey.* Unpublished manuscript.

Lee, J. C. K., Chiu, C. S., Poon, T. C., Tang, M. S., & Tam, M. K. (1999). *Hong Kong accelerated schools project and quality education* [in Chinese] (School Education Reform Studies Series No. 1). Hong Kong: Faculty of Education & Hong Kong Institute of Educational Research, The Chinese University of Hong Kong.

Lee, J. C. K., Chiu, C. S., Wong, H. W., Chan, P. L., Leung, C. W., & Poon L. M. (1999). Primary students' perspectives of classroom environments: A Hong Kong perspective. *Educational Practice and Theory, 21*(1), 109–127.

Lee, J. C. K., & Dimmock, C. (1998). Curriculum management in secondary schools during political transition: A Hong Kong perspective. *Curriculum Studies, 6*(1), 5–28.

Lee, J. C. K., Wong, H. W., Chiu, C. S., Chung, Y. P., & Lo, L. N. K. (1999, January). *Accelerated schools for teacher development: Challenges and opportunities.* Paper presented at International Conference on New Professionalism in Teaching: Teacher education and teacher development in a changing world, organized by Hong Kong Institute of Educational Research and Faculty of Education, CUHK and International Research Network "PACT," Hong Kong.

Levin, H. (1996a). Accelerated schools: The background. In C. Finnan, E. P. St. John, J. McCarthy, & S. P. Slovacek (Eds.), *Accelerated schools in action: Lessons from the field* (pp. 3–23). Thousand Oaks, CA: Corwin Press.

Levin, H. (1996b). Accelerated schools after eight years. In L. Schauble & R. Glaser (Eds.), *Innovations in learning: New environments for education* (pp. 329–352). Mahwah, NJ: Lawrence Erlbaum Associates.

Levin, H. (1998a). Accelerated schools: A decade of evolution. In A. Hargreaves, A. Lieberman, M. Fullan, & D. Hopkins (Eds.), *International handbook of educational change* (pp. 807–830). Dordrecht, Netherlands; Boston: Kluwer Academic Publishers.

Levin, H. (1998b). *Education and the ability to deal with change* (Education Policy Studies Series No. 15). Hong Kong: Hong Kong Institute of Educational Research, The Chinese University of Hong Kong.

Levin, H. (1999, October 30). *Report to the "Accelerated Schools for Quality Education Project"* (ASQEP).

Li, W. S., Yu, W. M., Lam, T. S., & Fok, P. K. (1999). The lack of action research: The case of Hong Kong. *Educational Action Research, 7*(1), 33–49.

Lo, L. N. K. (2000, October). *Teachers and teacher education in the currents of educational reform* [in Chinese]. Keynote paper presented at the International Seminar on Education and Basic Education, Nanjing Normal University, Nanjing, China.

Marsh, H. W. (1990). *Self-Description Questionnaire-II manual*. Campbelltown, Australia: Univesity of Western Sydney.

Marsh, H. W. (n.d.). *SDQII short form*. Unpublished document.

Mims, J. S. (1996). Principals speak out on their evolving leadership roles. In C. Finnan, E. P. St. John, J. McCarthy, & S. P. Slovacek (Eds.), *Accelerated schools in action: Lessons from the field* (pp. 208–218). Thousand Oaks, CA: Corwin Press.

Morris, P., Lo, M. L., & Adamson, B. (2000). Improving schools in Hong Kong — Lessons from the past. In B. Adamson, T. Kwan, & K. K. Chan (Eds.), *Changing the curriculum: The impact of reform on primary schooling in Hong Kong* (pp. 245–262). Hong Kong: Hong Kong University Press.

Mowday, R., Steers, R., & Porter, L. (1979). The measurement of organizational commitment. *Journal of Vocational Behavior, 14*, 224–247.

Pang, N. S. K. (1997, November). *Primary students' perceptions of quality of school life*. Paper presented at the 14th annual conference of Hong Kong Educational Research Association, The Chinese University of Hong Kong, Hong Kong.

Pang, N. S. K. (1998a). Managerial practices in Hong Kong primary schools. *Journal of Basic Education, 8*(1), 21–42.

Pang, N. S. K. (1998b). Organizational values and cultures of secondary schools in Hong Kong. *Canadian and International Education, 27*(2), 59–84.

Ramsay, W., & Clark, E. E. (1990). *New ideas for effective school improvement: Vision, social capital, evaluation.* London; New York: Falmer Press.

Rinehart, J. S., Short, P. M., Short, R. J., & Eckley, M. (1998). Teacher empowerment and principal leadership: Understanding the influence process. *Educational Administration Quarterly, 34* (Suppl.), 630–649.

Ross, S. M., Troutman, A., Horgan, D., Maxwell, S., Laitinen, R., & Lowther, D. (1997). The success of schools in implementing eight restructuring designs: A synthesis of first-year evaluation outcomes. *School Effectiveness and School Improvement, 8*(1), 95–124.

Sammons, P., Hillman, J., & Mortimore, P. (1997). Key characteristics of effective schools: A review of school effectiveness research. In J. White & M. Barber (Eds.), *Perspectives on school effectiveness and school improvement* (pp. 77–124). London: Institute of Education, University of London.

Smith, L., Maxwell, S., Lowther, D., Hacker, D., Bol, L., & Nunnery, J. (1997). Activities in schools and programs experiencing the most, the least, early implementation successes. *School Effectiveness and School Improvement, 8*(1), 125–150.

Smith, L., Ross, S., McNelis, M., Squires, M., Wasson, R., Maxwell, S., Weddle, K., Nath, L., Grehan, A., & Buggey, T. (1998). The Memphis restructuring initiative: Analysis of activities and outcomes that affect implementation success. *Education and Urban Society, 30*(3), 296–325.

Soler, P., & Levin, H. (1997, January–February). *Obstacles to inquiry.* Paper prepared for National Networking Meeting of Accelerated Schools Project, St. Louis, MO.

St. John, E. P., Meza, Jr., J., Allen-Haynes, L., & Davidson, B. M. (1996). Building communities of inquiry: Linking teacher research and school restructuring. In C. Finnan, E. P. St. John, J. McCarthy, & S. P. Slovacek (Eds.), *Accelerated schools in action: Lessons from the field* (pp. 124–138). Thousand Oaks, CA: Corwin Press.

Walker, A., & Cheng, Y. C. (1996). Professional development in Hong Kong primary schools: Beliefs, practices and change. *Journal of Education for Teaching, 22*(2), 197–212.

Walker, A., & Dimmock, C. (2000). Developing educational administration: The impact of societal culture on theory and practice. In C. Dimmock & A. Walker (Eds.), *Future school administration: Western and Asian perspectives* (pp. 3–22). Hong Kong: The Chinese University Press; Hong Kong Institute of Educational Research.

4

Improving the Quality of Education for All as an "Authentic" School Improvement Program[1]

David Hopkins

"Improvement occurs through organised social learning, not through idiosyncratic experimentation and discovery" — Richard Elmore (2000)

Abstract

The purpose of this chapter is to outline an approach to school improvement that has a medium term and systemic orientation, and to describe the principles on which it is based. Accordingly, school improvement is best regarded as a strategy for educational change that focuses on student achievement by modifying classroom practice and adapting the management arrangements within the school to support teaching and learning. It is only through viewing school improvement holistically and by adopting a strategic and inclusive response that the challenge of enhancing the level of student learning and achievement will be met. This specific approach to school improvement — termed here as "real" or "authentic" school improvement — is defined in some detail as is the "Improving the Quality of Education for All" (IQEA) program that exemplifies these principles in practice. In exemplifying the theory and practice of this approach to school improvement, the following themes are discussed in this chapter:

1. The current international educational policy context is briefly outlined.
2. Ten principles for authentic school improvement are proposed.

3. *The rationale behind the IQEA approach to school improvement is explained.*
4. *An example of the approach in action is provided.*
5. *The initial three phases of a school improvement intervention are described.*
6. *In conclusion the key features of the "third age" of school improvement are identified.*

Preamble

Those of us who spend much of our professional lives laboring in that part of the educational vineyard known as "school improvement" have recently been celebrating. For decades now we have been the poor relations of the field — tolerated, talked to at parties, but not really regarded as being a main player. But as Western societies have in recent years grappled with the challenges of economic growth and social dislocation, our particular contribution to educational change has increasingly been recognized as important and helpful. As societies continue to set educational goals that are, on current performance, beyond the capacity of the system to deliver, those whose work focuses on strategies for enhancing student learning through school and classroom intervention are taken more seriously.

Many of the educational initiatives that have been recently spawned under the school improvement umbrella are unfortunately, however, simply tinkering at the edges. Governments whose policies emphasize accountability and managerial change fail to realize that if teachers knew how to teach more effectively they would themselves have done so decades ago. Blaming teachers and delegating financial responsibility have little positive impact on classroom practice. Similarly, school heads or principals who restrict their influence to bureaucratic intervention and ignore the "learning level" should not be surprised when student achievement scores fail to rise. Even those consultants and others who do offer training on "thinking skills" and "learning styles" are missing the point when they fail to recognize that many of their prescriptions have a short shelf life. Even when there is a subsequent attempt at implementation following a "one-off" workshop, "tissue rejection" is usually the result.

This is the rather bleak context within which school improvement has to operate at the turn of the century. It is a situation that is predisposed toward short-term remedies for profound problems, in organizational settings not always conducive to enhancing levels of student achievement and learning. The emergence of school improvement from the shadows is therefore a mixed blessing. As with any new idea, much is expected of it, particularly from those desperately seeking for simple and rapid solutions to complex challenges. School improvement's time in the sun will be short lived unless it can persuade its newfound friends that it is not a "quick fix" response to educational change.

The International Policy Context

The last 10 or 15 years of this century have been a time of great challenge as well as considerable excitement for educational systems around the world. Governments everywhere have been embarking on substantial programs of reform in an attempt to develop more effective school systems and raise levels of student learning and achievement. Schools in many countries have been subject to a barrage of legislation and policy that has meant changes in curriculum, assessment, governance, and financing. Both England and Hong Kong have perhaps had more of this than most countries, but the phenomenon of large-scale reform by central governments is worldwide.

A general strategy has been to centralize educational policy while at the same time has placing the responsibility for implementation on the school. This tension has made the task of implementing change both complex and challenging. The balancing of centrally directed change and locally developed improvement has proved most difficult to achieve in practice. To the cynic this looks as if governments have created a situation where they can have their cake and eat it too! If policies fail to meet aspirations, the fault can then be attributed not to the policy maker, but to the schools, teachers, and local authorities that have failed to put them into practice.

This policy approach is widely referred to as "performance based" reform (Hopkins & Levin, 2000). There are a number of properties that characterize "performance based" approaches to reform that are familiar:

1. There are centrally determined and explicit goals and standards for student performance.
2. Curriculum frameworks and materials for use in accomplishing the goals are set for students.

3. Information about school and student performance is widely disseminated.
4. A system of finance and governance that devolves to the school responsibility for producing improvements in student performance is implemented.
5. A series of agencies are established to judge the extent to which standards have been met, and distribute rewards and sanctions, for success or failure in meeting specified standards.

There is now growing research evidence on the effectiveness of performance-based policies (Leithwood, Jantzi, & Mascall, 1999). For example, on the basis of a review of five well-known cases of performance-based reform — Kentucky, California, New Zealand, Victoria (Australia), and Chicago — two striking conclusions were reached:

1. On the available evidence there was no increase in student achievement in any case except Chicago, and even that was "slow in coming."
2. The contribution that performance-base reforms have made to improving the core technology of schooling was disappointing. These reforms did not:
   • adequately acknowledge local context,
   • take the school site seriously,
   • find incentives that work,
   • contribute to significant increases in professional capacity, and
   • address and diagnose opportunity costs.

Although the impact of large-scale reform on student achievement is notoriously fickle, the fact that these reform strategies neglected to focus on teaching and learning and capacity building must have contributed to their inability to impact positively on student achievement. In support of this argument, it is helpful to look at the case of Chicago where there were student achievement gains, but not until year 7 of a 10-year initiative.

The Chicago initiative has been well-documented (see, for example, Fullan, 2000). On examining the evidence it appears that for the first six years of the initiative, 1988–1994, the "system operated in a decentralized fashion with little functional contact between schools and the district. In other words too little structure characterized the operation" (Fullan, 2000, p. 11). Since 1994 however, the central district was reorganized, with decentralized development being retained within a context of capacity building and external accountability. During this time five extra school functions were developed that may help explain why students in Chicago began to achieve more during this period:

1. Policy making increasingly supported decentralization.
2. There was a focus on local capacity building.
3. A system of rigorous accountability was introduced.
4. Innovation was stimulated.
5. External support networks were established.

The Chicago case resonates with other analyses of large-scale reform efforts (for further examples, see Fullan, 2000; Hopkins, 2001; Leithwood, Jantzi, & Mascall, 1999). The Rand study of innovation (McLaughlin, 1990) for example concluded that:

> It is exceedingly difficult for policy to change practice, especially across levels of government. Contrary to the one-to-one relationship assumed to exist between policy and practice, the nature, amount, and pace of change at school level is a product of local factors that are largely beyond the control of higher-level policy makers.

When the implementation of central policies was effective, the following series of implementation strategies were usually in place:

1. Concrete, teacher-specific and extended training;
2. Classroom assistance from local education authority (LEA) and the University of Nottingham;
3. Teacher observation in other classrooms, schools or LEAs;
4. Regular meetings that focused on practical issues related to teaching and learning;
5. Teacher involvement in school improvement planning;
6. Local development of classroom materials; and
7. Head's participation in training.

The analysis of "performance based" approaches and centralized policy initiatives are entirely consistent with previous research on the implementation of large-scale reform efforts. It is however an irony of quite breathtaking proportions that the dramatic increase in educational reform efforts in most Western countries over the past decade is having insufficient impact on levels of student achievement. There are at least two reasons why educational reforms do not in general have the desired impact.

First, many reforms focus on the wrong variables. Any strategy to promote student learning needs to create a discourse around teaching and learning, and expand the teaching and learning repertoires of teachers and students respectively. Second, reform efforts have not paid sufficient attention to how to create a framework for implementation that leads to changes in practice; in particular they have neglected to exploit the synergistic potential at the local authority level.

Unless central reforms address the context of teaching and learning, as well as capacity building at the school level, within the context of external support, then as is seen in the following section, the aspirations of reform will never be realized.

It is for reasons such as this that one cannot be over-optimistic over the ability of current reform initiatives leading to dramatically enhanced levels of student learning and achievement. The argument being built in this chapter is that because policy prescriptions do not by and large impact on practice, new ways of formulating educational change needs to be developed.

The Principles of Authentic School Improvement

Ironically, we now know enough about the theory and practice of educational change to successfully improve schools and the achievement and learning of the vast majority of students. Approaches to school improvement that utilize this knowledge base are being called here "authentic school improvement." A values base that honors equity, advocates globalization, and articulates a systemic approach to change also underpins them.

These approaches to school improvement stand in contrast to "target setting" and "high stakes accountability" reform strategies, and short-term quick fix approaches, all of which are informed by different expectations, values and modus operandi. For example, reviews of successful school improvement efforts around the world suggest that they are based on a number of key principles (see, for example, Hargreaves, Lieberman, Fullan, & Hopkins, 1998). In general authentic school improvement programs are:

1. Achievement-focused — they focus on enhancing student learning and achievement, in a broader sense than mere examination results or test scores.
2. Empowering in aspiration — they intend to provide those involved in the change process with the skills of learning and "change

agentry" that will raise levels of expectation and confidence throughout the educational community.

3. Research-based and theory-rich — they base their strategies on programs and program elements that have an established track record of effectiveness, that research their own effectiveness and connect to and build on other bodies of knowledge and disciplines.

4. Context-specific — they pay attention to the unique features of the school situation and build strategies on the basis of an analysis of that particular context.

5. Capacity building in nature — they aim to build the organizational conditions that support continuous improvement.

6. Inquiry-driven — they appreciate that reflection-in-action is an integral and self-sustaining process.

7. Implementation-oriented — they take a direct focus on the quality of classroom practice and student learning.

8. Interventionist and strategic — they are purposely designed to improve the current situation in the school or system and take a medium-term view of the management of change, and plan and prioritize developments accordingly.

9. Externally supported — they build agencies around the school that provide focused support, and create and facilitate networks that disseminate and sustain "good practice."

10. Systemic — they accept the reality of a centralized policy context, but also realize the need to adapt external change for internal purpose, and to exploit the creativity and synergies existing within the system.

Taken together, these principles provide a framework for "authentic" school improvement taken in this chapter. Although the principles are based on an analysis across many programs, obviously not all programs will share these characteristics. Even the most successful school improvement efforts will not necessarily embody all of the principles, and there will be inevitable variation within the principles as well. The principles although empirically based, reflect an "ideal type" of school improvement profile. They can be used as a standard against which to assess a wide range of school improvement practice (for a more detailed discussion, see Hopkins, 2001, chapter 2).

To summarize briefly, most successful forms of school improvement are characterized by a relatively consistent set of values or principles. This approach to "school improvement" is being called "authentic" in order to distinguish it from other forms with different values, strategies, and expectations. Table 1 represents a first attempt to define the influences on authentic school improvement. Although illustrative rather than exhaustive, the table identifies some of the wide range of influences that have helped determine this particular approach to school improvement.

These principles of "authentic" school improvement therefore fulfill a number of important functions as follows:

1. Defining a particular approach to school improvement;
2. Able to be used to organize the theoretical, research and practical implications that define school improvement as a field on enquiry;
3. Providing a set of criteria that can be used to differentiate broad approaches to school improvement;
4. Able to be used more specifically to help analyze and define individual school improvement efforts or programs; and
5. Containing a series of implications for policy that could enable them to more directly influence the achievement and learning of all students.

In the following section an approach to school improvement that is consistent with these principles is described.

Improving the Quality of Education for All

The "Improving the Quality of Education for All" (IQEA) program has over the past 10 years collaborated with hundreds of schools in England, Hong Kong, and elsewhere in developing a model of school improvement and a program of support. The IQEA program aims to enhance student outcomes through focusing on the teaching-learning process as well as strengthening the school's capacity for managing change. IQEA is also a research-based program and reflects many of the principles of authentic school improvement as is seen in Table 2 (for an overview, see Hopkins, 2002).

At the outset of IQEA, a set of principles were articulated that provided a philosophical and practical starting point. These principles represent the expectations of the way project schools pursue school improvement, and serve as an *aide-memoire* to all those involved. The operation of these

Table 1 *The Principles of Authentic School Improvement*

Principle	Examples of theoretical, research, policy or practical influences on school improvement
Achievement-focused	The moral and social justice responsibility to enhance student learning, and the unrelenting focus on the quality of teaching and learning.
Empowering in aspiration	The moral imperative of emancipation, of increasing individual responsibility, the enhancement of skills and confidence in the tradition of Dewey, Freire and Stenhouse.
Research-based and theory-rich	The use of teaching and learning and organizational development strategies with robust empirical support for the development of a variety of curriculum and teaching programs or models; and the location of the approach within a philosophical tradition, for example, Critical Theory.
Context-specific	The influence of the contemporary school effectiveness research that points to the importance of context specificity and the fallacy of the "one size fits all" change strategy.
Capacity building in nature	The necessity to ensure sustainability, the nurturing of professional learning communities, and the establishing of local infrastructures and networks.
Inquiry-driven	The uses of data to energize inform and direct action. The influence of the "reflective" practitioner ethic and a commitment to dissemination and utilization.
Implementation-oriented	The research on the management of change, in particular the importance of individual meaning, the consistency of classroom effects, and the creation of a commitment to active implementation.
Interventionist and strategic	The influence of "Lewinian" Action Research and Organization Development principles and strategies, and the contemporary emphasis on development planning.
Externally supported	The centralization/decentralization polarity of most national educational policies places increasing emphasis on networking and external support agencies to facilitate implementation.
Systemic	This relates not just to the need to accept political realities, but also to ensure policy coherence horizontally and vertically, and the use of pressure and support to exploit the creativity and synergies within the system.

Table 2   *IQEA as an Authentic School Improvement Program*

Principle	Example of theoretical, research or practical influence
Achievement-focused	• Moral commitment to student learning • Influence of the school effectiveness research
Empowering in aspiration	• The focus on enhancement of skills, confidence and learning capability • Community involvement and responsibility
Research-based and theory-rich	• Models of teaching and learning • Organizational development strategies • General influence of socio-psychological and critical theory
Context-specific	• Emphasis on adapting external change for internal purpose • Works within school's own development plan • Program designed on basis of school-based data collection
Capacity building in nature	• Peer coaching and staff development • Cross-hierarchical working groups
Inquiry-driven	• Teacher as researcher • Action research
Implementation-oriented	• Importance of individual meaning • Consistency of classroom effects
Interventionist and strategic	• "Lewinian" Action Research • Development and maintenance distinction • Survey data feedback and organization development
Externally supported	• Consultancy support from the University of Nottingham • Facilitation of networking • Links with LEAs
Systemic	• Influence of National Reform agenda • Appreciation of local micro-politics • Searches to increase policy coherence

principles creates synergism — together they are greater than the sum of their parts. The five principles of IQEA are:

1. School improvement is a process that focuses on enhancing the quality of students' learning.

2. The vision of the school should be one that embraces all members of the school community as both learners and contributors.

3. The school will see in external pressures for change important opportunities to secure its internal priorities.

4. The school will seek to develop structures and create conditions that encourage collaboration and lead to the empowerment of individuals and groups.

5. The school will seek to promote the view that monitoring and evaluating quality is a responsibility which all members of staff share.

This approach to school improvement is underpinned by a contract between the partners in the project — the school and its teachers, and in some cases, the LEA or sponsoring agency, and the IQEA team. The contract defines the parameters of the project, and the obligations those involved owe to each other. It is intended to clarify expectations and to ensure the conditions necessary for success. In particular the contract emphasizes that all staff be consulted, that school coordinators are appointed, that a "critical mass" of teachers are actively involved in development work, and that sufficient time is made available for appropriate classroom and staff development activities. The IQEA team coordinates the support arrangements, provides training for the school coordinators and representatives, makes regular school visits, contributes to staff training, provides staff development materials, and monitors the implementation of each school's project. Handbooks and videos are produced to support staff development work, that includes training exercises and support materials (a selection of the published work that supports the IQEA approach to school improvement is contained in the reference list).

The IQEA approach to school improvement is not simply about the implementation of centralized reforms in a more effective way; rather, the emphasis is on how schools can use the impetus of external reform to "improve" or "develop" themselves. Sometimes, what a school chooses to do in terms of school improvement will be consistent with the national reform agenda, at other times it will not. Whatever the case, the decision to engage in school improvement, at least in IQEA schools, is based on an aspiration to create cultures that enable teachers to effectively pursue what is the best for the young people in that school. When this occurs school staff not only begin to meet the real challenge of educational reform, but as is seen in the following example, they also create classrooms and schools where both students and their teachers learn.

A Case in Point — Bigwood School Nottingham

Bigwood School serves an area described as "one of serious social need." Eight years ago Bigwood faced possible closure. Demographic trends coupled with a poor image in the community meant that the school had been steadily losing pupils and staff for several years. In January 1993 a new headteacher was appointed with a brief to arrest the decline. A rapid period of research — interviews with staff, questionnaires to pupils/parents/ local community, and meetings with primary link school staff — produced a picture of a school that was seen as caring but which lacked rigor. Three clear aims were quickly established:

1. To improve the school's image in the community,
2. To develop the links with primary schools, and
3. To tackle the underachievement culture.

The threat of possible closure, replaced after the first twelve months with the "threat" of an OFSTED inspection, proved to be powerful factors in focusing people's minds. A new staffing structure, clear policies, new uniform, well-structured Code of Conduct, and mentoring programs all began to show positive effects. Pupil numbers began to rise, examination results improved, and the "what-can-you-expect of ..." culture was being successfully challenged. The OFSTED report was, in the main, positive, but the quality of teaching and learning emerged as a major issue.

A start had been made. The school had begun to develop the capacity to accept change. However, the initiatives outlined above were, in many ways, only peripheral. It was recognized that for lasting improvement the school needed to bring about more sustainable change focused on the classroom.

At the critical moment the school learnt of the IQEA school improvement program. The program's emphasis on teaching and learning at the heart of sustained improvement was felt to be in total accord with where Bigwood was in its particular stage of development.

This approach to school improvement called for, among other things, the establishment of a School Improvement Group to act as the initial change agents. The first "cadre" group consisted of the headteacher and seven volunteers — a deputy headteacher, two heads of department, and four class teachers. Interestingly, and purely by chance, all areas of the curriculum except one were represented. During this time, several members of the School Improvement Group attended a summer school on models of teaching run by the IQEA team at the University of Nottingham and soon realized that the inductive model offered a possible way to address the issues facing the school. It seemed an ideal place to start, partially because it was a new approach, and therefore offered exciting possibilities, and also because it was applicable across the whole curriculum.

For the School Improvement Group, the first stage was to learn more about the model, to practice it and to observe each other. Lessons were then videoed and, when they felt ready, a day's in-service training (INSET) session was prepared for the whole staff. The model was explored inductively, videos shown and opportunities created for staff to begin to practice using the model in a safe environment, that is, with other groups of staff.

In order to encourage other people to adopt this approach, staff were clustered into small groups with a member of the cadre attached to each one to provide support and guidance. Opportunities were created for people to observe each other and some notable successes were recorded; when, for example, a member of staff, known more for his competence than his charisma, found himself surrounded by a group of eager pupils at the end of an inductive lesson wanting to continue with their work. As well as working with their support groups, staff also worked within their departments, reviewing schemes of work to see where the inductive approach might be used to greatest effect and planning lessons accordingly.

By the end of the first year the whole process was reviewed and several clear "messages" emerged.

1. Time was an issue:
   - The importance of creating a regular time for the cadre group to meet;
   - The need for time for staff to learn new models, to prepare new materials, to observe each other and visit other schools to observe good practice;
   - The fact that interviews/questionnaires all required time.
2. The power of the pupil voice. A 14-year-old pupil's calm statement on video that, "copying is a waste of time because the words go

from the board down your pen and onto the paper without going anywhere near your brain" is a more arresting message than any amount of exhortation and analysis from the headteacher on ineffective methodologies.

3. In the same way, showing in-house videos and persuading staff, not normally seen as the most inventive of teachers, to demonstrate effective approaches, had a powerful impact especially on the dissenting few.

4. The value of residentials and other twilight sessions in helping to develop a real group ethos among the members of the cadre.

5. The difficulty of maintaining momentum. It was not always easy to find regular development time.

In the second year a more structured model was developed. Creating more time required a radical rethinking of the way time was currently used in the school. The problem was resolved in the following ways:

1. The existing meeting structure was reviewed, and staff meetings, for example, were replaced by staff development time, and alternative methods were used to disseminate information. All remaining meetings, such as departmental meetings, were to devote 50% of the time to development issues relating to teaching and learning.

2. Staff were encouraged to "bank" some non-contact time by covering other colleagues. This time was then pooled so that all staff, either as individuals or departments, were given half-day slots for development.

3. Members of the senior management team were to provide a percentage of the cover time each fortnight, which could be booked by staff.

4. Adults other than teachers were to be used to supervise exams and thus free departments.

The careful positioning of INSET, twilight and staff development meant that staff were now meeting approximately every 4 weeks to look at development issues focused on teaching and learning. It was also agreed, following consultation with the staff, to broaden the range of activities.

It was during the second year that the real benefits of this approach to school improvement became apparent. Working in pairs and triads, the cadre used the expertise of university and LEA staff plus their own reading and research to develop their expertise in areas as diverse as the major components of a well-structured lesson, cooperative group work, whole class teaching, formative assessment, creating the learning classroom. The aim was to encourage staff to develop at their own pace, while providing the necessary expertise and support within a climate that encouraged risk taking.

As the school was preparing to enter its third year of the IQEA program, the inevitable brown envelope arrived and, while not totally subsuming everything else, it would be fair to say that the prospect of an imminent OFSTED inspection led to a period of consolidation rather than breaking new ground. The inspection results were better than the head and staff had hoped for. In a term with four Newly Qualified Teachers (NQTs) having had very little time to settle in and when two members of staff were off with long-term illness and being covered by supply staff, OFSTED deemed that, "Teaching is a strength of the school." A total of 97% of lessons were judged satisfactory or better, 64% were good or better, and 28% were very good or excellent. This was in sharp contrast with the picture four years earlier when only 75% of lessons were judged satisfactory and less than 30% were good or better.

As compared with 3 years ago, Bigwood School is now moving forward from a position where:

1. Teaching and learning is acknowledged by all as fundamental and is at the heart of the development agenda;
2. Classrooms are more open and people are more willing to observe and be observed;
3. Staff are developing a language to talk about teaching and learning; and
4. People feel part of the development process. They are involved in making it happen not just the unwilling recipients.

Obviously this is just part of a wider picture, but in working to improve education for all, the following comment from OFSTED encapsulates everything the head and staff have been working toward:

> The school is successfully challenging the non-achievement culture, noted in the previous OFSTED Report, through its major focus on raising the quality of teaching. This is having a major impact on pupils' attainment and progress.

The IQEA Framework for School Improvement

The Bigwood story is not unique. It represents the achievements of many schools who are managing to make a significant difference to the education of their students, despite the challenging circumstances in which they find themselves. What is interesting about the Bigwood experience however is the way in which they went about the school improvement process. Although each school's context is individual and in some senses unique, what we see in the Bigwood example is an approach that is relatively systematic and strategic and that can be replicated elsewhere.

There are six aspects to this school improvement strategy that need highlighting. First, the school set itself a clear and unifying focus for its improvement work. The direct emphasis on the quality of student achievement and learning became linchpin for all the school's development work and it was used to marry together all the various initiatives that the school engaged in. The school's development plan will usually provide the focus for such work, or a Raising Attainment Plan may have been specifically prepared for the purpose based upon an analysis of the school's improvement needs.

Second, in common with many other schools, Bigwood collected data on its performance as a precursor to initiating an improvement strategy. What perhaps was different in this case was that the data collected related not only to examination results and the type of information contained on PANDA (Performance and Assessment) forms, but also focused on the quality and range of teaching and learning and an analysis of the internal conditions or capacity of the school. This latter information provided not only a clear indication of how well the school was performing but also an indication of what needed to be done.

Third, at an early stage a school improvement group was identified. This group of about six members of staff represented a cross-section of views, experience and seniority in the school. It was not an existing group but was specifically established to carry forward the school's development agenda. Unlike other groups or committees in the school, the School Improvement Group or cadre as it is sometimes called is solely concerned with school improvement and staff development. Put another way, it becomes the school's "development capacity."

Fourth, the School Improvement Group subsequently receives specific training in the classroom practices most crucial to achieving the school's developmental goals. The focus of this training is on the teaching strategies most appropriate to the learning needs of the students in the school. These workshop sessions contain a variety of activities including presentations, demonstrations, practice, and feedback. In addition time is found during the school week for classroom observation, coaching, and support. Besides training in teaching strategies, the cadre also learn how to plan and provide staff development and to conduct school-based research on school improvement. Initially this training is often provided by an external agency, in our case a university, but once networks have been established, much of this support comes from other schools and one's own school.

Fifth, although the initial focus is on the preparation of the cadre group, very soon the improvement activity goes whole school. The range of staff development activities involved is considerable and is likely to include:

1. Whole staff INSET days on teaching and learning and school improvement planning as well as "curriculum tours" to share the work done in departments or working groups;
2. Inter-departmental meetings to discuss teaching strategies;
3. Workshops run inside the school on teaching strategies by cadre group members and external support;
4. Partnership teaching and peer coaching; and
5. The design and execution of collaborative enquiry activities, which are, by their nature, knowledge-generating.

When all these types of staff development are in place, schools find that their cultures become increasingly collaborative and a professional learning community within the school is well on its way to being established.

Lastly, the whole school emphasis is vital, because without it consistency of practice and high expectations is unlikely to be achieved. The move toward involving the whole school and the community is complex, demanding, and daunting. It involves the careful planning of the curriculum and teaching developments, the organization of staff development, sustaining momentum across the school, and evaluating progress and success. It involves carefully managing a change process that may have begun as a project restricted to a few, to a whole school improvement initiative, to a way of working that is natural and fits with the school's aspirations and the rhythms of the school year.

This approach to school improvement that focuses explicitly on enhancing the learning experiences, achievement and progress of pupils is summarized in Figure 1. The three inner circles represent the image of powerful learning, powerful teaching, and powerful schools. In the center of the concentric rings is powerful learning — the achievement and progress of students. The next ring is comprised of the essential ingredients of powerful teaching — the "holy trinity" of teaching strategy, curriculum content, and the learning needs of students. Powerful learning and powerful teaching are found in powerful schools that have organizational conditions supportive of high levels of teaching and learning. Some of the key elements of these conditions are found in the next ring — collaborative planning that focuses on student outcomes, staff development that is committed to the improvement of classroom practice, the involvement of students in their own learning, and the school community in the educational process. This activity usually takes place within the context of a national reform agenda,

Figure 1   *A Framework for School Improvement*

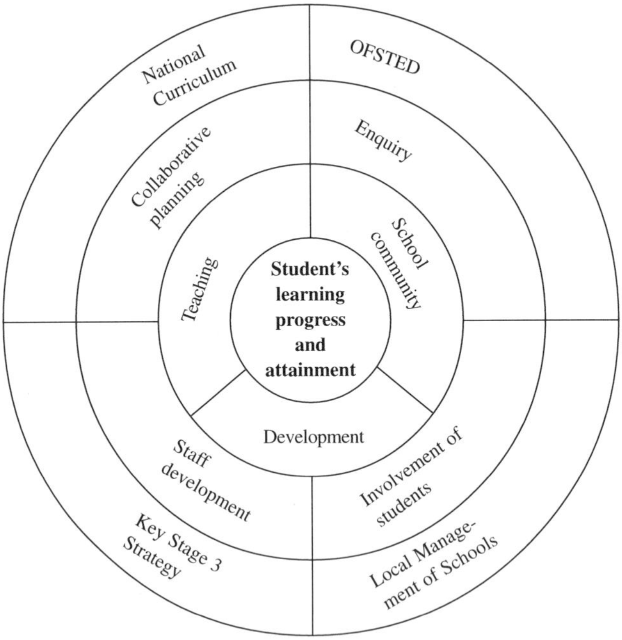

as depicted by the outer ring. This is represented in the diagram by reference to the English context, for example, the National Curriculum, OFSTED inspections, Local Management of Schools (LMS), and the Key Stage 3 Strategy. The similarities with the Hong Kong policy context are striking!

When all the circles are pulling in the same direction, then the aspirations of school improvement have much more chance of success. All need to exist in a reciprocal relationship if student achievement is to be enhanced. Unfortunately many teachers and schools feel that change comes from the "outside-in," that their role is to implement externally imposed initiatives, and that they have little control over. A more productive approach to school improvement is to start from the center of the circle and move outwards. Those schools that appear to be more successful than most at managing school improvement begin at the other end of the sequence — with student learning goals. It is as if they ask, "What changes in student performance do we wish to see this year?" Having decided these, they then discuss what teaching strategies will be most effective at bringing this about, and reflect on what modifications are required to the organization of the school to support these developments. Finally they survey the range of initiatives confronting the school to see which ones can most usefully be linked with in order to adapt external change for internal purpose. Such an approach to school improvement obviously requires a certain degree of confidence that places considerable demands on the *capacity* of the school to manage change.

It is by adopting such an approach that the most successful schools pursue their improvement efforts. While focusing on the learning needs of students in the context of systemic and environmental demands, they also recognize that school structures must reflect both these demands as well as offering a suitable vehicle for the future development of the school. In this sense the structure of the school provides the *skeleton* that supports cultural growth, rather than the framework which constrains it.

In the following section a practical three-phase approach to school improvement based on these principles is outlined.

The Three Phases of School Improvement

This three-phase school improvement process has at its core an unrelenting focus on learning and attainment. Given this central focus, the school improvement strategy encompasses both *classroom practice*, particularly the expansion of teacher's teaching repertoire, and the *building of capacity* at the school level, especially the redesign of staff development. While this is not a "quick-fix" approach, many of the activities involved will bring short as well as medium-term gains. The three phases are: Establishing the Process (Phase One), Going Whole School (Phase Two), and Sustaining Momentum (Phase Three).

Phase One — Establishing the Process

As IQEA is not a short-term approach, it is important that careful deliberation is given to the decision to embark on this way of working. Preparing for the project involves generating commitment, planning and gathering data on the school level conditions. Although it is important to move into action as soon as is practicable, it is vital that the cadre group is fully established and well-informed with management of change and teaching/learning strategies, and has carefully planned the whole school improvement strategy. This phase involves:

1. Commitment to the School Improvement Approach — It is particularly important that the leadership of the school is committed to the approach as they will need to make decisions about allocation of resources and the deployment of time. They will also need to be confident that the approach is consistent with the aspirations of the school and the values of most staff.
2. Selection of School Improvement Group or Cadre — The selection of the cadre group is crucial. They will be the drivers of school improvement over the next few years and their status and importance in the school will grow considerably over time.
3. Enquiring into the Strengths and Weaknesses of the School — Any school improvement strategy must reflect the specific context of the school. This means that as much data as possible on the school context, student attainment and learning, and the teaching approaches of staff must be gathered to help design the school improvement strategy. This includes information about examination results as well as diagnoses of the school's *capacity*.
4. Designing the Whole School Program — This approach to school improvement is not just another initiative or project. It is a way of carrying forward in a more systematic and strategic way the priorities

that a school has already set for itself. Consequently there needs to be a clear link between these school improvement activities and the school's development plan. In addition, involvement in the program should be used to integrate as many as possible of the other initiatives facing the school by using teaching and learning strategies as the common factor and point of reference.

5. Seeking Partners — At the start of such a school improvement initiative, support from an external agency (e.g., the University of Nottingham, LEA or commercial provider) is usually necessary. This kind of approach may be new to the school and advice and encouragement is therefore helpful. Also the school will need access, at least initially, to knowledge related to planning, teaching strategies, and staff development. The school will quickly develop its own expertise and confidence, but the "pressure and support" provided by an external partner will always be valuable.

6. Seeding the Whole School Approach — Inevitably in the early stages of the work, the energy will be coming from the senior management team and the cadre group. It is therefore essential that the whole staff is kept informed about developments and that expectations for their involvement in the near future are carefully nurtured. The emphasis should be that this is not just another initiative, but a more effective and collegial way of working.

Swanwick Hall School is a comprehensive school that caters for students of 11–18 years in age. It is in "ex-coal mining" Derbyshire with almost 1,100 pupils. The catchment area is mixed, which makes it a true comprehensive school, but there is a skew to the less able. The school has always been a caring institution and many parents were more concerned that their children were happy at school than they were about external examinations. The increasing emphasis on attainment was slow to arrive in the area, and 6 years ago the percentage of 5+ A–C grades was only 23%. A new headteacher changed this, and results improved by working with parents on numerous initiatives such as increased homework, and by pupil mentoring, changing school aspirations through assemblies etc.

However there was a major problem associated with the drive for improvement. Staff, and particularly heads of department, felt that change was being imposed on them from above, be it senior management team (SMT), LEA or national government. There was a resentment that lots of hoops had to be jumped through and a feeling that the main job — work in classrooms — was relegated to a low priority. The SMT had just decided that it was essential to give the ownership for change back to teachers, and particularly heads of departments. It was then that they heard about IQEA and the emphasis on "teaching and learning at the heart of sustained school improvement." The SMT also understood that initially IQEA involved establishing a common culture for change, and a temporary group of volunteers (i.e., a cadre) to spearhead the change.

IQEA seemed to address the school's needs at exactly the right time and the school joined the East Midlands IQEA network in summer 1997.

The SMT realized that to be successful they had to get the enthusiasm and commitment of the heads of faculty (HoFs). This was a relatively easy task as they were delighted to know that classroom practice was to be established as the school's main priority. Very soon they were spearheading our development because they were:

1. Talking as a group about their priorities for classroom-based school improvement;
2. Hearing experts reinforce their view that school improvement must be focused on teachers in classrooms, that is, if we do not concentrate on classrooms there will be no long-term improvement;
3. Collecting some evidence from pupils about their perceptions of learning, for example, what do you enjoy? what challenges you? and so forth;
4. Accountable because school improvement has to be internally driven;
5. Encouraging members of their department to volunteer for the cadre;
6. Given staff development time to establish new ideas within the departments, including planning and sharing lessons; and
7. Clear that the idea that the project would advantage their work but was not another initiative they were forced to lead.

By June 1997 a school improvement group was established. Five of the cadre members were given one "IQEA period" per week, and it was made clear that the group was a task group and not a permanent structure. It was essential to have some team-building time; this involved practicing new models of teaching among themselves before going public with the staff. This involved videoing, laughing, modifying, and so forth. The group was quickly given a high profile, by focusing on a clear task — in our case organizing a school INSET day around inductive teaching, the first new classroom-based model we chose to learn. The cadre group also systematically gathered information about student performance, teaching and learning styles, and the schools "internal conditions" in order to help them plan their work.

After extensive discussion, the IQEA group decided that the focus for the first year of whole school development should be on the "inductive" model of teaching. The main reasons for this decision were:

1. The model was applicable to all departments.
2. No one understood it previously so all staff were learning together and sharing ideas across departments.
3. The different phases catered for different styles of teaching, including individual and group work, so there was variety in the lessons.
4. The six phases made it quite a complex model, which required understanding, so the staff had something to talk about. Comments like "Phases 1–4 are fine but then I struggle with phases 5 and 6. Any ideas?" were often heard in the staffroom.
5. The latter phases involved higher-order thinking skills, which were underdeveloped in school.
6. Though the data for inductive teaching often required considerable time in planning, it could be used from year to year, once it existed. This meant that building the teaching model into schemes of work was not too difficult.

This example from Swanwick Hall School reflects the early flow of school improvement activity. This flow of activity is illustrated in Figure 2.

As seen in Figure 2, during this early phase strategies need to involve a clear and direct focus on a limited number of basic curriculum and organizational issues in order to build the confidence and competence to continue. These include:

1. Provision of early, intensive outside support;
2. Surveying staff and student opinion; gathering and disaggregating data on student achievement;
3. A focus on managing learning behavior, not on behavior management;
4. Intensive work on re-skilling teams of teachers in a limited but specific repertoire of teaching/learning styles; and

Figure 2   *Preparing for School Improvement*

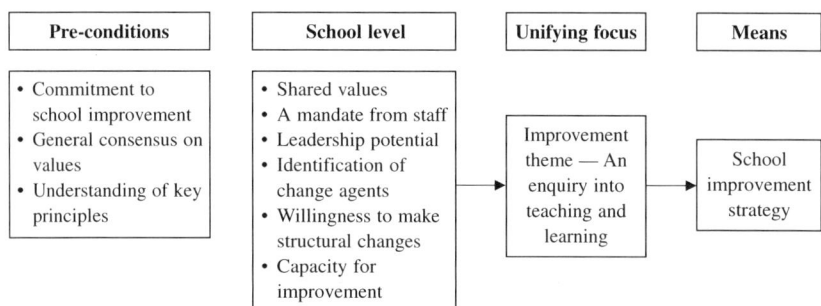

5. Progressive restructuring to generate new opportunities for leadership, collaboration and planning.

Phase Two — Going Whole School

This cycle of activity usually lasts between two and three terms. During this phase the focus is upon specific teaching and learning issues and on building the capacity within the school to support this way of working. These strategies usually involve a certain level of external support and comprise:

1. Innovations in teaching and learning that are new to most staff and are informed and supported by external knowledge and support; and
2. The sharing of and building on good practice within the school.

It begins and ends with a whole staff day. In the first, the curriculum and teaching focus and learning teams will be established. In the second, the staff will share with each other on a curriculum tour around the school the progress they have made. The activities in this phase are:

1. The Initial Whole School INSET Day(s) — This is the point at which the school improvement program formally goes "whole school." It therefore needs to be carefully managed and include a lot of "hands on" and practical activities. Colleagues, especially those who may be cynical, need to see the implications for their own teaching. The day should end with a clear understanding of the next steps and implications for individual action.

2. Establishing the Curriculum and Teaching Focus — This may have already been decided before the initial whole school INSET day. If so the opportunity needs to be taken to clarify its implications and applications to individual members of staff's own curriculum areas and classroom practice. It is also important to stress that unlike most other initiatives, this one focuses directly on the core purpose of schooling, that is, teaching and learning.

3. Establishing the Learning Teams — Different schools choose different ways of organizing the staff into "learning teams." Usually this, at least in the beginning, is departmentally based, but there are real advantages in cross-departmental groupings. There need to be two types of "learning team":

   • Curriculum grouping where teachers work together on planning schemes of work and integrating teaching strategies into the curriculum content; and

   • Peer coaching or "buddy" groups where staff in groups of two or three observe each other provide support and act as critical friends.

4. The Initial Cycle of Enquiry — This is the implementation phase of the work when the new or amended schemes of work are taught, and the peer coaching groups support each other and monitor and reflect on the impact on student learning and the development of classroom practice. Most schools aim to go through at least one cycle of such activity each half term.

5. Sharing Initial Success and Impact on Student Learning on the Curriculum Tour — there is a whole school INSET day where staff share the fruits of the work during the previous term or two. At the start of the day staff departmental groups set up a display in their area of schemes of work, videos and student work. They then form into cross-departmental groups and begin the tour around the school. At each display the member of staff from that group explains to others the work that they have done. Sometimes students are involved in the tour also. The "curriculum tour" is an efficient and exciting way to share developmental work and always engenders a great deal of enthusiasm.

The second phase of the school improvement work at Swanwick Hall School began with the whole staff INSET day. The day focused on inductive teaching, being the first new classroom-based model the staff were to enquire into. The INSET included videos of the group teaching and examples of pupils' work. It was much more powerful because teachers delivered it who had never talked to the whole staff before rather than experts from outside.

At the end of the day departments worked together planning lessons using inductive teaching. The SMT and staff realized that to establish new teaching models there had to be staff development time to:

1. Understand the model and plan lessons.
2. Share the experience across several staff which might be via joint teaching or observation.
3. Evaluate the lessons and build the successful ones into schemes of work for subsequent years.
4. Share ideas across departments by publishing lists of what has been planned/delivered; going round the table at heads of faculty meetings so every HoF contributed; and "curriculum tours" where every department put on a short display of teaching at a subsequent INSET days.

This has involved several INSET days or half days on teaching and learning each year. After each one an IQEA group member collects a return from each department so they know exactly what has been planned and when the teaching is likely to take place.

The process of school improvement moves forward by keeping a regular interchange between the permanent structures of the school (i.e., HoFs and department teams) and the development structures of the school as embodied by the IQEA (and other) groups.

The IQEA group realized that they had to keep the HoFs constantly in touch if they were expecting them to deliver certain aspects of the program in their departments. They knew they are accountable for their departments and that many IQEA developments would be published.

Certain departments have gained enormously by having a member of the IQEA group who has become an agent for change within the department. This was effective, whether or not the IQEA member was the department leader or just a member of the team.

The flow of activity during this phase of the process is illustrated in Figure 3.

Developmental activities at this stage include:

Figure 3   *Going Whole School*

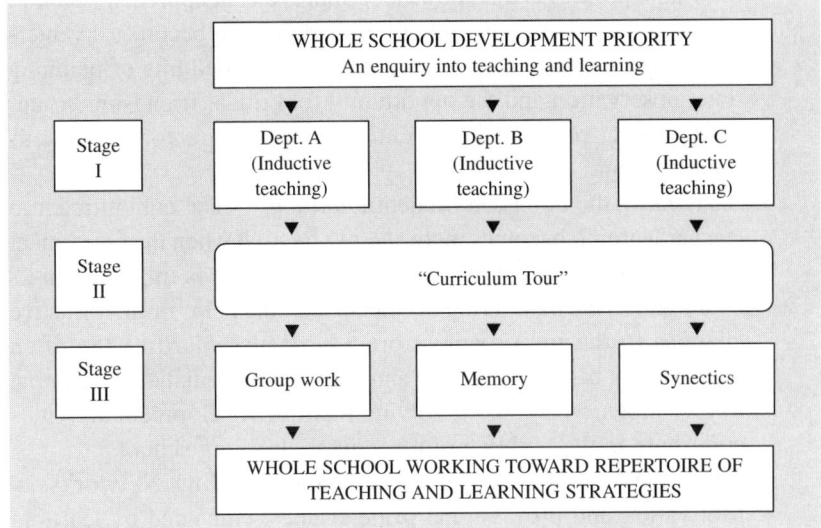

1. The use of whole school training days to focus on practical teaching and learning strategies,
2. The allocation of dedicated time for school improvement activities,
3. The organizing of staff into critical friendship groups,
4. Monitoring progress through a focus on student learning, and
5. Generating an on-going dialogue about values across staff and with key groupings such as HoFs.

Phase Three — Sustaining Momentum

It is in this phase that the capacity for change at school and classroom level becomes more secure. Learning teams become an established way of working and there is an expansion of the range of teaching strategies used throughout the curriculum. This activity includes:

1. Establishing Further Cycles of Enquiry — Following the first curriculum tour, most groups of staff will wish to enquire into other teaching models that may be more specific or relevant to their curriculum areas, or may address certain student learning needs. It is important to encourage such an approach to differentiation.

2. Building Teacher Learning into the Process — A crucial aspect of the whole process is that the school improvement approach becomes a "way of life" within the school. In particular, it becomes a vehicle for teacher learning and development. The embedding of planning time, observation and the opportunity for critical friendship groupings to meet provide the essential infrastructure for continuous improvement.

3. Sharpening the Focus on Student Learning — The commitment to teacher learning becomes more sharply focused when the assessment of student learning is built into the process. This is important in its own right, as the monitoring of student learning helps make formative changes to the improvement process. It also clarifies the often intuitive link between teaching and learning. Systematically listening to the student voice and involving them in development activities contribute to the building of a genuinely learning school.

4. Finding Ways of Sharing Success and Building Networks — Motivation and professional pride are best enhanced by learning from other teachers and from sharing good practice success. An important way of doing this is through the establishment of networks within and between schools. Networks are more than just opportunities to share "good practice"; they are characterized by a commitment to quality, rigor, and a focus on outcomes. They are also an effective means of supporting innovation in times of change. In education, networks promote the dissemination of good practice, enhance the professional development of teachers, support capacity building in schools, and assist in the process of restructuring and re-culturing the school.

5. Reflecting on the Culture of the School and Department — The point has already been made that this approach to school improvement is not another project but more a way of working. As such it needs building into the fabric of the school, its structures and culture, and the ways in which teachers work together and think about their own development. This involves:

   • New understandings about learning and the management of change;
   • More flexible and creative use of space, time, communication structures and people;
   • Widespread use of collaborative ways of working; and

- The redefinition and adaptation of ideas through the use of evidence.

When these ways of working are internalized then not only will student attainment have risen but also the school will have established itself as an effective learning organization.

In their second year of purposeful school improvement, Swanwick Hall School concentrated on consolidating inductive teaching into schemes of work, and introducing work on mnemonics (which was very successful for a few staff) and co-operative group work. As a result it is now accepted among pupils that staff will regularly group them and move them to suit the specific learning styles of the lesson in question.

By the third year, the cadre (membership had changed somewhat by then because other staff were interested in joining) felt that school improvement was more in-built into the fabric of the school, which was exciting but more difficult to manage and to monitor for effectiveness. In the third year school improvement work moved forward on several fronts:

1. Consolidation of the models from Years 1 and 2;
2. An INSET for all staff to discuss our own Preferred Learning Styles, which will reinforce the need for variety in the classroom;
3. Some departments worked to include a range of higher-order thinking skills and building them into schemes of work;
4. Members of the IQEA group experimented with other models so that they could run workshops for staff later in the year, for example, synectics, concept attainment, STAD (i.e., team games);
5. A group of staff began working on questioning techniques, which they piloted with two groups of Year 7; and
6. The IQEA group established links with the school's behavior task group to help staff train the pupils in listening skills.

Plans for next year involve:

1. Researching the effectiveness of what has been achieved so far; data is being collected from staff & pupils about progress and perceptions;
2. Pupil involvement especially in decision making; and
3. More observation of each others' lessons.

But there is only so much time in a school year and the cadre group has learnt that May to December is the best time for "development." After that there is only time for consolidation amid parents' evenings, reports, budget worries, and examination preparation.

However as IQEA has developed they claim to have learnt the following retrospectively:

1. School improvement is not about a dependency culture but about the school doing something for itself, which it wants to do. They have had a lot of help from university staff but, in the end, it is up to the staff. "We feel like colleagues with them, not just learners."

2. Development has to be built into the school's structure; for example, there are now teaching and learning meetings as part of the cycle of directed time meetings after school.

3. Staff development has changed to cover a wider variety of school activities which were never done before, for example, canceling an ordinary staff briefing to watch a colleague teaching on video, co-teaching, regular directed time meetings, talking to staff in other schools and at conferences.

4. Schools need to be learning communities; that is, pupils and staff are learning together.

5. It is essential to share ideas across the curriculum; departments have things to learn from each other.

6. Staff have got better at risking new ideas and talking about them to pupils in the classroom.

7. New models of teaching and learning may be hard work but if pupils respond well and are interested, they are easier and more fun to teach.

8. Despite the hard work, staff have had a huge boost through sharing ideas with other schools.

9. Although it cannot be proved that the continued improvement in both A–Cs and A–Gs is directly attributable to IQEA, it is clear that the departments that have substantially changed their modes of teaching now have GCSE grades which are well above the average for the school.

Figure 4 illustrates the range of activities that contribute to a capacity for learning within a school. It reflects the school improvement journeys of Bigwood and Swanwick Hall Schools who began their work facing "challenging circumstances." It also represents an attempt to capture how

Figure 4 *Establishing a Capacity for Learning*

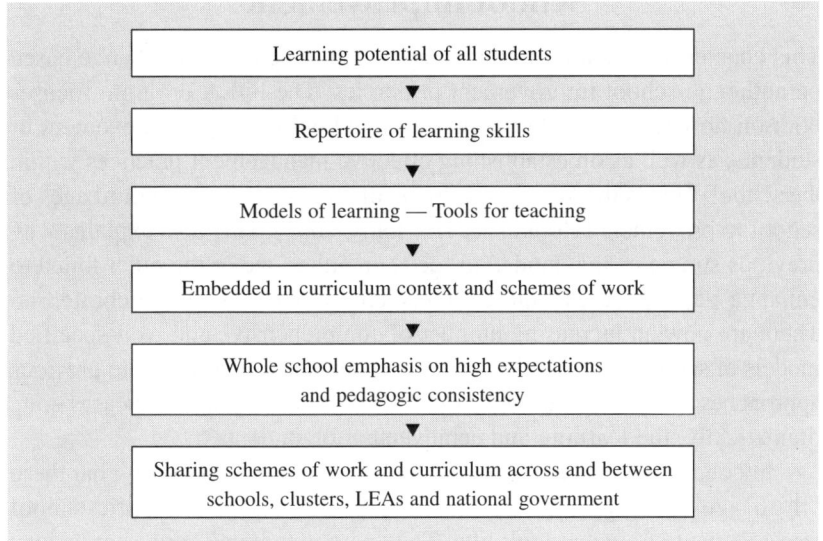

schools establish a "learning focus" and how a number of the elements of school improvement come together in practice. It begins from two assumptions. The first is that *all students* have a *potential for learning* that is not fully exploited. The second is that the students' learning capability refers to their ability to access that potential through *increasing their range of learning skills*.

This potential is best realized and learning capability enhanced through the range of teaching and learning models that the teacher uses with his/her students. The teaching and learning strategies are not "free-floating," but embedded in the schemes of work and curriculum content that teachers use to structure the learning in their lessons. These schemes of work also have the potential to be shared between schools and be available for wider dissemination.

Finally, this way of working assumes a whole school dimension through the staff development infrastructure the school has established, the emphasis on high expectations, the careful attention to consistency of teaching, and the discussion of pedagogy that pervades the cultures of these schools.

Conclusion — Toward the "Third Age" of School Improvement

This chapter has been outlining an approach to educational change based on authentic school improvement principles. The IQEA program focuses both on how to accelerate the progress and enhance the achievement of students, as well as on establishing effective management practices within the school. This is the key characteristic of what is called the "third age" of school improvement (Hopkins & Reynolds, 2001). This also explains why previous strategies that tended to focus on either one or the other failed to enhance pupil progress and achievement. What is being celebrated is: There are now an increasing number of comprehensive and well-specified models of school improvement that are so qualitatively different to previous approaches that they offer the prospect of accelerating, in some cases quite dramatically, the learning and achievement of students.

In conclusion it may be helpful to give some indication of what these "third age" programs that reflect the principles of authentic school improvement strategies look like. The "new paradigm" represents a new way of thinking about school improvement that embodies the following features:

1. There is an enhanced focus upon the importance of pupil outcomes. Instead of the earlier emphasis upon changing the processes of schools, the focus is now upon seeing if these changes are powerful enough to affect pupil outcomes.
2. The learning level and the instructional behaviors of teachers are increasingly being targeted for explicit attention as well as the school level. Specifications of curriculum and teaching are being adopted that extend current practice and that focus directly on the student learning goals that have been set.
3. There is the creation of an infrastructure to enable the knowledge base, both "best practice" and research findings, to be utilized. This involves an internal focus on collaborative patterns of staff development that enable teachers to enquire into practice, and external strategies for dissemination and networking.
4. There has been also an increased concern to ensure that the improvement programs relate to, and impact upon, practitioners and practices through using increasingly sophisticated training, coaching and development programs.

5. In addition there is an increasing consciousness of the importance of "capacity building." This includes not only staff development, but also medium-term strategic planning, change strategies that utilize "pressure and support," as well as the intelligent use of external support agencies.

6. The adoption of a "mixed" methodological orientation, in which bodies of quantitative data plus qualitative data are used to measure quality, effects and deficiencies, is becoming more common. This includes an audit of existing classroom and school processes and outcomes, and comparison with desired end states, in particular the educational experiences of different pupil groups.

7. Authentic school improvement stresses the importance of ensuring reliability or "fidelity" in the program implementation across all the organizational members within schools, a marked contrast with the past when improvement programs did not have to be organizationally "tight."

8. There is an appreciation of the importance of cultural change in order to embed and sustain this approach to school improvement. There is a careful balance between "vision building" and the adapting of structures to support those aspirations.

Note

1. The themes raised in this chapter are more fully explored in Hopkins (2001).

References

Elmore, R. (2000). *Building a new structure for school leadership*. Washington, DC: The Albert Shanker Institute.

Fullan, M. (2000). The return of large scale reform. *Journal of Educational Change, 1*(1), 1–20.

Hargreaves, A., Lieberman, A., Fullan, M., & Hopkins, D. (Eds.). (1998). *International handbook of educational change*. Dordrecht, Netherlands; Boston: Kluwer Academic Publishers.

Hopkins, D. (2001). *School improvement for real*. London: Routledge Falmer.

Hopkins, D. (2002). *Improving the quality of education for all*. London: David Fulton.

Hopkins, D., & Levin, B. (2000). Government policy and school development. *School Leadership and Management, 20*(1), 15–30.

Hopkins, D., & Reynolds, D. (2001). The past, present and future of school improvement: Towards the third age. *British Educational Research Journal, 27* (4), 459–475.

Leithwood, K., Jantzi, D., & Mascall, B. (1999). *Large scale reform: What works?* Unpublished manuscript, Ontario Institute for Studies in Education, University of Toronto.

McLaughlin, M. (1990). The Rand change agent study revisited: Macro perspectives, micro realities. *Educational Researcher, 19*(9), 11–16.

5

Quality Education Through Quality Teacher Education and Development: The Unified Professional Development Project

Lo Mun-ling & Edith Lai

Abstract

This chapter presents the Unified Professional Development Project for Teachers and Student Teachers (UPDP), an educational initiative at the Department of Curriculum Studies, the University of Hong Kong. UPDP attempted to link teacher education with school improvement and was committed to enhancing the professional development of teachers from teacher preparation throughout their entire teaching careers by means of collaboration between Hong Kong schools and the University of Hong Kong in partnership. This chapter describes the major components of UPDP — the School-University Partnership Scheme, the Unified Professional Development Fellowship, and the School-based Development Consultancy. It also examines the project's impact on schools, particularly student teachers and school mentoring teachers, and how UPDP interacted with the culture of the schools to contribute to teachers' learning and professional development. It also explores the possible contributions of the development of a mentoring force in schools to improving the quality of education in Hong Kong.

Over the last decade, initial teacher education has been re-conceptualized. There is an emerging perspective which advocates "teaching as the learning profession" (Darling-Hammond & Sykes, 1999). It is believed that "neither experience nor inquiry improves teaching" (Darling-Hammond & Sykes,

1999, p. 11). Teachers would also need to learn how to use the knowledge gained to improve their teaching, and that "the key to producing well-qualified teachers is to greatly enhance their professional learning across the continuum of a career in the classroom" (Sykes, 1999, p. xv). Shulman (1999) argues that "teachers are professionals precisely because they operate under conditions of inherent novelty, uncertainty, and chance" (pp. xii–xiii) so that teachers' behavior cannot be prescribed and no amount of theories or knowledge taught in any teacher education courses can fully prescribe appropriate or wise practice. Ball and Cohen (1999) argue that:

> Much of what they [teachers] would have to learn must be learned in and from practice rather than in preparing to practice. Or, perhaps better, they would have to learn, before they taught and while teaching, how to learn in and from practice. (p. 10)

Since student teachers are not clean slates without any knowledge or experience of classrooms, the learning experience of the student teachers must be powerful enough to counteract the conservative lessons that most have learned from their own past experience as students. Student teachers should be placed in schools that support their growth and learning and encourage innovative practices. Thus, a comprehensive approach to teachers' professional development is needed. This means that teacher education institutions must work in partnership with schools toward providing a conducive learning environment where student teachers' learning to teach can be situated in a culture which reflects the best of practice (Ball & Cohen, 1999).

New models of teacher education have developed involving partnership between schools and universities (e.g., Furlong et al., 1996; Murphy, 1997; Totterdell & Lambert, 1998). In England and Wales, school-university partnership is mandated for all initial teacher preparation (DES, 1992). Many examples of school-university partnerships can be found: The federally funded Innovative Links in Australia that focuses on school-based teachers' professional development and whole school improvement (Yeatman & Sachs, 1995); the Learning Consortium at the University of Toronto that takes on a systemic approach to teachers' continuous professional learning throughout their careers, in such areas as pre-service training, in-service training and working conditions of teachers (Swanson, 1995); and the Professional Development Schools (PDS) movement in the United States (Linn, 2000). PDS, modeled after teaching hospitals in medicine, are framed by the conception that schools and universities work together in partnership for the professional preparation of prospective and novice teachers as well as the professional development of veteran teachers. They would also carry out praxis-based research on school and instructional improvement (Holmes Group, 1990).

This chapter describes the Unified Professional Development Project for Teachers and Student Teachers (UPDP), a school-university partnership project for initial teacher education in Hong Kong, and examines its evolution as the teaching practicum was re-conceptualized. UPDP originated in a small-scale School-University Partnership Scheme that was initiated in the Department of Curriculum Studies at the University of Hong Kong in September 1996 with three schools. Then eight schools participated in this scheme in 1997, and it was here that the groundwork on school-based mentorship was undertaken. The successful application of the principles underpinning the scheme led to the proposal for UPDP. With funds from the Quality Education Fund, it was possible to appoint a development team initially for 2 years from 1998 to 2000 (UPDP Phase I) and then for another 2 years from 2000 to 2002 (UPDP Phase II). Although UPDP was not initially conceptualized with PDS in mind, it slowly took on many of the characteristics of PDS in its later stages.

Aims of the Partnership

The immediate reason for initiating the partnership was the expansion of the P.C.Ed. and B.Ed. programs in 1996, which created a drastic increase in demand for teaching practicum places. By establishing partnership ties with schools, the Department of Curriculum Studies was guaranteed of a certain number of teaching practicum places from our partnership schools because each partnership school was requested to take on a minimum of four to six student teachers each year upon joining the partnership scheme.

At the same time, the partnership idea was spurred by increasing concerns over the quality of support given to student teachers by placement schools during teaching practicum. Problems associated with the traditional mode of teaching practicum showed that student teachers were not guaranteed of quality support during the practicum, that mentoring teachers needed to be trained, and that partnership between schools and the University needed to be nurtured and maintained.

Two departmental projects, Quality Enhancement in the Teaching Practicum (QETP) and Quality Enhancement of Supervising Teaching (QUEST), contributed to the initiation and development of the partnership as a way of re-conceptualizing the teaching practicum. More specifically, the two projects contributed to a better understanding of student teachers' experiences during teaching practicum. QETP revealed different supervisory practices undertaken by university tutors (Kwo, 1998), whereas QUEST explored a framework for improving teaching practice supervision (Stimpson et al., 2000).

For a long time, teacher education in Hong Kong had been mainly the responsibility of tertiary institutions. Schools generally had not been involved in teacher education programs apart from taking on student teachers in practicum placement. Tsui (1997) in a discussion paper entitled "The University-School Partnership Scheme" formally introduced and documented the aim of the partnership in this Department. Firstly, the partnership was to enhance the quality of teacher education programs offered by the University by making the programs more relevant to school situations, making the teaching practicum component of the program a richer and more beneficial experience for student teachers, and encouraging schools to participate more in teacher education provision. Secondly, the partnership was to help schools to enhance the quality of teaching by providing input in the professional development of their teachers and addressing current issues in education. Therefore, from its very beginning, the partnership was intended to be a collaborative one.

UPDP Phase I —
A "Unified" Approach to Teacher Development

The partnership took on a "unified" approach to teacher development, which involved linking teacher education with school improvement. This was to be achieved through the development of a quality teaching force in schools by providing opportunities for teachers' continuing professional development at different stages of their career: from pre-service teachers, to beginning teachers, and to experienced teachers.

The unified approach to teacher development was to be achieved by the three major components in the first phase of UPDP: the School-University Partnership Scheme, the Unified Professional Development Fellowship, and the School-based Development Consultancy.

Component 1: The School-University Partnership Scheme

The School-University Partnership Scheme (hereafter called "the Partnership Scheme") offered a new mode of teaching practicum that was different from the one traditionally adopted in most teacher education institutions in Hong Kong. In the Partnership Scheme, schools and the University were close partners working collaboratively to provide a holistic school experience to student teachers during their initial teacher education, more specifically their teaching practicum. Schools that had established partnership ties with the University were called "Partnership Schools."

First, the whole school, instead of only individual subject departments or individual subject teachers, was involved as a partner in providing support to student teachers during teaching practicum. Second, a formal induction program for student teachers was built into the early part of the teaching practicum. Third, a mentor was assigned to each student teacher, which enabled student teachers to receive full support from their mentors who took up the roles of an observer, a provider of feedback, a role model, a counselor, a critical friend, an instructor, and a manager. Fourth, lesson observation (including student teachers observing mentors and other teachers, and student teachers being observed) as well as pre- and post-lesson conferences to discuss observed lessons were regular parts of the teaching practicum. Fifth, tripartite conferences involving a student teacher, a mentor and a university tutor to provide feedback on the teaching performance of the student teacher was an important initiative of the Partnership Scheme. Sixth, student teachers were involved in all aspects of school life.

On the one hand, student teachers were fully supported by mentors and Partnership Schools during teaching practicum. On the other hand, the University maintained close liaison with Partnership Schools on matters related to teaching practicum. The University also facilitated the training and growth of teachers as mentors of beginning teachers and student teachers through publishing mentoring handbook, UPDP newsletters and training videos, arranging general and subject-based mentoring workshops, organizing project conferences, and inviting mentors to work alongside university tutors in tripartite conferences.

The impact of the Partnership Scheme was evaluated using individual interviews, focus group interviews and questionnaires. In particular, the evaluation aims at finding out how the Partnership Scheme had changed the quality of support given to student teachers during the practicum, and how mentors, principals, and university tutors perceived the Partnership Scheme.

Support for Student Teachers

Findings from the various data sources indicated that most student teachers placed in Partnership Schools found pre- and post-lesson discussions with mentors very practical and constructive. In particular, student teachers appreciated that mentors took time and effort to go through their lesson plans and provide feedback on their teaching performance. In addition, student teachers appreciated the opportunity to observe mentors' as well as other teachers' classroom teaching, and to discuss the observed lessons with the teachers afterwards. Partnership Schools also made an effort to accommodate student teachers in various ways by, for instance, improving their facilities, arranging new furniture for student teachers, seating them near to their mentors in the staff room, inviting them to attend staff and subject panel meetings, and encouraging them to participate in various school activities.

The arrangement of tripartite conferences had achieved its purpose of providing a context for getting at mutual understanding between the three parties involved (a student teacher, a mentor and a university tutor) and for exchanges of ideas and experiences in teaching and mentoring. Many university tutors and mentors made an effort to adjust their schedules so that they could sit together with student teachers before, during and after lessons to review student teachers' strengths and weaknesses, listen to their concerns, and find out how things were going in their practice. Findings from interviews showed that student teachers generally found tripartite conferences beneficial for their professional growth. More specifically, they found that tripartite conferences provided a context for them to hear comments on their teaching performance from both mentors and university tutors, which enhanced reflection on their practice. For mentors that had been involved in tripartite conferences, they found that the conferences provided good opportunities for them to interact and share with university tutors regarding teaching methods, problems faced by student teachers in classrooms, and the challenges of teaching supervision. Some university tutors interviewed also found comments from mentors very practical and worthwhile.

The overall evaluation findings showed that student teachers placed in

Partnership Schools generally received more support than those placed in non-Partnership Schools. They reported more support from induction programs, more opportunities to take part in pre- and post-lesson conferences and tripartite conferences, and greater involvement in non-teaching duties.

Mentors' Perception of the Partnership Scheme

In the early stage of the implementation of the Partnership Scheme, most mentors were unclear about the rationale behind the partnership, how the partnership operated in schools, mentors' roles and responsibilities, the role of schools and the University in the partnership, and also how to go about mentoring student teachers. Consequently, they generally did not see how the partnership is different from the traditional mode of teaching practicum. Thus, in this early stage, mentors were mostly concerned with how the partnership affected them in both positive and negative ways, and some of these concerns were technical and procedural in nature. For instance, they were concerned about how seating space could be arranged for student teachers and the need for mentors to travel all the way to the University to attend mentoring workshops.

With time, the theme of mutual benefits began to emerge. Most mentors reported both benefits and costs by engaging in mentoring. For benefits, apart from having part of their workload alleviated by student teachers, mentors generally found that working with student teachers provided them with exposure to new teaching ideas and new teaching materials. They found the chance to see new teaching ideas being put in action in student teachers' teaching most rewarding. Mentors also found that the mentoring experience helped them rethink their own teaching, thus becoming more reflective of their own practice. In addition, mentors found that they gained mentoring experience and became more skilled at analyzing lessons and communicating with student teachers. One mentor reported that the arrangement of regular mutual lesson observation between mentors and student teachers had changed his view on lesson observation and now he felt more relaxed about being observed by colleagues in the school. Many mentors found it gratifying to see that their mentees made progress in teaching and classroom management and became more confident. They also enjoyed their friendship with student teachers and reported times when they felt touched by student teachers' enthusiasm, energy, and fresh outlook on life and the world. Some mentors perceived that their pupils benefited from better-prepared student teachers and their innovative teaching ideas.

In terms of costs, time was the biggest concern for most mentors. Extra time and effort were involved in mentoring, including preparation work before the arrival of student teachers, observing lessons, and participating in pre- and post-lesson conferences. Moreover, extra time was usually needed to help the class catch up after student teachers left. Some mentors were particularly anxious about losing contact with their own pupils.

Partnership Schools' Perception of the Partnership Scheme

Principals of Partnership Schools generally saw taking on student teachers for teaching practicum as their obligations toward teacher preparation. Through school visits and interviews with principals, it was found that they were becoming increasingly aware that mentoring benefits the professional growth of both pre-service teachers and serving teachers. After joining the Partnership Scheme, many schools explored ways to provide a more conducive environment for student teachers to practice teaching, such as devising an informative induction program, inculcating proper values of teaching, and providing a stimulating environment for professional learning. A principal, after joining the Partnership Scheme for 3 years, had the following comment:

> The interaction between in-service teachers and student teachers as well as classroom observations have opened up our teachers' attitude toward classroom observation which in turn, has changed the teaching culture in our school.

University Tutors' Perception of the Partnership Scheme

Since the inception of UPDP, university tutors in the Department of Curriculum Studies had been kept fully informed about the partnership and their roles related to it. Some of these university tutors were members of the project's Management Committee and/or Steering Committee. Others contributed to mentor training and the Fellowship component of the project. A series of formal interviews were conducted to gain a clearer understanding of the experience and understanding of the partnership by university tutors. The principal findings were reported below:

1. There was a high level of understanding by university tutors of the concept of partnership as developed in UPDP.
2. There was a general agreement that UPDP was a useful innovation in that it contributed to the introduction of a program of mentoring and tripartite conferences.

3. Some tutors stated that they had benefited from participation in the partnership; it had challenged their views about teacher education and helped to clarify their roles in schools.
4. University tutors generally spoke favorably about the improved relationships they were developing with principals and mentors in Partnership Schools.
5. University tutors generally agreed that student teachers benefited from the improvements in mentoring and from tripartite conferences.
6. Some university tutors expressed an interest in contributing to the work of the partnership, for example, running mentoring workshops and working with Unified Professional Development Fellows.

Therefore, the Partnership Scheme benefited at least three parties. The University benefited as student teachers in the initial teacher education programs received strong support from mentors and schools during their practicum placement in Partnership Schools. Mentors benefited by receiving training in mentoring and becoming more reflective of their own practices in the process of mentoring student teachers. Partnership Schools benefited by having staff trained to become mentors and getting a head start in the development of a mentoring force that will help these schools train new teachers and contribute to quality education in the long run.

Component 2: Unified Professional Development Fellowship

UPDP contributed to the continuing professional development of teachers by providing them with an opportunity to conduct research and/or development projects with university academics through the establishment of the Unified Professional Development Fellowship (hereafter called "the Fellowship"). Teachers that took up the Fellowship were called Unified Professional Development Fellows (hereafter called "Fellows"). Fellows were released from their teaching duties for a continuous period of 3 to 5 months to engage in studies that would contribute to the work of their schools and meet their own identified personal professional needs. They worked closely with a university partner who supported their work throughout the Fellowship period.

In UPDP Phase I, 19 Fellowships were completed. Among them, 14 were projects respectively in the areas of curriculum development, use of information technology in teaching and learning, and students' academic and social development, and 5 involved Fellows participating in an intensive program in teacher development, which focused specifically on teachers' professional development through mentoring (hereafter called "the Teacher Development Fellowship"). To illustrate the impact of the Fellowship on teachers, the Teacher Development Fellowship program is described and some of its impact on the participating teachers is highlighted.

The Teacher Development Fellowship was based on a conceptual framework of teacher development, which took into account different views about teachers' professional knowledge, including the technical, interpretive and critical perspectives (Hoyle & John, 1995) of how teachers gain professional knowledge, as well as both cognitive and affective elements in teaching and learning. The main aims of the Teacher Development Fellowship included: helping teachers make use of classroom observation as a means of improving teaching and learning, creating a learning community of teachers by engaging teachers in lesson studies (Stigler & Hiebert 1999), helping school improvement by providing schools with access to research findings on teaching and learning, and helping each participating school train a teacher who will be able to facilitate other teachers in their professional development in the school. The Teacher Development Fellowship program consisted of a series of seminars and workshops conducted by local and overseas teacher educators and visits to local schools, to be completed within a period of 3 months. Some of the main program components included sessions on mentoring, lesson analysis and lesson study, lesson observation as well as pre- and post-lesson conferencing, staff development and staff appraisal, and critical incidents as opportunities for professional development.

Fellows generally found the Teacher Development Fellowship beneficial for their professional growth. In particular, it helped open up their views on current issues in education and gain new perspectives on teaching and learning through exchanges with local and overseas teacher educators and other Fellows in seminars and workshops at the University, and exchanges with principals and teachers in school visits. In particular, Fellows found that the provision for them to be released from school duties for a continuous period of 3 months allowed them to have a quiet time to reflect on their own practice and role as a teacher. They also gained knowledge and skills in doing lesson analysis, lesson study, classroom observation and conferencing, which benefited their school. Positive feedback was received from all Fellows that had participated in the Teacher Development Fellowship program. Below were some typical sentiments:

1. I have benefited a great deal in the area of teaching and learning from these 3 months of studies in the Fellowship. I have come to understand more about what I can do to facilitate student learning. It also makes me realize that teaching effectiveness can be raised by engaging teachers in professional development programs, such as the Fellowship. Besides, the Fellowship helps me look at the relationship between teachers and students in a new way — the growth of students need our care, understanding and encouragement.
2. Fellows from different schools share experiences and opinions toward teaching. This is a very valuable opportunity for us to learn from each other in the profession. The space and time (3 months of full-time study) gives us chances to reflect on our practices in our work of teaching.
3. The Fellowship helps to re-ignite my passion for teaching. The interflow between Fellows makes me feel that I am not alone in teaching.
4. The Fellowship helps me reflect on my teaching and my philosophies behind it. The writing workshops help me realize that teaching is about establishing connection with people.

Component 3: School-Based Development Consultancy

UPDP contributed to school-based staff development through the School-based Development Consultancy (hereafter called "the Consultancy"). The Consultancy was intended to address school needs, benefit the professional growth of teachers, and contribute to school improvement by helping schools and teachers identify their needs; design and implement school-based staff development programs to address the identified needs, and evaluate the effectiveness of such programs in particular school contexts.

Among the nine Consultancies undertaken in UPDP Phase I, three were on the development of higher-order thinking skills, three on invitational education, two on the use of information technology in teaching and learning, and one on curriculum integration.

Participating schools and their staff generally found the Consultancies helpful in diagnosing their schools' needs, relevant to their school situations, and effective in addressing the identified needs. Most participating schools expressed that they would continue to adopt the plans developed in the Consultancies. Some schools expressed the desire to have a longer Consultancy period so that they could work out with their consultants specific guidelines and strategies for the sustainable implementation of the plans.

To illustrate the impact of the Consultancy, the area of invitational education and its impact on school are described below. Three schools undertook Consultancies in this area. Central to invitational education is the belief that "every person and everything in and around schools adds to or subtracts from the process of being a beneficial presence in the lives of students" (Wong, 2000). The Consultancy on invitational education aimed at creating a school environment that would enhance educational success in students through changing the five factors (the so-called 5Ps) in the invitational model: people, places, policies, programs, and processes. This was to be achieved through systematic staff development and ongoing consultation with local and overseas consultants. Evaluation of the Consultancy in each of the three schools showed that the Consultancy had made an impact on these schools.

School 1 was ready to put in systematic efforts to create a more inviting school environment and the school had already made efforts to bring about invitational changes in people and places. Examples of these efforts include: displaying students' work around the school, planning to change signages around the school to make the school environment more inviting, promoting positive attitudes in all school staff, and involving parents to facilitate Form 1 students in moving up to a secondary school. In addition, the staff became increasingly aware of the need to make the school a caring environment for students, as evidenced in demand from teachers for an expansion of pastoral care services for students and training sessions on counseling and guidance for teachers. The Consultancy also had a positive impact on developing among staff a culture of peer support in enhancing teaching and learning, through increased opportunities for the staff to work together and share ideas and experiences.

In School 2, the 5Ps were in great synergy and harmony. The school grounds were nicely decorated with plants and display of students' artwork, and people showed care and mutual respect for each other, creating a warm and caring school community. In terms of policies and programs, the school had positive regard for every individual student, encouraged positive peer relationship and mutual sharing, and involved parents as partners in education. The school won the "Year 2000 Inviting School Award" presented by the International Alliance for the Invitation Education in the United States.

In School 3, the staff became more aware that in the process of educational change, it was important to cater for students' needs. After the Consultancy, the school put emphasis on the expansion of counseling and pastoral care services for students in the coming year, and as a whole, the staff was found to be more receptive to changes.

To sum up, the first phase of UPDP had significance in a number of ways. First, UPDP initiated a new mode of teacher education in Hong Kong, in which student teachers could benefit from richer school experiences during their practicum placement. This was made possible by the collaboration between schools and the University. Second, UPDP contributed to a change in the culture of many Partnership Schools by initiating mutual classroom observation between mentors and student teachers. Teachers were now more ready to open up their classrooms for observation by peers and to engage in professional discussion about their lessons. This had great potential for improving the quality of teaching and learning in schools. Third, the initiation of tripartite conferences also helped to enhance the collaborative relationships between school teachers and university tutors in teacher education. This had great potential to help to re-conceptualize the relationship between theory and practice. Finally, UPDP demonstrated the potential for quality education by the establishment of a mentoring force in schools.

In order for these positive changes to be sustained and to gather momentum, much more work was needed to nurture the partnership and to continue with the professional development of mentors. The second phase of UPDP was devoted to strengthening the partnership and to building up a strong mentoring force in Partnership Schools.

Problems with UPDP Phase I

First, the Consultancy was to be highly responsive to the professional needs identified by individual schools. Initially, it was estimated that some Consultancy plans would be produced in each of the 2 years. It was intended to disseminate the Consultancy plans to Partnership Schools as a reference for other school-based staff development plans. Meeting this objective proved to be difficult. In the first year of the project (1998–1999), one Consultancy was undertaken and five Partnership Schools began to develop Consultancy plans. In the second year (1999–2000), these six Partnership Schools were joined by three additional schools, so that a total of nine Consultancies were undertaken in 2 years. School-based consultancy was a new development for most of the Partnership Schools and this unfamiliarity posed difficulties. Further, matching schools' needs with appropriate university expertise was a major challenge. As a result, expertise from other institutions had to be enlisted in order to fulfill the requirement for the number of Consultancies.

Second, the school-oriented Fellowship projects were found not to be contributing to the main theme of the "partnership" — the development of a mentoring force in schools. In view of this, a Fellowship in the area of teacher development was offered to Partnership Schools in the second year (1999–2000). The Teacher Development Fellowship aims at training a person for each school that would practice mentoring and train other teachers to become mentors and contribute to the professional development of teachers in the school. Five experienced teachers and one principal took up the Teacher Development Fellowship. The Teacher Development Fellowship served as a pilot and paved the way for the subsequent Unified Professional Development Fellowship in Mentoring in the second phase of the project.

Third, the quality of mentors and thus mentoring varied widely within and across schools. It became increasingly clear that the quality of mentors could not be ensured through a few mentoring workshops. In addition, attendance at mentoring workshops had not been satisfactory even if these workshops were run at different regions to make them more accessible to school teachers in remote areas. This pointed to the need for an "in-house" person in each school that would be responsible for mentor training.

UPDP Phase II — Toward the Development of a Mentoring Force for School Improvement

Phase II was refocused in order to streamline all activities to contribute to the aim of the project — creating a mentoring force in schools, which in turn should contribute to the professional development of student teachers, beginning teachers, and experienced teachers in Partnership Schools. The project still consisted of three components. The School-University

Partnership Scheme remained unchanged. The Unified Professional Development Fellowship was renamed the Unified Professional Development Fellowship in Mentoring and had the same nature as the Teacher Development Fellowship piloted in Phase I. The aims of the Unified Professional Development Fellowship in Mentoring were:

1. To help teachers make beneficial use of classroom observations for improving teaching and learning;
2. To create a community of teachers and researchers that learn and grow together;
3. To enable findings from researches on teaching and learning to be fed back to teachers and schools for school improvement; and
4. To help in the professional development of one teacher in each Partnership School, who would demonstrate understanding and leadership in teachers' professional development and appraisal.

Upon joining the project, each new Partnership School was offered a Fellowship. The Fellowship began in March and ended in June. Schools were given 3 months' supply teacher pay so that the Fellows were completely freed from their teaching duties for 3 months to work and learn together at the University. They took an intensive course that prepared them for undertaking professional development programs in their schools. They were introduced to the most current researches on teaching and learning, lesson analysis (Lo & Chik, 2000; Mok, Marton et al., 1999; Mok, Chik et al., 2001), and lesson studies (Stigler & Hiebert, 1999) undertaken by academic staff at the University, and encouraged to carry out similar studies in collaboration with university staff. Twenty-four Fellowships were offered over 2 years.

The School-based Development Consultancy, although found to be very successful in Phase I, was dropped because it did not contribute to the mission of creating a mentoring force. It was replaced by "Teacher Development in Clusters." All 50 Partnership Schools were grouped into five clusters based on geographical locations. A network was created in each cluster to encourage collaboration and dissemination of good practice among Partnership Schools of the same cluster. It was anticipated that Fellows would act as a binding force for schools in these clusters, contribute to coordination of cluster activities, and support each other in professional development work in their respective schools.

The stated aims of the project in this second phase were:

1. To facilitate school improvement through the development of a mentoring force in the school;
2. To provide principals and department heads with a framework for staff appraisal using classroom observations;
3. To provide schools with a framework for staff development using peer observations of lessons;
4. To achieve quality assurance in teaching and learning by engaging teachers in lesson studies; and
5. To enhance the professional development of experienced teachers through mentoring.

By the end of 2001, 50 schools joined UPDP as Partnership Schools. Many schools were receptive to the ideas behind UPDP. This was because in Hong Kong, many schools had introduced lesson observations as a component of staff appraisal, whereas some had introduced peer lesson observations as a means for teachers' professional development. Many schools joined UPDP because they envisaged that the large number of student teachers that came to their schools for teaching practicum would bring in new ideas and practices that would challenge the established culture of these schools. Some teachers actually became more open and receptive to classroom observations after engaging in mentoring student teachers, which was what most schools were trying to instigate. Schools also wanted to enlist the expertise of the University in helping them train their teachers for lesson observations. Some Partnership Schools had established an induction program and a mentoring scheme for their own new or beginning teachers.

Looking to the Future

Owing to the voluntary nature of the partnership, the strength of the partnership ties between schools and the University varies across schools depending on the schools' readiness to commit to the relationship and whether a common vision can be built between the partners. As a result, different levels of partnership have emerged, with some schools showing more commitment than others in maintaining and developing the partnership. In the years to come, it is anticipated that some mentors may be involved as examiners for student teachers' practicum performance, whereas some mature Partnership Schools may be developed into "Centers of Excellence" for teaching practicum in certain subject areas.

On the University's side, the Partnership Scheme remains part of a project despite the fact that it is already in its third action research cycle and its sixth year of operation. As long as the extra time and effort being put into the partnership by colleagues are not being recognized as part of their workload, future work related to the partnership still depends on goodwill. If the good work of UPDP is to continue and become institutionalized, it has to be given proper recognition as a formal structure within the Faculty of Education in the University.

References

Ball, D. L., & Cohen, D. K. (1999). Developing practice, developing practitioners: Towards a practice-based theory of professional education. In L. Darling-Hammond & G. Sykes (Eds.), *Teaching as the learning profession: Handbook of policy and practice* (pp. 3–32). San Francisco: Jossey-Bass.

Department for Education and Science (DES). (1992). *Initial teacher training: Secondary phase (Circular 9/92)*. London: Author.

Darling-Hammond, L., & Sykes, G. (Eds.). (1999). *Teaching as the learning profession: Handbook of policy and practice*. San Francisco: Jossey-Bass.

Furlong, J., Whitty, G., Whiting, C., Miles, M., Barton, L., & Barrett, E. (1996). Re-defining partnership: Revolution or reform in initial teacher education? *Journal of Education for Teaching, 22*(1), 39–55.

Holmes Group. (1990). *Tomorrow's schools: Principles for the design of Professional Development Schools. A Report.* East Lansing, MI: Author.

Hoyle, E., & John, P. (1995). *Professional knowledge and professional practice.* London: Cassell.

Kwo, O. (Ed.). (1998). *Professional learning together: Building a collaborative culture in teaching practicum supervision.* Hong Kong: Faculty of Education, University of Hong Kong.

Linn, D. (2000). *Integrating Professional Development Schools into state education reforms.* Washington, DC: National Governors Association.

Lo, M. L., & Chik, P. M. (2000, January). *What matters? Progressive versus traditional teaching styles.* Paper presented at the 13th International Congress for School Effectiveness and Improvement, Hong Kong.

Mok, I., Chik, P. M., Ko, P. Y., Kwan, T., Lo, M. L., Marton, F., Ng, F. P., Pang, M. F., Runesson, U., & Szeto, L. H. (2001). Solving the paradox of the Chinese learner? In D. A. Watkins & J. B. Biggs (Eds.), *Teaching the Chinese learner: Psychological and pedagogical perspectives* (pp. 161–180). Hong Kong: Comparative Education Research Centre, University of Hong Kong.

Mok, A. C. I., Marton, F., Ko, P. Y., Lo, M. L., Ng, F. P., Kwan, Y. L., Szeto,

L. H., & Chik, P. M. (1999). *The anatomy of a Chinese lesson*. Paper presented at 8th European Conference for Research on Learning and Instruction, Göteborg University, Göteborg, Sweden, August 24–28.

Murphy, D. S. (1997, March). *Teacher education for essential learning: A school/ university residency program for new teacher development*. Paper presented at the Annual Meeting of the Association for Supervision and Curriculum Development, Baltimore, Canada.

Shulman, L. S. (1999). Foreword. In L. Darling-Hammond & G. Sykes (Eds.), *Teaching as the learning profession: Handbook of policy and practice* (pp. xi–xiv). San Francisco: Jossey-Bass.

Stigler, J. W., & Hiebert, J. (1999). *The teaching gap: Best ideas from the world's teachers for improving education in the classroom*. New York: The Free Press.

Stimpson, P., Lopez-Real, F., Bunton, D., Chan, W. K. D, Sivan, A., & Wiliams, M. (2000). *Better supervision, better teaching: A handbook for teaching practice supervisors*. Hong Kong: Hong Kong University Press.

Swanson, J. (1995). Systemic reform in the professionalism of educators. *Phi Delta Kappan, 77*(1), 36–39.

Sykes, G. (1999). Introduction: Teaching as the learning profession. In L. Darling-Hammond & G. Sykes (Eds.), *Teaching as the learning profession: Handbook of policy and practice* (pp. xv–xxiii). San Francisco: Jossey-Bass.

Totterdell, M., & Lambert, D. (1998). The professional formation of teachers: A case study in reconceptualising initial teacher education through an evolving model of partnership in training and learning. *Teacher Development, 2*(3), 351–371.

Tsui, A. B. M. (1997). *Discussion paper: A University-School Partnership Scheme*. Hong Kong: Department of Curriculum Studies, University of Hong Kong.

Wong, K. H. P. (2000). *Consultancy report: The application of invitational education for school improvement*. Hong Kong: The Unified Professional Development Project, Department of Curriculum Studies, University of Hong Kong.

Yeatman, A., & Sachs, J. (1995). *Making the links: A formative evaluation of the first year of the Innovative Links Project between Universities and Schools for Teacher Professional Development*. Murdoch, Australia: Innovative Links Project.

6

Teacher Development and Empowerment Through School-University Partnerships

Irma J. Van Scoy & Christine Ebert

Abstract

This chapter focuses on how one university's Professional Development School (PDS) network, a type of school-university partnership, contributes to the professional development of in-service PDS teachers. Following an overview of professional development schools and theories of teacher development and empowerment, a description of the evolution of the University of South Carolina PDSs and key components of the partnership are described, including shared supervision of pre-service teachers, school-university action research, on-site courses for pre- and in-service teachers, and the organizational and committee structures of the network. PDS effects on teacher development and empowerment are explored through data collected during focus group sessions with university faculty, pre- and in-service teachers, and P-12 administrators in a variety of studies. The authors also draw on their 10 years of experience in developing and maintaining PDS relationships. Impact on teachers is described in two sections: (1) empowerment and change in teaching practices, and (2) leadership and expanded roles (e.g., clinical adjunct, practicum instructor). The chapter concludes with a summary of challenges related to maintaining school-university partnerships with strong professional development components for all parties.

There comes a time in the teaching of children when one wants to reach out and impact a different audience. I would like to do this without giving up my class of children. Working with USC [University of South Carolina] faculty at my school has given me the opportunity to move beyond the arena of the classroom ... PDS has changed my life and the lives of all the teachers at Hood Street. As I speak, 9 student teachers, 4 junior block students, and 50 practicum students are coming and going from our 14-classroom school ... We have all become teacher educators. (Chaplin, 1993, p. 4)

Professional Development Schools (PDSs) are a major focus of teacher education reform in the United States. The Holmes Group, the National Network for Educational Renewal, the National Education Association's Teacher Education Initiative, and the National Board for Professional Teaching Standards all advocate the development of PDSs. A PDS can be defined as an early childhood, elementary, middle, or secondary school in which prospective teachers, in-service teachers and administrators, and university professors work together to continually develop and provide exemplary learning experiences for pre-kindergarten through Grade 12 (P-12) students and pre- and in-service teachers. Levine (1997) describes the best PDSs as:

> Imbued with a vision of teaching as professional practice — knowledge-based, collegial, and inquiry oriented. Work in PDSs is guided by a commitment to a set of principles that include a student-centered approach to teaching and learning; the sharing of responsibilities between the partnering institutions; the simultaneous renewal of school and university; and a commitment to provide equal opportunity for all participants. (pp. 1–2)

It was suggested by the Holmes Group (1990) that PDSs would yield "in essence, a new institution ... a school for the development of novice professionals, for continuing development of experienced professionals, and for the research and development of the teaching profession" (p. 1). Though the result may in fact be a new institution, it might be more appropriately conceptualized as a new *educational community*. The difference is that people see themselves as working *for* an institution — an entity defined by its own set of characteristics. Community defines itself by the common interests of the community members. It involves a personal involvement, a personal concern for, and a sense of personal ownership in the activities of the group. In the context of a PDS, that involvement, concern, and ownership is the result of effectively demonstrating that activities of the PDS are of value to all participants. This chapter focuses on the benefits of PDSs to teachers.

Teacher development can encompass numerous elements such as technical competence, moral purpose, political adeptness, and personal development (Hargreaves, 1994). Fullan and Hargreaves (1992) contrast the limitations of narrow, innovation-focused attempts at teacher development (e.g., training in a new curriculum or teaching method) with a broader "total teacher and total school" (p. 5) framework for teacher development. This more comprehensive approach includes consideration of the culture of teaching and schooling, the purpose of teaching, the context of each teacher's work, and the teacher as a person (e.g., career stage). Teacher development as a component of PDSs holds promise, in part, because of the comprehensive way these larger issues are naturally integrated into PDS life. Isolationism that is prevalent in the "culture" of teaching is challenged in a PDS as teachers become part of teams working with pre-service teachers. Teachers are engaged in discussions on the *purpose* of teaching with pre-service teachers they are mentoring and with school- and university-based colleagues with whom they collaborate. As teachers work with university students and faculty, they consider education issues, curricula, and methods within the specific *context* of their students, grade level, and circumstances. Even teachers' *personal* needs for different types of participation and professional development can be accommodated as teachers make choices about the degree and type of university engagements in which they participate (e.g., limited work with beginning students, full-time mentoring, collaborative curriculum development/ research).

In further describing conditions of educational change, Fullan (1999) notes that "collaborative cultures are anxiety provoking and anxiety containing" (p. 26). Provoking anxiety is obviously necessary for change since existing ideas must be challenged for innovations to occur. However, it is important that challenges arise within supportive environments so that players can effectively consider courses of action. True PDSs provide both aspects of this equation. Dissonance is in ready supply as school and university faculties debate issues of best practice. Yet, these debates occur within the context of relationships that have been built over time. A school-based teacher may not hesitate to challenge his university-based colleague, because he knows she will put the challenge in context of their established respect for one another's expertise and efforts. Such debates evidence the empowerment of teachers. As stated by Comer (1980), "society does not grant public school careers status equal to university careers" (p. 214).

Consistent with this status differential, many P-12 teachers would be reluctant to challenge university professors.

Ideally, in a PDS, such challenges are a typical occurrence. This is consistent with the description of empowered teachers as having a sense of themselves as "critical consumers ... [who] get ideas, insights, and lines of thought and action from others," but who are confident in applying and adjusting innovations to their own particular situations (Fullan, 1999, p. 28). Other suggested characteristics of empowered teachers include assertiveness in relation to external pressures and demands, a strong sense of efficacy, risk-taking, the ability to create opportunities for collaboration and shared leadership, and the acceptance of responsibility for empowering others (Hargreaves, 1994).

Teacher development and empowerment are strong PDS goals. Although PDSs have been under development in the United States for over 10 years, assessment of the impact of PDSs is in very early stages. Thus far, effects of these partnerships have primarily been reported in terms of improvements to teacher education. Teitel and Abdal-Haqq (2000) note: "Most of the impact documentation focuses on pre-service teachers, with less attention paid to impacts on experienced teachers ..." (p. 2). We propose that PDSs have tremendous impact on teacher development and empowerment. Before focusing on specific descriptions of ways in which PDSs provide such professional development, the evolution of PDSs at the University of South Carolina is described.

University of South Carolina
Professional Development Schools

The University of South Carolina (USC) began to create PDSs in 1990 by inviting local schools to participate in conversations on what a PDS should be. The University worked *with* schools to create a definition of PDS based on the premise, as stated by Senge (1990):

> If people don't have their own vision all they can do is "sign up" for someone else's. The result is compliance, never commitment. On the other hand people with a strong sense of personal direction can join together to create a powerful synergy toward what I/we truly want. (p. 211)

Over time the school- and university-based faculty and administrators agreed that becoming a USC PDS means working toward key assumptions that define a PDS (Professional Development Schools, 2000):

1. Building a community of learning,
2. Appreciating diversity and promoting social competence and justice,
3. Creating flexible and innovative organizational structures that support shared decision making,
4. Demonstrating essential good practice based on professional knowledge including teaching for understanding,
5. Engaging in inquiry and reflection about teaching and learning, and
6. Providing high-quality clinical experiences.

As the USC PDS Network worked to put these ideas into practice, an operational definition of what it means to be a USC PDS was developed, including (Professional Development Schools, 2000):

1. Openness to curricular innovation (e.g., the "new ideas" of pre-service teachers) and a commitment to professional renewal through participation in research, conferences, and coursework;
2. University faculty involvement in the school through on-site courses for pre- and in-service teachers, teaching of pre K-12 students, and participation in curriculum development; and
3. School involvement in pre-service teacher education through significant numbers of clinical placements, teacher/administrator roles in developing teacher education programs, and teacher/administrator roles in teaching and supervising pre-service teachers.

The following sections provide greater detail on the collaborations that have occurred.

Shared Supervision of Pre-Service Teachers

A key to PDSs is for school and university partners to really listen to one another and share in decision-making (Harris & Harris, 1995). As summarized by Robinson and Darling-Hammond (1994), "Open dialogue about issues of practice allows colleagues to recognize each other's strengths and needs so that professional collaboration can occur" (p. 211). In a PDS, the relationship between school- and university-based faculties transforms to a focus on *shared* supervision and equal status. Both on-site teachers and university-based faculty members observe, confer with, and guide pre-service teachers. They reach consensus on the evaluation of pre-service teachers rather than one's evaluation being more important than the other's.

School-University Action Research

Offering mini-grants for research projects at USC has been a successful way to involve school- and university-based faculties in inquiry and reflection about best practice. These small grants, typically $1,000–2,000, are given to teams consisting of a teacher, an education faculty member, and an arts and sciences faculty member who agree to investigate an area of teaching and learning of particular interest to them. The funds are often spent for curriculum materials, but have also provided release time for teachers to participate in curriculum development or provided research equipment and supplies.

On-Site University Courses for Pre- and In-Service Teachers

On-site courses of two types have been an important means of increasing opportunities for collaboration and professional development. On-site courses for in-service teachers have provided a means for school and university faculties to engage in in-depth study and conversations related to both best practice for P-12 teaching and best practice in pre-service teacher education. Courses develop a shared language that avoids the mis-communication, or even alienation, that can occur when an exclusive language is used by a school or university culture. Courses offered have included advanced study of specific areas of curriculum (e.g., science, mathematics, literacy), supervision of student teaching, and teacher as leader. These courses save time and expense for teachers by being offered on-site and provide an opportunity for the instructor to be familiar with the teachers' work environment.

On-site courses for pre-service teachers provide a wealth of opportunities beyond a typical university campus-based course. Teachers and children from the school are readily available to participate in the on-site class for demonstration lessons or guest lectures. The school and the university easily share curriculum materials with one another when the university course is taught at a school. In-service teachers also have the opportunity to sit in on class sessions or attend pre-service students' presentations.

On-site courses for both pre- and in-service teachers put the university faculty member in the school on a regular basis. If the faculty member combines an on-site course with supervision of pre-service teachers at the school, he/she spends a significant amount of time each week on-site. The more time a university liaison spends at a school, the more opportunity is provided for contacts that lead to further collaborative efforts between the school and university.

Collaboration Through Organizational Structure and Committees

A USC PDS governance structure was created to provide a vehicle for school-university information sharing and decision-making. The governance structure centers on a Coordinating Council with subcommittees on pre-service teacher education, curriculum inquiry, technology, and conferences (Professional Development Schools, 2000). The Network's school-university committee meetings are held primarily in schools at times convenient to and suggested by teachers and administrators. The pre-service committee has been a particularly effective vehicle for collaborative decisions related to course content and clinical experiences. Beyond the formal PDS governance structure, school-based educators serve regularly on university admissions and search committees and task forces for specific projects (e.g., the revision of clinical evaluation forms). University-based educators serve on individual schools' PDS site councils and additional committees as requested.

PDS Effects on Teacher Development and Empowerment

Formal studies of the USC PDS Network (Carnes, 2000; Carnes & Boutte, 1998; Carnes & Chen, 1998–99; Van Scoy & Lippincott, 1997) verify the significance of PDS as reported through focus groups. Focus groups met in role-alike sessions in which P-12 teachers, administrators, university faculty, and pre-service teachers assessed various aspects of PDS. Van Scoy and Lippincott (1997) investigated one elementary PDS in-depth. Teachers and university students were interviewed in groups of five to eight members. Administrators and university-based faculty were interviewed separately for logistical reasons. All participants were asked a series of open-ended questions concerning number, type, and quality of school-university interactions in which they had engaged; benefits to and contributions from themselves and others; and a general evaluation of the school-university relationship. Categories of participant responses were developed from the data. The researchers found that all groups described professional development of teachers as an important benefit of PDS activities. Groups also consistently described teachers as "very near the center of all [PDS] activities. Teachers are more involved with more different players than anyone else [children, pre-service students, administrators, support personnel, university faculty]." Further data from the study is presented in the following sections.

The Carnes studies (Carnes, 2000; Carnes & Boutte, 1998; Carnes & Chen, 1998–99) included participant group discussions focused on effectiveness in implementing the nine principles of National Education Association's Teacher Education Initiative's (NEA-TEI). P-12 teachers came from four elementary PDSs, included a total of 19–22 teachers (depending on the year), and responded to research questions in focus group sizes of 5–8. Data are also reported from similar role-alike focus groups involving 5 PDS principals, 7 university teacher education faculty, and 11 pre-service teachers. Focus group leaders were trained in the research protocol and included PDS teachers, the lead researcher, and a graduate assistant. Data collection included responses to open-ended questions related to the NEA-TEI principles and participant ratings and rankings of the effectiveness of the implementation of the principles. In summary, the 2 highest rated and ranked principles were "partnerships with all stakeholders involved" and "professional preparation/development for pre- and in-service teachers." Each had a mean rating of 2.7 on a 3-point scale and was selected as one of the most effectively implemented principles by approximately 50% of all respondents. Expanded roles for university- and school-based educators each received a mean rating of approximately 2.6 with teachers rating university-based educators higher than themselves (2.7 vs. 2.55) and university faculty rating teachers higher than themselves (2.67 vs. 2.33). Narrative data is reported in the following sections.

Our observations and experience in PDS over the last 10 years are consistent with the findings from these studies that PDS positively impacts the professional development and leadership roles of teachers. We will describe the impact of PDS involvement on teachers in detail in both teaching practices and leadership roles and conclude with a section on continuing challenges. Evidence from the aforementioned studies and our further experiences are integrated throughout these sections.

Empowerment and Change in Teaching Practices

The USC PDS Network emphasizes that teachers must begin as mentor and coaching teachers with a willingness to learn from and with their pre-service students. As has been reported in many partner schools, practicing and emerging teachers learn from one another — modeling goes both ways (Barnhart et al., 1995). Teachers report that serving as a model for pre-service teachers makes them carefully consider the practices they are demonstrating. As stated by one teacher, "The constant presence of student teachers helps to keep one on his/her 'teacher toes' ... As we strive to maintain a cutting edge school, we have learned to evaluate our efforts and make changes ..." (Van Scoy & Lippincott, 1997). Another teacher noted, "In working with a student teacher, I had to think about my goals, my expectations, my organizational skills — in order to set a good example — and found that it improved my performance" (Van Scoy & Lippincott, 1997). These comments are consistent with teachers reflecting on the purposes of what they do. At the same time, pre-service teachers in PDSs find teachers are open to their ideas. This intern's comment is typical: "Teachers seem to respect our ideas — like they think we know what we're talking about" (Van Scoy & Lippincott, 1997). Teachers regularly reported that it is an advantage to hear fresh perspectives and learn from current educational ideas implemented by student teachers (Carnes & Chen, 1998–99; Van Scoy & Lippincott, 1997). One teacher expressed it this way:

> You know, you've been in this profession for years and years; you get in a rut. You start to view children in a certain way. [So], it's nice to have a fresh perspective as far as what children are able to do. These interns really have no expectations of what children can or can't do. So they come in and they have these, what looks like to us, unreasonable expectations, like the writing in the journals or the compliment box. We think, "They'll never be able to do that." Well, for me, I just have been kind of surprised. It's helped us get past our assumptions. (Carnes & Chen, 1998–99, p. 41)

Pre-service teachers sharing of innovations in teaching has evolved from informal sharing to more standardized procedures. For example, pre-service teachers now share the results of their curriculum inquiry projects with teachers in formal presentations at each PDS.

Another important element in curricular change has been the participation of university faculty in the day-to-day life of the school. As university faculty have had a greater presence in the school and become engaged in teaching lessons and working with children, they have an opportunity to be part of discussions about teaching strategies, classroom management, and other school issues. Here, again, the learning goes both ways as the school- and university-based teachers learn from one another. One university faculty member noted:

> I have learned from many people at Hood Street — the teachers, the principal, the children.... From the teachers I learn of the many ways teaching is different — and the same — as when I was a teacher.... I have seen many excellent strategies for teaching children and college students.... [Being at the school] is a wonderful opportunity for me to learn from children — I can try out some teaching techniques that I learned of after I left the classroom and see if I really think they work! (Van Scoy & Lippincott, 1997)

Mini-grants for action research projects, described in the first half of this chapter, have also been influential in impacting practice. The USC PDS Network has sponsored over 60 joint research projects that encompass a broad variety of disciplines in the last 9 years. Teachers have the opportunity to work with arts and sciences faculty as well as education faculty during these projects. All research teams present at local conferences and many present their work at state and national conferences as well. Studies have been published in a variety of journals. Presentation and publication experiences add to the professional development and empowerment of teachers. They see themselves as part of the broader educational community with an active role in generating and sharing the knowledge base of teaching and learning.

In one school, a series of mini-grants related to teaching mathematics grew from an interest of one teacher into changes in the teaching of mathematics throughout the school. The grants began when the university liaison asked for a teacher volunteer to collaborate in an investigation of teaching in any curricular area of his/her choice. The volunteer chose mathematics and said he especially wanted to get away from being controlling and directing children about what and how to do everything. The university liaison shared some current research in mathematics and supplied a variety of board and dice games for the classroom. A graduate assistant constructed some materials and also introduced games to small groups of children. The university liaison and the classroom teacher each taught lessons with the new materials that were observed by pre-service teachers, and they spent time discussing which strategies they thought were working well and why. Over time, other teachers in the school became interested in learning more about the mathematics activities. Ten of 14 teachers agreed to participate in a second grant centered on teachers meeting after school every other week to share how and why they teach mathematics as they do. Grant funds were used to purchase professional books and more mathematics materials. The teacher who originated the idea of studying mathematics described the impact of the grants this way:

> In one of our discussion groups at the end of the year, I overheard one of my peers say, "We can't stop now. Let's start a math club." As it worked out, we have been able to receive a small grant each year to support our inquiry into how math is taught best. Math games, the focus of the first grant, are now in every classroom. (Van Scoy, Chaplin, & George, 1997, p. 18)

As this teacher's confidence grew, and with encouragement from his university liaison, he went on to present his new understanding of teaching and learning in mathematics at local, state, and national conferences. The teacher's work in the grant also connected him to a mathematics professor who integrated the teacher's work in his course and invited the teacher to be a presenter in the university course each semester. The teacher and mathematics professor continue to share ideas that improve the instruction of both partners.

In another mini-grant, a faculty member from education and another from journalism worked with a fourth grade teacher to explore how to stimulate fourth grade students as writers. The journalism professor shared his career as a newspaper reporter, feature writer, and professor of journalism with the children. Each educator taught mini-lessons on authorship while the other two watched, and all worked with students in editing and peer conference groups. Grant money provided release time for the teacher to meet with the university faculty members for planning and reflection:

> We gave ourselves the gift of a day's retreat to the elegant downtown library to talk through what we had learned. Each of us brought a draft to share, and this talk led to new insights. Our conversation ranged widely, and led us to questions such as "Is writing an art or a craft and what do we mean by this?" (Busching, Gacek, & Wiggins, 1998)

The elementary professor noted, "The journalism professor and I both thought that the experience influenced our teaching of writing at the university because it caused us to think more deeply about what writing means and how to teach it. Seeing the teacher's commitment and standard of excellence in teaching made me more committed to improving MY teaching" (B. Busching, personal communication, September 1998).

To support more PDS teachers in continuing study of best practice, a unique tuition reduction system was designed for PDS teachers. In the old system, only one specific *cooperating teacher* could receive a tuition reduction from the university. In order to recognize the responsibility of *all* teachers in a PDS for nurturing pre-service teachers at their school, the university agreed to a system in which tuition reductions were committed to a *pool* in each school from which PDS participants could share tuition reductions more broadly. This system, combined with offering on-site courses at PDSs, has encouraged many PDS teachers to participate in courses and pursue advanced degrees. As described above, courses offered specifically for PDS teachers relate to current educational practices such as curriculum inquiry and teaching for understanding. The university's Educational Specialist Degree focuses on teachers as researchers in their own classrooms and is an increasingly popular degree for PDS teachers. The attainment of higher degrees empowers teachers to assume additional leadership roles.

Transforming practice in schools is a complex process. Our schools have varied in the degree of change that has occurred based on their individual circumstances. One certain conclusion is that curriculum change takes years and moves in small steps. However, PDS experiences engage school- and university-based faculties in significant work together, that at least some evidence shows, moves conversation, and ultimately practice, forward.

Leadership and Expanded Roles

The opportunities for teachers to assume a variety of leadership roles may be one of the most obvious impacts of PDS work. Leadership opportunities range from a teacher's initial steps beyond the classroom to influential roles in many educational arenas. For teachers who have had little experience in teaching future teachers, simply having pre-service students observe in their classrooms is a new leadership role. For many, the next step is becoming a coaching teacher. USC provides a course for coaching teachers to explore methods and issues related to mentoring pre-service teachers. The course emphasizes opportunities for teachers to share perspectives and consider the broader issues related to school-university collaboration.

As described above, teachers and university faculty work in much more collaborative ways in supervision than occurred in the past. In fact, PDS terminology at USC has changed to reflect this more collaborative approach. The former *cooperating teacher* (a passive term) has become the *coaching teacher* (a much more active term reflecting the primary role the teacher assumes in guiding the pre-service teacher). The *university supervisor* (a term which denotes superiority and a narrow role) is now the *university liaison* (a term communicating more equal status and the broader responsibilities of the university person in facilitating the school-university partnership).

A new role that has developed with the establishment of PDSs is that of *clinical adjunct*. A clinical adjunct is a school-based teacher who serves as *chief worrier* and facilitator for pre-service teachers in the school, works closely with the university liaison, and participates in formal observations and evaluations of pre-service teachers. Clinical adjunct's duties are similar to those of partner school facilitator described by Harris and Harris (1995), but are loosely defined so that each PDS and its university partner faculty can develop the role in a way that works best for them. Clinical adjuncts are listed as faculty in USC catalogs.

Teachers use the opportunity of being a clinical adjunct to lead changes at their schools and thus impact the professional development of others. One clinical adjunct worked with her university liaison to establish weekly *breakfast meetings* to facilitate communication. At 8 a.m. on the first and third Tuesdays of the month, all pre-service teachers meet for 45 minutes with the clinical adjunct and university liaison. Meetings, accompanied by plenty of coffee, juice and doughnuts, focus on the exchange of information, and provide opportunities to share "memorable classroom moments," and to learn from one another's successes and mistakes. On the second and fourth Tuesdays, coaching teachers meet with the clinical adjunct and university liaison. The conversations in this group focus on issues and concerns related to teacher preparation. The teachers are very supportive of the frustrations experienced by one another when, for example, teacher-student communication does not flow smoothly. Experienced coaching teachers offer advice and insights to those just learning the role. Various solutions and successes are discussed. While breakfast meetings began in just one school, their success was shared among teachers at pre-service committee meetings and soon spread to other schools.

Breakfast meetings are just one example of many innovations designed by clinical adjuncts that support the professional development of both pre- and in-service teachers. Others include service projects in which pre-service teachers construct curriculum materials for teachers throughout the school and weekly seminars with pre- and in-service teachers across discipline and specialty areas.

Another significant role for teachers that has developed through PDS is that of *practicum instructor*. This role was created as teachers on the pre-service committee reviewed syllabi and plans proposed for a new education minor. Teachers suggested that school-based educators, rather than university faculty or graduate assistants, lead practicum seminars for one of the proposed courses. Their input led to a new role for teachers:

> (O)ne unique feature of EDUC 402-P is the role played by the Practicum Instructors (PIs) who work with EDUC 402-P students and their teaching colleagues. They are responsible for 402-P's day-to-day operation. They assume the primary responsibility for students' experiences in their buildings, keeping records of students' attendance and participation, coordinating classroom placements, evaluating weekly directed observations, interacting with individual classroom mentor teachers, conducting weekly seminars based on directed observations, and exercising their professional autonomy within the framework of the collaboratively-developed assignments and evaluation rubrics. (Freeman et al., 2000, p. 81)

Once again, a teacher in a leadership role, Practicum Instructor, positively impacts other teachers' professional development by involving them as mentors for pre-service teachers. Practicum Instructors have written about the positive impact of 402-P on their schools: "Everyone learns in this amazing relationship. Our school is a better place because of this collaboration." Another writes: "One of our goals at Summit Parkway is to encourage our faculty to seek leadership positions as a means of professional growth. Our participation as a PDS and our involvement in EDUC 402-P, in particular, contribute to these goals" (Freeman et al., 2000, pp. 84, 90).

PDS teachers' expanded roles include many functions that were once only the domain of university faculty. PDS teachers participate in pre-service courses by providing demonstration lessons and serving as guest lecturers. As noted earlier, these opportunities are more readily available as more pre-service courses are taught in the schools. Teachers also serve on important decision-making committees throughout the pre-service program:

1. Admissions committees, assessing potential pre-service teachers in interview sessions that are a major component of acceptance into teacher education;
2. Consensus teams, assessing pre-service students progress throughout their internship year; and
3. Oral examination committees, being part of the assessment team in pre-service teachers' culminating presentations which are part of degree requirements.

Some P-12 teachers have progressed into advanced university roles by becoming course instructors or school-based supervisors. School-based supervisors assume primary responsibility for the supervision of interns in the school including formal observations and conferences, evaluation of projects, and final grades. This was formerly a role filled only by university-based personnel.

Teachers' involvement in PDSs also takes them beyond their own schools. Teachers' participation in the USC PDS governance structure provides opportunities for them to meet, teach, and learn from teachers in similar roles at other schools. Some teachers have moved beyond the USC Network to serve as national consultants to schools and universities that are developing PDSs in other parts of the state and country. These teachers return to their own schools and university partnership to infuse new ideas learned through their consultations. They are not only leaders in their schools, but also leaders in the greater school-university partnership.

PDS Challenges Related to Teacher Development and Empowerment

The issues of professional development for teachers in a PDS are intricately involved with the overall success of a school as a PDS. A number of challenges in sustaining PDSs, and the opportunities they provide for teachers, have been cited in the literature and are reflected in our own experiences. These include limited resources (time and money), turnover in personnel (losing administrative and teacher leaders at both schools and universities), and limited recognition or rewards for PDS efforts.

Teachers and administrators who have experience as school-based teacher educators can maintain many of the benefits of PDS that accrue to pre-service teachers, but full benefits for their own professional development require continuing, active participation by their university-based colleagues. This makes reward structures of universities particularly problematic since they are often focused on a narrow definition of scholarship that does not encompass PDS work. Concern for the reward structure of the university has been reflected in a number of comments at our site, such as a school administrator's view that "... we have not seen a change in the reward system. We have not seen the change in the mission and the purpose of the University" (Carnes & Chen, 1998–99, p. 38). Another administrator noted: "The other thing that has impacted on the level of involvement of the College is that the reward structure has been one of the weakest [components]" (Carnes & Chen, 1998–99, p. 46).

We must find ways to support on-site work at schools as a regular, and appropriately rewarded, component of university faculty positions, in order for PDSs to withstand the test of time. This includes promoting involvement of university faculty, not only within education, but in the arts and sciences as well. As stated by one teacher, "Our involvement [in PDS] is directly proportional to USC's commitment. My concern, and that of my colleagues, is that with budget cuts, change in educational focus, and loss of USC support personnel all our efforts will be for naught" (Van Scoy & Lippincott, 1997).

In recent years, the university has indeed been struggling with budget cuts and some key education positions have remained unfilled for long periods of time. This situation has caused an ebb and flow of direct university involvement in some schools rather than the constant presence that is required for continuing renewal. However, the strength of PDS is reflected in how well the system has been maintained despite such obstacles. As stated by a principal, "I think it's a success story that the Partnership has survived no [permanent] dean for a long time. I think the fact that we've managed to continue means that it's pretty viable that this group could continue to function and do things and prepare teachers in spite of wavering support ..." (Carnes & Chen, 1998–99, p. 44). While we can survive periods of drought, general progress and significant professional development of all parties require continued investment in *in-depth* school-university collaboration.

Conclusions

Despite all of the professional development opportunities that PDS provides within and beyond the classroom, the primary focus of all teachers is their P-12 students. As quoted from the educator at the beginning of this chapter, therein may lie the greatest value of PDS — allowing teachers to remain with their primary passion, teaching children, yet providing a mechanism for continuing professional growth and development. The partnerships created through the USC PDS Network have stimulated simultaneous renewal for the schools and the university. Because individual teachers in the schools within the Network helped to define what is meant by PDS, the teachers have always felt personal ownership of the concept. All of the constituents are perceived to be equally valuable and important to the philosophy and mission of the PDS. The resulting educational community, where collaboration such as inquiry is part of the daily activity, has empowered teachers to join in the discussion of teaching and learning with their university colleagues and to be leaders in decision-making regarding what is best for their children and schools. For these teachers, teaching is no longer the transferring of information and organizing of activities as directed by another. Teaching has become professional practice.

References

Barnhart, M. L., Cole, D. J., Hansell, S. T., Mathies, B. K., Smith, W. E., & Black, S. (1995). Strengthening teacher education. In R. T. Osguthorpe, R. C. Harris, M. F. Harris, & S. Black (Eds.), *Partner schools: Centers for educational renewal* (pp. 45–71). San Francisco: Jossey-Bass.

Busching, B., Gacek, T., & Wiggins, E. (1998, September). *Moving from active writing to purposeful authorship: Curriculum and inquiry in a fourth grade classroom.* Poster presentation at the Teacher Inquiry Conference, University of South Carolina.

Carnes, G. (2000). Implementation of NEA-TEI principles: A report from the USC PDS Network. In A. Donnelly (Ed.), *PDS partnerships: The promise of quality education proceedings* (pp. 39–58). Columbia, SC: University of South Carolina.

Carnes, G. N., & Boutte, G. S. (1998). Teachers leading the way. *Teaching and Change, 6*(1), 79–89.

Carnes, G. N., & Chen, L. (1998–99). *National Education Association–Teacher Education Initiative (NEA-TEI): The University of South Carolina 1998–99 Progress Report.* Columbia, SC: College of Education, University of South Carolina.

Chaplin, P. (1993). My Maine adventure. *PDS Proceedings*, pp. 4–5.

Comer, J. P. (1980). *School power: Implications of an intervention project.* New York: Free Press.

Freeman, N., Barnes, J., Carlton, S., Hawkins, D., Jameson, S., Markham, F., Outlaw, C., Siceloff, S., & Timberlake, C. (2000). A new kind of practicum:

Collaboration links the lecture hall with classrooms. In A. Donnelly (Ed.), *PDS partnerships: The promise of quality education proceedings* (pp. 80–93). Columbia, SC: University of South Carolina.

Fullan, M. (1999). *Change forces: The sequel.* London; Philadelphia: Falmer Press.

Fullan, M., & Hargreaves, A. (1992). *Teacher development and educational change.* London; New York: Falmer Press.

Hargreaves, A. (1994, April). *Development and desire: A Postmodern perspective.* Paper presented at the Annual Meeting of the American Educational Research Association, New Orleans, LA.

Harris, R. C., & Harris, M. F. (1995). Launching and sustaining a partner school. In R. T. Osguthorpe, R. C. Harris, M. F. Harris, & S. Black (Eds.), *Partner schools: Centers for educational renewal* (pp. 127–165). San Francisco: Jossey-Bass.

Holmes Group. (1990). *Tomorrow's schools: Principles for the design of professional development schools.* East Lansing, MI: The Holmes Group.

Levine, M. (1997). Introduction. In M. Levine & R. Trachtman (Eds.), *Making professional development schools work: Politics, practice, and policy* (pp. 1–11). New York: Teachers College Press.

Professional Development Schools — University of South Carolina. (2000). Retrieved December 13, 2001, from College of Education, University of South Carolina Web site: http://www.ed.sc.edu/pds/index.htm

Robinson, S. P., & Darling-Hammond, L. (1994). Change for collaboration and collaboration for change: Transforming teaching through school-university partnerships. In L. Darling-Hammond (Ed.), *Professional development schools: Schools for a developing profession* (pp. 203–219). New York: Teachers College Press.

Senge, P. (1990). *The fifth discipline: The art and practice of the learning organization.* New York: Doubleday.

Teitel, L., & Abdal-Haqq, I. (2000). *Assessing the impacts of professional development schools.* Washington, DC: American Association of Colleges for Teacher Education.

Van Scoy, I. J., Chaplin, P., & George, C. (1997). *The Hood Street story: A professional development school journey.* Unpublished manuscript, University of South Carolina.

Van Scoy, I., & Lippincott, S. (1997, April). *Perspectives of school- and university-based participants in a professional development school on university-school collaboration.* Paper presented at the Annual Conference of the Association of Childhood Education International, Portland, OR.

7

Promoting Equity in Education: Community Service Partnerships and Teacher Development

Jude Butcher, Peter Howard, Elizabeth Labone & Nicole Breeze

Abstract

Schools are committed to enhancing the learning of all students. The diversity of student backgrounds and the increasing number of students from low socio-economic areas require teachers to have an understanding of students' worlds and to be committed to social justice in the school's structures and curriculum as well as in the life of the wider community. It is important that school communities give priority to citizenship values and practices, are advocates for marginalized groups, and work with them in addressing the inequities they are experiencing. School teachers who listen to the voices of the community, particularly those of marginalized groups, are challenged to ensure that they and their schools become engaged citizens committed to justice and equity.

This chapter reports on a partnership between the Australian Catholic University and nationally based community agencies in the development of a community outreach program that includes the integration of social analysis theory with the practical applications of a social justice community placement. The chapter also reports on student outcomes from the community service program and shows how they vary from a richer and more personal understanding and appreciation of the world of the disadvantaged to a preparedness to address the sources of disadvantage.

Rationale

Society at local, national, and international levels is concerned with issues of poverty, unemployment, lack of or inequitable access to education, health and welfare services, and maintaining a sustainable environment. Many youth experience a deep hopelessness about their own lives and the future generally. Equity is a central issue as is seen with information and communication technology which is acknowledged as being effective in bridging worlds and being integral infrastructure for business, education, and people's lifestyles. Equity needs to be an explicit criterion in the development and use of these technologies if social issues are to be addressed, not aggravated (Loller & Butcher, 2000).

Two examples of social issues are poverty and discrimination. A total of 12.6% of children in Australia are living in poverty and 11% of Australians live in a household in poverty (Pax Christi Australia, 2001, p. 1). While many in society proclaim the importance of tolerance and multiculturalism, they emphasize the social, cultural, sexual, political, physical, religious, and other differences among people rather than the dignity of all people (Mackay, 1999). These two issues can be addressed at two different levels, the first being the social issue, and the second being the structures and policies which contribute to the social issue (Chomsky, 1991).

Mbilinyi (1977) claims that if educational reform is to be effective, it needs to not only address basic education goals but also critique social and structural issues which affect the lives and learning of people. Freire (1968/ 1972) also emphasized this social analysis role of education in his vision of education as a tool of liberation. Within this socio-educational framework, educators need to examine their curriculum, pedagogy, and evaluation procedures (Bernstein, 1996) to ensure that their students engage with social issues, such as poverty and unemployment, and the structural issues which contribute to them.

Teachers and schools committed to equity and empowerment and working within a liberation framework are potential agents for change in this world. Individually and institutionally they become engaged citizens who are actively involved in the issues of local and global communities and are committed to the transformation of self and society. Families and children at the margins in society will benefit from schools which provide curricula and pedagogies that empower them in their learning, work with them in addressing causes of injustice and marginalization, and offer an educational and socially transforming agenda concerned with the good of all in the community and school (Turnbull & Muir, 2001). This educational agenda is universal and relevant to people of different traditions and religions who are conscious of the global interconnectedness of people's lives (Borts, 1996).

Teachers and teacher educators need to be prepared so that they have the knowledge, skills, attitudes, and commitment to address the cultural diversity and inequities of their school and the wider community (Ball, 2000; Causey, Thomas, & Armento, 2000; Norberg, 2000). Teacher education institutions cannot succeed in this task in isolation but need to work closely and in partnership with their communities and community agencies to achieve this educational agenda (Butcher, Howard, Dockett, & Perry, 1999).

This chapter describes community service partnerships at one university, examines the nature of the partnerships, and reports upon the outcomes of the partnerships and program for all stakeholders. The community service learning program featured in this chapter was designed to provide students with opportunities to see themselves as engaged citizens who can develop an understanding of what is happening in communities through working with, listening to, and seeing through the eyes of others. The qualitative methodology presented in the chapter was designed by the research team to develop a valid category system for the identification of student learning outcomes. An initial report of outcomes or benefits from a partnership perspective for the community agencies and the university is also presented.

Evolution of Community Outreach

From the early 1980s till 1994, the School of Education, Australian Catholic University, was involved in the development of contextual studies for teacher education students. Such studies, though focused upon student community-based experiences, were incorporated as a separate strand within teacher education courses. In 1995 the Community Experiential Learning Program (CELP) was developed and offered to secondary teacher education students. The purpose of this program was for students to nominate a place of work within the community that they wished to be involved and to generate personalized learning from their experiences. In 1997–1998 this program was extended to include primary as well as secondary teacher education students.

In 1999 the Community Outreach Program evolved with social justice as its frame of reference. This was done with the belief that educators have a responsibility to empower their pupils so that inequalities and unjust social structures might be challenged. Classrooms are complex. Pupils face great academic and social challenges, often lacking experience and resources to deal with peer pressure and other harmful influences. Teachers must be prepared for this and go beyond curriculum knowledge and skills outcomes to educate for social action and empowerment (Oxley, Howard, & Johnston, 1999).

The involvement of students and staff in the community is an expression of the University's commitment to be actively involved with the wider community. The development of the Community Outreach Program is a continual process of identifying and establishing credible links between the University, particularly the School of Education, and the community. At the core of such links are effective community-university partnerships.

Forming the Partnerships

The School of Education through the Community Outreach Program continues to extend the number of social justice and community agencies with which it has informal or formal partnerships. The development of the partnership moves from initial establishment phase through a maintenance phase to a continuation phase (see Table 1). The organization of the partnership for particular students can be initiated by the University, community agencies, or the students themselves. While the University has formal links with over 100 agencies, students are able to propose other agencies for their community outreach experience.

A Community Outreach Advisory Committee has been established so that those agencies with which it has a more formal and continuing partnership can provide advice and guidance on the development and extension of the partnerships. This Committee also provides a community/university voice to advise on program development and evaluation. The Committee has also ensured that agency representation is integral to the life of the University including advising on the School of Education's research and development projects.

In the development of the community-university partnerships, explicit attention has been given to the following principles (Butcher, 1998):

1. There is a shared agenda.
2. Attention is focused on core rather than peripheral issues.
3. All levels of the organizations involved are committed to the goals and resource implications of the alliance.
4. An environment of mutual benefits and win/win is created for all participants/organizations.
5. There is an appropriate meeting and appreciation of cultures of all participants/organizations.
6. All aspects of the alliance are operational, actionable, and open to review.
7. New professional relationships and a constructive meeting of differing priorities and approaches are established.

The incorporation of these principles within a community service learning program involved the establishment, maintenance, and continuation partnership phases with the accompanying actions as presented in Table 1.

Social Analysis and Action

Throughout the development of the teacher education community outreach programs at the Australian Catholic University, the emphasis has been on building relationships with communities based on participant learning through service using the tools of social analysis and personal reflection. The Community Outreach Program challenges students to move beyond their comfort zones, exposes them to other peoples' life situations, and allows them to reflect upon this with respect to themselves and their teaching philosophy. The program endeavors to raise students' self-awareness and challenge their beliefs and stereotypes.

The current program consists of:

1. A series of lectures which involve participants from the community agencies and which expose students to the necessity for social engagement;
2. The field component of 80 hours during which the students are personally and actively engaged in challenging contexts;
3. The reflective journal which focuses student attention on their attitudes, skills, and successful experiences within the challenging contexts; and

Table 1   *Relationship of Partnership Phases, Principles and Actions in the Community Outreach Program*

Phase	Principle	Actions
Establishment	• Shared agenda	• Focus on benefits for all participants — community agencies, clients, student teachers, and university staff • Change the learning culture to greater openness to the gifts of the marginalized and critique of the causes of marginalization
	• Core issue	• Development of institutions and individuals as engaged citizens • Institutionalization of social analysis and action
	• Commitment	• At all organizational and field levels to personal, social, and professional development • Strategic planning for effective and collaborative work
Maintenance	• Mutual benefit environment	• Ensuring that experiences are beneficial for community agency, clients, teacher educators, and student teachers
	• Meeting of cultures	• Appreciation of and engaging with culture of community agency, clients, teacher education institution, and students
	• Management of partnership	• Commitment of time and people to maintaining effective communication and strategic planning and continuous formal evaluation of the initiative
Continuation	• Emerging professional relationships	• Greater respect for each other • Development of new forms of professional interaction • Joint ownership of initiative and commitment to review and research

4. The de-briefing session which creates a forum for gaining normative information about coping skills and levels of success as well as a deeper understanding of the situations and structures affecting marginalized people.

Students are provided with opportunities that enable them to develop an understanding of local structures that impact upon peoples' basic human rights. They are able to identify and analyze the functional and organizational elements of community agencies that assist the marginalized within the society. Further, it avails them of the opportunities to question government decisions, structures, and policies that affect the marginalized.

The students use the tools of social analysis to reflect upon their experiences. Through their contextual involvement, the students come to challenge and develop their personal, spiritual, and moral growth (Howard & Oxley, 2000). Throughout the program, students are challenged and confronted by the social justice issues they experience while also benefiting in personal and spiritual ways (Johnston, 2000).

Methodology

Based upon the partnership model of the Community Outreach Program, it was hypothesized that engagement in the program will impact differently on each of the three key participant groups. The hypothesized outcomes for each group were:

1. Community agencies
   - Nurtures an agency-university partnership and raises the profile of social justice and community organizations, and
   - Encourage students to maintain contact with the agency and many continue working on a voluntary basis.
2. School of Education
   - Raises awareness of issues impacting on children and their learning,
   - Has encouraged shaping of the school's learning agenda to become more inclusive,
   - Highlights the school's responsibility for the development of the students as engaged citizens, and
   - Encourages evaluation of priorities and activities with much more attention to its own community service responsibilities.

3. Students
   • Challenges and matures students in regard to issues of social justice, and
   • Promotes personal and professional growth in understanding and engaging with marginalized groups.

While addressing the outcomes of the Community Outreach Program for each of these participant groups, the major focus of the data analysis for this report has been on the personal and professional learning outcomes of students. In determining these learning outcomes, a three-cycle analysis of student data was adopted. The cycles are:

1. Cycle One: shaping and naming personal and professional learning outcomes for students,
2. Cycle Two: refining domains of learning for student outcomes, and
3. Cycle Three: validating the meaning and understanding of identified domains.

A set of 26 primary teacher education Year 1 student learning journals was analyzed to identify the types of learning outcomes expressed by the students. The journals were selected on the basis of their providing a range of agencies visited by the students. An iterative process was used for identifying and naming the outcomes with the students' journal entries being regularly revisited throughout the conceptualization and naming of the learning outcomes.

Cycle One: Shaping and Naming Personal and Professional Learning Outcomes for Students

Preliminary analysis involved scanning of student journals to identify recurring themes. Six major domains were identified and named. These are listed in Table 2. The domain categories were found to be effective in identifying differences in student development and learning which seemed to correlate with the type of placement. In other words, differences were found between the students placed in agencies engaged with disadvantaged groups and those students who were with educational agencies engaged with people with disabilities.

Table 2 *Student Comments and Related Domains*

Student comment	Domain name
• "It is hard to imagine that there are so many people in need of assistance."	• Awareness of the extent of disadvantage within society
• "It has been today that my stereotypical image of a 'bum' has been challenged ... medical problems, lack of education, lack of food ... there are many problems that each individual faces that causes him or her to turn to the streets and fall under this category of poverty."	• Challenges to personal experience and belief systems
• "I have learnt not to fear people with disabilities and keep my distance, but to truly admire and respect them ... I have learnt that these people can teach me a great deal about the human spirit and how to show kindness and love without words."	• Development of coping skills and social efficacy
• "We need social change so that everyone is given the same opportunities in life."	• Growth in understanding of social responsibility and engaged citizenship
• "The unit promoted acceptance, tolerance and sensitivity towards the students," and "Teachers should encourage students and provide support."	• Development of their own teaching identities
• "Teachers are a way to raise awareness of these issues ... by teaching children about those less fortunate and educating them on the effects of factors which lead to these issues."	• Growth in understanding the role of teachers

Cycle Two: Refining Domains of Learning for Student Outcomes

Cycle Two focused on refining domains of learning for student outcomes identified in Cycle One. Journals were classified according to the type of placement, disability, or disadvantage. Disability placements were usually schools for students with physical or mental disability, while disadvantage placements included organizations that provided services for homeless people, those suffering financial hardship, or new migrants. The analysis of the journals showed that student learning fell differently within the domains depending on the placement type.

Cycle Three: Validating the Meaning and Understanding of Identified Domains

To validate the categories determined through Cycles One and Two, the third cycle is to engage with the authors of the journals, namely the students, to ensure that the understandings and meanings are accurate representations of their intentions. This validation would involve three processes:

1. Clarification of understandings of statements,
2. Acceptance of domain names, and
3. Ensuring accuracy in classifications of these statements into accepted domains.

As the cyclical nature of this analysis implies, this process involves revisiting prior cycles and processes rather than simply a stepped process. Processes involved in validation are iterative in nature with continual returning to the data and the categories, and an openness to renaming the constructs to better reflect the reality of the learning outcomes which emerge.

Outcomes

The outcomes of the Community Outreach Program are presented with respect to three stakeholders in the partnership, namely the students, the community agencies, and the Australian Catholic University through the School of Education.

Student Learning

Student learning outcomes from the community service program indicate that field experience challenges and matures students in regard to issues of social justice. Based upon the first cycle of the analysis presented above, the students' reflections in their learning journals indicated a richer and more personal understanding of marginalized groups within our society, as well as the development of a strong sense of social responsibility and a recognition of the important role of teachers in being advocates for the disadvantaged and promoting equity in education. As indicated previously, these student learning outcomes were classified into six major categories:

1. Awareness of the extent of disadvantage within society,
2. Challenges to personal experience and belief systems,
3. Development of coping skills and in social efficacy,
4. Growth in understanding of social responsibility and engaged citizenship,
5. Development of their own teaching identities, and
6. Growth in understanding the role of teachers.

Each of these learning outcomes is discussed and supported below through analysis of the students' learning journals

Awareness of the Extent of Disadvantage Within Society

Initial reactions of the students at the beginning of their placement indicate a great deal of surprise at the extent of disadvantage within their community. While some students recognized their ignorance of this section of their community ("I am beginning to see a completely different side of Sydney"), others were simply stunned by the numbers of disadvantaged in society ("It is hard to imagine that there are so many people in need of assistance"). Such reflections clearly indicate that the students' perception of their community has been challenged and their awareness of the extent of disadvantage has developed greatly.

Challenges to Personal Experience and Belief Systems

While students' perceptions of the extent of disadvantage in our society developed, their journal reflections also indicated that their perceptions of membership of these disadvantaged groups were challenged. There was surprise that these people could be the people sitting next to you on the morning train as one student commented, "It was a shock to see some of the customers [for the soup kitchen] on the train this morning … this would be the last thing you ever think of when looking at these people."

Other students recognized that they held incorrect stereotypical images of the disadvantaged: "It has been today that my stereotypical image of a 'bum' has been challenged … medical problems, lack of education, lack of food … there are many problems that each individual faces that causes him or her to turn to the streets and fall under this category of poverty." Some others still showed surprise that disadvantaged groups included children ("I saw a grandmother and her grandchild come in today which I think it's sad as young children shouldn't be exposed to this") and young families ("A couple brought their 17-month-old baby today, and I felt bad that they had to stoop this low to feed their family").

Development of Coping Skills and Social Efficacy

Student responses during the early days of their placement show recognition of deficiencies in their coping skills. When confronted with the challenges presented by their placement, the students initially felt unsure of their efficacy to cope with these unfamiliar situations. Some comments indicated simply fear or nervousness ("I felt unsafe," "I was scared and nervous"), while other recognized deficits in their skills ("I felt limited in my ability to help in the classroom, I was unsure of myself").

Such comments, however, soon dissipated and were replaced by comments indicating enjoyment of their interactions during their placement: "I have learnt not to fear people with disabilities and keep my distance, but to truly admire and respect them ... I have learnt that these people can teach me a great deal about the human spirit and how to show kindness and love without words," and pride in being accepted: "Sarah ... would not leave my side let alone my hand. The other teachers told me that this was a great privilege from Sarah. It excited me that a student was accepting of my company."

Finally students recognized their development of skills in coping with situations encountered during their placement. These skills included self-regulation of emotional responses ("I have learned to remain calm when there are problems"), the development of assertiveness ("Another important lesson I learnt was that you need to be assertive if need be"), and the development of compassion ("I discovered a more patient and compassionate temperament for dealing with behavior problems"). The comments suggest that the students have internalized and generalized these skills resulting in enhanced levels of social efficacy.

Growth in Understanding of Social Responsibility and Engaged Citizenship

Recognition of the social responsibility for improving the quality of life of marginalized groups and the need for social change was also evident in the students' reflections: "We need social change so that everyone is given the same opportunities in life." Students recognized that there must be shared responsibility to improve the lives of the disadvantaged: "Society needs to be made aware of what is going on … government and big business should be donating more time and resources to needy causes."

Students' analyses of their experiences shows the development of a sense of engaged citizenship both in relation to their future careers as teachers ("My placement work has encouraged me to look at the avenue of special education and the rewarding nature of such a career") and to society generally ("I have made many new friendships that I will keep in contact with and will definitely volunteer again").

Development of Their Own Teaching Identities

While the students' reflections report a great sense of personal growth, their placement experiences have impacted on the development of their own teaching identities. Some reported changes in personal teaching philosophies that showed growth in their sense of social justice in education ("The first day of this placement quickly dispelled any preconceived notions I have of intellectually disabled people and challenged me in regard to my teaching philosophy to focus on the promotion of tolerance and awareness among my students"), others reported greater awareness of their pupils' concerns ("I will be more open and aware of problem that kids in my class face that may hinder their performance at school") and the development of compassion towards their future students ("The unit promoted acceptance, tolerance and sensitivity towards the students," and "Teachers should encourage students and provide support").

Growth in Understanding the Role of Teachers

An enhanced understanding of the broad role of teachers complemented development of the students' teaching identities. These understandings included the role of teachers as advocates for the marginalized and disadvantaged both in a general sense ("Teachers are a way to raise awareness of these issues … by teaching children about those less fortunate and educating them on the effects of factors which lead to these issues") and in their own classroom ("I will be more aware of the circumstances of my students and try to ensure that there is equity in my classroom"). Additionally there was development of an acceptance of responsibility for the inclusion of students with disabilities: "Teachers can learn new skills that will make them more capable and prepared to deal with the variety of learning disabilities and impairments found in children," and "I now believe mainstreaming these children [autistic children] is really important."

The benefits of the Community Outreach Program both in terms of engaged citizenship and in the development of teachers are clearly evident in the learning journals of the participating students, and support the importance of addressing issues of social justice and equity in the professional development of teachers.

Benefits to Community Agencies

During 2001, 300 teacher education students completed 80 hours of community service being placed with over 140 agencies. This is a total of 24,000 hours of volunteer work. The program nurtures the developing agency-university partnerships and raises the profile of social justice and community organizations. Students are encouraged to maintain contact with their agency and many continue working on a voluntary basis.

Benefits to the School of Education

The School of Education through the Community Outreach Program has taken more time to listen to the voices of the people in the community; become more aware of issues impacting upon children and their learning; shaped its learning agenda to become more inclusive; sees itself as being responsible for the development of the students as engaged citizens; and evaluates priorities and activities with much more attention to its own community service responsibilities.

A Partnership Perspective

The School of Education and the community agencies have developed and implemented Community Outreach Program as a genuine expression of their partnership and their commitment that the program is of mutual benefit to all participants. The data presented in this chapter has focused upon the student teachers, the agencies, and the School of Education. The agencies and the University include benefits to the "clients" as a core principle in the program. Indirect data from students and agency staff have indicated the general benefit of the program to the "clients." A formal study of these benefits has been identified as a focus in subsequent research into the Community Outreach Program and partnerships.

A core focus for the partnerships was the development of organizations and individuals as engaged citizens. Students and the teacher educators have begun to acknowledge their power as teachers and use it in social action and advocacy for the good of all citizens especially the marginalized. This shows the benefits of engaged citizenship as a goal of education in which "all intellectual work and research ... must be motivated and informed by a zeal to befriend the poor in their religiosity and culture, and in some way participate in their struggle for full humanity" (Pieris, 1999, p. 68). The vision for this University is embedded in the justice and integrity of "graduates who are sensitized to the values and principles of justice who must be highly responsible citizens in a world that happens to be increasingly challenged ethically" (Sheehan, 1998, p. 5).

The structure of the Community Outreach Program was found to be effective in achieving the goal of engaged citizenship for the teacher education students. The analysis of the students' learning journals showed their ability to articulate their experiences at the agencies, the challenges they experienced, and the learning derived from their participation in the program. The provision of a structured framework for self-reflection and research (Bengtsson, 1995; Cole, 1997; Zeichner, 1997) where students are asked to think about their learning expectations, describe their experiences, and reflect upon their learning has assisted them not only in the keeping of journals, but also in enhancing their awareness of their own learning. It is hoped that the students' experiences in this Community Outreach Program will lead to more attention being given to empowering school students to take more responsibility for setting and evaluating their own learning outcomes within a transformative agenda.

The maintenance and continuation of the partnerships has been fostered through agencies' active participation in the Community Outreach Advisory Committee. The extent of time devoted by the student teachers to their involvement with the agencies and their "clients" has been appreciated by the agencies as a genuine indication of a commitment to the marginalized by the students and the School of Education.

Conclusion

This chapter has shown how a vision of individual and organizational engaged citizenship can be achieved through genuine partnerships with communities and community agencies rather than through the university acting in isolation. Teacher educators and student teachers need to grow in their realization of what the marginalized can offer education, not only upon what educators can offer the marginalized. The role of community service in teacher education is one which is aware of the genuine partnerships and mutual learning that can exist between the marginalized and people in authority such as teachers, rather than a role in which the university profiles what its members give to communities. The partnerships between the community agencies, the University and its students are central to the development and implementation of community outreach programs and their accompanying research agendas.

References

Ball, A. F. (2000). Preparing teachers for diversity: Lessons learned from the U.S. and South Africa. *Teaching and Teacher Education, 16*(4), 491–509.

Bengtsson, J. (1995). What is reflection? On reflection in the teaching profession and teacher education. *Teachers and Teaching: Theory and Practice, 1*(1), 23–32.

Bernstein, B. (1996). *Pedagogy, symbolic control and identity: Theory, research, critique.* London: Taylor and Francis.

Borts, B. (1996). Repairing the world — A task for Jews. In J. A. Romain (Ed.), *Renewing the vision: Rabbis speak out on modern Jewish issues* (pp. 192–202). London: SCM Press.

Butcher, J. (1998, November–December). *Making a difference through effective educational alliances.* Paper presented at the annual conference of the Australian Association for Research in Education, Adelaide, Australia.

Butcher, J., Howard, P., Dockett, S., & Perry, B. (1999, July). *Alliances: A key to advancing educational agendas.* Paper presented at the ninth biennial conference of the International Study Association on Teachers and Teaching, Dublin, Ireland.

Causey, V. E., Thomas, C. D., & Armento, B. J. (2000). Cultural diversity is basically a foreign term to me: The challenges of diversity for preservice teacher education. *Teaching and Teacher Education, 16*(1), 33–45.

Chomsky, N. (1991). *Deterring democracy.* London; New York: Verso.

Cole, A. (1997). Impediments to reflective practice: Toward a new agenda for research on teaching. *Teachers and Teaching: Theory and Practice, 3*(1), 7–27.

Freire, P. (1972). *Pedagogy of the oppressed* (M. B. Ramos, Trans.). London: Penguin.

Howard, P., & Oxley, K. (2000, February). *Active citizenship: University-community partnerships.* Paper presented at the Change in Education Research Group Symposium, University of Technology, Sydney, Australia.

Johnston, K. (2000, August). *The relevance of Catholic higher education for the community: A university perspective.* Paper presented at the International Federation of Catholic Universities Satellite Meeting, Sydney, Australia.

Loller, M., & Butcher, J. (2000). Confronting global and local social justice issues: A challenge for educators. *Just Issues, 3*(1), 1–7.

Mackay, H. (1999). *Turning point: Australians choosing their future.* Sydney: Pan Macmillan.

Mbilinyi, M. (1977). Basic education: Tool of liberation or exploitation? *Prospects: Quarterly Review of Education, 7*(4), 489–503.

Norberg, K. (2000). Intercultural education and teacher education in Sweden. *Teaching and Teacher Education, 16*(4), 511–519.

Oxley, K., Howard, P., & Johnston, B. (1999). *Social Justice: Learning implications for teacher education. Tertiary Teaching: Doing it differently — doing it better.* Darwin, NT: Northern Territory University.

Pax Christi Australia. (2001). Poverty isn't a crime … Ignoring it is. *Disarming Times, 26*(2), 1.

Pieris, A. (1999). *God's reign for God's poor: A return to the Jesus formula* (2nd ed.). Kelaniya, Sri Lanka: Tulana Research Centre.

Sheehan, P. (1998). *Some challenges for Australian Catholic University.* Queensland, Australia: Federation of Parents and Friends Associations.

Turnbull, J., & Muir, E. J. (2001). The practice of citizenship: Embracing diversity in learning and teaching with implications for in-service training and professional development. *Journal of In-Service Education, 27*(3), 429–446.

Zeichner, K. M. (1997). Action research and issues of equity and social justice in preservice teacher education. *International Journal of PEPE, 1*(1), 36–52.

8

Alternative, Magnet and Charter Schools: Models for Creating Effective Partnerships

William Parrett & Scott Willison

Abstract

A remarkably effective approach to school restructuring in the United States has been the creation of alternative, magnet and charter public schools. These schools provide proven models of partnership-driven schooling which hold great value to all schools in the country. Starting in the mid to late 1960s, a number of schools and communalities in various parts of the country began to design new approaches to education, make them available by choice to parents and students, and implement small alternative public schools within their school districts. The first such schools tended to be dropout centers, dropout prevention schools, open schools or schools without walls. While only a dozen or so alternative schools were in operation during the mid to late 1960s, by the mid-1980s their numbers had grown to over 15,000, and today there are over 20,000 of these schools serving 15% of all public school students in the United States (Hardy, 2000).

The success and growth of the alternative/magnet schools concept can be seen in the number of school districts throughout the country that now use this concept to provide choice to students and families and to address the needs of many students including at-risk youth. Most have long waiting lists of parents and students who would like to participate. The success of alternative public schools coupled with the large numbers of parents and students unable to participate, due to the current supply/demand scenario, has fueled the growing national interest in providing all parents with educational options.

The most recent extension of the alternative/magnet school concept is the recent proliferation of charter schools. These schools represent a significant shift in public policy, permitting school districts or states to transfer responsibility for public education to groups of teachers and parents. Charter school legislation (now in 30 states) provides a process that allows for most state and local regulations that govern public education to be relaxed or waived in exchange for accountability standards that focus on student achievement. Many of the 2000 charter schools which have opened since 1992 are former alternative or magnet schools, and they rely heavily on home/community partnerships in their operation.

The charter school concept has emerged from the decades of alternative and magnet school development and the more recent public demand for increased choice in public education. Each of these public options — alternative, magnet and charter schools — are currently providing thousands of American children and their families with an important choice in their public education. Perhaps most significant is the nature and value of partnership each of these approaches relies upon to create optimal relations between the school, home, and community.

A remarkably effective approach to school restructuring in the United States has been the creation of alternative, magnet and charter public schools. These schools provide proven models of partnership-driven schooling which hold great value to all schools in the country. Starting in the mid to late 1960s, a number of schools and communities in various parts of the country began to design new approaches to education, make them available by choice to parents and students, and implement small alternative public schools within their school districts. The first such schools tended to be dropout centers, dropout prevention schools, open schools or schools without walls. While only a dozen or so alternative schools were in operation during the mid to late 1960s, by the mid-1980s their numbers had grown to over 15,000, and today there are over 20,000 of these schools serving 15% of all public school students in the United States (Hardy, 2000).

For a concept that has had such a significant impact on public education in the United States, the concept of alternative schooling and public schools of choice is actually quite simple. Programs and schools are created with distinctive educational offerings designed to meet the needs and interests of groups of students, parents, and teachers through voluntary choice. Through the recent development of charter schools, the concept of school choice has provided the opportunity for an individual school to exchange state and district regulations and requirements for contractually specified student performance outcomes (Barr & Parrett, in press).

The development and growth of alternative schools reflect a significant shift in the organization of public schools in the United States. These schools of choice, including magnet and charter schools, now serve 11–13% of the students attending public schools in the United States (Hardy, 2000). The total number of actual schools has grown to over 15,000 alternative schools, 3,200 magnet schools, and 2,000 charter schools (Barr & Parrett, 2001, in press; Hadderman, 1999).

Since the first alternative public schools were created in the late 1960s, the organizing principles and characteristics of schools of choice have remained constant. The essential components of these public schools of choice include:

1. Voluntary participation — Students, parents, and teachers choose to voluntarily participate in a school or program.
2. Small size — Schools of choice personalize learning by creating small learning communities. Average enrollments for schools of choice continue to be in the range of 200–250 students per school/program.
3. Caring teachers with high expectations — Based on a teachers' voluntarily participation in a school of choice, they become highly invested and committed to the success of all parts of the program. These teachers also tend to be very dedicated which translates into a powerful motivation to both care for students, and hold high expectations for their achievement.
4. Customized curriculum/Personalized instruction — Schools of choice offer students, parents, and teachers opportunities to participate in a highly focused curriculum which is geared toward student needs. Students enrolled in these schools participate in a curriculum designed to motivate student learning and provide relevant experiences that relate to individual needs, interests, and career aspirations.
5. Safe learning environment — Alternative, magnet and charter schools report a remarkable lack of violence, vandalism, and disruptive behavior. Students and their families report feeling both physically and emotionally safe to participate and learn.

These five components are consistently found in alternative, magnet and charter schools. They both drive school practice and serve as the foundational block upon which the programs are built (Barr & Parrett, 1997, 2001, in press; Raywid, 1983, 1994; Wehlage, Rutter, Smith, Lesko, & Fernandez, 1989).

Alternative Schooling in the United States

By the year 2002, alternative schooling opportunities had grown to include thousands of schools of choice available throughout the nation. Three particular models represent the vast majority of public alternatives. They are:

1. Alternative schools — Over 15,000 established alternative schools serve multiple levels and kinds of students. These schools range from programs for at-risk, expelled, and violent students to schools for the gifted and talented. Many alternative or optional schools serve heterogeneous student populations with typical public school achievement profiles (Barr & Parrett, in press).
2. Career-theme or technical magnet schools — Magnet schools have emerged over the past 30 years to provide focused programs which emphasize career themes. Students complete district academic curriculum requirements through a focus on and application of a career theme, academic discipline, or area of emphasis. Students further participate in internship and service experiences related to the theme (Barr & Parrett, in press).
3. Charter schools — The most recent extension of the alternative/ magnet school concept is the recent proliferation of charter schools. These schools represent a significant shift in education policy, which now permits the transfer of responsibility for schooling to teachers and parents. Charter school legislation (now in 38 states) provides a process that allows for most state and local education regulations to be waived in exchange for student achievement accountability standards. A significant number of the 2,000 plus charter schools which have opened since 1992 are former alternative or magnet schools. These "new" charter schools continue to highly value home/community partnerships in their daily operation.

The charter school concept emerged from the decades of alternative and magnet school development and the recent demand for increased choice in public education. Each of these options — alternative, magnet and charter schools — currently provide thousands of children and their families with their first choice in public education. Partnerships are central to each of these approaches in their effort to create optimal relations between the school, home, and community.

These schools are represented by thousands of working models which serve as benchmarks for success. Replication and modeling continue to be the most common approaches employed by districts and individuals in the creation/expansion of alternative schools.

Alternative and Magnet School Models

It is virtually impossible to distinguish between an alternative and a magnet school as the terms are often used interchangeably: alternative referring to different and magnet referring to a program or school that "attracts or draws" its students by providing something unique or different. Each school typically serves heterogeneous populations of students. Yet, within these schools exist a wide variety of approaches to implementing curriculum, instruction, school governance and management (Barr & Parrett, 1997, in press). Alternative and magnet schools typically employ one of the following models as their primary focus:

1. Specific curricular and instructional approaches — These schools include: Montessori Schools, based on the theories of Italian Physician/Educator, Maria Montessori; Open Schools, outgrowths of the British Infant School design; Waldorf Schools, inspired by German educator, Rudolph Steiner; Multiple Intelligence Schools, founded on the theories of Harvard psychologist, Howard Gardner; Paideia Schools, established by the philosopher, Mortimer Adler; free schools and self-directed education based on the concepts of British educator, A. S. Neill; as well as a variety of continuous progress schools, schools without walls, and traditional "back-to basics" schools.

2. The needs and interests of students — The vast majority of these schools were developed to address the specific needs of children. These alternatives include: Teen Parent schools, Dropout and Dropout Prevention schools, schools for expelled or incarcerated students, technical schools, bridge or transition programs, and schools for gifted and talented students.

3. Career-themes and professional relevance — Career-theme schools compliment academic studies with intensive experience in workplace/career settings. These schools, which operate primarily at the secondary level include: Performing Arts schools, Radio and Television Broadcasting schools, Health Professional schools, Law/Legal schools, Science/Technology schools, and dozens of other career-focused educational options as well as academic, disciplinary-focused programs in International Studies, Multi-Cultural issues, Environmental Studies, and many of the other traditional academic disciplines.

4. Experiential learning — Based on the philosophies of John Dewey, many schools in the United States emphasize learning by doing. Examples of these programs include Schools Without Walls, where students learn in banks, businesses, courtrooms, museums and government agencies rather than in typical school classrooms; Foxfire schools and programs, where students learn by collecting and publishing the folklore of their region; and Outward Bound/Expeditionary Learning, where students learn through academic expeditions and experiences in their communities.

A number of established models for organizing, administering, governing and funding alternative schools exist. These include district-wide choice programs delivered through clusters of alternative and magnet schools, like those found in Louisville, Kentucky, Houston, Texas, Los Angeles, California and Vancouver, Washington. These districts and others like them serve as many as 30% of the total student enrollment.

While alternative schools are greater in total number, magnet schools are on the increase due in part to recent research which has focused on student achievement. It is within this domain that some differences do exist. Alternative schools tend to enroll disparate academic groupings of students. Magnet schools, in some cases, require performance auditions or demonstrations of achievement which might result in an absence of "low performing" or at-risk students. Several recent studies have found that students in magnet high schools outperform their peers in conventional public schools and private, parochial counterparts (Flaxman, Guerrero, & Gretchen, 1999; Gamoran, 1996). No two alternative or magnet schools are exactly alike as a primal characteristic of these programs is their unique identity.

While all of these schools share the previously identified common characteristics, actual operations may vary considerably. Nonetheless, the basic organizational principles of these schools are very difficult if not impossible to separate, and in reality, closely unite the two models.

International Alternative Schools

As alternative schools were created in the 1960s in the United States, a similar development was occurring around the world. *The Handbook of Alternative Education* (Mintz, 1996) identified alternative schools in 23 nations including the Americas, Europe, Middle East, Russia, Asia, Australia, Micronesia and the West Indies. Canada, with 114 programs reported throughout its provinces, held the largest number as most other nations reported 5 or fewer programs. Most of the programs identified, represented the categories of independent, Montessori, Waldorf, open/choice programs and/or schools for at-risk students. While the handbook represents the most recent source for documenting the existence of international alternative schools, many schools undoubtedly were not identified. Denmark, for example, operates hundreds of Tvind Alternative public schools, and other nations such as Hong Kong, Brazil, Japan, and Australia have multiple examples of alternative schools. Charter schools have also begun to appear in other nations, such as Canada.

An example of one such alternative school is the Kinokuni Kodomo No Mura, which became the first alternative school in Japan to gain public school status and financial support over a decade ago. The school, whose name translates to Kinokuni Children's Village, joins alternative schools around the globe in basing their philosophy and operations on the writings of A. S. Neill and John Dewey. Democracy in learning and a project-centered curriculum drive the K-12 instructional focus which embraces a blend of out-of-school learning and the acquisition of basic skills (Potter & Potter, 1998).

As most countries provide public education through national systems of organization and governance, it is important to note that local control, as is practiced in the United States, clearly appears to foster dramatically higher numbers and types of alternative and magnet schools. Yet, as of 2002, interest in and the growth of these schools in other nations are clearly on the increase. The public demand for choice in schooling appears to be significantly impacting educational systems throughout the world (Barr & Parrett, in press).

Charter Schools

To create charter schools, state legislatures first must pass enabling legislation. These new laws permit school districts or other authorized agencies to assume responsibility for operating public schools. Charter school legislation allows for most state and local regulations that govern public education to be waived in exchange for documentation of student achievement.

For decades, school districts have contracted with private firms to provide such services as transportation and food. Charter school legislation has moved the contract concept a dramatic step further. As of 2002, 38 states now grant teachers, business people, nonprofit organizations, parents, public agency personnel, and a host of others the opportunity to create a partnership to design, seek approval, and operate their own public school. According to the specific legislation in each state, these charters can be authorized by local school districts, state boards of education, a college or university, or other authorizing agencies (Barr & Parrett, in press).

Characteristics of Charter Schools

Not all charter school legislation is created equal. In fact, there is considerable variation in the 38 states that have enacted charter laws. Critics argue that only 50% of the states provide for "true" charter schools that clearly offer the flexibility and support necessary to operate schools, while the other states have "diluted" the concept. Some states require local school boards to be the sole entity to authorize charters. This practice often stringently dictates the terms of the charter and ensures continuing local control. The result is few charter schools are created. Despite variations in state laws, there are a number of elements that are common among existing schools.

First and foremost, a charter school is a public school. Charters must be nonsectarian, may not charge tuition, and cannot use admission tests or any other device to screen student applications. They must take all who apply as long as there is room in the school and after full, they must maintain waiting lists. However, once a charter school is established, it becomes virtually autonomous; thus it is like a one-school district (Barr & Parrett, in press).

Because they are legal entities, charters provide for comprehensive site-based management through the creation of local governing boards.

Teachers usually can choose to join the local bargaining unit (teachers' union), form their own bargaining unit, or decide that, as owners, they no longer need a bargaining unit.

Charter schools are schools of choice and partnership. The element of choice in public education likely accounts for a larger portion of the success of charter schools. In order to continue operation, charter schools must achieve the student performance objectives that are agreed to in the charter and must obviously attract sufficient numbers of parents and students to maintain operation. Most approved charters require students to comply with district testing policy as the determinant of student achievement.

Another common characteristic of charter schools is the waiver of many state and local education regulations. With the exception of health, safety, and fire codes, almost all of the rules and regulations, including union contracts are waived. The amount of regulations waived differs from state to state. For example, many states do not require charter schools to hire certified teachers while others do.

By virtue of being public schools, charter schools receive state and local educational funds. Charter school funding is based like other public schools on a state formula. In many states, these funds flow through local districts who hold back a percentage pay for those services that the district provides to the charter, such as transportation, special student services, purchasing, personnel, payroll, and so forth (Wilt, 1993).

Charter schools typically receive their state funds without the line-item restrictions that are placed on funds for other public schools. This allows the charter school's funds to be used in the most flexible, creative, and beneficial manner. For example, charter schools may choose not to hire multiple administrators and, instead, use these savings to pay for facilities, hire increased numbers of paraprofessionals or to purchase educational technology.

Teaching in a charter school demands that teachers and staff assume multiple roles. They become planners, managers, and coordinators of learning. In addition to the traditional responsibilities of instruction, each professional teacher often supervises and coordinates a number of instructional aides and other paraprofessionals who assist in some aspect of student instruction. Techniques of shared decision-making, coupled with small school size and a staff that chooses to participate, often reduces the need for more than one school administrator. Parents and volunteers also provide considerable help with the tasks of operating the school.

Charter schools also make extensive use of volunteers from business, industry, the arts, and nearby colleges and universities to supplement the curriculum, mentor students, and provide tutorial services (Barr & Parrett, in press).

ANSER Charter School:
A School Designed for Partnerships

ANSER Public Charter School is located in Boise, Idaho, the states' capitol and a city of approximately 165,000 people. Following the almost unanimous passage in 1998 of charter school legislation in Idaho, a group of veteran teachers, a former Boise principal of the year, and members of the community organized ANSER, Boise's first charter school, in 1999. The charter school currently has 138 students enrolled in a K-6 program and at the completion of its second year has a waiting list of 250 students. ANSER's educational philosophy emphasizes educating the whole child in a collaborative environment of partnership where all of the school's community is responsible for teaching and learning.

While the Latin translation of the word ANSER is geese, the school was named ANSER because of the way that geese take turns leading the flock, with the lead goose exerting more energy and effort than others for a period of time and then upon tiring another will assume the leadership role. It is through the development of partnerships that a collaborative educational environment is possible. It requires communication, trust and respect for the gifts and talents that individuals and organizations can contribute. ANSER's philosophy extends into the school's efforts to engage students in learning activities within the greater Boise community and to partner with community businesses, social agencies, and governmental agencies.

ANSER seeks to establish partnerships with parents, members of the community, and with institutions such as the local university, area businesses and social agencies. For ANSER, an effective partnership is evidenced by mutual support of the parties involved, carrying out classroom and school improvement activities, conducting collaborative curriculum and participation together in various decision-making activities. Out of the partnership evolves a curriculum that promotes a shared learning process among all partners. Regardless of who initiates an ANSER partnership, all partnerships have a common goal, directly or indirectly, of improving the education of children. The benefits of an effective partnership are shared and valued by all. It is understood that while there may be specific benefits for each of the partners, the shared goal of enhancing students' learning is the critical criteria for solidifying partnerships.

All ANSER partnerships are developed through well-established communication. To ensure that individuals are comfortable working outside of their normal level of comfort, trust and confidence between each party must be established. Thus, partnerships are well defined and organized with roles, expectations and outcomes agreed upon prior to the formal partnership being established. ANSER partnerships clearly identify from each of the partnering organizations an individual, with the necessary decision-making capacities and resources at hand, responsible for the welfare and nurturing of the partnership. Regardless of the nature of the partnership, ANSER partnerships regularly celebrate their success and reflect upon their effectiveness with the intent of improvment.

ANSER's relationships with parent volunteers, community board members and university educators are all developed within the partnership context. Additionally, ANSER's curriculum is influenced through two partnerships, one with Expeditionary Learning Outward Bound (a school improvement organization) and the other in which community organizations participate in enrichment activities.

Expeditionary Learning Outward Bound (ELOB)

ANSER's organizing philosophy and design are based on the nationally recognized school improvement model, ELOB. This comprehensive school reform model, found in over 100 school districts throughout the United States, is organized around 10 foundational principles (Mednick & Wainwright, 1999). The principles are woven throughout the curriculum, drawing on students' personal experiences and intellectual growth to promote self-discovery and construct knowledge. ANSER recognizes that learning occurs in many contexts and that school partnerships are closely related to bringing the principles into a practical existence.

Principle 1: The Primacy of Self-discovery

ELOB schools demonstrate that learning happens best when there is emotion, challenge, and the requisite support. People discover their abilities, values, grand passions, and responsibilities in situations that offer adventure and the unexpected. In addition, learners need tasks that require, among other things, significant achievement. A primary job of educators is to help students overcome their fear and discover they have more in them than they think.

Principle 2: The Having of Wonderful Ideas

This design principle focuses on the notion that teaching should build on children's curiosity about the world by creating learning situations that provide matter to think about, time to experiment, and time to make sense of what is observed. This principle calls upon learning to take place in a community where students' and adults' ideas are respected.

Principle 3: The Responsibility for Learning

While learning occurs in the context of a social activity, this principle draws attention to the goal of having learners to become responsible for directing their own personal and collective learning.

Principle 4: Intimacy and Caring

Learning is fostered best in groups where there is trust, sustained caring, and mutual respect among all members of the learning community. Thus, there should be consideration given to the size of the learning community and the deliberate connection between adults and children as well as between children themselves.

Principle 5: Success and Failure

To nurture and develop students' self-efficacy and capacity to take risks, it is necessary for them to regularly experience success. Likewise it is necessary for students to experience failure, to overcome negative inclinations, to prevail against diversity, and to learn to turn disabilities into opportunities.

Principle 6: Collaboration and Competition

ELOB school design embraces the development of relationships between learners as well as the development of the group as a whole. Rather than competing against each other, students are encouraged to challenge their own personal best and to strive to reach rigorous standards of excellence.

Principle 7: Diversity and Inclusivity

To ensure the understanding of multiple perspectives, resources and solutions, schools and learning groups should be heterogeneous. Likewise, the curriculum should incorporate multiple perspectives from a variety of sources.

Principle 8: The Natural World

This design principle helps focus students on their relationship with the natural world and the students' responsibility to become stewards of the earth.

Principle 9: Solitude and Reflection

Developing a habit of reflective inquiry is critical to the cognitive, emotional, spiritual, and psychological development of a learner. ELOB schools intentionally provide opportunities of solitude and silence for children and adults to reflect on matters at hand. Additionally, opportunities to share reflections are also built into the curriculum.

Principle 10: Service and Compassion

ELOB philosophy recognizes that all are responsible for the well-being and care of others, as well as the well-being and care of the natural world. The power of consequential service to others — the attitudes and skills to learn from others and be of service to others — is/are fundamental to ELOB schools.

The ELOB partnership enables ANSER's teachers and staff to work with ELOB educators to ensure thoughtful reflection on teaching practices as well as governance structures and to ensure that the organizing principles are considered in curriculum and other decision-making processes. An ELOB school designer observes teachers and provides feedback, models lessons, and participates in problem-solving all in the interest of enhancing student learning. ANSER's interpretation and application of ELOB's school design model has provided ELOB with valuable examples of how the principles can be connected to community-based learning. Additionally ANSER's enrichment curriculum provides ELOB with a community partnership model that can be duplicated by other ELOB schools.

The Enrichment Program

An integral part of ANSER's curriculum is a weekly enrichment program. The school's enrichment coordinator, a half-time (certified teacher) employee, helps community groups and ANSER parents develop enrichment modules, which are offered to all students. Students participate in a module for 6 consecutive Wednesdays. Every 6 weeks students choose from a new list of 12 to 15 module offerings. Enrichment modules are designed to address one of the school's learning principles and incorporate specific cognitive and social skills/concepts into the lesson. For example, during a module students may be asked to write to specific prompts that incorporate the particulars of the module. Throughout the week, classroom teachers use the students' writings as a resource to examine the authors' skills and to engage students in further literary development. In 2001, ANSER's second year of operation, the enrichment portion of the school partnered with over 30 community businesses and agencies. Examples of the types of partnerships developed include: students participating in workshops by members of the community's theatrical group, students studying with biologists from the community's power company and the state's Department of Fish and Game, and a module facilitated by the community's district attorney who helped students study the judicial system by examining the fable of *Goldilocks and the Three Bears*. This module ended with a mock trial in which students assumed roles varying from Goldilocks to the trial judge.

During one 6-week period, each of the enrichment modules offered centered around the school's principle of "service and compassion." This principle stresses the importance of contributing to a community. Students participated in modules that focused on volunteerism and the importance of being responsible for others. Examples include students planning, planting and tending of a community garden; students grooming dogs at the community's animal shelter; students reading to senior citizens living in care centers; students recording the biographies of residents of the veterans' hospital; students working with area bicycle mechanics in a project that repaired discarded bicycles and then donated them to immigrants that had settled into the Boise area; and students working with children in an area *Head Start* program, helping them complete art projects.

ANSER Public Charter also engages parents in a partnership relationship. Besides parents volunteering in the classroom to help with various tasks, parents are engaged in facilitating, chaperoning, and developing enrichment modules. During the 2000–2001 academic year, 49 parents developed and coordinated modules and another 70 assisted in one way or another. Of the parents that contributed to the enrichment curriculum, two-thirds were employed full time or part time outside the school. Parents of ANSER report that they feel valued and that because their role in the school goes beyond that of just doing clerical work or monitoring the playground, and that they are likely to continue to partner with the school.

Partnerships at ANSER go beyond just the enrichment curriculum. Parents and community members serve on advisory councils, community boards which govern the policy of the school, strategic planning and growth committees and other groups designed to contribute to the well-being of the school. The largest university in Idaho has partnered with ANSER to provide doctoral students an opportunity to study the school's organizational structure and policy. Additionally, the university has used ANSER as a lab school in which professors of education engage pre-service teachers in a variety of hands-on learning/teaching experiences including teaching nontraditional physical education curriculum such as rock climbing and camping. To help pre-service teachers better understand the nuances of children's literacy, one professor engages his students in a weekly written journaling exchange with entire classrooms of ANSER students. This literacy partnership provides pre-service teachers an opportunity to observe the developmental growth of a student's writing within the context of authentic writing samples. In return ANSER students are engaged in meaningful correspondence and partnership with an adult. Through this experience, an ANSER student will write to and receive a minimum of 15 letters from their partner.

ANSER's status as a charter school has provided the opportunity to rethink the role of curriculum and to serve as a model for other education institutions interested in developing partnerships beyond those normally associated with schools. In the spring of 2001, ANSER was recognized by the U.S. Department of Education with an award of $150,000 to serve as a demonstration site for other schools interested in raising student achievement through the use of partnerships and other nontraditional ways of educating.

Conclusion

The vital constructs of alternative, magnet, and charter schools are choice and partnership. These schools have clearly become an integral component of public education in the United States and are gaining increasing popularity in many other nations. The success and growth of the alternative/magnet/ charter schools concept can be observed throughout school districts in the country that actively employ this approach to provide choice to students and families. Most schools of choice in these districts have extensive waiting lists of students who would like to participate. The success of alternative, magnet, and charter public schools coupled with the large numbers of parents and students unable to participate, due to the current supply/demand scenario, has fueled the growing national interest in providing substantially more families with educational options.

The driving force which continues to foster this growth and development evolves from grassroot efforts by parents and educators, striving to find better ways to create partnerships with the schools that educate their children. Recognizing the present movement for its substantial educational success, President George Bush, in his 2002 proposed budget for the federal support of education, recommended continued, dramatic support to further develop choice in public education. Budget recommendations include: 21st Century Learning Centers — $846 million; Choice and Innovative State Grants — $472 million; Charter Schools — $375 million; Magnet Schools — $110 million; Comprehensive School Reform — $260 million (Education Department et al., 2001). Federal support of this nature has fueled the growth of choice programs through annual increases since the late 1970s. Education has continued to occupy a top priority on most political agendas as nationally elected officials of the United States, representing their public constituencies, continue to support school reform have identified schools of choice as a valued priority.

The beginning of 2002 signals a patently clear message that alternative, magnet and charter public schools, with 3 decades of development and success, both work, and are highly desired as preferred vehicles of choice and partnership by the citizens of the United States. The experiences and lessons learned by schools are now propelling local, state, and national efforts to look to their success as models to improve public education in the United States. Based on these realities, the continued growth and expansion of alternative, magnet, and charter schools is eminent.

References

Barr, R. D., & Parrett, W. H. (1997). *How to create alternative, magnet and charter schools that work*. Bloomington, IN: National Education Service.

Barr, R. D., & Parrett, W. H. (2001). *Hope fulfilled for at-risk and violent youth: K-12 programs that work* (2nd ed.). Boston: Allyn & Bacon.

Barr, R. D., & Parrett, W. H. (in press). Alternative schooling. *Encyclopedia of education*. New York: McMillian Reference Publishing.

Education Department, House Appropriations Committee, Senate Appropriations Committee. (2001, October 15). Fiscal 2002 education funding. *Education USA*, p. 11.

Flaxman, E., Guerrero, A., & Gretchen, D. (1999). *Career development effects of career magnets versus comprehensive schools* [MDS-803]. Berkeley, CA: National Center for Research in Vocational Education, University of California.

Gamoran, A. (1996). Student achievement in public magnet, public comprehensive, and private city high schools. *Educational Evaluation and Policy Analysis, 18* (1), 1–18.

Hadderman, M. (1999, October). *Trends and issues: School choice.* Retrieved December 10, 2001 from University of Oregon, Clearinghouse on Educational Management Web site: http://eric.uoregon.edu/trends_issues/choice/index.html

Hardy, L. (2000). Public school choice. *American School Board Journal, 187*(2), 22–26.

Mednick, A., & Wainwright, C. (Eds.). (1999). *Expeditionary Learning Outward Bound: A design for comprehensive school reform.* Cambridge, MA: Expeditionary Learning Outward Bound.

Mintz, J. (Ed.). (1996). *The handbook of education.* New York: Macmillan.

Potter, J., & Potter, A. C. (1998). Kinokuni children's village: A child's view (Part 2) — An interview with Akirachan by his father. *SKOLE: The Journal of Alternative Education, 15*(3), 1–7.

Raywid, M. A. (1983). Schools of choice: Their current nature and prospects. *Phi Delta Kappan, 64*(10), 684–688.

Raywid, M. A. (1994). Alternative schools: The state of the art. *Educational Leadership, 52*(1), 26–31.

Wehlage, G., Rutter, R., Smith, G., Lesko, N., & Fernandez, R. (1989). *Reducing the risk: Schools as communities of support.* London: Falmer Press.

Wilt, J. (1993). Charter schools: An entrepreneurial approach to public schools. *Changing Schools, 21*(3), 10–12.

9

A Higher Education Institution-School Collaboration Program for the Enhancement of Teaching

Iasonas Lamprianou & Bill Boyle

Abstract

This chapter uses data collected by the Centre for Formative Assessment Studies (CFAS) of the University of Manchester. These data indicate that since national tests were introduced in England in 1990, schools have evidenced a perceptible move from teaching for learning to test-preparation strategies. This has an obvious potential to narrow the curriculum and reduce the purpose of testing to the testing of coaching.

Concerned at this development, the CFAS took the initiative of establishing a collaboration (intervention) program with schools for the promotion of enriched teaching strategies based on the interpretation of scrutinized national examinations results.

The major aim of the program is to involve the schools in a collaboration program, which will facilitate a change of culture, where appropriate (or at least an evaluation of their existing policy about teaching and testing) and contribute to a movement toward assessment for learning. Supplementary aims are to help schools to enhance their teaching with diagnostic feedback from the National Curriculum tests and to encourage the professional development of the teachers.

The schools involved are already engaged in an on-going dialogue with the CFAS and are being given the opportunity to steer and shape the future program. The collaboration is designed to evolve at a slow pace in small and careful "confidence building steps" and it is a non-commercial initiative with costs borne by the CFAS.

The program is in its second year and comprehensive evaluation procedures have not yet been fully implemented. This has been because of a concern to minimize the workload on schools in these early stages. There are indicators which suggest that the program is successful although it is still in its infancy.

Introduction

Since the introduction of the National Curriculum (NC) in England in 1988 and its associated system of statutory assessment tests, many academics have been pressurizing for more "use" of the annual test results (Gipps, 1994; Murphy, 1996). Educationalists, teachers, policy makers, and parents have regularly emphasized that the NC tests cause too much disturbance and anxiety (Denscombe, 2000), cost too much time and money, and that their results should be more efficiently used to benefit the education of the pupil. Close, Furlong and Swain (1995) investigated and presented headteachers' opinions about the Key Stage 3 NC tests in Science. A number of headteachers reported a very negative attitude toward the tests and one stated that the implementation of the tests was "a criminal waste of educational resources." Another stated: "The tests have been an unnecessary and unwanted interruption to our program of teaching and learning. We do not expect the results to be helpful, diagnostic, constructive, formative or informative."

Since the Task Group on Assessment and Testing (TGAT) report in 1988, there has been a long running debate about the multiple purposes of a national assessment system, that is, support of learning, reporting individual achievement and public accountability agenda. The TGAT recommended that: "The promotion of children's learning lies at the heart of this process. It can provide a framework in which educational objectives may be set and pupils' progress charted and expressed ... By facilitating dialogue between teachers, it can enhance professional skills and help the school as a whole to strengthen learning across the curriculum" (DES, 1988). Ten years later, Black (1998) reconfirmed these recommendations: "Teachers ... need to differentiate their teaching as they collect evidence that some have grasped ideas and want to go ahead, whereas others are trapped in confusions ... teachers need sound information on which to base differentiation decisions. Ideally assessment should provide short term feedback so that obstacles to pupil learning can be identified and tackled" (p. 25).

In 1997 the government White Paper "Excellence in Schools" stated that: "The use within a school of reliable and consistent performance analyses enables teachers to assess progress by their pupils and to change their teaching strategies accordingly" (DfEE, 1997, p. 27).

Nothing is new! Since the TGAT report the education community has extensively discussed or questioned whether there is any formative or diagnostic role for the results generated by national tests (Black, 1998). There has been much discussion of the negative effects of the tests on the teaching and learning of pupils, on teachers and their style of instruction, and on the role of the schools (Black & Wiliam, 1998; Jennings, Price, & Pankhurst, 1999; Kluger & DeNisi, 1996; Shepard, 2000; Whitford & Jones, 2000; Williams & Ryan, 2000). The "one-shot" end-of-the-year nature of the tests has caused much concern since a central, basic characteristic of formative assessment is the provision of information at point of use to enable teacher intervention and remediation strategies within a continuous feedback loop. Related questions were asked such as: how can a summative end-of-the-year test provide educationally meaningful formative feedback? Are the NC tests designed in such a way to provide meaningful and useful cognitive/diagnostic feedback? "The traditional dominance of the summative function means that formative assessment struggles for its status and development. The summative function can inhibit the growth of the formative function because external tests are accepted as the model for teachers' assessments so driving these toward techniques appropriate only for summative use" (Black, 1998, p. 120).

There has been much research on pupils' common errors and misconceptions (Clausen-May, 1998; Clerk & Rutherford, 2000; Cumming, 1998; Kinchin, 1998; Pine, Messer, & St. John, 2001; Sanger & Greenbowe, 2000; Taber, 1995, 2001). Clausen-May (1998) attempted to investigate the reasons that make pupil misconceptions in certain topics of science so difficult to change. Error analysis strategies utilizing samples of the NC scripts would inform teachers about possible misconceptions of their pupils and would be valuable in helping teachers to employ different teaching strategies to avoid similar problems.

Unfortunately, the NC test results have not yet been systematically used on a large scale for in-depth feedback to schools. The Qualifications and Curriculum Authority (QCA)[1] has published detailed annual cohort question analysis reports (numeric and descriptive) disseminated directly to schools (Standards Reports, QCA) for a long time but schools were not very enthusiastic (or confident) about using this feedback for formative purposes since they were not customized for each school or school department.

Williams and Ryan (2000) analyzed the errors from more than 1,200 key stage 1 (KS1) and key stage 3 (KS3) mathematics scripts from the 1997 national tests for 7 and 14 years old to provide "a resource to help raise teachers' awareness of their children's thinking and present openings for diagnostic assessment and teaching" (p. 1). The main findings of the study were reported to all primary and secondary schools although no customized feedback for each individual school was prepared.

Such focused research is only a small element of the vast body of literature, which deals with national assessment problems and issues. Furthermore is this more specific assessment feedback actually what individual schools and classroom-teachers need in order to identify and resolve their specific needs and problems? Or can the existing more general-purpose error-analysis style reports inform and guide the curriculum and the teaching strategies adequately enough?

Individual schools in the United Kingdom have very diverse characteristics, for example, different economic circumstances, ethnic mix, catchment area, geographical location, percentage of qualified and experienced teachers, school size, and so forth. It is highly possible that an individualized feedback strategy, taking into consideration the specific characteristics of each school, may be a step forward that could multiply the positive effects of such feedback. An in-depth question level error analysis of — at least a large random sample — the scripts of each individual school, although costly, will be of significance. Is it however more beneficial for all schools to make their own arrangements for the preparation and the use of item-level error analysis reports? Could external bodies of professionals organize and facilitate such a strategy at local or national levels?

History indicates that partnerships between schools and external bodies (i.e., universities and colleges) for such a purpose are not common practice. Generally, the route for the establishment of partnerships between schools and universities has been tortuous and laborious. It has, quite often, been the case, that schools may even regard their "partner" as an intruder rather than an ally. Kirk (1996) wrote that:

> Schools and their teachers have been known to be highly critical of "irrelevant theory," to criticise university staff as "refugees from the classroom," and

even to have encouraged beginning teachers on taking up their first appointment "to forget all of that stuff you learned up there: you are now in the real world." (p. 5)

Usually, "expert teachers" are perceived to have a more informed view across the range of pupils' errors and misunderstandings. However, it is very difficult to argue that experienced or "charismatic" teachers could help their colleagues to use pupils' test results for the enhancement of their own teaching strategies without any external support. It has long been testified that teachers work in an environment of intensification (Robertson, 1996), isolation (Lortie, 1975) and "busyness" (Sharp & Green, 1975). Therefore, rather than waiting for teachers to accumulate this knowledge year after year, the support of an external body may act as a catalyst in enhancing and enriching personalized teaching strategies by providing in-depth error identification through analysis of the pupils' NC test results.

The Basic Principles of the Collaboration Program

Supported by the accumulated evidence of the positive impact of feedback on performance (Bangert-Drowns, Kulik, Kulik, & Morgan, 1991; Black & Wiliam, 1998; Kluger & DeNisi, 1996), the authors established an on-going collaboration (intervention) program between the CFAS and the national sample of schools involved in the QCA's School Sampling Project (SSP).[2] The aim was to enrich curriculum delivery strategies using analysis of national examinations results.

The authors, however, fully appreciated that under certain circumstances feedback can have negative effects as far as the attitudes of the teachers were concerned. Coe (1999) carried out an experiment involving teachers of "A" level[3] in six volunteer schools. The experiment sought to record the attitudes of the teachers who were provided with student performance feedback. Coe found that the feedback could actually have a negative effect on teacher attitude, that is, teachers could develop a negative attitude toward feedback if they regarded it as too detailed or as incomprehensible.

For the authors this was another indication of the importance of the need to establish an efficient communication system between the schools and their external collaborators. It was decided that one of the basic characteristics of the project would be its flexibility. Schools would be given the power to steer and shape the program according to their own needs in a culture of equality, collaboration and democratic dialogue.

It was also decided that the establishment of the collaboration program between the CFAS and the SSP schools should be patiently planned in small and careful "confidence building steps." The collaboration/intervention program should be given the opportunity to evolve at a pace dictated by the participating schools themselves. It was appreciated that change in the culture of schools would be a slow process and that some schools might feel threatened or targeted if asked to invest resources and effort from the very inception — resources which in many cases do not exist.

Schools would be able to set their own terms and conditions of partnership and participate or withdraw from the program at will. No formal contract or any other kind of bureaucratic arrangements would be established. Participation in the program and the relationship between the CFAS and the schools will remain informal and loose in an effort to overcome defense-mechanisms arising on behalf of the schools. Such defensive reactions have been frequently observed in practice in formal collaboration programs between schools and external bodies and are also documented in the literature.

It was also determined that "altruism" would be a crucial and fundamental principle of the program. The collaboration between the CFAS and the SSP schools would not involve any form of financial relationship and the program would maintain its non-commercial nature at the expense of the CFAS.

The Aims of the Program

The major aim of the program was to engage the schools in a collaboration, which would facilitate an evaluation of existing policy and a change of culture, where appropriate, and contribute to the development of a philosophy of assessment for learning. It is anticipated that because of their involvement, the trend of schools to move from teaching to test-preparation strategies will be questioned and then gradually weaken and more schools will move toward a culture of teaching to promote learning rather than teaching merely for better test results.

Another aim of the collaboration program was to help schools to enhance their teaching with diagnostic feedback from the NC tests and to invest more time on reflecting and improving their teaching strategies.

Finally, the third aim of the program was to encourage the professional development of the teachers. For the teachers, the provision of feedback and error-analysis reports for their pupils at the end of every year may be regarded as a valuable type of formative feedback. Teachers have the opportunity to evaluate and enhance their teaching strategies at the end of every year so that the following years' cohorts will avoid similar errors. Teachers are also expected to become more enthusiastic about studying the feedback from the NC tests and possibly to attempt their own in-depth research about possible causes of mistakes and possible remedies for the future.

Indicators of the Success of the Program

A comprehensive system of indicators has been designed to evaluate the collaboration program. The evaluation of the success of the movement of schools away from test-preparation strategies that do not promote learning to more teaching will be done by means of questionnaires. Questionnaires that assess schools' use of various test-preparation strategies to prepare their pupils for the NC tests are already administered to schools by the CFAS every year as part of a survey funded by the QCA. Moreover, it is expected that any change in attitudes will be identified through regular monitoring interviews with subject teachers and heads of departments.

The evaluation of the aim of helping schools to enhance their teaching with diagnostic feedback from the NC tests and to invest more time on reflecting and improving their teaching strategies will be done by means of interviews with teachers and heads of departments. Avoidance of the repetition by schools of the same errors across years in national tests will be monitored by detailed item-level analysis. According to recent research pupils tend to repeat the same errors year after year possibly because the teachers are too busy to prioritize the digestion of the annual error analysis reports (Jennings et al., 1999).

Another indicator of the success of the intervention program is the development of enthusiasm among teachers for scrutinizing and using formatively (i.e., to implement changes in their teaching strategies) the error analysis reports. Recent literature states that approximately one-sixth (15%) of the teachers in the United Kingdom read and take into account the feedback from the national test results (Jennings et al., 1999) and only just under one-fifth (19%) of the teachers in the United States admit that they have the professional development to deal efficiently with supplied technical data on test items, for example, facility and item discrimination indices (Smith et al., 1997). According to our data, the percentage of schools that use detailed item-level feedback from the previous NC tests to prepare pupils for their exams was rather small and lied between 12–24% for the three subjects, namely English, mathematics and science in 1998. However, these percentages increased to 19–37% in 2001.

Research Results That Support the Need for This Collaboration Program

According to the analysis of the CFAS Head of Department questionnaire data (for a brief summary of the questions included in the questionnaire, see Appendix 2), most schools in 1998 and 1999 used a large variety of test-preparation strategies. These findings are evidenced from the responses to the question from the Head of Department questionnaire (see Table 1).

As shown in Figure 1, the percentage of schools using an "analysis of previous years' performance on a question-to-question basis" is relatively small and ranges from 12% to under one quarter of the sample (24%) in 1998, from 16% to 28% in 1999, and rises from 19% to over one-third (37%) in 2001 (see Appendix 1). At this stage we should mention that this strategy was consistently the penultimate least popular (out of nine strategies

Table 1   *The Question About the Test-Preparation Strategies of the Schools*

How do you prepare for the end of KS3 mathematics tests? Tick as many of the following which apply in your department.

A. Review last year's test papers
B. Teacher originated test to replicate question format
C. Revise question types which appear to reoccur
D. Preparation by ability
E. No additional preparation outside normal teaching
F. Make use of mark schemes and exemplar material from previous years
G. Analysis of previous years' performance on a question-to-question basis to identify strengths and weaknesses in provision
H. Analysis of SCAA/QCA standards booklets
I. Analysis of returned marked scripts

Note: In each case the respondents were given space to write their comments.

Figure 1   *Analysis of Previous Years' Performance on a Question-to-Question Basis*

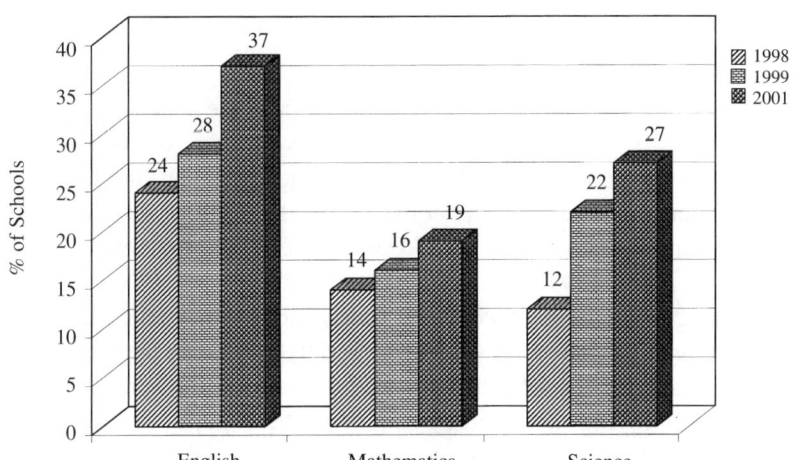

offered) for all three subjects (English, mathematics and science) for 1998, 1999 and 2001.

Apparently, from the percentages above, there was an increase in the number of schools using detailed feedback on a question-to-question basis for all three subjects from 1998 to 2001. However, many of the schools which admitted employing this strategy to prepare their pupils for their KS3 test style accompanied their response by comments which showed that they did not use the strategy to its full potential. We quote some of these comments:

1. "Not done on a question by question basis."
2. "Limited due to time restrictions."
3. "Some — particularly those pointed out in report on test perform-ance."

If we take all those schools with similar qualifying comments into account, the percentage of schools who employed this strategy will reduce even more.

What is the main comment of the schools that did *not* use this strategy? According to the data, there was one main reason for schools not to use analysis of previous years' performance on a question-to-question basis: *lack of time*. Below, we quote some of their more interesting comments:

1. "Lack of time prevents this. It might be nice in an ideal world."
2. "Has anyone seriously got time to do this?"
3. "It would be good to do all of this but this is restricted by lack of time."

The option "analysis of returned marked scripts" is the second preparation strategy that is based on feedback from the analysis of pupils' NC test results. This technique was employed by a relatively small percentage of schools, especially in mathematics. It is very interesting to mention that this strategy was consistently the sixth or seventh most popular (out of nine) for all three subjects (English, mathematics and science) for 1998, 1999 and 2001 (see Appendix 1).

Figure 2 indicates that there was a consistent increase in the percentage of schools analyzing the returned marked scripts to improve the preparation of their pupils for the KS3 test. However, many of the schools which admitted employing this strategy to prepare their pupils for their tests accompanied their response by comments. These reveal that they did not use the strategy to its full potential. For example, we quote some of their comments:

1. "Limited by time" or "Haven't got the time" or "Limited due to time restrictions"

Figure 2   *Analysis of Returned Marked Scripts*

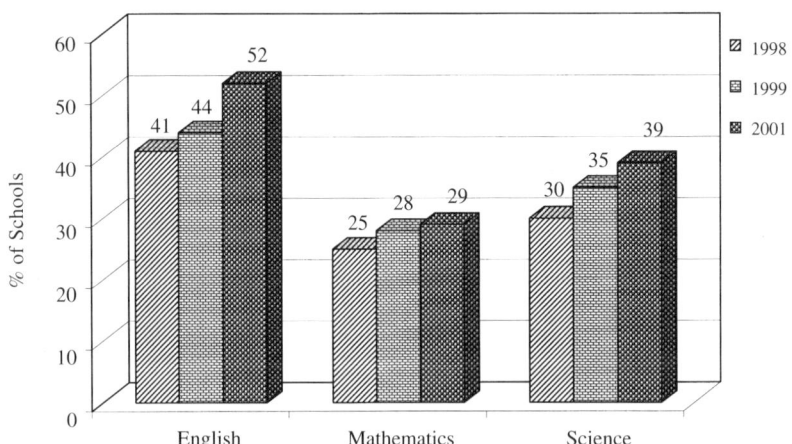

2. "We do this in a few surprising cases" or "Some of this is beginning"

As far as the schools that do not use that technique are concerned, the main reason for not doing so is obvious from their most frequent comment: *not enough time for this.*

From the above, it can be suggested that the schools liked the idea of reviewing and enhancing their teaching techniques using the feedback supplied from detailed error analysis of their pupils' scripts. They benefited most when they had some help and support especially in focusing activities, possibly from an external organization like the CFAS. A detailed error analysis may take the form of comprehensive tables of the types of errors the pupils make on each item. The tables could include the most common errors of the pupils on each sub-domain and various statistical analyses could then be run to establish relationships between the different categories of errors and the most prominent pupil characteristics.

Such detailed feedback and error analysis reports would be extremely valuable to school leaders, assessment coordinators, and teachers. However, the time for gestation of such a detailed form of feedback may not be available for schools. It is indicative that a head of a science department wrote the following comment about all of the test-preparation strategies: "All good ideas but we don't have the time/staffing/structure to implement them yet."

Lack of time is the major problem listed by schools when completing the Head of Department questionnaire on their test-preparation strategies. However, over the period surveyed schools interestingly gradually increased the number of test-preparation strategies they employed. This increase has been very obvious especially in English and science for the period from 1999 to 2001 as shown in Figure 3.

Although schools seem to increase the number of different strategies that they employ, it is interesting to investigate whether they tend to move toward certain strategies and abandon others. The change in the number of schools employing each of the test-preparation strategies from 1999 to 2001 was studied.

Mathematics and science were found to be the two subjects that had the most significant changes. In mathematics, schools gradually abandoned strategies like "preparation by ability," "review last year's test papers" and "analysis of SCAA/QCA standards booklets." On the contrary, schools adopt less time-consuming but more traditional and apparently "successful"

Figure 3   *The Average Number of Test-Preparation Strategies Employed by Schools*

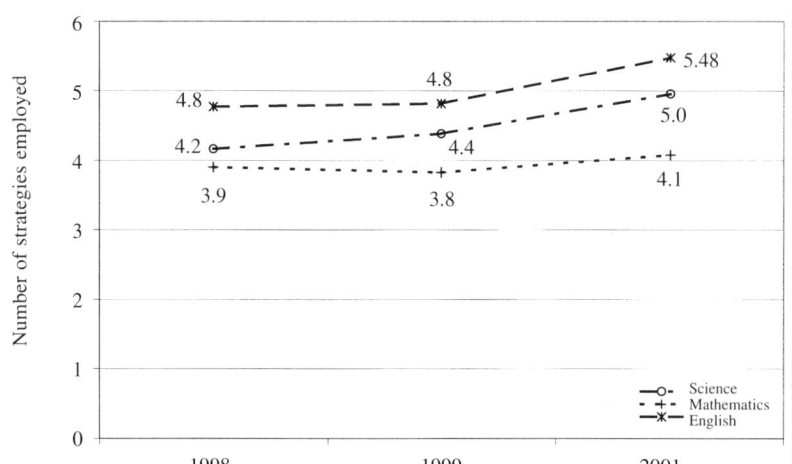

strategies like "revise question types which appear to reoccur." The number of schools employing this strategy has increased by approximately 13% since 1999, a very large increase, compared to the changes in the other test-preparation strategies. A summary of these changes is presented in Figure 4.

The increase in the number of schools employing the "revise question types which appear to reoccur" strategy implied that schools are moving in KS3 testing toward the same traditional methods employed usually in the GCE "A" level examinations in which the teachers tried to predict types of questions and areas of the curriculum that might be examined. However, this strategy, although superficially efficient and successful (as far as the key stage test results are concerned), does not shed light on pupils' individual weakness and cannot help teachers to deal with pupils' misconceptions or to evaluate their teaching strategies.

Unfortunately, the same pattern appeared in science. Schools abandoned the "preparation by ability" strategy and also stopped preparing their own tests to simulate the NC tests. On the contrary, they focused on the "revise question types which appear to reoccur." The increase for this strategy was again 13%. A summary of these changes is presented in Figure 5.

Figure 4 *The Change (%) in the Number of Schools Employing Each Test-Preparation Strategy in Mathematics From 1999 to 2001*

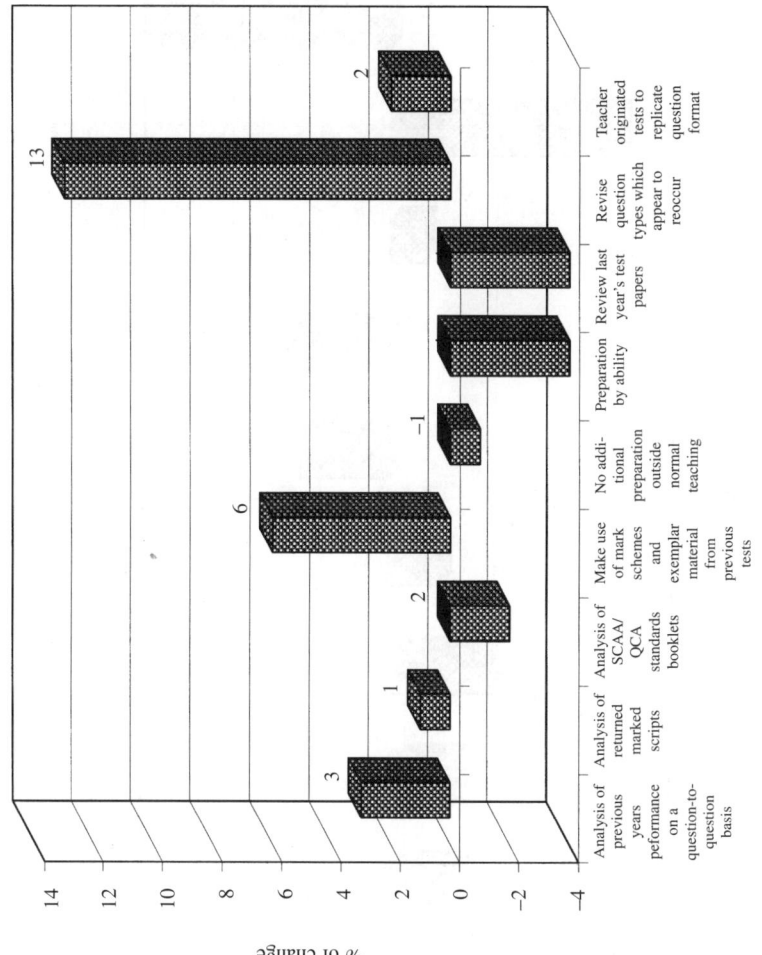

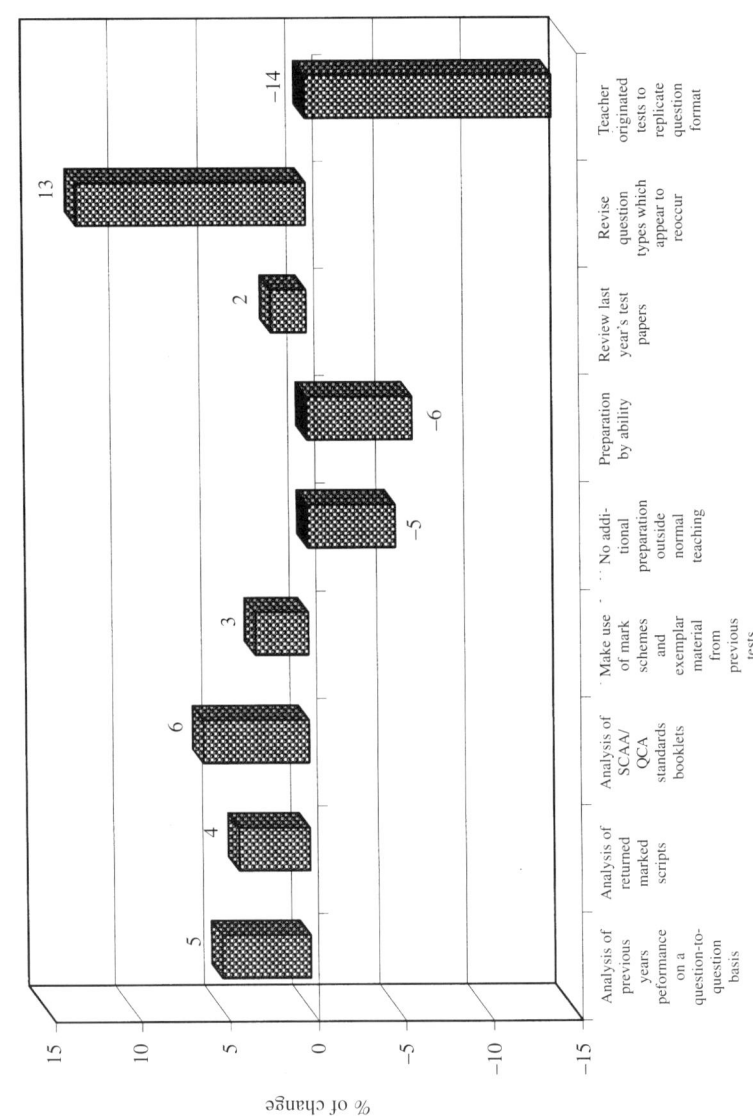

Figure 5 *The Change (%) in the Number of Schools Employing Each Test-Preparation Strategy in Science From 1999 to 2001*

The consistency of the results for mathematics and science might well be regarded as alarming since it may be a sign of the side effect the testing culture is having on the educational system. Fifty percent of the schools employed the "revise question types which appear to reoccur" strategy to prepare their pupils for the mathematics and science tests. However, 80% of the schools used that strategy to prepare their pupils for the English tests in 2001, an increase of 14%, consistent with the increase in the other two subjects. A continuous increase in the percentage of schools which employed this strategy as their only or their main test-preparation strategy might have the effect of narrowing the curriculum and converting an ostensible teaching course to a coaching one in actuality.

For all those reasons, the CFAS decided to develop a collaboration project which would aim for enriched teaching strategies by providing the schools with appropriate, formative and cognitive feedback. The most fundamental issue of this collaboration program was to ensure teachers' willingness to participate of their own volition — not under the pressure of the headteacher (principal) of the school. History has shown that teachers' attitudes toward the national tests have not been very positive (see Gipps, Clarke, & McCallum, 1998). Many teachers feel that the results from the national tests have not been used in an educationally positive way and in some instances have been overtly negative, for example, through "name-and-shame" league tables (Murphy, 1996). Even 10 years after the first national tests took place, teachers can still be disconcerted by experts challenging the validity of the NC testing (Morrison & Wylie, 1999), or addressing "teaching to the test issues" by arguing that even "excellent tests" may not help to improve education just as better speedometers do not make for faster cars (Froomkin, 1998). Therefore, we decided that our first task would be to approach schools carefully, not as "National tests experts," but as a partner who is willing to spend enough time with them during both the pre- and post-test period to collaborate in a process which should "reward" them by the achievement of better test results and in making better use of those test results to inform future teaching.

The Establishment of the Cooperation

The first step was to establish trust and cooperation between the researchers and the schools participating in the longitudinal SSP. In the 1999–2000 academic year, the schools were provided with detailed feedback on their pupils' results. The feedback concerned the overall achievement levels of the sample pupils in the tested cohorts by subject and compared each school and the national results by subject. Item-level information was provided for a school cohort but there was no personalized feedback for individual pupils at this stage.

Questions, proposals and communication with the CFAS were encouraged by a personalized letter accompanying each feedback report. Each school was encouraged to use the feedback and to raise issues about their report. Some schools asked for additional analysis or clarification of the data supplied and the CFAS responded promptly and fully.

For the 2002 assessment cycle, the schools will be offered participation through a more personal, on-going form of support. This will include one or all of the following:

1. The schools will receive much more detailed feedback and they will have the opportunity to invest in one of the CFAS's experienced staff to help them understand and digest the reports.
2. Customized reports for individual pupils will be prepared comparing their achievement on English, mathematics and science;.
3. Each individual school will be enabled to organize its own agenda for the development program, for example, group discussions between teachers and a CFAS assessment specialist.
4. Focused group discussions between statistically neighboring schools[4] in the same geographical area may be set up to facilitate the identification of common problems, to disseminate successful teaching strategies on specific curriculum sub-domains and to promote the collaboration and the exchange of the ideas.
5. Detailed error analysis reports for individual tested domains, customized for each school, will be available to be used to identify ways of evaluating and refining teaching strategies for the avoidance of repetition of the same type of errors in future year's exams. These error analysis exercises will always seek to positivize the exercise and focus on "ways forward" for improved performance.

Evaluation of the Program

Although specific evaluation procedures were designed since the beginning of the programs, a comprehensive evaluative system has not yet been fully implemented. This has been through a concern to minimize the workload on schools in these early stages. There were fears that very frequent correspondence and intense involvement on behalf of the schools would probably discourage a number of them from participating in the program.

Therefore, a single evaluative survey was conducted during the first term of the academic year 2001–2002 in order to collect some indications of the success or the weaknesses of the program. The philosophy underpinning the questionnaire was for it to function as a vehicle by which the schools would be enabled to contribute their ideas to steer the program and shape it according to their own needs and desires. The questionnaire was kept short in order to encourage the schools to participate to the survey. Open-ended questions were deliberately used to give the schools the opportunity to respond as fully as possible. The questionnaire consisted of three open-ended questions (see Table 2), which covered important aspects of the program.

Table 2   *The Evaluative Questions Sent to Schools*

1. The feedback we have supplied compares your school results with the SSP results. How do you plan to make use of the feedback?

2. In terms of content (sub-domains, mean achievement, etc.) and format (tables and graphs) how could the feedback be presented to be more useful to you?

3. If there are any issues (or comments) you would like to raise either about the SSP or the feedback we have supplied about your school please comment below (use the back of this page if necessary).

The first question was intended to enable schools to give information about the ways they used the feedback received — if they used it at all. It was anticipated that this might help the identification and dissemination of good ideas and practice between schools. It was also expected that this question would give the CFAS the opportunity to identify schools which used the feedback in a sub-optimal way so that more support or guidance might be offered. The second question aimed to gather schools' opinions about the content and the format of the feedback and requested ideas for improvement. Finally, the third question intended to give the schools the opportunity to raise any issue they considered important in order to give them the chance to contribute to the steering and the shaping of the program.

The questionnaire was posted to each individual school approximately 1 month after the feedback was sent in order to ensure that schools would have enough time to study and digest the feedback and plan ways forward. Up to that time, not all schools had the opportunity to receive, complete and send the questionnaire back. Although the flow of questionnaires to the CFAS is still going on, a first qualitative analysis was attempted based on 30 fully completed questionnaires. The results presented here may be regarded as provisional leading toward a final report which will be completed and sent to all schools at a later stage.

The analysis of the responses to the open-ended questions resulted in the identification of three major areas: (1) the use of the feedback, (2) attitudes to the programs, and (3) involvement in the development of the program.

The Use of Feedback

According to the responses to the questionnaire, the most important use of the feedback was to define areas where the teaching and learning taking place in the school was rather weak. The schools also used the feedback as a guide to inform and adapt their curriculum planning and teaching. Schools appeared to be particularly involved in identifying areas of the curriculum where the children scored below the "average SSP score." They also found the comparisons of school-SSP results by item as very interesting and useful.

Many schools also concentrated on organized procedures for the involvement of the whole school staff in the interpretation of the feedback. There are indications that schools got seriously involved in the interpretation and use of the feedback. The following passage is an extract from the response of a headteacher:

> I, as Headteacher, have looked through it [the feedback]. I have also given copies to curriculum coordinators. We will share this information with the whole staff at our staff meeting when we look at SATs [the tests] results & papers & how we can do better next year.

Schools also reported enhanced cooperation between KS1 and KS2 teachers. The returned feedback for the KS1 pupils was used to inform the next year's teachers about the weaknesses of children and to guide the target setting. The following passage is an extract from response of a KS1 school:

These data will be used by Y2 [Year 2] teachers to target perceived weaknesses. Y1 [Year 1] teachers will also be involved in the process with their pupils ...

The general message the authors received from the responses was that almost all schools were prepared to make changes to their curriculum, target setting and teaching plans in the view of the feedback they received. The following extracts are from the completed questionnaires of three different schools and may be regarded as typical responses from the sample:

1. The feedback will be analyzed by the coordinator for mathematics and the literacy and numeracy consultants with the Senior Management Team in order to provide additional evidence for target setting and teaching plans. The results are in line with our tracking data and reinforce key areas for future improvement and action.
2. The interesting initial findings that seem to stand out are that in English our writing score is very similar to the whole sample while a reading score is lower. We have been investing a considerable amount of energy in enhancing writing. Perhaps we ought to be thinking about reading instead.
3. We will use the information to inform our teaching, learning and planning. The results clearly show where the weaknesses lie.

The above extracts also give evidence that schools do not only use the feedback they receive but also attempt to use it as a base to generate their own further analysis according to their own needs and perceptions. The following four extracts indicate the tendency of the schools to use the feedback provided by the CFAS as a base or supplement to their own analysis and are typical of the general philosophy of the responses:

1. Useful to feedback to the Governors' Curriculum Committee for discussion with the governors. I particularly note science physical processes and mental maths as being close on the average. This poses questions for all the staff to consider. It will also be discussed at a staff meeting and comparison between KS1 and KS2 will be studied.
2. It will be used as part of our analysis of results. It will be used to focus on specific areas/questions which may indicate a weakness in teaching/learning. It's already been used as part of evidence in my deputy's performance management.
3. We found it very useful [the feedback] as it stands and are now keen

to find out *why* [emphasis is the school's] our girls performed as they did and how we can *improve* [emphasis is the school's] that performance.
4. [We used the feedback] … to support our own analysis of areas of need.

Attitudes Toward the Program

Most of the schools appeared to have a very positive attitude toward the program. This was clear throughout their responses and was explicitly stated verbally. Some schools regarded the feedback as very useful and wrote comments such as: "Helpful feedback at no cost to school. Thank you." Other schools were even more enthusiastic and wrote: "Continued participation in the scheme is a must."

A school was also very enthusiastic about the time that the program saved her. The teacher who completed the questionnaire also foresaw the usefulness of the program if applied in a national scale. She wrote:

> Many people across the country are spending hours and hours doing this sort of thing. As a teaching head and Y6 teacher I do not have the time or energy this year! If it was done nationally by the QCA we could save ourselves such time and be specific in our analysis. An extended simple table like the CFAS English one would be fine. The QCA Standards booklets at KS1 and KS2 are very useful but are rather too late in the academic year. Difficulties need to be pinpointed to inform planning and teaching.

Another school also commented along the same lines: "Useful analysis and time saving for school."

However, the schools not only regarded the program as useful and time saving but also suggested that they found the feedback easy to read and understand. Short comments like the following were very common in the questionnaires:

1. "We like the simple format you use."
2. "The format is very useful, clear to read, good use of graphs."
3. "We found it easy to understand."
4. "I like it as it is simple!"

The enthusiasm of the schools about the program is also evident in the way they asked for more involvement in the program and more feedback.

There are indications that the schools recognized the usefulness of the program and would like its extension. Schools that did not provide data for their whole cohort, sometimes wrote comments like the following:

> We sent scripts for one Y2 [Year 2] class of 30 pupils but it would be useful for us to be able to send the scripts of the whole cohort to make best use of the feedback.

Involvement in the Development of the Program

A common factor for almost all of the responses of the schools was their desire for changes and improvements to the program. This was in parallel with one of the aims of the authors which was to give to the schools the right to be involved in steering and shaping the program.

Some schools suggested that the mark schemes (e.g., examples of the ideal handwriting for a full mark) should accompany the feedback report in order to give to the teachers a more clear idea about the ideal responses to the tests. One school commented that:

> [The average mark for our school in] handwriting seems to be less than SSP mean — I would really like to see styles of handwriting that receive 5 — I've looked at the QCA examples, we have some good handwriters and yet in all the years of KS2 SATs [the tests] we have never had a pupil with 5 points.

Other schools suggested that the feedback should include sections with feedback broken down according to gender. For example, one school proposed that:

> Breakdown according to gender would be useful to determine gender difference and if some results (e.g., writing) were influenced by a large gender imbalance taking the tests.

Another school suggested that for the generation of the report statistical information like the percentage of pupils having English as an additional language (EAL), the percentage of Special Educational Needs (SEN) pupils, and the percentage of impoverished pupils (those who have free school meals) should be taken into account. That way, schools with poor catchment areas or schools with large percentages of SEN pupils would be compared with their statistical neighbors.

One school also proposed that the feedback should be available on-line or by a disk so that the schools will be able to cut and paste sections to create their own reports, possibly by adding results of their own analysis. The following extract was from the KS1 school which proposed the availability of the reports on-line:

> … should prefer to access the feedback either via the Internet or by disk so that we could cut and paste sections of it into reports for Governors and staff. Also it would be helpful to have more specific guidance on what constitutes a significant difference in results.

Some schools were very careful to offer constructive criticism for the format of the feedback. Those schools focused mainly on the type of graphs provided and generally expressed their preference for the pie charts. Some of the comments are the following:

1. "Pie charts are easy to read — otherwise its fine."
2. "I feel the graphs to be useful — not too enthusiastic about the 3D image, a pie chart might be useful."

A common pattern in schools' responses was also the demand to accompany the comparisons for every item with the exact skill or sub-domain tested. That way — the schools argued — the use of the feedback will be much easier. Although overall comparisons between the school–SSP performance for different sub-domains was provided, the schools insisted that the exact sub-domain or skill tested by each individual item should be explicit. Some of the comments were the following:

1. "It would be helpful if each question were given the Attainment Strand so that we did not have to cross-reference the results against the questions."
2. "It would be helpful if the tables gave an indication of the type of question instead of just the question number, e.g., RL2 Q1 Literal retrieval, RL2 Q5 Inference. This would help us to identify trends more easily for both Comprehension and Mathematics."

Moreover, several schools expressed their desire for a summary and possibly some verbal explanations of the statistical results and the tables. Two short comments are presented below:

1. "Short readable summary explanation in addition to analysis."
2. "It seems fine to me, but I might like a few more words."

The Conclusions of the Evaluation

Overall, the schools had very constructive suggestions and more feedback is expected to be accumulated while more completed questionnaires are received. The final report of the short evaluation will be sent to all interested parties (e.g., the schools, the QCA, the staff of the CFAS involved in the program) and all the suggestions will be taken seriously into account for the next year's feedback reports.

Only two schools expressed their concern about the usefulness of the feedback from the CFAS. The first school was one of the schools that did not supply the CFAS with results with the whole cohort of its pupils. The school did not regard the feedback appropriate and commented that "The school results don't reflect the performance of the whole cohort so therefore they are of limited use."

The second school was a special school, that is, all its pupils were pupils with SEN. Therefore, the school did not consider the feedback relevant and commented:

> I am sure the feedback is valuable to non-special schools. I am more likely to find the comparisons with PANDA [Performance and Assessment] data more relevant as I am able to compare our results with like special schools.

The fact that only 2 schools (out of 30) did not regard the feedback to be of any use this year may not however reflect the true "overall" feelings of the schools participating to the project. Although the flow of returned questionnaires to the CFAS continues, it is possible that the final percentage of returned questionnaires will be relatively low, perhaps lower than 30%. This may be explained in a variety of ways.

A number of schools that will finally fail to return a complete questionnaire may do so because of excessive workload. Both the feedback reports and the questionnaire are usually sent during the first months of the academic year where the schools are busy with the fresh start. This was, however, predicted by the authors and the avoidance of extra workload to the schools was one of the reasons that prevented a full-scale evaluation this year.

Another possible cause of the low return rate may indicate lack of interest on behalf of the participating schools. This is appreciated by the CFAS which will attempt to interpret with a more in-depth investigation the reasons that prevented the school to complete and return the questionnaire. The possibility that some schools may not be highly interested in the program should not be regarded as a surprise. It was predicted that several years should be given to the schools in order to change their culture to a culture of assessment for learning.

It is also possible that a number of schools might have been using item-level feedback to inform their teaching strategies for some time now. Those schools would probably feel self-sustained and their interest to the program may be limited although it could save them valuable time and resources.

Finally, it is appreciated that a comprehensive evaluation procedure with a more detailed questionnaire, interviews and other measurable indicators might be more appropriate for the evaluation of the program. However, it was the decision of the authors that the demand on schools' time and resources should be kept at the minimum for the first years of the program.

The results of the short evaluation questionnaire were very encouraging. It could, however, be claimed that "the silent majority" of the schools have not yet been convinced by the usefulness of the program. However, time should be given to the schools to get to know the program and to reflect on its usefulness. As it has been suggested in the beginning, the change of the culture of the schools may well be torturously slow especially when the change involves extra resources and time.

Discussion

Test coaching seems to be an efficient mechanism for the achievement of higher test results and schools seem to be well aware of that. The phenomenon of test coaching, however, is not new and specialized material to prepare students for various exams has been widely published. For example, Diane (1995) authored a paper offering guidance to students who aimed to achieve top test scores on public tests. Diane presented various test-wise advices and strongly encouraged students to employ educated guessing whenever in doubt in multiple-choice tests. The author also provided a whole list of steps that would help students reach a successful and educated guess to test items.

Stricker and Emmerich (1999) evaluated the connection between gender Differential Item Functioning (DIF) and gender differences in familiarity about the content of the items of a test. The researchers sampled 730 college students from 19 psychology courses. Each student was administered an achievement test, the Advanced Placement Psychology Examination test and was asked to rate his/her familiarity with what the item asked. The researchers found that there was a statistically and educationally significant correlation between the familiarity of what the item asked and the achievement. For example, a DIF effect against boys was identified for the items that boys were less familiar than the girls showing that coaching on the possible content or the context of the items might help examinees raise their scores.

Allalouf and Ben-Shakhar (1998) suggested that worries about unfairness and possible effects on the predictive validity of the tests might be unjustified. They claimed that, in general, test coaching may have some beneficial aspects since it involves elements like acquiring familiarity with the test, reviewing material that is relevant to the test content and learning "test-wiseness."

Although several authors' attitude toward test coaching was not negative, other researchers warned about the artificial inflation of test scores because of test coaching (Alliger & Dwight, 2000). However, the English NC tests are too high-stakes for schools to ignore and the trend toward "results-raising" test-preparation strategies (test coaching) will probably continue in the near future. The CFAS acknowledges the fact that many teachers do not at the present use diagnostic feedback to make the test-preparation procedure educationally more meaningful. On this issue, Williams and Ryan (2000) say that

> ... many teachers do not use diagnostic methods, and seem to be unaware of their potential for improving classroom practice. (p. 50)

Researchers such as Whitford and Jones (2000) and Shepard (2000) ask all the stakeholders within the educational community to employ more thought on the diagnostic use of the plethora of data generated from the national test results. The authors propose that careful interpretation of test results and immediate diagnostic feedback to schools through a collaborative program may be one way of promoting the enhancement of their teaching strategies.

Our findings have a close similarity with the results presented by Swain (1996). Swain presented the responses of 15 teachers from different schools in telephone interviews about the use of the returned pupils' marked scripts. According to Swain the two most typical comments on the use of the returned marked scripts were:

1. "Time factors prevent real diagnosis."
2. "In an ideal world we would like to but it is not likely." (Swain, 1996, p. 89)

Moreover, Swain reported that only 1 out of 15 schools was intending to use the returned scripts for diagnostic purposes (lack of time was given by the other schools as the main reason for not doing so).

From the above, it is suggested that the schools might actually like the idea of enhancing their teaching techniques with feedback from a detailed error analysis of their pupils' scripts, provided they have some help and support especially in focusing activities, possibly from an external organization. A detailed error analysis may take the form of comprehensive tables of the kind of errors the pupils make on each item. The tables could include the most common errors of the pupils on each sub-domain of the curriculum being tested and various statistical analyses could then be run to establish relationships between the different categories of errors and the most prominent pupil characteristics.

Such detailed feedback and error analysis reports would be extremely valuable to school leaders, assessment coordinators and classroom teachers. However, the digestion of such a detailed form of feedback may prove to be too time-consuming for schools. It is very indicative that a head of science department wrote the following comment concerning all of the test-preparation strategies: "All good ideas but we don't have the time/ staffing/structure to implement them yet."

Swain (1996) has also presented very similar findings and, as an example, cites the exact comments of a teacher on preparing pupils to sit the KS3 science tests:

> Revision time had nothing to do with learning science; it was done to familiarize pupils with the format of the tests. The pupils could have been learning new work in the time spent. (p. 80)

For all the above reasons, the CFAS decided to become involved in a collaboration project which would aim to enrich teaching strategies by providing the schools with appropriate, formative and cognitive feedback. However, it is important to note that all the above information reflects only the views of the heads of departments who completed the Head of Department questionnaires and their views do not necessarily correlate with the views of their individual subject teachers.

The most fundamental issue of this collaboration program was to ensure teachers' willingness to cooperate voluntarily and sincerely — not under pressure from the senior management of the school. History has shown that teachers' attitudes toward the NC tests have not been very positive (see Gipps et al., 1998). Many teachers still feel that the results from the national tests have not been used in an educationally positive way and in some instances have been reduced to ranking data lists for the "name-and-shame" league tables (Murphy, 1996). Even 10 years after the first national tests took place, teachers are still alarmed by experts challenging the validity of the NC testing (Morrison & Wylie, 1999) and arguing that even "excellent tests" may not help to improve education at all in the sense that better speedometers do not make for faster cars (Froomkin, 1998).

Therefore, we decided that our first task would be to approach schools step-by-step, not as "national tests experts," but as a partner who is willing to spend enough time with teachers during both the pre- and post-test period for the collaboration to achieve better test results and to make better use of the test results.

The first step was to establish trust and cooperation between the researchers and the schools participating in the SSP. For the 1999–2000 academic year, the schools have been provided with feedback on their pupils' results. The feedback concerned the overall achievement levels of the pupils by subject and compared the school and national results by subject. It was based on a sample of pupils' scripts randomly selected (using the date of birth of the children) and provided by the schools. Often the feedback took the form of tables with comparisons between the aggregated school results and the national results. Examples are presented in Tables 3 and 4.

The tables were usually accompanied with graphs, which aimed to visualize the results and make it easier for the teachers to conceptualize and digest. An example is presented in Figure 6.

Moreover, separate sheets provided item-level information for a school cohort but not personalized feedback for individual pupils at this stage.

Questions, dialogue and any form of communication with the CFAS (via e-mail, telephone or letter) are encouraged and schools are encouraged to use the feedback and to raise issues about their report. Moreover, some schools ask for additional analysis or clarification and the CFAS is willing to help.

Table 3   *An Example of the Comparison Between the School and the SSP Mean Achievement on the Main NC Domains in Mathematics*

Curriculum domain	SSP mean score**	School mean score	Statistically significant difference?*
Total score	103.7	62.5	Yes
Shape	22.3	20.5	No
Algebra	30.0	29.3	No
Data handling	22.5	15.0	Yes
Number	28.9	13.5	Yes

*   The significance of the difference is judged according to 95% Confidence Intervals of the school mean score.

** The mean score is based on a nationally representative sample of approximately 3,000 pupils.

Table 4   *An Example of Feedback to Schools (Item-level Comparison between School and National Performance)*

Question no.	SSP level			School level		
	No marks or omitted (%)	One mark (%)	Two marks (%)	No marks or omitted (%)	One mark (%)	Two marks (%)
Q1	7.2	92.8	–	6.7	93.3	–
Q2	13.3	66.2	20.5	26.7	60.3	13.0
Q3A	16.6	83.4	–	6.7	93.3	–
Q3B	5.9	94.1	–	0	100.0	–

* KS2 Mathematics Test B Level 3–5.

Conclusion

Although the NC testing program has a relatively short history of not much more than a decade, schools seem to be under such accountability pressures and so anxious to achieve high overall levels that they are willing to sacrifice valuable teaching time for test-preparation strategies which narrow the curriculum and detract from learning. It is the responsibility of all the stakeholders in the education system not to ignore such an important issue.

Figure 6   *A Comparison Between the School and the SSP Mean Achievement on the Main NC Domains in Mathematics*

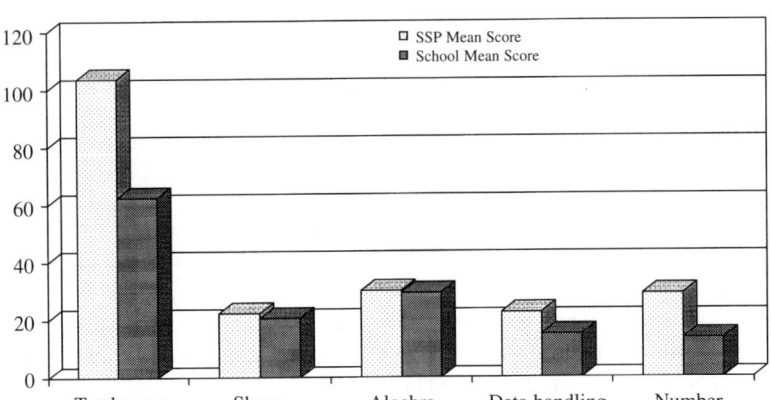

One possible strategy to address the problem might be the establishment of collaboration programs between schools and external facilitators to empower the teachers themselves to monitor and evaluate their curriculum delivery strategies within the provision of individualized, tailored information on pupils' performance. The changing of attitudes and culture within a high stakes accountability system which bases its judgments of quality on test outcomes measures might be a slow process, but the only sustainable changes will be the ones that come from within the schools after self-reflection.

Notes

1. The Qualifications and Curriculum Authority (QCA) is a government organization based in the United Kingdom responsible to guard the standards in education and training. The major aims for the QCA are to maintain and develop the school curriculum and its associated assessments, and to accredit and monitor qualifications not only in schools and colleges but also at work. For more information see http://www.qca.org.uk.
2. The SSP is a longitudinal study, which the CFAS has managed for the QCA since 1996, monitoring curriculum provision and analyzing the NC test results at question level for a nationally representative sample of primary and secondary schools in the United Kingdom.

3. "A" level is the "gold standard" examination for 18+ pupils usually regarded as the entrance qualification for higher education.
4. "Statistical neighbors": Schools are clustered into "statistical neighborhoods," using socio-economic and demographic information. This is expected to enable schools to better understand and interpret their own results and to identify potential areas for improvement.

References

Allalouf, A., & Ben-Shakhar, G. (1998). The effect of coaching on the predictive validity of Scholastic Aptitude Tests. *Journal of Educational Measurement, 35* (1), 31–47.

Alliger, G. M., & Dwight, S. A. (2000). A meta-analytic investigation of the susceptibility of integrity tests to faking and coaching. *Educational and Psychological Measurement, 60*(1), 59–72.

Bangert-Drowns, R. L., Kulik, C. C., Kulik, J. A., & Morgan, M. (1991). The instructional effect of feedback in test-like events. *Review of Educational Research, 61*(2), 213–238.

Black, P. J. (1998). *Testing: Friend or foe? The theory and practice of assessment and testing.* London; Washington, DC: Falmer Press.

Black, P., & Wiliam, D. (1998). Inside the black box: Raising standards through classroom assessment. *Phi Delta Kappan, 80*(2), 139–144. Retrieved November 28, 2001, from http://pdkintl.org/kappan/kbla9810.htm

Clausen-May, T. (1998, August). *Common errors, common understanding: The development of KS3 mathematics tests for fourteen-year-olds.* Paper presented at the British Educational Research Association Annual Conference, The Queen's University of Belfast, Northern Ireland.

Clerk, D., & Rutherford, M. (2000). Language as a confounding variable in the diagnosis of misconceptions. *International Journal of Science Education, 22* (7), 703–717.

Close, G., Furlong, T., & Swain, J. (1995). The Key Stage 3 tests and tasks: Head-teacher opinions on the impact, effect on the curriculum, teaching and learning, and teachers' assessments. *British Journal of Curriculum and Assessment, 6*(3), 19–25.

Coe, R. (1999, September). *The effects of feedback on teachers' attitudes: Difficulties of measurement.* Paper presented at the British Educational Research Association Annual Conference, University of Sussex, Brighton, the United Kingdom.

Cumming, J. (1998, August). *Why are misconceptions in science so hard to change?* Paper presented at the British Educational Research Association Annual Conference, The Queen's University of Belfast, Northern Ireland.

Denscombe, M. (2000). Social conditions for stress: Young people's experience of doing GCSEs. *British Educational Research Journal, 26*(3), 359–374.

DES. (1988). *Science at age 11. A Review of APU Survey Findings from 1980–84.* London: HMSO.

DfEE. (1997). *Excellence in schools: Education White Paper presented to Parliament by the Secretary of State for Education and Employment, July 1997.* London: Stationery Office. Retrieved December 3, 2001, from http://www.dfee.gov.uk/wpaper/mindex.htm

Diane, L. (1995). *Making the A: How to study for tests.* Abstract accessed through ERIC/Assessment and Evaluation Digest [ERIC Identifier: ED385613].

Froomkin, D. (1998). Tests are key to the Clinton education agenda. *The Washington Post.* Retrieved December 5, 2001, from http://www.washingtonpost.com/wp-srv/politics/special/testing/testing.htm

Gipps, C. V. (1994). *Beyond testing: Toward a theory of educational assessment.* London; Washington, DC: Falmer Press.

Gipps, C., Clarke, S., & McCallum, B. (1998, April). *The role of teachers in National Assessment in England.* Paper presented at the Annual Meeting of the American Educational Research Association, San Diego, CA.

Jennings, S., Price, N., & Pankhurst, K. (1999). To what extent can National Curriculum tests in Mathematics inform and guide teaching? *International Journal of Mathematics Education in Science and Technology, 30*(1), 1–10.

Kinchin, I. M. (1998, August). *Constructivism in the classroom: Mapping your way through.* Paper presented at the British Educational Research Association Annual Conference, The Queen's University of Belfast, Northern Ireland.

Kirk, G. (1996, September). *Partnership: The sharing of cultures?* Keynote address at the 21st Annual Conference of the Association for Teacher Educatiuon in Europe (ATEE), University of Strathclyde, Glasgow, the United Kingdom.

Kluger, A. N., & DeNisi, A. (1996). The effects of feedback interventions on performance: A historical review, a meta-analysis, and a preliminary feedback intervention theory. *Psychological Bulletin, 119*(2), 254–284.

Lortie, D. (1975). *The schoolteacher: A sociological study.* Chicago: University of Chicago Press.

Morrison, H. G., & Wylie, E. C. (1999). Why National Curriculum Testing is founded on a methodological thought disorder. *Evaluation and Research in Education, 13*(2), 92–105.

Murphy, R. (1996, September). *Drawing outrageous conclusions from national assessment results: Where will it all end?* Paper presented at BERA Annual Conference, University of Lancaster, the United Kingdom.

Pine, K. J., Messer, D. J., & St. John, K. (2001). Children's misconceptions in primary science: A survey of teachers' views. *Research in Science & Technological Education, 19*(1), 79–96.

Robertson, S. L. (1996). Teachers' work, restructuring and postfordism: Constructing the new "professionalism." In I. F. Goodson & A. Hargreaves (Eds.), *Teachers' professional lives* (pp. 28–55). London; Washington, DC: Falmer Press.

Sanger, M. J., & Greenbowe, T. J. (2000). Addressing student misconceptions concerning electron flow in aqueous solutions with instruction including computer animations and conceptual change strategies. *International Journal of Science Education, 22*(5), 521–537.

Sharp, R., & Green, A. (1975). *Education and social control: A study in progressive primary education.* London; Boston: Routledge and Kegan Paul.

Shepard, L. A. (2000). The role of assessment in a learning culture. *Educational Researcher, 29*(7), 4–14.

Smith, M. L., Noble, A., Heinecke, W., Seck, M., Parish, C., Cabay, M., Junker, S., Haag, S., Tayler, K., Safran, Y., Penley, Y., & Bradshaw, A. (1997). *Reforming schools by reforming assessment: Consequences of the Arizona student assessment program (ASAP): Equity and teacher capacity building* [CSE Technical Report 425]. Los Angeles: National Center for Research on Evaluation, Standards, and Student Testing, University of California.

Stricker, L. J., & Emmerich, W. (1999). Possible determinants of Differential Item Functioning: Familiarity, interest, and emotional reaction. *Journal of Educational Measurement, 36*(4), 347–366.

Swain, J. R. L. (1996). The impact and effect of key stage 3 science tests. *School Science Review, 78*(283), 79–90.

Taber, K. S. (1995, September). *Prior learning as an epistemological block? The octet rule — An example from science education.* Paper presented at the European Conference on Educational Research, University of Bath, Bath, the United Kingdom.

Taber, K. S. (2001). The mismatch between assumed prior knowledge and the learner's conceptions: A typology of learning impediments. *Educational Studies, 27*(2), 159–171.

Whitford, B. L., & Jones, K. (2000). Kentucky lesson: How high stakes school accountability undermines a performance-based curriculum vision. In B. L. Whitford & K. Jones (Eds.), *Accountability, assessment, and teacher commitment: Lessons from Kentucky's reform efforts* (pp. 9–24). Albany, NY: State University of New York Press.

Williams, J., & Ryan, J. (2000). National Testing and the improvement of classroom teaching: Can they coexist? *British Educational Research Journal, 26*(1), 49–73.

Appendix 1

Preparation of the Pupils for the National Tests

(1998–1999 Head of subject department questionnaire)

English	1998 (%)	1999 (%)	2001 (%)
Analysis of previous years' performance on a question-to-question basis	24	28	37
Analysis of returned marked scripts	41	44	52
Analysis of SCAA/QCA standards booklets	44	47	50
Make use of mark schemes and exemplar material from previous tests	63	73	83
No additional preparation outside normal teaching	14	12	13
Preparation by ability	41	46	51
Review last year's test papers	78	82	85
Revise question types which appear to reoccur	56	66	80
Teacher originated tests to replicate question format	52	57	64

Mathematics	1998 (%)	1999 (%)	2001 (%)
Analysis of previous years' performance on a question-to-question basis	14	16	19
Analysis of returned marked scripts	25	28	29
Analysis of SCAA/QCA standards booklets	16	19	17
Make use of mark schemes and exemplar material from previous tests	68	58	64
No additional preparation outside normal teaching	17	12	11
Preparation by ability	67	66	62
Review last year's test papers	86	82	78
Revise question types which appear to reoccur	47	45	58
Teacher originated tests to replicate question format	45	45	47

Science	1998 (%)	1999 (%)	2001 (%)
Analysis of previous years' performance on a question-to-question basis	12	22	27
Analysis of returned marked scripts	30	35	39
Analysis of SCAA/QCA standards booklets	29	25	31
Make use of mark schemes and exemplar material from previous tests	72	73	76
No additional preparation outside normal teaching	14	11	6
Preparation by ability	70	69	63
Review last year's test papers	82	80	82
Revise question types which appear to reoccur	46	45	58
Teacher originated tests to replicate question format	63	58	65

Note: $N_{1998} = 224$, $N_{1999} = 219$, $N_{2001} = 140$

Appendix 2

A Brief Summary of the Most Important Questions Included in the "Head of Department" Questionnaire

Question	1997/8	1998/9
Please indicate the actual number of staff (not the FTE) that teach \<subject\> this year who:		
HAVE a recognized pre-service qualification in \<subject\>	Yes	Yes
DO NOT have a recognized pre-service qualification in \<subject\>	Yes	Yes
TOTAL number of staff that teach \<subject\>	Yes	Yes
Are you able to manage (<u>Note</u>: 1997 is "cover") the program of study at KS3 given the teaching time your school allocates?	Yes	Yes
Explain Why	No	Yes
Are you able to go beyond the program of study at KS3 and incorporate other material, given the teaching time your school allocates?	Yes	Yes
Explain Why	No	Yes
Please indicate what you think about the amount of detail in the program of study for teaching \<subject\> at KS3? (Not detailed enough/About right amount of detail/Too detailed)	Yes	Yes
What do you think about the expectations set out in the level descriptions for mathematics for the majority of pupils at KS3? (Too high/About right/Too low)	Yes	Yes
In general, how useful do you consider the level descriptions for \<subject\> to be for the following purposes at KS3? End of KS3 statutory teacher assessment Planning targets for year groups } Useful/Not useful Assessment at the end of the year	Yes	Yes
Have any of the following changes in provision taken place in your subject since last year \<year\>? Timed allocated in timetable Staffing } Increased/No change/Decreased (Non-staff) courses	Yes	Yes
Do you use IT in your teaching \<subject\>? (Not at all/A limited amount/A lot) (Give examples) – Note: Qualitative data probably not analyzed yet	Yes	Yes

Question	1997/8	1998/9
If you indicate that you make little or no use of IT this is because of (problems of access to hardware/inappropriate software/lack of staff experience/lack of time?)	Yes	Yes
Has statutory Teacher Assessment in <subject> had an impact on the way you plan and organize your curriculum? (Yes/No)	Yes	Yes
If yes, where has the impact been felt? (The teaching time, the way of teaching ... etc)	Yes	Yes
Which of the following approaches to standardizing Teacher Assessment judgments are used in your department? (Teachers make their own arrangements, follow departmental guidelines ... etc.)	Yes	Yes
How do you prepare for the end of KS3 <subject> tests? Tick as many of the following which apply in your department (Review last year's papers, analysis of returned marked scripts ... etc.)	Yes	Yes
How useful do you consider the level description information from KS2 <subject> statutory assessment? (Useful/Not useful)	Yes	Yes

Note: "Yes" means that the question was included in the questionnaire; "No" means that the question was NOT included in the questionnaire. All the major questions also appear in the 2001 questionnaire.

10

Young Children Starting School: A Fine Example of Home-School Partnership

Sue Dockett, Bob Perry & Peter Howard

Abstract

The Starting School Research Project, based at the University of Western Sydney, involves a group of researchers and a wide ranging Advisory Committee representing peak early childhood organizations, early childhood employer groups, parent associations, school organizations, community and union perspectives (Dockett, Howard, & Perry, 1999). Over the past 3 years, the project has investigated the perceptions and expectations of all those involved in young children's transition to school. This has been done through a comprehensive literature review, extensive focus group interviews with adults and children and a wide-ranging survey of prior-to-school and school teachers, and parents with children who had just started school or were about to start.

In this chapter, we report on data gathered from parents, prior-to-school and school teachers, and children in response to the question "How much involvement should the following people have in a child's transition to school?". Analysis of the data has resulted in a clear view that the planning and implementation of transition to school should involve many players, including parents, school and prior-to-school educators, other local community members, and most importantly of all, the children themselves. Examples of transition programs which involve as many of these groups as possible are presented to highlight the importance of educational partnerships at this critical change point for young children.

Introduction

Thousands of Australian children start school every year. For each of these children, their families and educators, starting school is an important time. Most children display eagerness and excitement at finally going to "big school." Sometimes, this can be overtaken by a sense of being lost or not knowing what will happen. Other times, the excitement continues as children feel valued within the school community.

Each of these outcomes can have an impact on later school success. Children who start school feeling happy and eager to be there, who believe their teacher likes and is interested in them, and whose family also reflects a positive attitude, have a good chance of succeeding at school. On the other hand, children who are anxious and afraid about school, who don't feel as if they belong there, or that anyone cares about their well-being at school, or whose family is confused and anxious about school, are unlikely to succeed at school without some extra assistance. Starting school is a key experience, not only for the children starting school, but also for educators — both in schools and in prior-to-school settings — and for their families. Bailey (1999) summarizes the importance of this experience in the following way:

> Kindergarten [the first year of school] is a context in which children make important conclusions about school as a place where they want to be and about themselves as learners vis-à-vis schools. If no other objectives are accomplished, it is essential that the transition to school occur[s] in such a way that children and families have a positive view of the school and that children have a feeling of perceived competence as learners. (p. xv)

Since 1997, the authors, as part of the Starting School Research Project, have been investigating who should be involved in children's transition to school and what they should be doing. It is this which is the major emphasis of this chapter. However, it is worth noting that the research project itself is an excellent example of a partnership between researchers, educational practitioners in school and prior-to-school settings, parents, and many other interested parties (Borg, Dockett, Meredith, & Perry, 2001; Dockett, Howard, & Perry, 1999; Dockett & Perry, in press-a). For example, the Advisory Committee for the project consists of representatives of all the peak employer, government, parent, teacher, union and other groups across the entire state of New South Wales which have some involvement in the transition to school. This committee has been very influential not only in suggesting directions for the research but also in the funding of that research and its dissemination. Through the committee, and because of the active involvement of the committee members in the research agenda of the project, changes in policy have been made with a speed and effectiveness not often seen in the nexus between research and policy and practice (Dockett, Howard, & Perry, 1999). Another example of how the project has developed key partnerships and used them to further its aims and influence is through the establishment and maintenance of groups of early childhood educators and parents in 15 locations across New South Wales. These locations include remote, rural and urban communities which differ in terms of cultural diversity and socio-economic status (Dockett & Perry, in press-a).

In this paper, we report on data gathered from parents, prior-to-school and school teachers and children in response to the question "how much involvement should the following people have in a child's transition to school." Analysis of the data has resulted in a clear view that the planning and implementation of transitions to school should involve many players, including parents, school and prior-to-school educators, other local community members and, most importantly of all, the children themselves. Examples of transition programs which involve as many of these groups as possible are presented to highlight the importance of educational partnerships at this critical change point for young children.

What Are Transition-to-School Programs?

To ensure that the use of "transition-to-school programs" is clear in this chapter, we have included the definition used by the Starting School Research Project. In this definition, a clear distinction is made between "orientation" and "transition" programs. Orientation programs are typically designed to help children and parents become familiar with the school setting. They may involve a tour of the school, meeting relevant people in the school, and spending some time in a classroom. Orientation programs are characterized by presentations by the school to the parents and children. While transition programs may include an orientation time, they tend to be longer term and more geared to the individual needs of children and families than orientation programs. Transition programs can be of indeterminate length, depending on a particular child or parent's needs. They recognize that starting school is a time of transition for all involved:

children, families, and teachers. Transition programs may be planned and implemented by a team of people representing all those involved in the change.

Who Are the Stakeholders?

There are many stakeholders in children's transition to school. As part of the Starting School Research Project, an extensive survey was developed which included, among many others, a question which asked about who should be involved in the transition to school and how much involvement those people should have. The list of groups of people in this question was developed from the literature and from the pilot studies for the project (Perry, Dockett, & Howard, 2000). Table 1 shows this list along with the average response from each of four groups of respondents — parents/ guardians ($n = 232$), prior-to-school educators ($n = 33$), school teachers ($n = 87$), and representatives of the peak early childhood bodies which comprise the Advisory Committee for the project ($n = 42$). The respondents were given four possible responses to the question of how much involvement each group of people should have (i.e. no involvement, a little involvement, a lot of involvement, total involvement), and the average score was

Table 1   *How Much Involvement Should (Groups of) People Have in a Child's Transition to School?*

People	Parent/ guardians	Prior-to-school educators	School teachers	Representatives of peak bodies
Parents/guardians	3.60	3.73	3.45	3.71
The child	3.54	3.53	3.75	3.68
School teachers	3.17	3.28	3.33	3.41
Prior-to-school teachers	2.71	3.09	2.57	2.93
Child's siblings	2.67	2.94	2.67	2.67
Child's friends	2.33	2.38	2.38	2.61
Grandparents	2.30	2.47	2.38	2.38
Other members of extended family	2.10	2.22	2.26	2.20
School staff other than teachers	2.08	2.52	2.21	2.21
Government bodies	1.79	2.03	1.72	2.13
Doctors	1.65	1.75	1.79	1.87
Religious groups	1.59	1.81	1.63	1.51

determined by assigning scores of 1, 2, 3, 4 to each of these respectively. For convenience, the results are listed in order of the means obtained from the parent respondents. This is not the order in which the different groups were listed in the questionnaire.

Three features of this table are worth discussion. Firstly, the figures across the four sets of respondents are remarkably similar for each group of possible participants in the child's transition to school. Hence secondly, the orders in which the different sets of respondents have placed the groups of people are quite similar. Thirdly, there is a clear understanding among the different sets of respondents about which groups of people should have the major involvement with the transition to school. Government bodies, doctors and religious groups — all of which were rated on average to be needed for less than "a little involvement" — seem to be seen to play at most a peripheral role in children's transition to school. On the other hand, parents/ guardians, the child, school, and prior-to-school educators were all rated as having "a lot of involvement" through to almost "total involvement." The other five groups of people listed — the child's siblings, friends, grandparents, other members of the child's extended family, and school staff other than teachers — all rated at least some involvement in the transition from each set of respondents. Probably the most telling result coming from this table is the large number of different groups of people who are seen to have a legitimate role to play in this transition.

It is clear that respondents believed that educators, parents, and children should have input into transition-to-school programs. Educators from prior-to-school settings as well as teachers of kindergarten (the first year of school) and other grades and school staff, such as community languages teachers, librarians, staff of the out-of-school-hours program, support/ clerical staff and general staff can all make valuable contributions to a transition program. Parents know their children well and can provide a great deal of valuable input to a transition program. Young children too, can make a significant contribution as they indicate areas of interest or concern. Educators in prior-to-school settings also know the children well. They may have developed comprehensive records as part of their planning process and often, have become trusted friends of the parents and the child in the years before school. Further, in some contexts, members of the broader community may be involved with the program.

To ascertain which members of the broader community should be involved, respondents to the survey were asked to indicate people other than those listed who might have some involvement in a child's transition to school. The suggestions included all staff in prior-to-school settings, bus drivers, out-of-school-hours care personnel, and families other than that of the child. No doubt, there are many more groups which could be included. Some of these, as well as the major stakeholders, are discussed below.

Parents and Families

Parents play a significant role in the education of their children. Not only are they their children's "first teachers," but also their attitudes and approaches to learning contribute a great deal to children's approaches to school and education. Children are quick to gauge how comfortable parents are in the school environment. This also impacts on their own sense of comfort and belonging. If children feel that their parents are not well accepted in a school community, or that they do not fit in, they may transfer this feeling to themselves. On the other hand, school communities which welcome and accept parents, where teachers and parents are accorded mutual respect, and where children feel that parents and teachers are working together for them, promote a sense of belonging and acceptance that is conducive to learning (Greenberg, 1989).

There are many ways in which parents can be involved in transition programs. These include:

1. Parents of children already at school meeting with parents whose children are about to start school;
2. School staff making time to visit parents, in whatever forum is most comfortable for all;
3. School staff meeting with parents in prior-to-school settings; and
4. Parents having a role in transition programs, such as helping with some activities, asking questions, making suggestions, organizing sessions, or identifying areas they would like to have discussed.

Many of these aspects can be extended to include other family members, such as grandparents. Some children spend a great deal of time with grandparents, and it is important for them to know that people who are special to them, such as grandparents, are welcome, and respected, in school settings. Schools gain a lot from recognizing the diversity of family experiences and welcoming family members to share in the education of the young child at school. Most importantly, families need to feel that someone cares for their child and will treat their child with respect.

Much is said of the need to maintain continuity of learning across contexts, whether it be from home to school, or from prior-to-school setting as well as home to school. This is particularly important when there is a clear divide between some or all of these contexts. Sometimes, parents will not feel comfortable visiting a school, perhaps because their own recollections of school are not so positive. Others may perceive teachers as the experts and consider that they have nothing to offer. In these cases, extra efforts are needed on the part of school staff to reach parents and to involve them in the school community.

Some parents have had a great deal of involvement in prior-to-school programs. In community-managed centers, they may have had a responsible role on the management committee as well as some input into the educational program. A number of parents are concerned that when their children start school, they will lose that ability to have such a "hands-on" approach in their children's education (Westcott, Perry, Jones, & Dockett, in press). Some even feel that they are actively discouraged from being involved in the educational program.

Children

Interviews with children who are about to start school, children who have just started school, and children who have been at school for several years, have been a feature of the Starting School Research Project and have identified several issues of concern (Dockett & Perry, 1999; Perry, Dockett, Clyde, & Tracey, 1998). Our interview methodology with young children involves small focus groups of up to 5 children in a familiar context such as their school or preschool. The consent of parents is always obtained but we also seek the permission of the children before the interview commences. On a number of occasions this has not been given and the interview has not proceeded. A range of questions is used to stimulate discussion among the children about their thoughts on starting school. Sometimes a question may be simply "Can you tell what you think about when you think about starting school?" and at other times it might be a hypothetical question such as "I wonder what would happen if children didn't come to school?". Our experience is that children are quite willing to share their experiences and feelings about something as important as starting school and that there is no need for detailed questioning. Data is analyzed through a grounded theory, constant comparative methodology which also links with the factors which have been found through analysis of the survey data arising from the adults. However, it is important to note that the children have generated new categories of response beyond those generated by the adults and have not used all of the adult categories in their own responses.

The major issues of concern which the children have identified include:

1. Children not knowing what is going to happen when they start school, for example, where they go, who their teacher will be, what they will do, whether or not they will be with their friends, or even where they will put their bags; and
2. Issues about the playground, such as the rules about where to go and who to play with. Major concerns for children about playgrounds relate to the "big kids," the number of children and the noise of the playground.

Children have views about what parents and educators can do to help them start school. Comments from children indicate that parents ought to:

1. Help do names and cutting out;
2. Know where the office is and which school you are going to;
3. Buy uniform;
4. Tell kids that they are going to school;
5. Wash clothes and get them ready;
6. Wake me up in the morning; and
7. Pack the lunch box, look at things you have been working on.

Children also indicate that educators in prior-to-school settings have some role in helping them start school. In particular, children suggested that these educators:

1. Have to sign something, write some letters for mum and dad to look at; and
2. Teach you some letters, teach you to say "thank you" and "goodbye."

According to these same children, teachers in schools:

1. Have to clean up the school and read us a story;
2. Make some more activities before we start school, set the place up nice, get some more things for us;

3. Help with writing names; and
4. Tell you what to bring in our lunch box, to eat breakfast every morning so you have enough energy to play.

When children who had been at school for some time were asked what they would tell children about to start school, the following advice was forthcoming:

1. You play;
2. Not to have friends is a bad thing;
3. Don't be sad, your mum will pick you up when it's afternoon;
4. Don't run away;
5. You need to know the rules;
6. You have to do homework, can't expect as many activities (as preschool). We do lots of fun activities. We play games. Our mums go home when the bell rings and we have to sit on the floor;
7. If they don't want to go I'll tell them it's good and they will have a lot of fun;
8. It's brilliant you can do lots of fun things, and you can sit next to a friend; and
9. It's fun, you do a little bit of homework and that's how you learn and then you go to high school and you are a bit better in high school.

These comments are included here to emphasize that children are actively trying to understand what is happening around them. They are concerned about what will happen, about having friends, and about knowing the rules. They are capable of sharing their perceptions, feelings and understandings with others. Sensitive adults, who seek information in appropriate ways can be privy to many of the interpretations and understandings children are developing. Equipped with such knowledge, we can plan appropriate transition experiences. Further, we can involve children in the development of those experiences.

Educators

Transition-to-school programs are most effective if they are not thought of as the responsibility of only one person, such as the teacher of the first year of school. Effective programs often reflect the involvement of teachers across the school, as well as from prior-to-school settings. In schools, this involvement may take the form of visits of teachers and classes to classrooms, the principal or executive teacher spending time with the new students, and a reorganization of the duty roster to relieve teachers of playground duty or bus duty.

Educators can be involved in transition programs in many ways. These include:

1. Meeting with other educators to plan, discuss and reflect upon transition programs;
2. Identifying stakeholders and inviting them to participate in transition programs;
3. Emphasizing the importance of transition programs within school and prior-to-school settings; and
4. Acting as an advocate for children, by listening to children's concerns and responding to these in an appropriate way.

In order to maintain the continuity of transition programs, it is important that there is more than one teacher from the school involved on an ongoing basis. In many instances, programs orchestrated by one teacher cease when the teacher moves to a different school. The status of the transition program within a school also is enhanced if a whole school commitment is made to the program. Despite this, it is vital that teachers who will be teaching children in their first year of school be involved in the transition program. Children and parents are interested and concerned to know who the child's teacher will be, and disconcerted if they have met and become familiar with one teacher, only to find at the beginning of the school year that that teacher is not the teacher with whom they will be working.

It is not only the teachers in school settings who become important participants in transition programs. At a recent conference of early childhood educators, groups of participants were asked to nominate stakeholders in the transition to school. One group proceeded to draw a picture of a bus driver and bus. Their explanation was that the bus driver was a consistent feature of school life and often the first and last person associated with the school, to be seen each day by the children. A bad trip to school on the bus does not augur well for the school day. On the other hand, a friendly caring and happy driver can make a not-so-good start to the day so much better. In country areas where children spend several hours on a bus each day, the driver assumes a great deal of importance.

Other school staff are also stakeholders in the transition to school.

Many parents have indicated that the response they receive to their initial telephone inquiry, or how they are welcomed as they arrive at the school office, has played a major role in determining whether or not they wish to send their child to a particular school. Children, too, have reported feeling lost in school, and sometimes seeking the help of office staff to find their teacher or classroom. Staff who know what transition programs are about, who meet children and parents as part of these programs, and who can contribute to them, are more likely to respond to these situations in a positive and welcoming manner. School librarians are often important contacts for children starting school because of their links to what many children see as the key reason for coming to school: learning to read. A relaxed atmosphere in the library can sometimes provide a much-needed oasis for young children (Immroth & Ash-Geisler, 1994).

Several school personnel have the potential to establish close connections with the community. Staff such as community liaison officers, home school liaison officers, education assistants, and community workers work very hard to interact with the broader community. Their expertise and their knowledge of the local community can be invaluable in transition programs.

Essentially any member of the school staff, be they teaching staff, support staff, cleaning staff, garden or maintenance staff can be stakeholders in transition programs. All will encounter children and families and all need to be familiar with what happens and why and how they can help assist children and their families in their transition to school.

Out-of-School-Hours Care

Some children in Australia commence out-of-school-hours care[1] at the same time as they start school. Sometimes, before and after school care is provided on the school site. Other times, children may have to be transported to or from a different location. Children may spend several hours each day in this form of care. When considering continuity of experiences for children, and smooth transition to school, we cannot forget about out-of-school-hours care.

Community Members

The entire community benefits when children and families start school and see it as a useful, productive and relevant experience. On this basis, it makes sense that community members are considered stakeholders in transition programs. Community members from church groups, professional associations such as librarians, service organizations and community groups — especially sporting groups — may be keen to be a part of such programs. Librarians can emphasize the importance of having friends with whom to go to school and can help develop these friendships through reading groups, for example. Sporting groups also help develop such friendships as well as the healthy life style and stamina needed for a full school day. Promoting a close connection between community and school involves an awareness of what is considered important in each area. When communities are familiar with what happens in schools, they are often more supportive of schools and those who work there as well as those who attend school. When schools make connections with the communities, they can make a significant contribution to community life.

Doctors and Community Health Professionals

As children attest, spending a full day at school can be a tiring experience. This is even more so if children travel for long distances or attend out-of-school-hours care. Children need to be healthy and well rested to benefit from school programs, including transition programs. The input of doctors and other health professionals can help promote this.

In some communities, there is a strong history of health screening as part of the transition to school. In other communities, this may occur at a later stage, or not at all. As well as identifying any health concerns, health professionals can provide useful input to transition programs on issues like providing nutritious and interesting lunches for children as well as appropriate health and dental care for young children and families.

Summary

Children starting school should be able to access assistance from as many people as is possible during what can be a very exciting and/or scary time. It follows from this that all of these people are at least aware of the basis for the organized transition to school program even if they are not integral in its planning and implementation. Transition programs which are left up to one teacher to run are almost certainly doomed to failure in the ever-changing world in which all of us live. Too much can occur which will destabilize even the best-planned program. By having as many people actively involved in the program as possible, the chances are that it will be successful, and it will be much more fun for all stakeholders, especially the children.

Implications for Practice

1. There are many stakeholders in the transition to school. These include families, children, educators in prior-to-school and school settings, other staff in these settings, government and other organizations, community members, health professionals, and other significant people from particular contexts. Different people can be involved in transition programs in different ways, as each brings a unique perspective and makes a unique contribution.
2. The inclusion of all the stakeholders relevant to children's transition to school in a particular context promotes a sense of working together in which children, families, and communities benefit.
3. Children develop positive attitudes about school and about themselves as learners more readily when they see their families and educators working together.
4. Listening, and responding, to the voices of children is an important part of effective transition to school programs since it is the children who are most affected by such programs and it is they who need to make the greatest changes when starting schools.

There are many examples of transition to school programs which have been developed as a result of the work of the Starting School Research Project and which do reflect the importance of involving all stakeholders, especially the children in their development and implementation. Some examples of these are given in other publications by the authors (Dockett & Perry, in press-a, in press-b).

Acknowledgments

The research on which this chapter is based was made possible through funding from the University of Western Sydney, Macarthur, the NSW

Department of Education and Training, the NSW Department of Community Services, and the Australian Research Council. These financial contributions are gratefully acknowledged by the authors, as is the assistance of all members of the project Advisory Committee and the Starting School Research Project team. The opinions expressed in the chapter are those of the authors.

Note

1. Formal care for school-aged children before and after school hours.

References

Bailey, D. (1999). Foreword. In R. C. Pianta & M. J. Cox (Eds.), *The transition to kindergarten* (pp. xv–xvi). Baltimore, MD: Paul H. Brookes Publishing.

Borg, T., Dockett, S., Meredith, H., & Perry, B. (2001). Do teachers who are parents have different perceptions about what is important in children's transition to school than those who are not parents? *Journal of Australian Research in Early Childhood Education, 8*(1), 11–22.

Dockett, S., Howard, P., & Perry, B. (1999). Research partnerships in early childhood: Forming the bonds. In S. Schuck, L. Brady, C. E. Deer, & G. Segal (Eds.), *Challenge of change in education* (pp. 122–131). Sydney: University of Technology, Sydney.

Dockett, S., & Perry, B. (1999). Starting school: What do the children say? *Early Child Development and Care, 159,* 107–119.

Dockett, S., & Perry, B. (in press-a). Starting school: Effective transitions. *Early Childhood Research in Practice.*

Dockett, S., & Perry, B. (in press-b). *Starting school in Australia.* Canberra: Australian Early Childhood Association.

Greenberg, P. (1989). Parents as partners in young children's development and education: A new American fad? *Young Children, 44*(4), 61–74.

Immroth, B., & Ash-Geisler, V. (1994, July). *Preschool partnerships: School and public library cooperation to facilitate school readiness.* Paper presented at the 23rd annual conference of the International Association of School Librarianship, Pittsburgh, PA.

Perry, B., Dockett, S., Clyde, M., & Tracey, D. (1998, August). *"Teachers aren't mean": Young children starting school.* Paper presented at the OMEP XXII World Congress, The Child's Right to Care, Play and Education, Copenhagen, Denmark.

Perry, B., Dockett, S., & Howard, P. (2000). Starting school: Issues for children, parents and teachers. *Journal of Australian Research in Early Childhood Education*, 7(1), 41–53.

Westcott, K., Perry, B., Jones, K., & Dockett, S. (in press). Parents' transition to school. *Australian Research in Early Childhood Education*.

11

Partnership in Staff Development: A School-Institute Project in Shanghai and Hong Kong

Hui Leng-han, Sin Kuen-fung, Ho Fuk-chuen &
Chan Hung-ki

Abstract

The importance of school-institute partnerships for professional development is widely acknowledged by many studies. Through partnership, tertiary institutions can gain access to schools' teaching practices, while schools can gain new ideas and knowledge. Such collaboration not only ensures teacher development but also makes action research feasible, which in turn promotes teaching and learning effectiveness in schools. The resultant school improvement is notable in the achievement of high quality education in Hong Kong. This chapter describes the successful experience of building a professional partnership in staff development between The Hong Kong Institute of Education and the Shanghai School for the Blind. Although there are dissimilarities in terms of vision, mission and target students between the two partners, the collaborative arrangement was found to be workable as a result of the explicit aims and shared goals. The experience gained in the partnership was meaningful and productive. Sharing responsibilities between partners not only minimized misunderstandings but also maximized the sense of involvement and contribution of the partners. The conclusion highlights the essential elements of a successful partnership, that is, mutuality, trust and reciprocal benefit (Anderson & Cheung, 1999; Fullan, Erskine-Cullen, & Watson, 1995; Goodlad, 1985; Osguthorpe, Harris, Black, Cutler, & Harris, 1995).

The Notion of School-Institute Partnership

The importance of school-university partnerships for professional development is widely recognized in many studies (Anderson & Cheung, 1999; Clark, 1988; Fullan et al., 1995; Goodlad, 1985; Osguthorpe et al., 1995). As early as 1892, the concept of the school-university partnership was devised by a committee under the chairmanship of Charles Eliot, then president of Harvard University. The committee recommended "a conference of school and college teachers of each principal subject" in order "to consider the limits of its subjects, to consider the best methods of instruction, the most desirable allocation of time for the subject, and the best methods of testing the pupils' attainment therein" (Clark, 1988). However, it was not until the 1980s that educators began to promote the "formation of school-university partnerships as the primary means of affecting widespread improvements in public education" (Stallings & Kowalski, 1990).

Following the recent trends in education reform, tertiary institutions, particularly teacher education institutes, have made great efforts to build up partnerships with schools. This collaboration not only provides tertiary institutions with a base for practice and research, but also assists with school improvement and staff development. "This movement has been particularly fast in countries like the U.S.A., Canada, the U.K. and Australia. Other countries and regions, like Hong Kong, though not moving very fast, have already started off initiatives aiming at more productive collaborations" (Anderson & Cheung, 1999).

With the professional support and resources of tertiary institutions, the outcome is invariably positive in local QEF (Quality Education Fund) projects (Sin, 1999; Sin & Tso, 1999). Following the advice of consultants from tertiary institutions and the school management, teachers were mobilized to try innovative approaches (e.g., the Snoezelen program in a school for severely mentally handicapped children) in their teaching.

The Significance of Partnership

In the field of education, partnership commonly refers to the collaboration between schools and tertiary institutions. During the process of a partnership, how to put theory into practice is the focus of teaching and learning in teacher education. For example, in Hong Kong, the common goal of partnership is to promote the more effective training of teachers, and simultaneously to improve the practices of schools (Anderson & Cheung, 1999). This idea is always fully supported by educators. Oettinger (1998) stated that "The premise of these partnerships is that the mutual enterprise of school teachers and university faculty working together to further develop theory and practice in the field [of] education will result in better prepared teachers for our nation's schools" (p. 23). Osguthorpe et al. (1995) also maintained that "In their simplest form, school-university partnerships are organized collaboration that brings university and public school teachers and administrators together to promote more effective preparation of preservice teachers and, at the same time, to renew conditions and curricula in the public schools" (p. 3).

Looking at the Hong Kong situation, Anderson and Cheung (1999) further explained that "These partnership initiatives are planned to go beyond the traditional idea of co-operating teachers supervising student teachers to a more genuine collaboration in improving teaching and learning within schools, at the same time creating a strong foundation for the continual professional growth of teachers and the lecturers" (p. 2) and "Through inquiring together into common interests in educational practices, school teachers and lecturers often can derive benefits which generate new knowledge or understanding of effective teaching learning, curriculum design and related practices" (p. 1).

Goodlad (1985) also supported this type of partnership and points out some of the benefits to both school and institution:

1. The continuous of knowledge relative to provision of good education in schools and in programs preparing educators.
2. The cultivation of site-based staff development activities designed to foster continual school renewal, particularly of the curriculum and accompanying pedagogical practices.
3. The creation of internships and residencies for educational specialists (including administrators) through which these professionals may observe and gain experience with the best possible education practices.
4. The creation of exemplary sites in which future teachers are educated that demonstrate the best we know about how schools should function. (p. 27)

However, it should be noted that schools and tertiary institutions are organizations with different missions, visions and target groups. Without explicit aims and shared goals, the link between tertiary institutions and schools is bound to be fragile. Goodlad (1985, 1988) stated that partnership could be explained as a deliberately designed, collaborative arrangement between different institutions working together to advance self-interests and solve common problems. The basic characteristics of partnership include:

1. A degree of dissimilarity between partners,
2. Mutual satisfaction of self-interests as the goal, and
3. A state of selflessness to ensure the satisfaction of these self-interests.

In short, it is worthwhile encouraging such a partnership movement. Schools and tertiary institutions both benefit, with improved quality of education for students and teachers alike.

The Relationship Between the Partner Schools

According to Osguthorpe et al. (1995), participants in school partnerships may include educators, students, families and university faculty members, community professionals, and volunteers. They all work together to achieve the four major goals of partnership (i.e., professional development, educator training, curriculum development, and research inquiry), the ultimate goal being to promote students' learning. The four goals may be described as collaborative activities between partners designed to:

1. Ensure that those entering the education profession are well enough prepared to serve all students effectively,
2. Provide opportunities for teachers to strengthen their ability to teach the students they serve,
3. Improve the educational and school life experience of all students, and
4. Raise questions and conduct research that will promote educational renewal in both the school and the university.

Successful Partnership

Although partnership is beneficial to professional development, there may be hurdles to be cleared in order to ensure that the success of the partnership is maximized. It is a fact that schools and tertiary institutions are two different entities with different target groups, goals and missions. Very often, a lot of hard work is involved and frustration among partners is not uncommon. To collaborate effectively is therefore not easy. What partners are concerned about, then, are the methods and strategies for ensuring an effective and successful partnership. Woloszyk and Davis (1993) suggested five favorable factors for partnership:

1. Representative student population,
2. Previous successful partnership relationship,
3. Strong commitment to the community,
4. Joint commitment to higher learning goals for all children, and
5. Innovative and progressive.

In addition, three elements were identified as being crucial to successful partnerships in teacher education by the Association of Teacher Education and the American Association of College Teacher Education (Oettinger, 1998):

1. Mutuality — All participants must feel a sense of ownership and investment in the partnership.
2. Trust — All participants must feel they can depend on each other for cooperation and fulfillment of responsibilities. Commitment from both parties enables one party to entrust the other party with responsibilities affecting domains traditionally perceived as belonging to the first.
3. Results — Each party must perceive benefits from the collaboration. These include intellectual stimulation and the satisfaction of knowing that one is effecting and being affected by improvements in teaching and learning.

Wood (1996) also summarized elements and strategies that are essential for the long-term success of a partnership:

1. Leadership recognized by both partners;
2. A set of clear and focused goals shared and accepted by both partners;
3. Economic factors (including resources and financial support) for initiating and maintaining the partnership;
4. Project selection and fostering ownership in addressing the needs of both partners;

5. Governance and communications of both parties;
6. Commitment to evaluation;
7. Support, rewards and recognition;
8. Networking; and
9. Relative advantage to both parties.

In short, it is clear that a successful school-institute partnership requires that both partners develop the knowledge, skills, values, attitudes, and behavior that will ensure effective and competent collaboration. Both partners need to understand each other's strengths and expertise and to be aware of those aspects that need to be developed further. Culture and ways of thinking need to be shared.

Effective Partnership

Certainly, partnership takes time to develop and the progress is often slow, so that often a partnership will flourish only with a long-term commitment. The following are three basic questions that are useful in guiding the establishment of an effective partnership:

1   Is there a clear mission for the partnership?
    A clear mission is one of the most important elements in a successful partnership. It is the first step in partnership and both partners should collaborate to identify a common mission that they can both accept.
2. What does each partner give and receive?
    The partnership will not last long if one partner always gives and the other always takes. It would be fatal to the partnership if only one partner is perceived as having wisdom, while the other is perceived as having little or none.
3. Can a trusting relationship be established?
    A trusting relationship can help both parties to avoid many misunderstandings resulting from different expectations and cultures. It also means that both partners are willing to think from different perspectives or from different viewpoints.

In conclusion, the above discussion presents a framework of analysis for understanding the school-university partnership, that is widely recognized as part of professional development. The significance of partnership is explained as a consciously designed, collaborative arrangement between different institutions working together to advance self-interests and solve common problems. Such a relationship enhances the growth of both partners. Schools and tertiary institutions both benefit from the improved quality of education for students and teachers alike. However, the relationship between the partners and how to establish a successful and effective partnership are necessary concerns during the process of development.

The Trial of a School-Institute Partnership

The Hong Kong Institute of Education (HKIEd) is a local tertiary institution providing teacher education in Hong Kong, while the Shanghai School for the Blind is a special school for students with visual impairment in Shanghai, Mainland China. In 1998, these two organizations made their professional contact. At the invitation of the Hong Kong Society for the Blind (HKSB), the HKIEd successfully co-organized a three-day school-based staff development program for teachers at the Shanghai School for the Blind. In the light of the identified contextual needs and in the interests of professional development, the team conducted a follow-up staff development program at the school, and also visited a number of mainstream schools for students with special needs in Shanghai in May 2000. This collaboration represented a trial of the type of school-institute partnership elaborated in the previous sections.

The Objectives of the School-Institute Partnership

Considering the similarities between the two cities, the development and support in the field of special education is quite dissimilar. Initially, the Shanghai School for the Blind expected to receive support in terms of the professional development of their staff, with the gradual development of the partnership. In turn, this would promote the learning of their students. The team from the HKIEd aimed to build links with special schools in Shanghai and thence to launch local studies in Mainland China. The objectives accepted and agreed were similar to those described by Goodlad (1985, 1988), in terms of advancing self-interests and solving common problems. This initial collaboration, if well developed, would support further collaboration in various areas, such as seeking solutions to educational problems, applying innovative strategies, promoting effective curriculum planning and development, and improving classroom practices. A mutually supportive relationship between the partners would be nourished with gradually increasing collaboration. In the long term, the HKIEd team expected to be able to build up links with other education organizations in Shanghai.

A Summary of Activities

The goals in terms of professional development, educator preparation, curriculum development, and research inquiry (Osguthorpe et al., 1995) became the model used to build up the relationship during the trial period. All these goals were integrated into the following activities.

Staff Development Program

At the invitation of the Shanghai School for the Blind, the first staff development program was organized in November 1998. Before planning the program, a small-scale survey was conducted to study the training needs of the teachers of the Shanghai School for the Blind and the difficulties they were facing in teaching students with poor vision. A three-day school-based training program, with the major objective of introducing the fundamental concepts and generic skills required for teaching students with poor vision, was conducted in Shanghai. Participants included government officials, teachers of visually impaired students, and teachers from regular schools. The program consisted of vision assessment, assessment of visual efficiency, effective teaching, and the use of optical aids and technology to promote learning. Experiences in teaching and difficulties encountered were shared among the participants. In the evaluation, the HKIEd team learnt about the practical difficulties the teachers had, while the teachers furthered their professional development. Both parties achieved an understanding of each other. The practice satisfied the three basic requirements of a successful partnership highlighted by Oettinger (1998).

Follow-up Staff Program

Supported by the principal and staff of the school, the second staff development program was organized in May 2000. This was a follow-up to the previous staff development program and aimed to empower teachers by supplying them with recent knowledge, instructional techniques, and helping them to become familiar with advancing technology and research related to the education of students with poor vision. It also aimed to widen the horizons of the teachers, as well as to initiate more reflexive teaching. The program included seminars, workshops, and experience-sharing sessions. There was active discussion among the teachers highlighting difficulties in teaching (e.g., how to increase the speed of reading and word-recognition ability of students with low vision). In addition , directions for future investigation into the topics were explored by both parties. In short, a closer relationship was built up between the team and the staff of the school, and the positive outcome, for example, in the areas of feasibility of research and competency enhancement, was similar to that described by Osguthorpe et al. (1995).

Classroom Observation

During the visit, particularly in classroom observation, the team developed a better understanding of both successful experiences and the difficulties encountered by the special education teachers. For example, it was noted that in the Shanghai School for the Blind, all the seats in the classroom were fully equipped with audio-visual resources. The students could easily see what the teachers were teaching from the computer monitor in front of them. However, in some instances, the team was of the opinion that the application of technology restricted teacher-pupil interactions. Dynamic interaction between students and teachers became a major concern in classroom teaching. The outcome of identifying this dilemma was fruitful to both parties as other issues on classroom interaction, pedagogy, learning environment, and curriculum development were highlighted in the sharing sessions. The gains from this process supported Goodlad's (1988) view that schools could acquire new ideas and knowledge, while tertiary institutions would have access to schools with best practices.

Visits to Regular Schools With Special Needs Children

Inclusive education is an area of interest to the team. With the help of the Shanghai School for the Blind, visits to teachers and students at regular schools with students with special needs were arranged. The team observed lessons in the classroom, and discussed and shared views with principals and teachers in meetings. It was observed that most school principals significantly played a leading role in the development of inclusive education. With the principal's strong belief and supportive attitude toward inclusive education, teachers were also found to be enthusiastic about inclusive education. In Shanghai, the focus of education was on the individual needs of students; principals often gave high priority to students with special needs, by, for instance, arranging for the most experienced teachers to teach those students. Some schools prepared a computer database for children with special needs, particularly in the areas of individual educational programs, learning progress, and special needs. The determination on the part of the authority and the successfully implemented practices provided good examples for Hong Kong teachers. The team was able to acquire a deeper knowledge of the practices in Shanghai, and the gain again supported Goodlad's (1988) view regarding accessing schools with good practices during the process of the partnership.

Exchange Visit

Three members of staff from the Shanghai School for the Blind came to Hong Kong in April 2001 and visited the HKIEd. This was a good opportunity for the teachers to learn about the education system and teacher education in Hong Kong. The team regarded this visit by the Shanghai School for the Blind's teachers as a strategy for strengthening or fortifying the partnership between both parties. Such visits are essential for the enhancement of a partnership. A full understanding of each other's culture and practices did help to build a trusting relationship (Oettinger, 1998; Wood, 1996).

Shared Responsibility of the Partners

During the process of establishing the partnership, the experiences gained supported the ideas discussed in previous sections, particularly those concerning the growth of both partners. The approach in establishing both the partnership and mutual trust was explicit. It started with an initial short-term collaboration and some irregular follow-up contacts, followed by a self-initiated collaboration, which further built up friendship and trust between the two parties. It continued to develop into a more stable relationship with regular contacts.

Table 1 *The Different Roles in the Partnership Between the Shanghai School for the Blind and The Hong Kong Institute of Education*

Role of the Shanghai School for the Blind	Role of The Hong Kong Institute of Education
• Administrative support for staff development program	• Professional support for staff development program
• Provision of venue and technical equipment for staff development program	• Planning, organization and implementation of staff development program
• Coordination with local authority and related education organization in Shanghai	• Seeking financial support for the trip to and from Shanghai
• Communication and correspondence with teachers in Shanghai	• Evaluation of staff development program
• Transportation support for HKIEd staff in Shanghai	• Conducting review research
• Translation support for HKIEd staff at staff development program	• Writing paper on the project
• Arrangement of accommodation for HKIEd staff in Shanghai	• Sharing partnership experiences at seminars and conferences

In drawing conclusions on the results achieved during the process of the partnership, the team felt that the importance of shared responsibility by the partners was paramount. Although both members of the partnership shared the common goal of building up links with the professionals and local teachers in the two cities, the partners took on different roles in view of the nature of the work and the limitations of resources. These roles corresponded mainly with the nature of the activities conducted and the professionalism of the partners. It was in line with the thought of Osguthorpe et al. (1995) that the "university" would be more concerned with promoting more effective preparation of pre-service teachers, and the "school" with renewing conditions and curricula in the public schools, and that both parties could work together to achieve the same target. In the process of "give and take," it was anticipated that the roles would change when the activities differed and when the partnership became mature. However, the clear division of labor not only minimized misunderstandings during the process but also maximized the involvement and contribution of the partners.

Elements Contributing to a Successful Partnership

During the course of the project, a number of elements that played a major role in the successful development of the partnership were identified. Some of these elements were similar to those suggested by educators discussed in the previous sections (e.g., Oettinger, 1998; Watson & Fullan, 1992; Wood, 1996):

1. Need-based request — The request of the Shanghai School for the Blind for assistance with the development of staff working with students with poor vision was a need-based request.

2. Initiative in actively seeking advancement in quality — Both partners were very concerned with the promotion of effective learning for students with poor vision and their teachers.

3. Opportunity for professional and academic exchange — Activities organized by both parties provided plenty of opportunities for professional and academic exchange among the members of staff of the two partners. These opportunities were regarded by the staff as valuable and useful.

4. Administrative and financial support from both organizations — Without the grant for research by the HKIEd and the administrative support from the Shanghai School for the Blind, most of the project activities could not have been conducted successfully.

5. Research-based project — The staff of the HKIEd took on the task of conducting an evaluation and review of the project, and this greatly facilitated further planning for collaboration.

6. Matching professional expertise and concerns — Both partners had the same professional expertise and concerns for students with visual impairment and their teachers.

Conclusion

The partnership trial was a worthwhile experience for both parties, particularly for the team members of the HKIEd. The notion of partnership was of significance for professional development (Anderson & Cheung, 1999; Fullan, Erskine-Cullen, & Watson, 1995; Osguthorpe et al., 1995). Effective partnership was supported in terms of clear mission, mutual contribution and trust. However, difficulties were also encountered. First, the language barrier was one of the major difficulties for the team members, who might have difficulties in communicating with teachers in Mainland China. Secondly, both parties had little knowledge of the education system of their partners. This caused unnecessary problems in planning the staff development program, especially in using the right terminology and giving appropriate examples and illustrations. Thirdly, the lack of adequate financial support was fatal to further collaboration. Finally, the geographical distance between Hong Kong and Shanghai (a 3-hour flight) hindered frequent contact between the two parties.

Although there were difficulties and uncertainties, the team treasured the opportunity and understood the contextual limitations, particularly the five "truths" for effective collaboration identified by Watson and Fullan (1992):

1. Schools/school systems and universities need each other in order to be successful.
2. They are dissimilar in key aspects of structure, culture and reward systems.
3. Working together may potentially provide the coherence, coordination, and persistence essential to teacher and school development.
4. Both parties must work hard together, by, for example, forging new structures, respecting each other's culture, using shared experiences to solve problems, and solving problems by incorporating the strengths of each culture.
5. Strong partnerships will not happen by accident, nor simply by good will or by establishing *ad hoc* projects. They require structures, new activities and a rethinking of the internal workings of each institution, as well as of their inter-institutional workings.

The team is looking forward to establishing a more permanent relationship with the Shanghai School for the Blind, as well as a closer link with the education organizations in Shanghai. Indeed, the team reflected the views of school-institute partnership (Anderson & Cheung, 1999; Fullan, Erskine-Cullen, & Watson, 1995; Goodlad, 1985; Osguthorpe et al., 1995; Wood, 1996) and learnt the strategies for the long-term success of a partnership (Wood, 1996). It is hoped that more regular activities could be conducted during the process of partnership development, which is essential for a successful partnership. It is also appropriate to review the process of the partnership, in order to determine the following: whether there is a structure for the partnership that is favorable to both partners; whether the mission needs to be changed; in which areas and in what ways both partners could give more; and whether more collaborative opportunities could be arranged to foster trust between the two partners. As a matter of fact, with a clear mission and mutual trust, the two partners successfully co-organized an international conference on the education of the visually impaired in Shanghai in July 2001.

References

Anderson, R., & Cheung, F. W. M. (1999, February). *Enhancing institute-school partnership: Lecturer-school attachment in Hong Kong.* Paper presented at the International Conference on Teacher Education at The Hong Kong Institute of Education, Hong Kong.

Clark, R. W. (1988). School-university: An interpretive review. In K. A. Sirotnik & J. I. Goodlad (Eds.), *School-university partnerships in action: Concepts, cases, and concerns* (pp. 32–65). New York: Teachers College Press.

Fullan, M., Erskine-Cullen, E., & Watson, N. (1995). The learning consortium: A school-university partnership program. An introduction. *School Effectiveness and School Improvement, 6*(3), 187–191.

Goodlad, J. I. (1985). *Reconstructing schooling and the education of educators: The partnership concept.* Unpublished manuscript, University of Washington.

Goodlad, J. I. (1988). School-university partnerships for educational renewal: Rationale and concepts. In K. A. Sirotnik & J. I. Goodlad (Eds.), *School-university partnerships in action: Concepts, cases, and concerns* (pp. 3–31). New York: Teachers College, Columbia University.

Osguthorpe, R. T., Harris, R. C., Black, S., Cutler, B. R., & Harris, M. F. (1995). Introduction: Understanding school-university partnerships. In R. T. Osguthorpe, R. C. Harris, M. F. Harris, & S. Black (Eds.), *Partner schools: Centers for educational renewal* (pp. 1–22). San Francisco: Jossey-Bass.

Oettinger, L. M. (1998). *A case study of an emerging school-university partnership.* Unpublished doctoral dissertation, Ohio University.

Sin, K. F. (1999). How can we make full use of the multisensory room? *Hong Kong Special Education Forum, 2*(2), 45–55.

Sin, K. F., & Tso, A. (1999). *Snoezelen: Utilization of the multisensory room.* Hong Kong: Caritas Jockey Club Lok Yan School.

Stallings, J., & Kowalski, T. (1990). Research on professional development schools. In W. R. Houston (Ed.), *Handbook of research on teacher education* (pp. 251–263). New York: Macmillan.

Watson, N., & Fullan, M. (1992). Beyond school district-university partnerships. In

M. Fullan & A. Hargreaves (Eds.), *Teacher development and educational change* (pp. 213–242). London; New York: Falmer Press.

Woloszyk, C. A., & Davis, S. (1993, February). *Restructuring a teacher preparation program using the professional development school concept.* Paper presented at the Annual Meeting of the Association of Teacher Educators, Los Angeles, CA.

Wood, D. B. (1996). *School-university partnerships: An exploration of the relationship.* Unpublished doctoral dissertation, The College of William and Mary, Williamsburg, Washington, DC.

12

Between "Uniprofessionalism" and "Multiprofessioanlism": Where Is the School?

Gunnar Berg

Abstract

The multiprofessional perspective focuses on school as a compendium of all the personnel groups active within that organization. These groups are analyzed individually from the perspective of their specialist as well as generalist roles. To explicate further, the teaching profession can be viewed from a uniprofessional and a multiprofessional perspective. The former focuses on the specialist function of teachers as it deals with the way teachers traditionally practice their occupation, which is based on good knowledge of subject, and method. The multiprofessional teacher role combines this specialist role with a generalist role, which presupposes that teachers also have good knowledge of and insight into the school's basic mission and how this mission can/should be achieved in cooperation with teacher colleagues as well as other school personnel.

A similar discussion can be applied to all occupational groups active within the school (school leaders, service personnel, recreational personnel, pre-school teachers, student care personnel, etc.). All of these groups can be analyzed individually in their specialist and generalist roles, respectively. Multiprofessional analysis of this type allows comparative studies with regard to if — and in that case how — the respective professions relate to the collective mission that is achieved or should be achieved by the school organization in which these groups are active.

The range between uniprofessionalism and multiprofessionalism makes up an abstract scale that is meant to serve as an (in a Weberian sense) ideal type for studies of school organizations from the perspective of the personnel.

Background and Purpose

As of 1976, the author has been — and still is — engaged in educational research projects within the following main areas:

1. The relation between education and organization theory;
2. The school as an institution, as an organization and as a work organization;
3. Teachers in the perspective of profession;
4. Strategies for development and change; and
5. Educational reforms and the implementation of reforms.

Earlier, this research (for a composite description of the research, see Berg, 1993) concentrated on the primary school, but in later years it also has focused on the high school, local adult education, personnel training companies, and folk high school education. This research has concentrated on the content and forms of steering *of* and *in* the school (Berg, 1999), and if — and in that case how — this steering has consequences for the school's organization and its actors. This research has also had an important influence on the project "Steering, Leadership and the activities of the School" (the so-called "SLAV 2-project"). This project is now completed and described in a final report (Berg, Groth, Nytell, & Söderberg, 1999).

The SLAV 2-project led to conclusions about the existing professional relations between teachers and school leaders. This paves the way for studies of other school personnel from the perspective of professionalism, and how the personnel (including teachers and school leaders) relate to one another. Research of this type sets the school, as a more or less markedly multiprofessional organization, in the center. A research direction of this type marks a desire to continue the development of the school organizational research that was started approximately 20 years ago. The following text therefore has a somewhat programmatic character, as it aims to formulate some of the points of departure for a similar, future research direction.

The Various Meanings of the Concept "Profession"

Traditionally the concept "profession" has been associated with a freer way of practicing an occupation. Take the lawyer as an example, a lawyer enthusiastically representing his/her client in legal disputes without interference from the state or a higher authority is a symbol of professional practicing. In everyday language, to practice an occupation professionally is often seen as the opposite of amateur practice. Just as in the world of sports, the "pro" carries out his/her occupation with skill and competence, while the quality of the amateur's — in an extreme case the dilettante's — occupational practice is more variable. In a societal perspective, professions can be regarded as providing key qualifications for modern societies. With the development of industrialism, professions began to take over certain key-functions in society, which earlier, in the pre-industrial farming society, had been held by the guilds.

Research on Professions

Roughly speaking, the research on professions can be divided into two main categories, namely the quantitative and the qualitative approaches. The former presupposes that all occupations have more or less a professional character, while the latter rests on the assumption that certain occupations are professions while others are not. The concept "profession" can be further used partly to study the conditions for the occupation itself, and partly to illuminate the occupational functions within the organization they belong to. Studies of professions that focus primarily on the occupations themselves are regarded here as having a "uniprofessional" approach, whereas research on the relations between the occupational groups and the organization they are part of is viewed as having a "multiprofessional" approach. By combining the above-mentioned approaches in studies on professions, Table 1 can be constructed.

Table 1 *Four Types of Professional, Occupational Practice*

	Occupational groups outside their organizational context	Occupational groups within their organizational context
Qualitative approach/ Quantitative approach	Uniprofessionalism	Multiprofessionalism

An example of a uniprofessional/qualitative approach can be seen in the following definition: "Professions are those occupational groups which are permitted to institutionalize a monopoly of knowledge and occupational skills" (Hellberg, 1978, p. 27). The approach behind this definition is qualitative in the sense that it rests on the assumption that certain occupations are professions while others are not, and it is uniprofessional in the sense that the occupational group or groups as such is in focus.

A uniprofessional/quantitative approach is expressed in the following definition of a profession: "... an occupation whose members (a) possess a high degree of special theoretical knowledge, plus certain methods and techniques with which to apply this knowledge in the daily work life, (b) are expected to carry out their work duties with consideration for a certain ethical code, and (c) are united by a corps spirit which stems from one and the same education and one and the same adherence to certain doctrines and methods" (Abrahamsson, 1971, pp. 11–12). This definition is uniprofessional/quantitative in the sense that it maintains that, in principle, all existing occupational groups can be studied in relation to certain criteria, and that conclusions about the type and degree of professionalism are relative, not absolute.

The reports on teachers and school leaders as more or less professional practitioners of their occupation (Berg, 1983, 1990), which our research resulted in, rest basically on a multiprofessional/quantitative approach. In accordance with Table 1, this implies that school leaders and teachers have been studied on the premise that they are active participants in the organization (and the institution) of the school. That the approach itself is multiprofessional does *not*, however, mean that the school by definition should be regarded as a multiprofessional organization. It simply implies that the method used to carry out a study of professions allows the specific school organization to be located on a scale ranging between the two extremes of uniprofessionalism and multiprofessionalism. In order to do this, clear research criteria have been formulated to characterize the uniprofessional and the multiprofessional school organization, respectively. These criteria — which have the character of ideal types in a Weberian sense (Weber, 1947) — will be discussed in the following sections.

The School's Occupational Groups in the Uniprofessional Organization

Our research on teachers and school leaders as more or less professional actors within the school as an organization has been based on the following variables of profession:

1. Autonomy,
2. Esprit de corps, and
3. Knowledge base.

Simply put, autonomy concerns the type and amount of scope for individual and independent actions, which the professional worker enjoys within the organization. The corps spirit concerns possible, existing, informal systems of rules, and the knowledge base deals with the specific level of competence that is linked to the profession in question. A uniprofessional school organization is described in Table 2.

Table 2 shows a traditional occupational relation between the teaching profession and the school leader profession, which in our research reports (Berg, 1996) is expressed by the concept "the invisible contract." This implies a clear division of labor between school leaders and teachers. The main responsibilities of the school leaders are limited here to managing the school's administrative apparatus (distribution of work duties, formation of schedules, etc.) for teachers to conduct the traditional, solitary type of instruction. In other words, teachers are responsible for the activity in the classroom and school leaders for the activity that takes place outside the

Table 2   *The School as a Uniprofessional Organization*

	Teachers	School leaders	Student care and student health personnel	Pre-school teachers, service personnel, recreational personnel, etc.
Autonomy	Classroom	Work organization	?	?
Corps spirit	Solitary	Administrative "back-up"	?	?
Knowledge base	Specialist knowledge	Autodidact	?	?

classroom, and the two parties to a limited extent intermingle in each other's areas of activity. The teachers' knowledge base for dealing with a work situation of this type primarily concerns specialist knowledge of subject content and method, and so forth. The traditional school leader is an "autodidact" in the sense that he/she as a rule does not have — at least not when beginning the occupation — a special education to function as a school leader. The "invisible contract" is strengthened by the fact that most school leaders have their occupational origins in the teaching profession.

If an empirical study had revealed that the work relation between teachers and school leaders is just as strictly divided as the contents of Table 2 implies, then the conclusion would have demonstrated a high degree of uniprofessionalism. Table 2 also shows that it is not enough to draw such a conclusion solely on the basis of ("biprofessional") studies of teachers and school leaders. Other occupational groups within the school should be analyzed in the perspective of profession. The results from studies of occupational groups such as student care and student health personnel, pre-school teachers, recreational personnel, service personnel, and so forth, will ideally create a base for evaluating the type of autonomy, corps spirit, and knowledge base in these groups. In turn, this allows comparative analyses among all the occupational groups within the school for the purpose of checking whether other "invisible contracts" exist — and in that case between which of the occupational groups. Also, it can be seen whether the occupational relations are characterized by at least some degree of multiprofessionalism in accordance with the criteria discussed below.

The School's Occupational Groups in a Multiprofessional Perspective

The above discussion of the school as a uniprofessional organization lies at one extreme on an abstract scale of the type and degree of professionalism among the different occupational groups in the school. One can also say that our studies can lead to the conclusion that there exists a strict *division of labor* ("invisible contracts") among all occupational groups in the school. This represents the extreme uniprofessional organization. The opposite is when there exists a thorough *integration of labor* among these occupational groups. In this case, the relations between these occupational groups are characterized by a lack of invisible contracts

Table 3 *The School as a Multiprofessional Organization*

	Teachers	School leaders	Student care personnel	Student health personnel, etc.
Autonomy	WITHIN THE FRAME OF THE EXISTING SCOPE OF ACTION			
Corps spirit	Teaching ↓ Overall school activities	Overall school activities ↓ Teaching	Student care ↓ Overall school activities	Student health care ↓ Overall school activites
Knowledge base	COLLECTIVE KNOWLEDGE OF THE SURROUNDING WORLD COUPLED WITH A SPECIALIST KNOWLEDGE SPECIFIC TO THE OCCUPATIONAL GROUP			

representing the other extreme on our hypothetical scale, that is, the multiprofessional organization in its "purest" form.

As a contrast to Table 2, this type of organization can be illustrated in Table 3.

Table 3 illustrates that, in the ideal multiprofessional organization all groups of personnel have the same attitude toward the school's basic *mission*, and they must fulfill *tasks* that are considered to be in line with this mission. Because the school leadership has the overall responsibility for activity, it also has the main responsibility to ensure that the mission is converted into operational tasks. This does not necessarily mean that the school leaders personally have to put this process into effect. It simply implies that they must lead the way to activate the personnel groups in this "transformation process." The multiprofessional organization requires the respective professions to maintain and develop their specialist knowledge. This implies that the teacher remains a good specialist in the subject and strives to develop this competence, but also that he/she has the ability to view the subject from the perspective of the school's mission. The school psychologist, the pre-school teacher, and the caretaker all have their respective specialist knowledge, but the practicing of these specialist roles is related to insights into the school's basic mission. This demands a broader base of knowledge for all the occupational groups in the school; in addition to good specialist knowledge, school personnel must possess knowledge directly related to the school's mission. In Table 3 this knowledge base is expressed by the concept "knowledge of the surrounding world."

Empirical Studies of Professions

The above discussion can be summarized in Table 4. Table 4 illustrates an ideal type (a "measure") by means of which the different results of school-organizational studies of professions can be contrasted. The procedure for such studies is that the various occupational groups in the school (see Tables 2 and 3) are studied individually with regard to the respective groups' autonomy, corps spirit, and knowledge base. The results of these studies are compiled, and thereafter comparisons are made between the groups with respect to the above-mentioned profession-variables (autonomy, etc.). These comparisons lead to conclusions about the type and degree of multiprofessionalism within the school organization under study.

Methodologically, profession-studies of this type can be carried out as interviews with selected representatives of the respective professions. Ideally the interviews can start out from "basic questions" of the following type: "Give a general picture of your work-life today and in the past. Has the occupation changed over time and, in that case, how and why? Will the occupation change in the future and, in that case, how and why? What are your views and attitudes toward the nature of the presumed change?"

Table 4   *The Range Between the Uniprofessional and the Multiprofessional Organization*

	Uniprofessionalism ◄──────────► Multiprofessionalism	
	Labor-divided professionalism	Labor-integrated professionalism
Autonomy	On the terms of the occupational functions	On the terms of the occupation and organization's mission
Corps spirit	Loyalty to those in the same occupation	Loyalty to those in the same occupation as well as to the organization's mission
Knowledge base	Specialist knowledge	Specialist knowledge and knowledge of the surrounding world

Scope of Action and Multiprofessional Development Work

Using the so-called scope of action model as a starting-point, the above discussion can be illustrated in Figure 1.

In the models in Figure 1, the outer, dashed lines symbolize the limits of the school's (multifaceted) mission, which is synonymous with the activity sanctioned by the state. The dotted lines within the outer limits illustrate the operational tasks that are fulfilled *de facto* by a specific school organization. On the left-hand side of Figure 1, the professions within the school relate in different ways to the mission as well as to the operational tasks. This is an expression of a high degree of uniprofessionalism; that is, in practice the professions act according to their own terms. On the right-hand side of Figure 1, the professions are gathered inside the frame of a task-structure shared by all, and further, the tasks are more in line with the overall mission (that is, the available scope of action is exploited to a greater degree) (for details, see Wallin & Berg, 1983). In this case we have a high degree of multiprofessionalism.

With this reasoning, the development work in multiprofessional organizations can be described as activity which:

Figure 1   *The school's Mission, Tasks, and the Practicing of Professions*

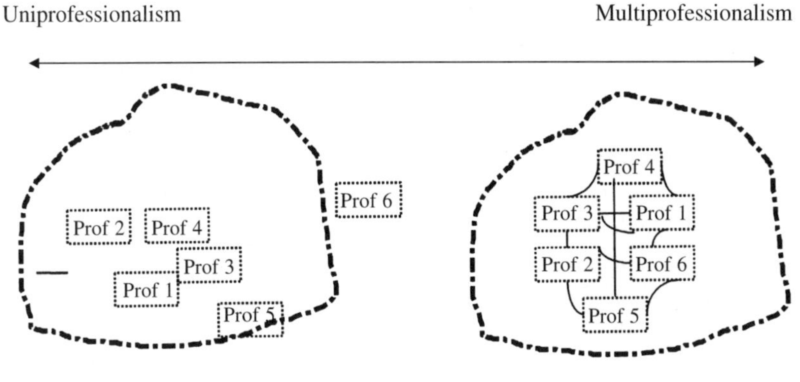

Uniprofessionalism   Multiprofessionalism

Source: Wallin & Berg (1983).

1. Links together the relevant professions without threatening the solidarity within the respective occupational groups;
2. On an operational level, accomplishes tasks that lie within the frame of the organization's mission;
3. Aims for greater exploitation of the available scope of action; and
4. Encompasses critical reflections on the content and implications of the mission/tasks.

The view of development work can be linked directly to the scope of action models in Figure 1. It implies that the common denominator among the professions in the organization is that they are united by one collective mission (or several missions) operationalized in a number of collective tasks. Development work entails the linking of operational tasks to the mission, to the greatest possible extent through making use of the available scope of action. In turn, this provides more opportunities for the professions to examine, critically, the basic implications of the mission and its content (i.e., the outer limits). Such critical examination can pave the way for dialogue between the task-assignors (in the school's case, the state and community) and the task-receivers (the relevant professions). This does not rule out opportunities for the respective professions to develop on their own terms as well; teachers develop their knowledge of subjects, school leaders their administrative skills, and so forth. On the contrary, the so-called labor-divided professionalism mentioned above is almost a prerequisite for a broadening of the labor-integrated, professional, occupational role.

The Complex Occupational Roles in the Multiprofessional Organization

Strictly speaking, the uniprofessional occupational role implies that loyalty is directed inward toward one's own profession and its internal system of norms (corps spirit). Basically this is a matter of a marked *specialist* function in which the professional practices his/her occupation in the range between the "content" of the knowledge base, which forms the basis of specialist competence, and the "work forms" which emanate from this competence. In the multiprofessional organization, this occupational role is broadened to become a combined specialist and *generalist* function. As discussed earlier, an occupational function of this type will also encompass aspects of the content and form of the collective mission, which must be fulfilled by the relevant organization.

In their work the multiprofessional individual must in essence relate to a base of knowledge shared by all the professions within the organization, and to the forms of work that arise from this base and are also shared by all. This knowledge base can be described concretely as adequate knowledge of the surrounding world with regard to missions and tasks, and the work forms are the way in which the different professions carry out their tasks in their daily work. However, the multiprofessional worker is also compelled to "keep an eye" on the content of his/her specialist role and the forms for practicing it, in parallel with the above-mentioned multiprofessional matters. This means that the multiprofessional individual in his/her daily work must be able to relate to the different combinations of the "specialist and the generalist" dimension, respectively. As a concrete example of this the teaching profession can be considered in this multiprofessional perspective. A teacher's specialist knowledge can be a question of having good knowledge of a subject within, for example, the field of social studies. This teacher has additional (methodological) knowledge as to how instruction in the subject should be given to enable students to learn as much as possible. The teacher also has knowledge of and insights into the school's basic mission ("equal opportunity/a school for everyone"), and how he/she, in cooperation with fellow teachers as well as other school personnel, can carry out operational tasks that correspond to the mission's content and implications. In accordance with what is said above the professional dilemmas that this teacher must therefore confront can be of the following type:

1. How can the content of the subject of social studies be related to the school's mission of equal opportunity?
2. How can the work that is carried out collectively by the school personnel within the frame of, for example, the work units be linked to the content of the subject of social studies?
3. Are the work methods/work forms I apply in my instruction consistent with the school's mission of equal opportunity?
4. How can the work methods and work forms which I and my colleagues apply in, for example, work units and personnel conferences be linked to the methods of instruction I practice?

Discussion

The multiprofessional perspective discussed in this chapter is naturally associated with the school as an institution and as an organization (for details, see Berg, 1992). However, it is also applicable to other institutions and organizations, which encompass a multitude of professions. One example is the health care organization, which includes a great number of specialist functions (doctors, nurses, psychologists, physiotherapists, occupational therapists, administrators on various levels, etc.). For these specialist professions, to tackle the question of a collective, multiprofessional attitude, which is linked to the overall mission ("good care"), is at least as important as within the school. A multiprofessional approach might even be used as a constructive method — and possibly an alternative method to the different existing economic strategies — in relation to quality and quality assurance in public organizations. It should be noted that the multiprofessional approach has the limitation that, when questions about quality and quality assurance arise, the organization is viewed primarily from the perspective of the personnel, not the "users" or clients. Nevertheless, from the perspective of democracy the professions' striving toward "professionalization," toward strengthening their positions of social power, can be problematic. Advancing the power of individual professions can, in some cases, be viewed as corporative striving with anti-democratic overtones.

As noted earlier, the multiprofessional perspective presented here does not only imply that the profession regards the practicing of its occupation on its own terms. The occupation is also seen in relation to the mission and the operational tasks deriving from the mission. The profession shares these with other professions active within the relevant organization. It is therefore not consistent with the profession's corps spirit to regard the occupation only on its own internal terms, but rather, the occupation must be practiced and coordinated with the practice of other professions.

This implies multiprofessional functions between the profession as such, and the surrounding organizational and institutional world in which the profession's activity is concentrated. This occupational ethic does not encourage the development of an occupation solely on its own terms. Ultimately, the multiprofessional perspective presented here is therefore inconsistent with anti-democratic strivings in a corporative direction.

References

Abrahamsson, B. (1971). *Military professionalization and political power.* Stockholm: Allmänna förlaget.

Berg, G. (1983). Developing the teaching profession: Autonomy, professional code, knowledge base. *Australian Journal of Education, 27*(2), pp. 173–186.

Berg, G. (1990). *Skolledning och professionellt skolledarskap [School leading and professional leadership]* (Pedagogisk forskning i Uppsala nr 92). Uppsala: Pedagogiska institutionen, Uppsala universitet.

Berg, G. (1992). Changes in the steering of Swedish schools: A step towards "societification of the state." *Journal of Curriculum Studies, 24*(4), 327–344.

Berg, G. (1996). Steering, school leadership and the invisible contract. In J. Kalous & F. van Wieringen (Eds.), *Improving educational management* (pp. 39–54). De Lier, the Netherlands: Academic Book Center.

Berg, G. (1999). Steering in and steering of the school. In C. Day, A. Fernandez, T. E. Hauge, & J. Moller (Eds.), *The life and work of teachers: International perspectives in changing times* (pp. 195–209). London; New York: Falmer Press.

Berg, G., Groth, E., Nytell, U., & Söderberg, H. (1999). *Skolan i ett institutionsperspektiv [The school in an institutional perspective].* Lund: Studentlitteratur.

Hellberg, I. (1978). *Studier i professionell organization [Studies in professional organization]* (Monografi nr 20). Göteborgs: Sociologiska institutionen, Göteborgs universitet.

Wallin, E., & Berg, G. (1983). Research into the school as an organization. III: Organizational development in schools or developing the school as an organization? *Scandinavian Journal of Educational Research, 27*(1), pp. 35–47.

Weber, M. (1947). *The theory of social and economic organization.* New York: The Free Press.

13

The Learning Capacity of Primary Schools in Hong Kong

Nicholas Sun-Keung Pang and Mary Cheung

Abstract

Never before in history have Hong Kong schools been confronted with so many rapid changes. The recent far-reaching educational reforms have precipitated many schools and their staff into a crisis situation. These reforms have urged schools to re-engineer their infrastructures in order to become learning organizations. In view of the possible impacts of the school as a learning community on the life-long learning of teachers, developing a set of performance indicators to evaluate schools' learning capacity is meaningful and an absolute must. A 78-item questionnaire was developed based on Peter Senge's five disciplines of a learning organization, namely Personal Mastery (PM), Mental Models (MM), Shared Vision (SV), Team Learning (TL), and Systems Thinking (ST). Schools' learning capacity was assessed accordingly at both teacher and organizational levels. The five scales developed were statistically reliable, with most of them having reliability coefficients above .7. The evidence shows that the 25 schools which participated in the study placed a different emphasis on each of the five disciplines, with Personal Mastery being accorded the most emphasis and Mental Models the least. It also indicates that whole-day primary schools have a higher learning capacity than bi-sessional schools. The study contributes theoretically to school improvement by providing an instrument with which to assess a school's learning capacity, and also by providing a theoretical framework that sheds light on practical steps schools may take towards becoming learning organizations.

Introduction

Successful people have the ability to, and are prepared to change and adapt. Successful people are people who learn. Organizations are no different, successful organizations are learning organizations (Lassey, 1998, p. 1).

The 21st century is an era of unpredictability, where change is the only constant, and uncertainty is the norm. Surrounded as they are by such a vast number of technological, economic and social changes, occurring at ever-increasing speeds, it is no longer enough for organizations simply to react to them. Change is a mixture of growth, opportunity, innovation, threat, disorientation, and upheaval, and whether an individual is able to appreciate it or not depends very much on that individual's attitude in perceiving it. As far as an organization is concerned, its ability to deal with change lies entirely in how it equips itself to help its members prepare themselves for change. This means that the organization must possess the capability to undertake an on-going process of change. This capability is not intrinsically possessed, it must be learned, not only by individuals, but also, most importantly, by the group, by the whole organization.

This is a pilot study, based on Peter Senge's five disciplines, carried out in the context of Hong Kong primary schools. The five disciplines of organizational learning were initially conceptualized by Senge (1990) for business organizations. Foreign empirical studies based directly on Senge's five disciplines model of a learning organization are in fact far too limited. Locally, as far as we are aware, no similar studies have been conducted, either on a school's learning capacity or on the school as a learning community. It is hoped that this research will provide certain insights for those schools that aim to provide good quality education by creating ongoing collective learning opportunities.

Education Reform in Hong Kong

Hong Kong is not exceptional; like many societies, it is undertaking a major restructuring of its school systems (Education Commission, 1999, 2000). Ever since the report *A Perspective on Education in Hong Kong, 1982,* proposed by an international panel of experts, which gives a very detailed systematic analysis of the strengths and defects of the Hong Kong education system, educational reforms in Hong Kong have risen to prominence. The Education Department has taken an active role in its follow-up work. With the publication of the seven successive *Education Commission Reports* (Education Commission, 1984, 1986, 1988, 1990, 1992, 1996, 1997), *The School Management Initiative* (Education and Manpower Branch & Education Department, 1991) and *Information Technology for Learning in a New Era* (Education and Manpower Bureau, 1998), the city has experienced a pervasive and influential transformation of its education system.

The school reform movement began by remedying the inadequacies of teacher training (Education Commission, 1984). Then came the School Management Initiative, that required schools to enhance their practice of delegation, empowerment, teacher autonomy, accountability, and parental involvement (Education and Manpower Branch & Education Department, 1991). The upgrading of 35% of primary school teachers to the level of bachelor or higher degree immediately followed the initiative (Education Commission, 1992). Five years later, the achievement of high quality education through schools performing self-evaluations and quality assurance inspections was highlighted (Education Commission, 1997).

In the face of the global challenges of an unprecedentedly vast flow of information, and of high technology, schools are urged to promote information technology throughout all aspects of learning and teaching, so that our young people will be well-prepared to meet these challenges (Education and Manpower Bureau, 1998). Recently, the reforms have finally touched the essence of education — the development of a school-based curriculum that emphasizes helping students to develop a global outlook and equipping them with a repertoire of skills and the positive attitudes required in order to respect knowledge and to learn how to learn (Curriculum Development Council, 2000, p. 1). It is believed that with these aims, school education can enable our young people to enjoy learning, enhance their effectiveness in communication, and develop their creativity and sense of commitment.

Paradigm Shifts in Managerial and Teaching Practice

Senge (1990, p. 4) advised government and educational leaders that the new challenges of the Information Age demand that businesses, the teaching profession and the government radically transform themselves. In a learning community, everybody can be a leader. The role of leader moves from being one of monitoring and supervising staff to one of coaching and developing staff (Lassey, 1998). It is essential that school leaders be committed to these changes in their role. They have to be supported and equipped so that they are able to make the changes happen. However, this does not mean that school leaders have to possess exceptional accuracy in terms of predicting future consequences based on current trends. It means, rather, that in developing visions for schools, that will be capable of responding effectively to the challenges of change, concepts such as decentralization, teamwork, accountability, innovation, and quality assurance should be accorded a very high value in practice. In order to put these concepts into practice successfully, principals and personnel at managerial levels need to change their management practices. The type of leadership that emerges in these settings is similar to Sergiovanni's (1987) concept of "cultural leadership." School leaders have to support an organizational culture that facilitates both the formal and informal learning processes, which are intrinsic to a learning organization (Marsick, 1987; Marsick & Watkins, 1996).

With regard to teachers, they also have to think about their work very differently from traditions (Louis & Kruse, 1998). They need to perceive themselves as peers as well as teachers of children, so that collaborative work, discussions, and group decisions will become part of their normal practice. Students' learning and the development of the school-based curriculum will be at the center of their dialogues. As a result, the teachers' sense of collective responsibility will subsequently be increased.

Research Framework

Peter Senge's Five Disciplines

In his book *The Fifth Discipline*, Senge (1990) defined a learning organization as one that possesses five core-learning disciplines, namely Personal Mastery, Mental Models, Shared Vision, Team Learning, and Systems Thinking. The combination of these five disciplines forms a life-long program of practice for individuals, groups, and organizations as well, if their aim is to enhance their learning capacity. He pinpointed the idea that an ideal learning organization is one that involves its members in continually expanding their capacity to create the results they truly desire. The organization should nurture expansive patterns of thinking so that collective aspirations are set free and so that its members are continually learning how to learn together (Senge, 1990). The meanings of the five disciplines of a learning organization are given as follows (Senge, Ross, Smith, Roberts, & Kleiner, 1994, p. 6):

1. *Personal Mastery* is the capacity to learn to expand our personal capacity to create the results we most desire, and to create an organizational environment that encourages all members to develop themselves toward the goals and purposes they choose.
2. *Mental Models* is the capacity to reflect upon, continually clarify and improve our internal pictures of the world, and see how they shape our actions and decisions.
3. *Shared Vision* is the capacity to build a sense of commitment in a group, by developing shared images of the future we seek to create, and the principles and guiding practices by which we hope to get there.
4. *Team Learning* is the capacity to transform conversational and collective thinking skills, so that groups of people can reliably develop intelligence and ability greater than the sum of individual members' talents.

Figure 1   *Peter Senge's Five Disciplines of a Learning Organization*

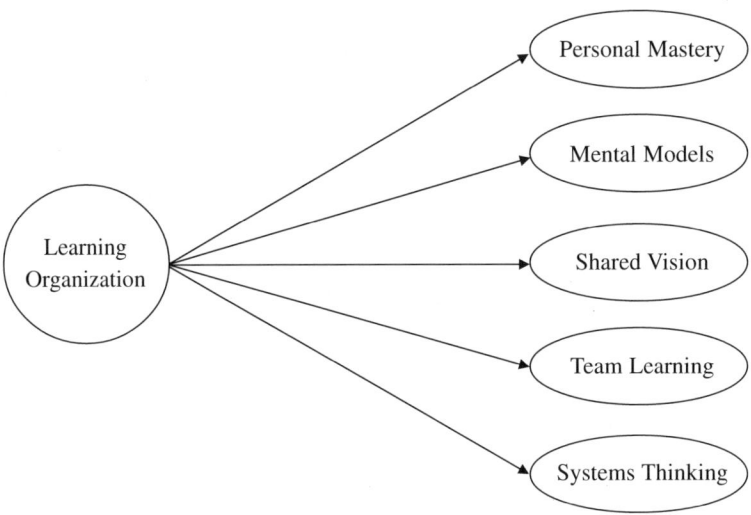

5. *Systems Thinking* is the capacity to foster a way of thinking about, and a language for describing and understanding, the forces and interrelationships that shape the behavior of systems. This discipline helps us to see how to change systems more effectively, and to act more in tune with the larger processes of the natural and economic world.

Getzels–Guba's Model of Social Behavior

Getzels–Guba's model, the dimensions of social behavior, helps to explain the phenomenon of the acquisition of knowledge necessary for one's survival inside a social system such as a school (Getzels & Guba, 1957). Getzels–Guba's model claimed that the institutional role (the nomothetic dimension) and the individual's personality (the idiographic dimension) determined the organizational behavior. In school, people take on certain

Figure 2   *The Getzels–Guba's Model of Social Behavior*

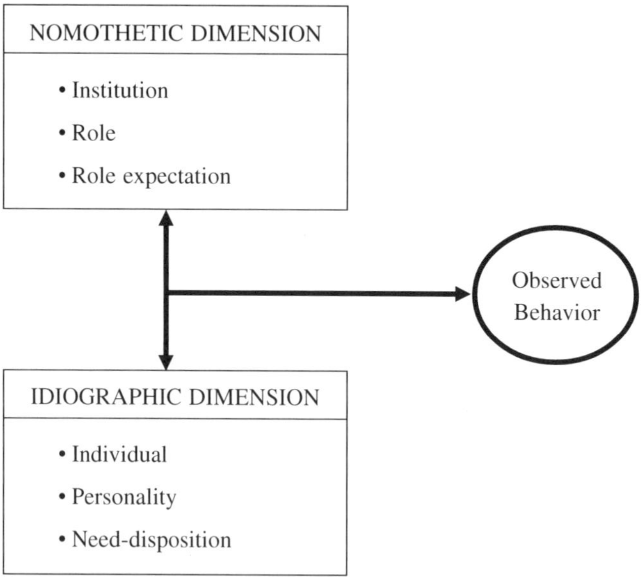

Source: Adapted from Getzels & Guba (1957), p. 429.

roles and expectations that will help to achieve the goals of the system. Simultaneously, the particular personalities and dispositions of individuals also affect the system. That is to say, when people embed in a social system, on the one hand, they are independent individuals; but on the other hand, they are actually interdependent on one another and on the environment around them. The interactions between them combine to determine social behavior. In fact, "changes" in a way may be identified as the nomothetic elements of organizational expectations of reaching the organizational goals, whereas "learning" may be seen as the idiographic elements of an individual's motives to achieve both personal and organizational goals.

Efficient leadership is the result of the interaction of role and personality in the context of value (Getzels & Guba, 1957). Tension will inevitably exist between personal and collective interests within any organization. It is the school administrators' responsibility to structure arrangements at group/school levels parallel with the individual level, so that not only are organizational expectations and individual needs maintained, but also the divergent interests of participants to achieve desired school goals are reconciled. Nonetheless, the concepts of learning as a social activity and knowledge as social property should always be central to the two-level arrangement.

Pang's Framework for the Operationalization of a Learning Organization

Even if the majority of employees in a school are knowledgeable and competent academically, this is not sufficient to guarantee that the school will be a learning community. Swieringa and Wierdsma (1992) declared that only when the change in the behavior of one individual had an effect on the behavior of others could the organization be defined as a learning organization. By the same token, individual teachers' learning should never be misinterpreted as the school's having developed into a learning community. It is the continuous growth of the group that is the essential requirement of a learning organization. Since individuals and groups/ schools learn differently, it is necessary for schools to nurture an environment that facilitates the maximal diversified learning of the learners at the different levels. Figure 3 shows how a learning organization actually works from a systematic perspective.

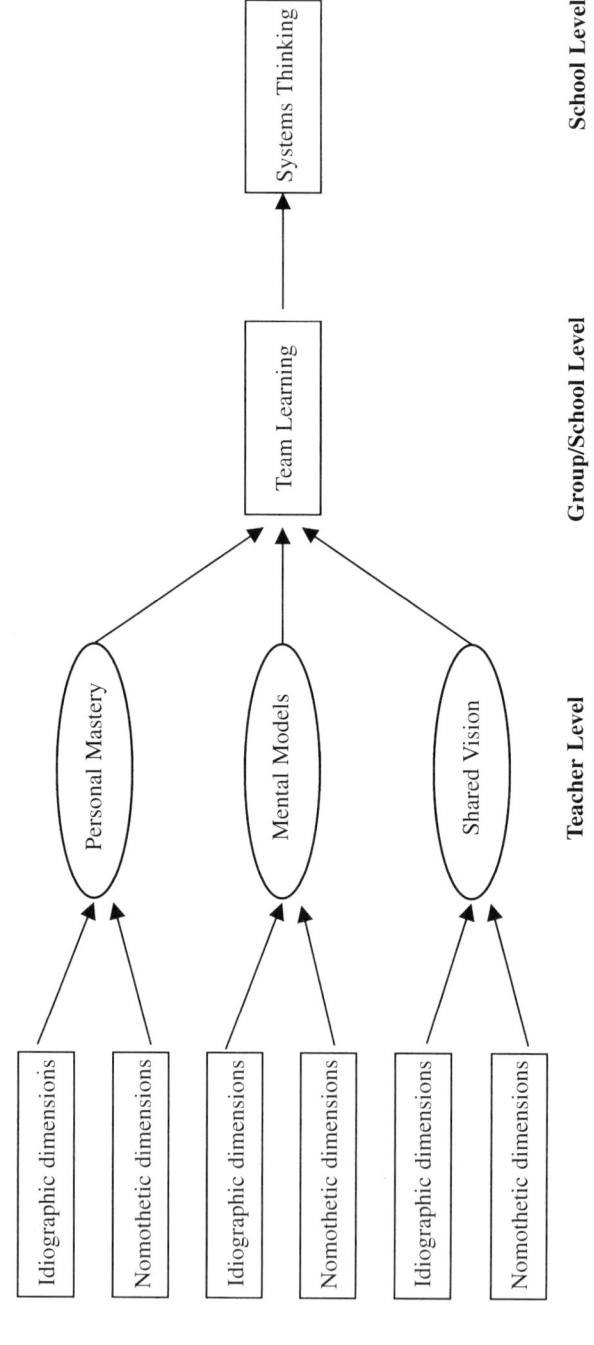

Figure 3 *Pang's Framework for Operationalization of a Learning Organization*

The Implications of Senge's Five Disciplines in the School Context

Senge (1990) advised people to put aside their old ways of thinking (Mental Models), learn to be open with others (Personal Mastery), understand how their organization really works (Systems Thinking), form a plan everyone can agree on (Shared Vision), and then work together to achieve that vision (Team Learning). He suggested these five disciplines should be developed as an "ensemble" (Senge, 1990, p. 21). He emphasized the fact that responsibility for Systems Thinking is not to be vested in one person but that in a sense the responsibility should be spread throughout the organization. People in the organization have to see the whole rather than parts of the system and must be able to see how the problems are linked. Senge put forward Systems Thinking as the discipline that integrates all the other disciplines. When we put these five disciplines into the context of a school, both the individual and the group/school levels need to be carefully considered.

Personal Mastery

The main role of teachers is to equip themselves with the competency to convey knowledge in class and to try all possible methods of facilitating the learning of their students. A teacher's personal mastery of his/her subject is as consequential as his/her possessing a wide range of knowledge. A well-planned staff professional development program at both school and individual levels should be implemented. It would be most desirable if teachers' participation in profession-related training activities could be stated in the school's annual plan as an essential issue fully supported by the school authority.

Schools that intend to enhance the practice of the discipline of Personal Mastery among their staff members should aim to offer support and encouragement for individuals' on-going learning. Empowering teaching staff to make changes in their schools, promoting and publicizing the ideas put forward by members of staff, and reinforcing work and initiatives across different boundaries are crucial to strengthening the professional development both of individual teachers and of the whole school. School administrators can formulate certain policies or set up working teams to deal with the practices of the discipline of Personal Mastery. For example, teachers may be invited to share experiences among themselves, or even to demonstrate what they have learnt on courses or in seminars to their colleagues. The establishment of a mentoring system is also a good measure for enhancing teachers' personal mastery. The mentor acts as a guide to newcomers, so that the newcomers' confidence in areas of expertise and knowledge can be built up and reinforced as time goes by.

Mental Models

School administrators need to bring about a radical transformation of their personal paradigm in the light of school organizational structures, processes, and power patterns. They have to develop a scenario that emphasizes the importance of "activeness over passiveness," "autonomy over dependence," "flexibility over rigidity," "collaboration over competition," "openness over closeness," and "democratic inquiry over authoritarian belief" (Morgan, 1986, p. 109).

Argyris and Schon (1978) argued that most people practice defensive reasoning in order to avoid embarrassment or threats, which in turn prevents them from being open-minded. Possessing flawed mental models leads people to act inappropriately. Thus, if the learning capacity of teachers is to be enhanced, the expectation of infallibility should not be encouraged and the application of penalties should be abolished. School administrators indeed should help teachers advocate their assumptions and beliefs by creating ample opportunities for teachers to speak out about their problems, fears, worries, and questions. Working in an environment surrounded by open-mindedness, mutual support and trust, teachers will be willing to take risks, to focus on finding all possible workable strategies, rather than just sitting back when difficulties are encountered.

Shared Vision

Senge (1990) stressed the fact that vision could not be sold. If a shared vision is to develop, members of the organization must cooperate in the building of such a vision. School visions must not be created solely by administrators or from the top down; rather, visions must be created by means of a comprehensive interaction among the individuals in the school, and through challenging and on-going dialogues. It is only by reaching a compromise among the individuals and by further developing the vision in a common direction that a shared vision may be honored with the teachers' commitment. When teachers have actually participated in the mission- and vision-building of the school, they will possess a strong sense of ownership, which in turn will encourage them to achieve the school goals with enthusiasm. School administrators must, on a continuous basis, share their own vision with the teachers, be assessed on their commitment to the vision, and be sufficiently open-minded to accept and welcome divergent opinions.

Team Learning

With regard to a successful learning relationship with others, a climate of trust for open dialogues is a minimum requirement, and an awareness of the factors that facilitate or inhibit individual and group learning is also imperative (Senge, 1990, p. 233). School administrators should rely not only on the learning, commitment and efficacy of individual teachers, but also on the team's learning capacity, so that the whole school will always be ready to face educational innovations. Nowadays, teaching can no longer be carried out alone behind closed doors. Individual teachers and teams must learn how to examine and validate their values, beliefs, and assumptions in public .

Team Learning is a team skill that can be learned (Senge, 1990, p. 245). School administrators should foster an environment in which members of staff are able to present their points of view in thorough discussions before decisions are made. Relevant structures like dual channel communication, evaluations, reflections, and experience sharing would best suit the purpose of providing opportunities for teachers to work in collaboration with one another, to learn from one another, to learn together, and to reinforce the teams' learning. In order to develop this further, school administrators might even help to form a network including all the teachers in the neighborhood, so that relevant information could be exchanged and teaching experience shared among schools.

Systems Thinking

By Systems Thinking, Senge (1990) meant the ability to understand the complex causal relationships among a set of organizational factors, that is, nothing in an organization stands alone. Systems Thinking integrates the other four disciplines and fuses them into a coherent body of theory and practice. School administrators should have a distinct understanding of Systems Thinking, perceiving it as a discipline for seeing the whole, with its essence lying in a paradigm shift. The discipline emphasizes seeing interrelationships rather than linear cause-effect chains, and seeing processes of change rather than snapshots (Senge, 1990, p. 73).

School administrators should employ a systemic thinking in their work. For example, when they want to carry out a new plan, they should take all their stakeholders' interests into careful consideration. These stakeholders include teachers, supporting staff, parents, students, the neighboring community, and the public. School administrators should also formulate strategies to help teachers acknowledge the relationship between things and operations. The most compelling of this discipline is the ability to see the world as a complex system. When teachers are able to appreciate the interrelationships among the components of an event or an idea, they will then be able to make decisions that are better-informed.

The effectiveness of a learning community lies in how it merges the disciplines of Mental Models, Personal Mastery, Shared Vision, and Team Learning into its routine practice by means of Systemic Thinking.

Aims of the Study

In view of the current global trend for schools to become learning communities, and in view of the fact that self-evaluation is of vital importance to all learning organizations, this study had two main aims. First, it was intended that a pilot study should be carried out in order to develop a set of performance indicators (Education Department, 1998) to measure the learning capacity of schools in the Hong Kong educational context. The second aim was to determine which conditions are favorable for a school to become a learning community. The questions addressed in the study were:

1. What is the learning capacity of the sampled primary schools?
2. What are the patterns and characteristics of the schools in terms of Senge's five disciplines?
3. What are the contextual factors that contribute to primary schools in Hong Kong becoming learning organizations?

Research Methodology

Instrument and Sample

This study employed a quantitative research method. It involved the participation of 25 primary schools in Hong Kong selected by using the convenient sampling method. These schools, with different histories and backgrounds, are scattered over various districts of Hong Kong. These districts include Hong Kong Island, Kowloon, and the New Territories. A total of 628 questionnaires were sent to the 25 primary schools, 523 of which were returned, giving a return rate of 83.3%. The respondents, who were designedly allowed to remain anonymous, were asked to rate the description of all the items according to the actual practice of their working school. The questionnaire, consisting of 78 items, employed a 5-point Likert scale running from one to five, denoting "very seldom," "seldom," "sometimes," "often" and "always" respectively. The findings obtained were supported by statistical data. Although the findings may not be generalized to the whole population of Hong Kong primary schools, the study does provide an insight into schools that make every effort to become learning organizations.

Factor Analysis

The 78 items in the questionnaire were spread over the five subscales that represented Senge's five disciplines of a learning organization. Each of these subscales included 13 to 18 items. For example, the subscale PM represented Personal Mastery with 14 items; MM represented Mental Models with 18 items; SV represented Shared Vision with 16 items; TL represented Team Learning with 16 items; and ST represented Systems Thinking with 16 items. The subscales PM, MM and SV were set at two levels, the teacher level (idiographic dimension) and the school level (nomothetic dimension). The subscale TL was set at the group level and the school level, while the subscale ST was set at school level only. After having gone through factor analysis, invalid items were eliminated, leaving a total of 66 useful items.

Pedhazur and Schmelkin (1991) claimed that a meaningful and essential question to be raised about a measure was whether it was consistent with the definition of the construct it was meant to be tapping. Factor Analysis is an analytic statistical tool that enables us to determine the chief underlying dimensions of a set of variables, attributes, responses, or observations (Oppenheim, 1992, p. 166). In applications of factor analysis, research often treats loadings exceeding .3 as meaningful. Principal Component Analyses were conducted for the items of the five disciplines. Oblimin

Rotation with its suppressed absolute values less than .3 and with Eigenvalues above 1 was set for the analysis.

The instrument finally consisted of 56 positive items and 10 negative items, rather than 64 positive items and 14 negative items as originally designed. The extraction method used was Principal Component Analysis. Items retained after extraction from the five subscales separately were 11 in Personal Mastery (PM), 14 in Mental Models (MM), 13 in Shared Vision (SV), 14 in Team Learning (TL), and 14 in Systems Thinking (ST).

Reliability

Reliability means consistency. It is important that the characteristics of the measuring instrument and the conditions under which it is administered be consistent. Cronbach's Alpha is the most commonly and routinely applied index in the measurement of reliability, and the goal for reliability at the initial stage of development of the instrument was a minimum of .70 (Pang, 1995, p. 170). The reliability coefficients (Alphas) of all the five scales in this questionnaire ranged from .72 to .91. Table 1 provides a detailed description of the coefficient alphas of the five subscales.

Correlations Among the Five Subscales

Table 2 shows that the five scales correlated positively and significantly to one another, ranging from .48 to .84, indicating that they were strongly associated with one another (Pang, 1999). The results reveal that Personal Mastery had the highest correlation with Team Learning ($r = .67$), while Mental Models had the highest correlation with Systems Thinking ($r =$

Table 1 *Means, Standard Deviations and Reliability Coefficients (Alphas) of the Subscales of Organizational Learning*

Subscales	M	SD	n	Alpha	No. of items
Personal Mastery (PM)	36.44	5.29	523	.79	11
Mental Models (MM)	38.67	5.66	523	.72	14
Shared Vision (SV)	40.97	7.30	523	.89	13
Team Learning (TL)	43.70	7.34	523	.86	14
Systems Thinking (ST)	43.06	8.58	523	.91	14

Table 2 *Correlation Coefficients Among the Five Subscales of Organizational Learning and the Scale of Learning Capacity*

Subscales	Personal Mastery	Mental Models	Shared Vision	Team Learning	Systems Thinking	Learning Capacity
Personal Mastery	1					
Mental Models	.477	1				
Shared Vision	.650	.734	1			
Team Learning	.670	.730	.784	1		
Systems Thinking	.644	.771	.841	.807	1	
Learning Capacity	.765	.842	.920	.913	.938	1

Notes: All correlation coefficients are significant at the .01 level (2-tailed); n = 523.

.77), Shared Vision with Systems Thinking ($r = .84$), Team Learning with Systems Thinking ($r = .8$), and Systems Thinking with Shared Vision ($r = .84$). The figures imply that Systems Thinking is highly associated with the other four scales in a learning community. The finding is in accordance with Senge's fifth discipline discourse, that is, Systems Thinking is the crucial criterion for continuous learning and improvement in any organization (Senge, 1990).

In this study, a composite score measuring the learning capacity of each school was generated by integrating the five subscales of organizational learning with different regression coefficients computed from LISREL one-factor congeneric modeling (Jöreskog & Sörbom, 1989). Table 2 reveals that the associations between the five individual subscales with the scale of Learning Capacity were also positively high and significant, ranging from .77 to .94. Since the correlations were well above .71, this is sufficient for us to say that more than 50% of the variance of the scale of Learning Capacity was predictable from the variance of all these individual subscales (Ferguson & Takane, 1989). The unexplained variances ($1 - r^2$) between the five individual subscales of organizational learning and the scale of Learning Capacity were: Personal Mastery 41%, Mental Models 29%, Shared Vision 15%, Team Learning 17%, and Systems Thinking 12%. From the above figures, Systems Thinking still demonstrated the highest level of association with Learning Capacity, explaining almost 88% of the learning capacity of a learning organization.

Results

The Learning Capacity of the 25 Primary Schools

A composite score measuring the learning capacity of each school was generated by aggregating the five subscales of organizational learning with different weightings. It is often desirable to describe the relative position of an observation within a distribution. One way of describing the location of a case in a distribution is to calculate its standard score. This score, sometimes called the Z-score, indicates how many standard deviations above or below the mean an observation falls. The mean of Z scores is 0 and the standard deviation is 1. Standardization permits a comparison of scores from different distributions. The standardized scores of the schools' learning capacities were their Learning Capacity Indices (LCIs). These indices were plotted for comparison according to the ascending order of the schools' assigned numbers. Figure 4 shows the comparison of the learning capacities of each of the schools.

The 25 schools were arbitrarily divided into three groups based on their LCIs in terms of a high, moderate, or low learning capacity. Those schools (9 schools) with LCIs greater than or equal to +.20 were classified as schools with a high learning capacity, while those (6 schools) with LCIs lower than or equal to –.20 were schools possessing a low learning capacity. Those schools (10 schools) with their LCIs lying between –.2 and +.2 were

Figure 4 *Learning Capacity of the 25 Primary Schools in Hong Kong*

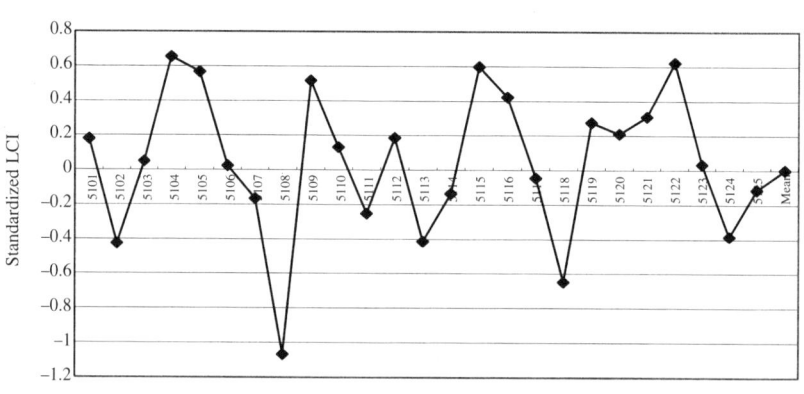

School No.

said to possess a moderate learning capacity. Figure 5 shows the profiles of the schools with different learning capacities in terms of Senge's model of a learning organization.

Figure 5 reveals that in all the schools, teachers' Personal Mastery was stronger than the other disciplines, but the schools all appeared to be weak in Mental Models. The distribution of the five scales displayed more or less the same pattern at all three levels, that is with the Personal Mastery scale the highest, followed by Shared Vision, Team Learning, Systems Thinking, and finally Mental Models as the lowest of all.

Chincotta (1992) declared that with the publication of the *Education Commission Report No. 5*, which highlighted the demand for professionalism among teachers, significant progress toward professionalization would be within reach. In these few years, Hong Kong teachers have had many opportunities to participate in seminars and conferences of all kinds, engaging in higher levels of learning in a quest for knowledge that will help them to meet the challenges of the new era. Life-long learning is recognized not only as necessary for self-improvement and as a means of dealing with social and global trends, but also as a path for better advancement in ones' career. Now that creativity, innovation, information technology, and communication have become essential elements in the school curriculum, teachers' personal mastery of these areas is of crucial importance.

Figure 5 *Profiles for Schools of Different Learning Capacity*

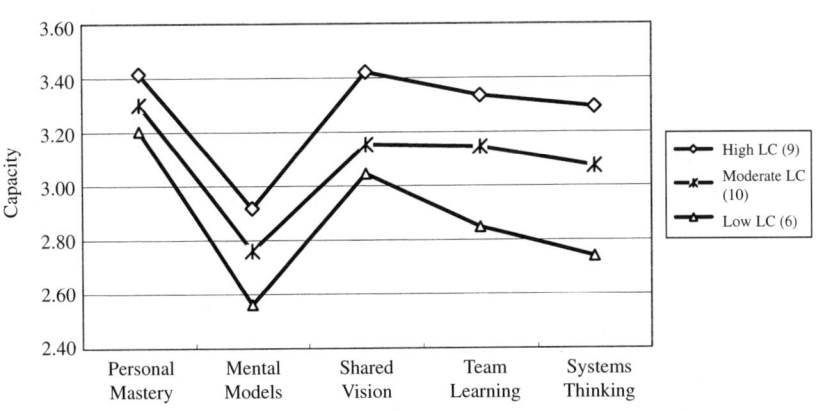

We are quite often unaware of the extent to which our behavior is affected by our Mental Models, by our individual personality/ need-disposition (idiographic dimension) and by our institutional role (nomothetic dimension). Senge (1990) described this discipline as assumptions and generalizations that influence how we understand the world, how we determine right from wrong, how we evaluate others and ourselves, and which help us to decide what to do in the myriad of situations in which we find ourselves. Our attitudes and beliefs indeed become a part of our thinking and are major factors in our perceptions of reality.

People in Hong Kong have benefited from two diverse cultures: Eastern and Western. On the one hand, we have adopted from the West the concepts of individualism and humanism, outspokenness, openness and freedom; on the other hand, our Chinese characteristics are still deeply rooted in us, and thus, compared to our Western counterparts we are more passive, conservative, defensive, indecisive and doubtful when facing challenges. It could be these typically Chinese characteristics of self-restraint, introversion, procrastination, and resistance to change (Xing, 1995) that might explain the poor Mental Models of the teachers. Schools that provide teachers with opportunities to examine their beliefs and assumptions on both individual and group bases usually experience a great leap in school improvement. However, the majority of schools in Hong Kong are not aware of the importance of cultivating teachers' Mental Models, nor of their influence over teachers' behavior.

The Effects of the Five Disciplines on Schools' Learning Capacity

The effects of the five subscales on the scale of Learning Capacity are shown in Table 3. The weighted set of the scales (independent variables) to the scale of Learning Capacity (dependent variables), in descending order of importance, were Systems Thinking (.28), Team Learning (.24), Shared Vision (.24), Mental Models (.19), and Personal Mastery (.18). As expected, the effect of Systems Thinking on Learning Capacity ranked the highest. Team Learning and Shared Vision ranked second, since there is little if any difference between their effect on Learning Capacity. Mental Models are the conceptual and operational representations that teachers develop while interacting with the school systems. A shift in one's paradigm is not easy

Table 3   *Multiple Regressions of the Five Subscales of Organizational Learning on Schools' Learning Capacity*

Learning Capacity (Dependent Variable)	Independent Variables				
	Personal Mastery	Mental Models	Shared Vision	Team Learning	Systems Thinking
Standardized Coefficients	.175	.187	.241	.242	.284

Notes: All regression coefficients are significant at the .001 level; n = 523.

to achieve. It usually happens as a result of the influences brought to bear by the former three disciplines in the organization. Although Personal Mastery weighed the least among the five scales, without it, it would be impossible for any organizational learning to take place. Nonetheless, although Personal Mastery is necessary, it alone will not produce a learning organization. Braham (1996) and Leithwood (1998) claimed that high Personal Mastery among members of staff does not imply that the organization has a high learning capacity.

The Learning Capacity of Whole-Day Schools Versus Bi-Sessional Schools

By using a one-way ANOVA, the differences between the means of the five scales and the scores of the Learning Capacity of the whole-day schools and the bi-sessional schools (the morning session [AM] schools and the afternoon session [PM] schools) were obtained, and these are shown in Table 4. Whole-day schools, in all aspects of organizational learning, scored higher than the bi-sessional schools. There were significant differences between whole-day schools and bi-sessional schools in terms of capacity in organizational learning. Most of these differences were significant at a .05 level of significance.

Table 4 shows the comparison between whole-day and bi-sessional schools in terms of their learning capacity. Generally, whole-day schools had a greater learning capacity than bi-sessional (both AM and PM) schools, in terms of both general learning capacity and four of the specific subscales of organizational learning, that is, Personal Mastery, Mental Models, Team Learning, and Systems Thinking. The results confirmed that whole-day schools had a significantly higher learning capacity and a better development

Table 4   *The Learning Capacity of Whole-Day Schools Versus Bi-Sessional Schools*

Subscales	Means			S.D.			Significance
	WD	AM	PM	WD	AM	PM	
Personal Mastery	**3.36**	3.23	3.35	.47	.49	.47	.019*
Mental Models	**2.83**	2.70	2.74	.36	.42	.42	.007*
Shared Vision	3.20	3.11	3.14	.51	.59	.59	.357
Team Learning	**3.23**	3.04	3.09	.48	.54	.55	.002*
Systems Thinking	**3.21**	2.98	3.03	.55	.66	.61	.001*
Learning Capacity	**3.16**	3.00	3.06	.42	.48	.47	.005*

Notes: 1. Figures in bold type are significantly higher than those in normal type.
2. The asterisk (*) denotes the significance at .05 level.
3. WD = whole-day schools (n = 184); AM = morning session schools (n = 181); PM = afternoon session schools (n = 158); total n = 523.

in terms of organizational learning than both the AM schools and the PM schools, except with regard to the scale of Shared Vision.

That whole-day schools obtained higher scores in most of the subscales of organizational learning may be understood when we think of the space and time that whole-day schools possess in their utilization of the school premises. Whole-day schools have a greater flexibility and capability in allocating a time and place for teachers to develop group interactions than bi-sessional schools could conceivably have. Teachers working in whole-day schools usually have longer working hours, which implies that there is more time available for intensive interaction with their colleagues. The infrastructure of whole-day schools helps to make it possible for the culture of learning to be established throughout the school, and enables teachers to learn together by interacting in a deeper and more thorough sense. As a matter of fact, time is a vital element in developing mutual understanding and deeper communication in human relationships. Whole-day schools provide more favorable conditions than do bi-sessional schools for developing both the teachers' and the schools' learning capacity.

The findings of the research also indicate that there were no significant differences in Shared Vision between the whole-day schools and the bi-sessional schools. This shows that the various infrastructures of the three types of school have no significant impact on the vision building of these schools. The essence of building a shared vision among teachers is to sustain an on-going process that aims to inculcate in the whole school a sense of commitment, a desire to achieve recognized goals, and a sense of ownership. School leaders, regardless of the type of school they are working in, provided that they understand the vital importance of shared vision to a successful school, will overcome all obstacles to build up a shared vision in their schools. The transmission of the vision is usually done via official meetings, the school's annual plan, disseminated documents, or by constant reviews of the students' performance and the school's effectiveness.

Discussions and Conclusion

The 21st century is an era overflowing with information, innovation, creativity, changes and unpredictability, that seep into almost every part of our daily lives, including the places where we work. The best way to deal with this problematic situation is to become a constant learner. An individual must employ a life-long learning strategy embedded in a life-long learning process. An organization is no different. It needs to develop a strategic plan to enhance both its employees' and the organization's learning capacity.

Schools in Hong Kong are confronted with more or less the same challenges, brought about by the huge flow of information and vigorous innovative moves due to globalization. It is thus necessary for schools to be transformed into learning communities so as to meet the expectations of their stakeholders (Lam & Pang, 2003). For a school to become a learning community, it must redesign its infrastructure in such a way as to nurture a learning culture and to equip its teachers. An important concept that every school leader needs to bear in mind is: All reforms are for improvement (Pang & Lam, 2000). In this regard, a school should enhance its own learning capacity in such a way that the whole school is always striving towards betterment and organizational improvement. We should also bear in mind that improvement takes time and that it is a process, not an event (Bollen, 1996). First of all, school leaders have to commit to their change in role, which implies much more than simply having a positive attitude. School leaders must carry out a paradigm shift from a hierarchical, supervising, controlling role to a role of facilitating and supporting individual and group learning with careful planning, not merely letting it happen by chance (Gamage & Pang, 2003).

Although this was a pilot study of Senge's five disciplines of organizational learning, the findings of this study highlight certain aspects which school leaders and educationists of the Hong Kong Special Administrative Region (HKSAR) should ponder. If they want to help schools develop their effectiveness in teaching and learning to the utmost, they should give due consideration to the following points.

1. Senge's five disciplines are vital to establishing a learning community. In the findings of this study, the five disciplines correlated positively with one another. Ignorance of any one of them will certainly lessen the development of the other four, and, consequently, reduce the learning capability of the school. Effective learning organizations should, therefore, put great emphasis on all the five disciplines in the community and place equal importance on each single discipline.

2. According to Senge (1990), Systems Thinking is the key discipline for a successful learning organization. This was also found to be true in the context of Hong Kong schools. The results of the study showed that Systems Thinking correlated positively and fairly high with all the other disciplines, and that it is the principal factor in the explanation of the learning capacity of an organization. Systems Thinking explains the concept of independence and interdependence within a system, that is, that all parts of a system are not only independent but also closely related to and influenced by one another. School leaders should encourage their teachers to think from a systemic perspective. If the whole school is able to consider all the issues presented from a holistic point of view and take into account the impact they might have on the various parts of the school system, the school is on its way towards becoming a learning community.

3. Schools should cultivate a milieu that fosters learning among their staff members. People usually work with deep commitment in an organization where priority is given to mutual respect, where mistake-making is treated as part of the learning process, where there is little fear of failing, and where risk-taking is encouraged. In such an environment, teachers will be more motivated to take the initiative in implementing new educational ideas in their schools, and to focus their attention on pursuing high quality teaching and learning. Since learning and improvement take time, school leaders should

have the consideration to allocate sufficient time and space for teachers to do these things.

4. The Chief Executive of the HKSAR, Mr. C. H. Tung, in his first policy address (October, 1997), clearly stated that whole-day schools possessed better conditions than bi-sessional schools for their transformation into learning communities. This study confirmed this. Whole-day schools have more opportunities to be flexible. It is the time factor as well as the physical factor that enables whole-day schools to offer ample opportunity for members of staff to communicate and interact with each other. Undoubtedly, the transformation of all bi-sessional schools into whole-day schools will help to achieve not only a high quality of education, but also a high quality of culture.

5. Senge's five disciplines serve as an effective tool for schools to use to re-engineer their infrastructures in order to become learning communities in which the learning capacity of both individuals and groups is continuously enhanced. If these disciplines are to operate effectively and productively, schools should deal with them as an "ensemble" and handle them all simultaneously with carefully planned strategies and supportive measures. Attention should be paid to the setup of infrastructures (the hardware) and the preparedness of the human factor (the software). School leaders should gradually guide all the components to work to promote the development of the five disciplines. They should aim to nurture a culture that encourages communication, support, trust and collective thinking, together with a perception of seeing mistakes as part of the learning process. However, none of the above will take a deep root if the above-mentioned culture and supportive infrastructures for promoting learning throughout the school are not established with the commitment of all parties in the schools.

References

Argyris, C., & Schon, D. A. (1978). *Organizational learning: A theory of action perspective*. Reading, MA: Addision-Wesley.

Bollen, R. (1996). School effectiveness and school improvement: The intellectual and policy context. In D. Reynolds, R. Bollen, B. Creemers, D. Hopkins,

L. Stoll, & N. Lagerweij (Eds.), *Making good schools: Linking school effectiveness and school improvement* (pp. 1–20). London; New York: Routledge.

Braham, B. J. (1996). *Creating a learning organisation.* London: Kogan Page.

Chincotta, D. M. (1992). Education Commission Report No. 5 and the organization of teachers: A strategy of limited professionalism. *New Horizon, 33,* 56–62.

Curriculum Development Council. (2000). *Learning to learn: The way forward in curriculum development (consultation document).* Hong Kong: Author.

Education and Manpower Branch, & Education Department. (1991). *The School management initiative: Setting the framework for quality in Hong Kong schools.* Hong Kong: Government Printer.

Education and Manpower Bureau. (1998). *Information technology for learning in a new era: Five-year strategy 1998/99 to 2002/03.* Hong Kong: Printing Department.

Education Commission. (1984). *Education Commission Report No. 1.* Hong Kong: Government Printer.

Education Commission. (1986). *Education Commission Report No. 2.* Hong Kong: Government Printer.

Education Commission. (1988). *Education Commission Report No. 3: The structure of tertiary education and the future of private schools.* Hong Kong: Government Printer.

Education Commission. (1990). *Education Commission Report No. 4: The curriculum and behavioural problems in schools.* Hong Kong: Government Printer.

Education Commission. (1992). *Education Commission Report No. 5: The teaching profession.* Hong Kong: Government Printer.

Education Commission. (1996). *Education Commission Report No. 6: Enhancing language proficiency — A comprehensive strategy.* Hong Kong: Government Printer.

Education Commission. (1997). *Education Commission Report No. 7: Quality school education.* Hong Kong: Government Printer.

Education Commission. (1999). *Review of education system — Framework for educational reform: Learning for life (consultation document).* Hong Kong: Printing Department.

Education Commission. (2000). *Review of education system — Reform proposals (consultation document).* Hong Kong: Printing Department.

Education Department. (1998). *Education indicators for the Hong Kong school education system.* Hong Kong: Printing Department.

Ferguson, G. A., & Takane, Y. (1989). *Statistical analysis in psychology and education* (6th ed.). New York; London: McGraw-Hill.

Gamage, D. T., & Pang, N. S. K. (2003). *Leadership and management in education:*

Developing essential skills and competencies. Hong Kong: The Chinese University Press.

Getzels, J. W., & Guba, E. G. (1957). Social behaviour and the administrative process. *School Review, 65,* 423–441.

Jöreskog, K. G., & Sörbom, D. (1989). *LISREL 7: A guide to the program and applications* (2nd ed.). Chicago: SPSS.

Lam, Y. L. J., & Pang, S. K. N. (2003). The relative effects of environmental, internal and contextual factors on organizational learning: The case of Hong Kong schools under reform. *The Learning Organization: An International Journal, 10*(2), 83-97.

Lassey, P. (1998). *Developing a learning organization.* London: Kogan Page.

Leithwood, K. (1998). Team learning processes. In K. Leithwood & K. S. Louis (Eds.), *Organizational learning in schools* (pp. 203–218). Lisse; Exton, PA: Swets & Zeitlinger Publishers.

Louis, K. S., & Kruse, S. D. (1998). Creating community in reform: Images of organizational learning in inner-city schools. In K. Leithwood & K. S. Louis (Eds.), *Organizational learning in schools* (pp. 17–46). Lisse; Exton, PA: Swets & Zeitlinger Publishers.

Marsick, V. J. (1987). *Learning in the workplace.* London: Croom Helm.

Marsick, V. J., & Watkins, K. E. (1996). Adult educators and the challenge of the learning organization. *Adult Learning, 7*(4), 18–20.

Morgan, G. (1986). *Images of organization.* Beverly Hills, CA: Sage.

Oppenheim, A. N. (1992). *Questionnaire design, interviewing and attitude measurement* (new ed.). London; New York: Printer Publishers.

Pang, N. S. K. (1995). The development of the school values inventory. In R. Cotter & S. J. Marshall (Eds.), *Research and practice in educational administration* (pp. 160–186). Hawthorn, Victoria: Australian Council for Education Administration.

Pang, N. S. K. (1999). Students' perceptions of quality of school life in Hong Kong primary schools. *Educational Research Journal, 14*(1), 49–71.

Pang, N. S. K., & Lam, J. Y. L. (2000). *How can schools tackle the challenges from the reform proposals?* [Educational Policy Studies Series No. 35; in Chinese]. Hong Kong: Faculty of Education and Hong Kong Institute of Educational Research, The Chinese University of Hong Kong.

Pedhazur, E. J., & Schmelkin, L. P. (1991). *Measurement, design, and analysis: An integrated approach.* Hillsdale, NJ: Lawrence Erlbaum Associates.

Senge, P. M. (1990). *The fifth discipline: The art and practice of the learning organization.* New York: Doubleday.

Senge, P. M., Ross, R., Smith, B., Roberts, C., & Kleiner, A. (1994). *The fifth discipline fieldbook: Strategies and tools for building a learning organization.* New York: Doubleday.

Sergiovanni, T. (1987). The theoretical basis for cultural leadership. In L. T. Sheive & M. B. Schoenheit (Eds.), *Leadership: Examining the elusive* (pp. 116–127). Alexandria, VA: Association for Supervision and Curriculum Development.

Swieringa, J., & Wierdsma, A. (1992). *Becoming a learning organization: Beyond the learning curve.* Wokingham, England; Reading, MA: Addison-Wesley.

Xing, F. (1995). The Chinese cultural system implications for cross-cultural management. *SAM Advanced Management Journal, 60*(1), 14–20.

14

School Self-Evaluation as a Strategy for Developing Teaching and Learning: A Hong Kong Case Study

Richard Dyer & Cheung Siu-ming

Abstract

This chapter describes the case of an international school in Hong Kong involved in developing school self-evaluation methods for school improvement.

In 1996 West Island School joined a consortium of local and international schools in a project called "Ensuring Excellence," which aimed to develop school self-evaluation practices in the member schools. In 1998, the Hong Kong government's Quality Education Fund provided a grant to the consortium to pursue its work and produce staff development materials for use in other schools.

This chapter is a retrospective analysis of the experience of West Island School's teachers in the project. It describes the evolution of the concept of "evaluation as development" and the attempts that have been made to ensure that evaluation practices lead to the collaborative professional development of teachers and enhanced learning for pupils. The model that has resulted from the work involves teachers in developing their practice through action research and peer observation. Evaluation is conducted in order to provide evidence grounded in teachers' personal professional knowledge. This is then used in collaborative professional development efforts. The purposes and processes contrast sharply with traditional modes of external inspection, which commonly provide feedback on performance rather than feedback for the development of performance and which are focused more on public accountability than on school development.

> *The authors suggest that involvement in structured school self-evaluation can be part of the professionalization of teachers and can lead to enhanced teaching and improved learning. It can have a positive impact on professionalism, collegiality, school culture and approaches to professional development.*
>
> *A dilemma exists on the role of such self-evaluation practices in relation to wider systems of quality assurance in schools. The chapter highlights the need for clarity over the purpose of quality assurance systems. In particular, it argues that regarding quality assurance as the exclusive domain of agencies external to the school continues to de-professionalize teachers and that an integrated form of quality assurance which places teachers at the center is needed.*
>
> *The authors suggest that it may be possible to integrate the school self-evaluation process with other quality assurance processes such as school audit, external inspection and staff appraisal in a coherent way, but that the purposes of external inspection and quality assurance will need to be redefined.*

Introduction

In 1996, a pilot project on school self-evaluation called "Ensuring Excellence" was initiated by the English Schools Foundation (ESF). While a good number of staff in the group of pilot schools were already familiar with self-evaluation concepts and practices, the project introduced a particular framework, based on the work of MacBeath in Scotland (see, for example, MacBeath, 1999). The framework and its key concepts of "Indicators of Excellence" and associated "Observable Features" enabled participating schools to develop and share a common understanding, language and process for self-evaluation. Moreover, the framework was sufficiently flexible to enable individual institutions to take into account the specific contexts of their own situations, and pilot and implement the initiative in different ways.

The early success of the project encouraged the ESF to apply for a grant for Ensuring Excellence from the government's Quality Education Fund (QEF). This bid was successful and the initiative entered a new 2-year phase in 1998, when a number of new schools, from both the international and local sectors, joined the project. After the QEF funding ended, the project continued in 2001–2002 within the ESF, and other ESF schools joined in.

West Island School is one of the original schools participating in the Ensuring Excellence project. This chapter seeks to outline developments in West Island School over these past 6 years in order to make a start in understanding the processes which have occurred.

Ensuring Excellence in West Island: A Chronology

The First Phase — Piloting the Initiative

In 1996, West Island School was in its sixth year of existence, the newest of the five ESF secondary schools. The school was undergoing rapid growth and development. While its first set of GCSE (General Certificate of Secondary Education) public examinations were very pleasing and a huge morale booster to all concerned, the school wanted to know more about how well it was progressing — it needed to establish its own system of evaluation. This was why it was eager to join the ESF self-evaluation project when it started that year. During this first phase, the use of Indicators of Excellence and Observable Features was piloted in a number of small-scale evaluations of different areas of school life.

However, after just one year, self-evaluation activity took a back seat when the school was informed that it was to be inspected by an external team of inspectors, using the OFSTED (Office for Standards in Education) inspection framework for schools in England and Wales (see, for example, OFSTED, 2000). The inspection took place in November 1997. The report was received in February 1998. It validated the positive achievements of the school to date, and signaled a number of key issues for action. It is not the purpose of this chapter to discuss the details of the inspection report; the key point was that for the rest of the 1997–1998 school year the energy of the staff was totally preoccupied with responding to the report's recommendations. Meetings, action plans, and more meetings. Self-evaluation, a young and exploratory development, was almost brought to a halt by the inspection process. In retrospect, it was inevitable that the self-evaluation initiative was marginalized that year. It could not possibly have had much credibility in the eyes of the school community, compared with the weight and authority of the inspection. (The inconsistent quality of internal monitoring and evaluation systems in schools was a key theme that featured in a large number of OFSTED inspection reports in the United

Kingdom. Ironically here was an example where an inspection had effectively taken a year out of the school's attempt to develop just such an approach.)

The Second Phase — Moving Toward Whole School Implementation

In 1998–1999, the Ensuring Excellence project expanded to include more schools from local and international sectors, thanks to the success of a bid to the QEF. At West Island, the project's coordination was transferred from the Principal and the coordinator (who returned to a promoted position in the United Kingdom) to the authors of the present chapter. Another ESF Deputy Principal centrally involved in the QEF project joined West Island School on a 2-year secondment. During these 2 years, the project's development was characterized by the following.

The school continued to expand rapidly — its development plan encompassed quite a number of changes and initiatives necessitated by the school's growth as well as its need to respond to key developments in the ESF and in the United Kingdom. Self-evaluation was therefore just one strand of development, and it needed to make relevant connections with other strands or risk being perceived by staff as one more "bolt-on" activity imposed on their already busy schedules.

The staff numbers grew dramatically as the school roll had increased by over 50% during those 2 years. The school culture was one that was receptive to change; colleagues on the staff clearly understood that West Island was a growing school and realized that change management was on everyone's agenda. Nevertheless, keeping the initiative going, inducting a significant number of new staff year after year and facilitating the further involvement of existing staff was quite a developmental effort.

Small pioneer teams of staff took active ownership of the project; the number of staff teams involved in self-evaluation activities grew as other teams saw the benefits of this approach and began to engage with the project.

The foci of teams were related to teaching and learning in the classroom; observation of each other's lessons and professional dialogue about teaching and learning were core features of the developmental work of teams. Indicators of Excellence and associated Observable Features which had been discussed, developed, and refined by these teams and subsequently shared with other staff were key processes and outcomes.

The senior management team's commitment to the project was not negotiable, but it adopted a flexible approach over the pace and scope of the school's involvement. It saw its role as providing support to pioneer teams, keeping an overview of the development and maintaining contact with the QEF-funded project. Teams were not compelled to be involved against their professional judgment of what were the most urgent developments in their curriculum area. Thus, the pace and focus of self-evaluation projects were determined by the teams and were not linked initially to the school's major developmental priorities. People were encouraged to take risks and experiment with the processes of self-evaluation within teams consisting of their closest colleagues. Secondary schools are not mono-cultural and the levels of trust, openness, collaboration and collegiality at West Island varied (Siskin, 1994). Some subject teams were able to engage in lesson observations and frank discussions of pedagogy whereas others were not. A flexible approach by the senior management was intended to allow teams to develop in ways appropriate to their initial position. Insisting that self-evaluation was taken on without regard to other priorities was seen as counter-productive. The belief was that if teachers were to engage in a rigorous examination of their practice, and to develop their practice as a result, then a strong sense of ownership should prevail.

It was not the intention that this disparate pattern of involvement should continue ad infinitum, however. Key staff promoting Ensuring Excellence within the school were conscious of the need to link self-evaluation activities with major strands and processes in the school's development. This complemented the wider project's increasing emphasis of linking self-evaluation explicitly to school improvement, as well as developing a view about the relationship of self-evaluation to external inspection.

So, in the second year of the project, attempts were made to move from empowered pioneer teams working in various areas of the curriculum to a whole-school approach. This met with limited success. The background to these attempts was one of significant, rapid and unpredictable change. This may have been the key limiting factor. It is recognized that change in schools is endemic and ubiquitous (Nias, Southworth, & Yeomans, 1989) and this was certainly true in the case of West Island School as it expanded from 96 to 800 students in 8 years. Against this, there are times when large-scale changes occur in the foreground. In the case of West Island School at this time, the substantive changes included the introduction of a newly structured and rapidly planned AS- and A-level examination system for post-16 education according to an externally imposed time scale, a change in the timing of the school week from 40 to 45 lessons, and a significant expansion in the numbers of post-16 students in the school. Most importantly, 16 teachers out of 53 left the school at the end of 1998–1999 and there were 20 new teachers out of 57 staff at the start of the school year 1999–2000. These combined to provoke considerable uncertainty and anxiety. As Fullan (1999) points out, successful reforms "… must take into account multiple priorities that continuously impinge on individuals and organization" (p. 66). At this time, the changes to post-16 education became the main priority (and in some cases, the only priority) for teachers at West Island.

At the same time, an additional change was imminent which also distracted attention from the development of Ensuring Excellence. Very soon after the year started the staff learnt that the Principal had resigned and was leaving midway through the year. In fact all four members of the senior management team were likely to leave as the three Deputy Principals were all seeking jobs elsewhere, albeit for professionally positive reasons, even before the new Principal had joined the school. It was no surprise, then, that attempts in 1999–2000 to move toward a whole school approach to self-evaluation were not met with great success.

The Third Phase — Moving Toward Embedding and Consolidation

In the last 20 months, under the leadership of the new Principal, the staff have recharged their batteries and renewed their professional commitments to the school. While the pace of change remains almost relentless, the school's climate has moved toward one of optimism, energy, openness and trust; staff morale has strengthened and the school's confidence in managing change has grown. The school's key priorities were reviewed and updated. The senior management team as a whole is now even more focused on school improvement. A change of emphasis with Ensuring Excellence has been to link it with other key processes and developments in school. This has included the professional development of individual teachers (a process called "Staff Review & Development (SRD)" within the ESF), whole school initiatives such as the celebration of the English language across the curriculum, and the drive to enhance the quality of teaching and learning.

Senior management and the project's coordinator are now quite clear that self-evaluation at West Island is a means to achieve the ends of school improvement, and no longer a development priority in itself. It will coexist with other systems of quality assurance within the school, including those with a focus on accountability rather than development.

When the school is next due for an external audit or inspection, the visiting team may be invited to validate the school's internal systems of monitoring and self-evaluation, and not just gather and interpret evidence against generic performance indicators developed without reference to the school.

The Self-Evaluation Process at West Island School

The Ensuring Excellence model of self-evaluation is specifically designed to develop teaching. It engages teachers in developing a shared understanding of good practice in a particular area and in the collection of evidence relating to that good practice. Teachers compare current practice against defined Indicators of Excellence to determine priorities for development.

The process can be summarized as involving the following stages:

1. *Initial choice of an aspect of teaching and learning to focus on.* This involves the professional judgment of teachers in an area of the school. They examine priorities from the school's development plan and from the development plan for their area of the school. The development plans may have been informed by earlier evaluations. The decision is also influenced by which area is best suited to an Ensuring Excellence type of evaluation. In some cases, teachers decide that the evaluation and development of a particular aspect of teaching interests them and this subsequently becomes part of the development plan.

2. *The use of existing professional expertise to draft statements which attempt to capture the essence of excellent practice in the area.* This is usually in the form of a brainstorm where judgments are withheld in order to facilitate openness and creativity. A small sub-group of teachers will then work on clarifying the language of the statements and make a first attempt to place them within the Ensuring Excellence framework of Indicators of Excellence and Observable Features. Examples of this appear in Tables 1 and 2.

3. *An extended cycle of lesson observations using the draft Indicators*

of Excellence and Observable Features. The purpose here is to extend the Observable Features by drawing upon actual practice and to work toward a shared understanding of the statements relating to good practice contained in the Indicators of Excellence and Observable Features. This is regarded as a key developmental phase of the process.

4. *An evaluation of one aspect of the area of teaching and learning.* Only one aspect is chosen for pragmatic reasons: teachers have limited time. This evaluation is usually multi-method, involving semi-structured or structured interviews with students, observations of lessons, and short questionnaires. The evaluation can be conducted by any of the teachers involved.

5. *An analysis of the evidence gained from the evaluation and the setting of development targets and strategies.* The evaluation is intended to result in a focus for professional development which links to an improvement in teaching and learning. In practice, much development work occurs throughout the process.

6. *The whole set of Indicators of Excellence and Observable Features can subsequently become a policy document.* This policy document is a clear statement of good teaching and the Observable Features provide unequivocal and understood descriptions of what this looks like in practice.

Professional and Conceptual Rationale for Self-Evaluation at West Island School

This section attempts to locate the Ensuring Excellence methods within contemporary research paradigms and also makes some initial comparisons with some of the current thinking on professional development, organizations, school improvement, evaluation, and school cultures. We expect that this may provide some insights into the reasons behind the success of the work and some starting points for more substantial analyses. It may also inform future developments with self-evaluation efforts and the wider agenda of school improvement within the participating schools.

The Ensuring Excellence framework was developed from the work of John MacBeath (1999) but schools were given considerable latitude in evolving their own ways of using it. The particular ways in which the framework was used at West Island School had much to do with the

Table 1   *Indicators of Excellence and Observable Features for Effective Questioning*

Effective Questioning	
Indicators of Excellence	Observable Features
Different categories of questions are used purposefully.	• More higher-order, open questions are used with all students than lower-order, closed questions. • The following types of questions are used deliberately for different reasons: data recall, naming, observation, control, speculative or hypothesis generating, evaluation, and problem solving. • Question sequencing is used to develop concepts and generalizations. • Probing and prompting are used to get students to: clarify, support a viewpoint, seek consensus, test accuracy, ensure relevance, provide examples.
Students' responses are valued.	• Adequate thinking time is provided. • Students' responses are listened to attentively by everyone involved. • Students are encouraged to rephrase answers and questions which are unclear. • Students are given genuine affirmative feedback.
Questions are expressed effectively.	• Key language is modeled in questions. • Attention is drawn to key language. • Teachers' expression of questions is clear and concise.
Students have equal opportunities to respond to questions.	• The whole geography of the classroom is covered reasonably equally. • There is a gender and culture balance. • Students of all levels of attainment are provided with a range of question types of appropriate difficulty and challenge. • Quiet students are progressively encouraged to respond.

experiences of the teachers involved and the particular leanings of the teachers who led the evaluation efforts. The specific circumstances that existed each year allowed evaluation to evolve in a unique manner.

Thus, we have an innovation that is free of any significant external or central control. House's (1979) perspectives on educational innovation do

Table 2 *Indicators of Excellence and Observable Features for the Celebration of Cultural Diversity*

The Cultural Diversity of Our School is Promoted and Celebrated

Indicators of Excellence	Observable Features
Cultural diversity is used to enhance classroom teaching and learning.	• Schemes of work indicate where multiculturalism should enhance learning. • Teachers know the cultural backgrounds of the students in their classrooms.
The cultural diversity of the school is reflected in the environment.	• Students mix in multicultural friendship groups. • Displays contain references to a variety of cultures. • The school diary includes cultural festivals for all students in the school. • The library contains books from representative cultures. • The school website contains pages devoted to representative cultures. • The school yearbook contains work which represents our cultural diversity.
The cultural diversity of our school is promoted and celebrated through regular events.	• Assemblies have items that celebrate cultural diversity and calendar events. • The school fair includes a celebration of cultural diversity. • Cultural events occur throughout the year.
Opportunities are provided in school for students to promote and celebrate their culture.	• Students, parents and teachers run cultural clubs through the activities program. • Students use their first language to help with mentoring, parents' meetings, PTA newsletter, web pages and displays.

not readily apply. Aspects of House's technological, political and cultural perspectives interact in a manner unique to the context. However, disentangling these influences and perspectives is not possible in this short retrospective analysis.

Self-evaluation in practice at West Island has not been informed by any single, coherent professional or theoretical rationale, but is a serendipitous combination of several. This chapter may contribute toward explicating not only what happened and how it happened, but also why it occurred in the way it did.

Comparison With Research and Evaluation Paradigms

The process adopted by West Island School has many of the key features of "illuminative evaluation" as first described by Parlett and Hamilton (1977). In particular, as a method for discovering in detail what is happening in a classroom, its focus is the same: "Its primary concern is with description and interpretation rather than measurement and prediction" (p. 10).

The process of defining and then refining Indicators of Excellence and Observable Features is akin to Parlett and Hamilton's "progressive focussing" (1977, p. 15) which allows the flexibility to concentrate attention on important emergent features of the area being evaluated. As the starting point for the evaluation consists of the professional and personal perceptions of the teachers involved, the Ensuring Excellence process has more in common with qualitative research than with classical positivist agricultural-botany approaches to program evaluation. This is thought to be a more appropriate approach to evaluating and developing classroom practice: "Parlett and Hamilton's approach provides a much more professional and educationally relevant set of parameters within which educators can work" (Hopkins, 1989, p. 25).

Moreover, the teachers themselves conduct the research and evaluation. This suggests that the language conventions, jargon and metaphors that characterize conversation and interaction within the learning milieu can be readily decoded, leading to a deep understanding of the area being evaluated and to grounded explanations (Glaser & Strauss, 1967; Parlett & Hamilton, 1977).

One particular West Island School project illustrates this well. The Mathematics Faculty conducted an evaluation of differentiation in the classroom, looking at the effectiveness of teachers' strategies for adapting classroom activities and work to account for the range of abilities and learning styles of the students in the mathematics classes. An initial brainstorm activity drew upon teachers' personal professional knowledge to provide an eclectic and unstructured list of good teaching strategies. Teachers then engaged in a round of mutual observations where they visited each other's lessons and noted anything of interest relating to the broad theme of differentiation. In this way, the list was expanded and grounded in the day-to-day realities of their classrooms. The initial brainstorm followed by observations of contrasting classrooms could be considered to sensitize the teachers to features of practice in the tradition of grounded theory development (Strauss & Corbin, 1998).

The list was subsequently re-worked through discussion. Features of good practice were clustered into broader themes under the title of "Indicators of Excellence." This is analogous to the processes involved in developing theory from coded text, which are familiar to qualitative researchers. Shared understanding and increasing clarity emerged from rounds of discussion, observation and re-drafting. Some of the initial unstructured list and the finished list of Indicators of Excellence and Observable Features appear in Table 3.

This was ultimately used to conduct an evaluation. The statement "All students are adequately challenged" was evaluated by interviewing a cross section of students, and the statement "A variety of teaching strategies is used" was evaluated using focused lesson observations.

Such evaluation work is epistemologically and methodologically akin to qualitative research in the social sciences. It contrasts with analyses of test scores, examination results, and studies of relative "value-added" (see, for example, Fitz-Gibbon, 1996).

The evaluations are rooted in the anti-positivist view that knowledge is personal, subjective and unique. This view recognizes that individuals are autonomous in their actions and that their actions and intentions can be best understood by a researcher who is in some way involved in the social world under scrutiny. It embraces subjective reality and acknowledges the relationship between the researcher and the researched (Cohen & Manion, 1994; Denzin & Lincoln, 1998).

This raises questions about the assumptions made by external schools inspection bodies such as OFSTED in England and Wales that they may meaningfully *validate* a school's self-evaluation findings (OFSTED, 2000). If this validation process means that external inspectors use a school's own criteria to see if they come to the same conclusions, then this provides a check on internal *reliability* rather than *validity*. The conclusions reached by teachers doing self-evaluation with their own criteria have high internal validity by necessity. More clarity is needed from all parties on whether the inspection process is intended to provide an alternative measure of the same things which can be used to compare with a school's self-evaluation conclusions. Or, conversely, whether the inspection looks at a school's

Table 3   *The Development of Indicators of Excellence for Differentiation*

Part of the initial unstructured list from the brainstorm:

- A range of tasks is used for a class
- Tasks differentiated by outcome
- Different methods of grouping students
- Schemes indicate core and extension objectives
- Varying teaching styles

- Tiered exam papers used
- Use of extension questions
- Tasks vary in amount of structure
- Special needs and language support
- Flexible setting

The final working document:

Differentiation

Indicators of Excellence	Observable Features
A variety of teaching strategies is employed which allow for different preferred learning styles.	• Mixed ability classes could work on different topics. • A variety of styles and strategies is employed within a topic. • KS3 classes have a variety of styles and strategies within a double lesson. • Grouping of students according to need is employed within lessons.
Work is planned to allow for the range of student attainment within a class.	• Particular needs of students are recorded and used in planning. • Schemes of work provide core, extension and low attainer objectives for years 7 and 8. • Quantity of work expected in a given time is varied • The quantity of structure provided is varied (low achievers → more structure; high achievers → less). • Homework accounts for ability (e.g., different amounts are set for different students — core and extension; a set time is given for all allowing different amounts within that time). • Questioning is differentiated (see "Effective Questioning"). • Tiered assessments are used (see "Assessment"). • Different assessment strategies are used (see "Assessment"). • Differentiated targets are set. • Starting points are adjusted according to prior learning.

Table 3   *(Cont'd)*

Indicators of Excellence	Observable Features
Setting is an effective means of differentiation.	• Set placement is flexible. It is reviewed in October and at 1/2 terms thereafter. Individual cases are considered at any time. • Teachers identify core needs and objectives for the set and all students can achieve these. • Teachers differentiate within the sets and all students are appropriately challenged and supported.
Teachers' expectations are matched to the students' abilities.	• Teachers' responses to students' oral and written work are differentiated to provide support, challenge and encouragement. • Teachers are aware of the special and individual needs of students in their classes and take appropriate action (e.g., individual learning, support teacher, help club, home help program).

self-evaluation *processes* (Is the school doing it? Is the school doing it well?).

Professional Development, Professionalism and Professionalization

The Ensuring Excellence framework appears to be a powerful mechanism for the continuous professional development of teachers. The process of developing Indicators of Excellence and transforming these into Observable Features is a direct and explicit means of developing practice. As teachers work together to define high quality teaching in a particular area they develop a precise language for discussing teaching and learning. As they do this they draw upon their professional knowledge and that of their colleagues and make their theories and beliefs about effective teaching explicit: "The maturing professional teacher is one who has taken some steps toward making explicit his or her theories and beliefs ..." (Clark, cited in Hargreaves & Fullan, 1992, p. 76).

Teachers research further and make use of expertise available in journals, books, local authority advisers, and university lecturers. Throughout, this is a developmental process.

Teachers are involved in lesson observations, either at the stage of developing Observable Features or at the stage of gathering data and evidence. This is a learning experience in itself. Teachers learn from observing each other teach, but if this learning is to go beyond the level of picking up tips and useful techniques then the observations must be tightly focused. The Ensuring Excellence model provides a very precise focus for observations through the Observable Features.

One immediate outcome of evaluation is the identification of areas for improvement. This leads to training needs, but in the Ensuring Excellence model two things stand out. First, considerable professional development will have gone on *throughout* the process of evaluation so some form of school improvement may have already occurred. Second, the involvement of teachers at every stage of the process means that the development needs are recognized and understood. This gives any subsequent training or development work a much higher chance of succeeding and having an impact on classroom practice. As Hopkins, Ainscow, and West (1994) note, staff development initiatives have a greater chance of success if located in the teachers' own classrooms.

Such a process is best described as "evaluation as improvement" (Hopkins, 1989, p. 27). This contrasts with Hopkins' promotion of "evaluation *for* improvement," where evaluation outcomes are linked in a formative manner to the school improvement but *not* to the change process itself (Hopkins, 1989, p. 27). In "evaluation *for* improvement," the evaluation and the resulting change are distinct. In "evaluation *as* improvement" the change and the evaluation are facets of the same process. It is interesting to note that Hopkins' more recent work, in particular with the Improving the Quality of Education for All (IQEA) project, links forms of evaluation more holistically with change and the change process (Hopkins, Ainscow, & West, 1994).

It has become clear from our experiences that involvement in peer evaluation of classroom practice may be connected with enhanced professionalism. It is not so clear, however, how much the involvement enhances professionalism, and in what ways. It would be glib and naïve to suppose that when teachers engage in more frequent, more informed, concrete and precise discussion about practice they become more professional in any meaningful sense of the word. The concept of professionalism and the meanings and motives of professionalization need to be clarified in any given context. This is not the place to engage in a review of the literature on teacher professionalism. Interested readers will find much on this in the works of Donald Schön (e.g. Schön, 1983), a discourse on the moral aspects of professionalism in Sockett (1993), and a contemporary edited debate in Goodson and Hargreaves (1996).

Particularly relevant to our discussion, however, are some of the six elements of professionalism described by Lee Shulman. Of these, the fifth is "the need for learning from experience, as theory and practice interact in the presence of chance and unpredictability" and the sixth is "a professional community to monitor quality and aggregate knowledge" (Shulman, 1998, p. 9, cited in Day, 2000). These certainly occur during an evaluation using the Ensuring Excellence framework. Classical descriptions of professions also describe professionals as having a specialized knowledge base or "shared technical culture" (Hargreaves & Goodson, 1996; Lortie, 1975; Rosenholtz, 1991). Lortie (1975), Rosenholtz (1991) and others provide evidence, however, that this shared technical culture is limited or lacking in many, if not the majority of schools. Hargreaves (1984) suggests that even when some form of shared technical culture exists, it is based primarily on personalized and localized experience rather than on any form of information emanating from outside individual teachers' classrooms. This view is echoed by Little (1990) in her review of the literature concerning collegial relations among teachers.

A contrasting and more positive view is that some of the perceived successes of Ensuring Excellence are substantially due to the emphasis placed on this personalized and localized experience as the starting point for the evaluation process. In legitimizing personal craft knowledge, it gains the support and commitment of the teachers. It has been suggested that teachers make judgments about change and development based on practicality in context rather than abstract rationality. They maintain a powerful sense of what works and what doesn't, not in the abstract, but in their specific context (Doyle & Ponder, 1978, cited in Hargreaves, 1994). If this is so, then rooting evaluation criteria in teachers own classrooms and then supplementing this with more general theory may well be a more successful route to self-evaluation than using general theories as starting points. Moreover, teachers' anecdotal "storytelling" may be regarded as a weak substitute for more robust forms of deliberation about practice but it may also be a widely underestimated source of rich, cumulative knowledge (Little, 1990).

So, at West Island School, evaluative criteria for such things as "use of

ICT in technology," "effective life-skills teaching," "group speaking and listening in languages," and "promoting linguistic diversity" have been developed from teachers' own observations of what was occurring in their classrooms, explicitly using *what works here, for us* as exemplars of good practice.

The processes of school self-evaluation also need to be understood in the context of teachers' professional lives and the political and economic contingencies surrounding them. Hargreaves and Goodson (1996) make a distinction between "professionalism" and "professionalization" in the context of teachers' work. Professionalization involves (among other things) the push to establish professional status for teachers. However, contemporary projects that seek this professionalization of teachers' work are, they say, paradoxical, confused and contradictory in intent and outcome.

Examples of such professionalization projects include the establishment of sets of "professional" standards of practice. These seek to *enhance* professional standards but contribute to a *reduction* in teacher autonomy and empowerment. Examples include projects such as the National Board of Professional Teaching Standards in the United States, the Australian standard-certifying Council of Teachers, the report by Hay McBer (2000) on teacher effectiveness, and the establishment of pay thresholds based on judgments of competence and expertise in the United Kingdom. These all have the potential to lead to de-professionalization (Hargreaves & Goodson, 1996).

Increasing public accountability and the imposition of centralized and prescriptive curricula in some contexts may have weakened teachers' professional confidence and left them uncertain of their right to take curriculum decisions (Helsby & McCulloch, 1996). The increased complexity and intensification of teachers work and roles (through such initiatives as site-based management, development planning, increasing nationally administered testing) have the potential to de-professionalize teachers by burdening them with administrative trivia (Hargreaves, 1994; Hargreaves & Goodson, 1996).

Teachers at West Island School have worked in a context that is comparatively free from externally imposed initiatives and have retained a considerable degree of autonomy in their professional lives. Pay and working conditions are good and the students highly motivated and well behaved. This may go some way toward explaining the accepting and relaxed adaptation of the Ensuring Excellence initiative spanning 6 years.

School Culture and School Climate

A school's culture and climate are of central importance in any self-evaluation work (Hopkins, Ainscow, & West, 1994; Stoll & Fink, 1996). Though the terms continue to lack rigor and agreement among academics is difficult to find, they are too important to ignore (Little, 1990; Strivens, 1985). Our experiences in the wider QEF-funded Ensuring Excellence project have led us to concur with this view. Different schools have adapted the Ensuring Excellence framework in fundamentally different ways and this appears to be linked to teacher cultures.

It has become common to associate change with cultural change and to regard cultural change as involving some period of traumatic instability. Hopkins, Ainscow, and West (1994) argue that for any school improvement to take place as a result of an innovation, some form of destabilization of the culture must inevitably take place. They describe this destabilization as a period of "turbulence" (p. 197). This particular model for change and improvement appears to draw upon Kurt Lewin's (1952) notion of "freezing → cognitive restructuring → refreezing" for personal and cultural change, and Cuban's (1988) and Watzlawick, Weakland, and Fisch's (1974) descriptions of first-order and second-order change. Schein (1992), who regards culture as a stabilizing force formed from collective solutions to common problems in the past, appears to agree that "… the system must experience enough disequilibrium to force a coping process that goes beyond just reinforcing assumptions that are already in place" (p. 298).

It is our experience, however, that little of this *turbulence* or *destabilization* has taken place in the culture, or cultures, of West Island School as a result of Ensuring Excellence. A closer look at Lewin (1952), Schein (1992) and others indicate that destabilization and turbulence are terms to describe a change in culture and are *not necessarily* experienced negatively by the individuals involved. Schein (1992, p. 304), for example, proposes eleven hierarchical cultural change mechanisms that may operate at various levels of organizational maturity. The first of these typically occur, according to Schein, in the early stages of an organization's development and thus appear more appropriate to a developing school like West Island. These changes are not described as turbulent and include incremental change through evolution, change through systematic promotion from subcultures, planned change through development and parallel learning structures. This latter process creates new learning alongside existing shared assumptions and provides a psychological safety net for a change in basic shared assumptions to take place. The ways in which Ensuring Excellence has been introduced in schools appears congruent with this process. Only changes in basic assumptions occurring in mature organizations with well-embedded cultures involve any turbulence of the types implied by Hopkins, Ainscow, and West (1994).

It is possible that the philosophical assumptions of Ensuring Excellence when it was introduced were not particularly at odds with the prevailing culture of West Island School. The Ensuring Excellence project members viewed school self-evaluation as best occurring in a climate of trust and openness, where risk-taking was acceptable and where teamwork was an integral part of the modus operandi of the teachers. Where this was not the case, the self-evaluation projects could be developed sensitively and be part of the deliberate creation of such a climate.

At West Island School, a young, confident and talented teaching staff charged with the common goal of starting and developing a new school found the ideas surrounding school self-evaluation to be consistent with their "basic assumptions," the building blocks of culture (Schein, 1992, p. 22). Since the school's inception, teams had been formed and re-formed and given considerable autonomy to develop major areas of the school. Among teachers in some department teams, trust was high, visiting others' lessons was accepted, and risk-taking was encouraged. This was supported and developed in part through the introduction of a teacher appraisal model based on peer-supported action research. A study by one faculty head during 1997–1998 revealed that teachers at West Island School were keen to receive feedback on their performance in order to develop and improve teaching and learning and that the appraisal model was accepted and appreciated (Stanley, 1998). There was little suspicion or defensiveness over evaluation.

Thus the Ensuring Excellence innovation was assimilated with ease into the school. Moreover, the process was introduced initially into *volunteer* subject departments. These departments were those which had already developed cultures which allowed the easy assimilation of self-evaluation practices. Siskin (1994) provides evidence from the United States that single secondary school cultures are not as prevalent as departmental cultures and that these departmental cultures can vary widely within a single school.

Some could argue that no real change has occurred through the introduction of Ensuring Excellence. Certainly, as yet, none of the types of second-order change as described by Watzlawick, Weakland, and Fisch (1974) appear to have occurred. We would tentatively propose, however, that it is possible for Ensuring Excellence to cause a fundamental change in the technical cultures of teams within the school through an examination of pedagogy. In defining Indicators of Excellence, teachers confront their basic assumptions about education and make these explicit to colleagues. In exceptionally open and trusting teams, teachers experience conflicting models of teaching and learning. For example, Bottery (1990) describes four "codes" of education, which are founded on differing and mutually exclusive views of the *purposes* of education:

1. Cultural transmission: the transmission of cultural heritage;
2. Child-centered: development of the individual's own construction of reality;
3. Social reconstruction: development of rational criticism and change; and
4. Gross National Product: the child as contributor to the nation's economic well-being.

Fenstermacher and Soltis (1998) provide a similar analysis with the emphasis on approaches to teaching resulting from the teacher's underlying purposes in educating:

1. Executive approach: preparing students to learn particular knowledge and develop particular concepts and skills;
2. Liberationist approach: freeing the mind of the student; and
3. Therapist approach: development of the self.

Similarly, Bruner (1999) proposes four models of pedagogy that emphasize different educational goals:

1. Seeing children as imitative learners (the acquisition of know-how),
2. Seeing children as learning from didactic exposure (the acquisition of propositional knowledge),
3. Seeing children as thinkers (the development of intersubjective change), and
4. Seeing children as knowledgeable (the management of objective knowledge).

Ongoing research by one of the present authors suggests that teachers focus on the practicalities of teaching (timing of topics, availability of resources, etc.) during meetings for the planning of teaching. Questions of fundamental purpose and implications for practice do not typically form part of the conversation. This supports Little's (1990) findings that generally teachers' collaborative activity does not add up to much. There have been glimpses during the Ensuring Excellence process that point to the possibility of more substantial debates among teachers regarding purpose and pedagogy.

For example, one of the authors was witness to a debate among mathematics teachers, which sprung from an evaluation of investigational work with 11- and 12-year-old students. Such work typically involves students working over an extended period of around a week on an open-ended problem like using a given piece of card to make a box with the largest possible volume. It was agreed that the objectives of such tasks should be clear and achievable and that two types of objectives were pertinent: objectives relating to process, and objectives relating to outcome. In other words, the students should solve a particular problem (outcome) but they should also use and be aware of a range of strategies for solving the problem (process).

This led to a debate that temporarily polarized opinion among the teachers. Several believed that the students should *discover* effective methods and strategy through experience and that they should gain such experience over an extended time and several tasks. Others believed that the students should be *provided* with a selection of tried and tested methods and strategies at the start of the year and that they should choose from these when working on the problem. This revealed fundamental differences in how members of this team of teachers conceptualized such work, differences in their beliefs about how children learn to problem-solving, and differences in the purposes of this part of the curriculum. Moreover, this team of teachers had been working together for a number of years under the assumption that there was consensus in this area.

It is possible that the Ensuring Excellence process can provide a forum for teachers to confront their assumptions about the purposes of teaching, their theories about how children learn (constructivist, transmission, etc.), and the resulting methods used in the classroom as in the example above. Moreover, the collaborative structure to the process encourages and assists teachers in articulating these theories and assumptions. It is highly likely that in most cases teachers may not express their assumptions in these technical terms and that strong and expert leadership may be needed to facilitate discussion along these lines. This creates possibilities for school-university partnerships whereby researchers and lecturers in education may collaborate in self-evaluation efforts.

The roles taken in such partnerships are still far from clear. Stoll, MacBeath, and Mortimore (2001) call for outside critical friends to help schools become more self-sufficient in their own self-evaluation and improvement efforts and suggest a need for high-quality critical friendship. What exactly constitutes high quality critical friendship is still problematic. de Lima (1999) discusses the notion of the friendly critic, emphasizing an essential distinction. In de Lima's view, friends are rarely critical but it is possible to be critical in a friendly way. He believes that cognitive conflict is essential for the growth of teacher communities and true collegiality and that this is brought about through relationships that are largely free from strong affective ties.

This leads to a possible additional or alternative role for researchers and lecturers in school-university partnerships. That is as a friendly critic who challenges groupthink (Janis, 1972) and helps teams of teachers surface and debate fundamental differences in conception and perception of purpose and pedagogy, as in the example on investigational work above. Whether this role is in addition to that suggested by Stoll, MacBeath, and Mortimore (2001) or is an alternative is a question worth exploring through action.

Finally, engagement in professional dialogue of this order may lead to the form of strong collegiality described by Little (1990) as "joint work" (p. 159), and the "situated certainties of collected professional wisdom" enthusiastically promoted by Hargreaves (1994, p. 248).

Quality Assurance — For What Purpose?

A dilemma exists on the role of self-evaluation approaches such as Ensuring Excellence in relation to wider systems of quality assurance in schools generally. In essence, the dilemma is between accountability and development. For a particular school, at any given specific moment in its life cycle, the key questions are as follows:

1. Is the *purpose* of its self-evaluation activity to *prove* or to *improve* quality? In other words, is the school seeking to demonstrate that its current practices already meet certain quality criteria, or is it

attempting to achieve an improvement in the quality of its current practices?

2. Who are the *audiences* of the school's self-evaluation activity? Is it the school's governing council, the organization which acts as the school's sponsoring body, the school principal and senior management team, the staff of the school, the parents, the students, the Education Department, or the wider community? Which audience and whose agenda is the evaluation activity primarily serving?

A school which tries to prove and improve quality with the same evaluation exercise, or tries to address the often competing and conflicting agendas of different audiences with just a single process, or is simply unclear about either purpose or audience is more than likely to achieve confusion. In today's climate, no school can afford to dissipate precious time, energy, resources and the goodwill of its stakeholders.

The more self-evaluation tends toward being a low-risk, politically safe, cut-and-dried procedural activity, the less likely it is going to serve as a vehicle for change and school improvement. Yet high-risk, open-ended self-evaluation could potentially lead to losers and casualties. It therefore needs to be managed with political sensitivity, and is best conducted within a school culture which values not just the quality of learning, but also the key people who facilitate that learning. The senior management needs to give clear support to such self-evaluation activity, and have an acute awareness of its likely impact on various constituents of the school community and beyond.

On the other hand, no self-improving school has the luxury of operating purely in developmental mode without needing to be accountable to the students it serves and to its other stakeholders. Within a framework of quality assurance, there must exist strategies and processes that validate the soundness of a school's policies and practices and the competence of its staff, to the satisfaction of all concerned. Internal audit, external inspection, and staff monitoring and appraisal are examples. The key question is — be it accountability or development, to what extent should teachers be professionally involved? Or is quality assurance the domain of management, consultants and inspectors?

There are schools in many different education systems that have periodically taken part in externally administered quality assurance or quality control procedures, such as inspections. In systems such as the

U.K.-based OFSTED inspection systems, there is evidence in the OFSTED database that schools address areas of concern identified by inspectors and many subsequently improve (for example re-inspection findings, and outcomes such as attendance and examination results). It is, however, not the intention that the inspection team is responsible for facilitating the improvement efforts. Further evidence would need to be sought, in the United Kingdom and elsewhere, for changes in classroom practice following external inspections.

In the case of West Island, the strong involvement of teachers in teams was the driving force for exploring and enhancing teaching and learning approaches in the classrooms. In the view of the authors, such involvement of teachers as empowered professionals is an essential ingredient to school improvement. How this complements or supplements external inspections is a question which is worthy of more detailed consideration.

There are a number of educational systems within which teaching is considered a profession in only but name. This is because, in comparison with other professions,

1. Teachers are not involved in any significant way over entry to and governance of the profession,
2. Teachers collectively do not assert sufficient influence over their field of professional activity, and
3. Teachers seldom have the opportunity to engage in critical reflection and dialogue over their professional practice.

The last point is the most important as far as developing the professionalism of teachers is concerned. Whatever the other outcomes may be in terms of school improvement, such as student attainment and adding value, there is considerable evidence within this case history that self-evaluation activity has provided substantial opportunities for teachers to be engaged in professional talk about what goes on within their classrooms, thus contributing to the professionalization of the teachers involved.

How then does the particular experience of West Island School inform the wider discussion about school improvement? Different education systems can cite their own examples of externally driven attempts to raise standards. Teachers "teach to the test" or focus their attention on the variable to be measured, like numeracy or literacy, and for a short period, pupil attainment improves. The authors contend that where teachers have been deployed as technical instruments and not as empowered professionals, these improvements are seldom sustainable. Far too often teachers have not been involved professionally in gathering and interpreting the evidence which points to the need for improvement, have had no input on the purposes or approaches for achieving improvement, and rarely become involved in sharing their reflections through professional dialogue on whether and how their professional activity is making a difference to students' learning. The teacher teams at West Island School experienced those empowering processes in their involvement with the Ensuring Excellence project and now continue to do so as part of their regular professional work.

Policy makers should be aware that in practice, schools and teachers have redefined, accommodated or subverted externally imposed innovations more often than they have embraced and internalized them. As an innovation, the Ensuring Excellence initiative is successful not just because of its sound conceptual framework and its perceived relevance to the schools, but because participating schools were empowered with the freedom to explore how best to apply it. Strategic decision-makers for educational reforms at systemic level should therefore recognize that desired change comes through an engagement with each school's unique culture and explicitly empower teachers to actively interpret how improvements are best implemented in their specific contexts. The example of West Island indicates that involvement in self-evaluation activity engages teachers in reflective practice and professional dialogue in teams. It is this which empowers teachers as professionals and sustains school improvement.

References

Bottery, M. (1990). *The morality of the school: The theory and practice of values in education*. London: Cassell.

Bruner, J. (1999). Folk pedagogies. In J. Leach & B. Moon (Eds.), *Learners and pedagogy* (pp. 4–20). London; Thousand Oaks, CA: Paul Chapman Publishing.

Cohen, L., & Manion, L. (1994). *Research methods in education* (4th ed.). London; New York: Routledge.

Cuban, L. (1988). A fundamental puzzle of school reform. *Phi Delta Kappan, 69* (5), 341–344.

Day, C. (2000, December). *Teacher professionalism: Choice and consequence in the new orthodoxy of professional development and training*. Paper presented at the Continuing Teacher Education and School Development Symposium, Aristotle University, Thessaloniki, Greece.

de Lima, J. A. (1999, July). *Teacher collegiality as a lever for school change*. Paper presented at the International Study Association on Teachers and Teaching 9th Biennial Conference, Dublin.

Denzin, N., & Lincoln, Y. (Eds.). (1998). *Collecting and interpreting qualitative materials*. Thousand Oaks, CA: Sage.

Fenstermacher, G., & Soltis, J. (1998). *Approaches to teaching* (3rd ed.). New York: Teachers College Press.

Fitz-Gibbon, C. T. (1996). *Monitoring education: Indicators, quality and effectiveness*. London: Cassell.

Fullan, M. (1999). *Change forces: The sequel*. London; Philadelphia: Falmer Press.

Glaser, B. G., & Strauss, A. L. (1967). *The discovery of grounded theory: Strategies for qualitative research*. Chicago: Aldine.

Goodson, I., & Hargreaves, A. (Eds.). (1996). *Teachers' professional lives*. London; Washington: Falmer Press.

Hargreaves, A. (1984). Experience counts, theory doesn't: How teachers talk about their work. *Sociology of Education, 57*(4), pp. 244–254.

Hargreaves, A. (1994). *Changing teachers, changing times: Teachers' work and culture in the postmodern age*. London: Cassell.

Hargreaves, A., & Fullan, M. (Eds.). (1992). *Understanding teacher development*. London: Cassell; New York: Teachers College Press.

Hargreaves, A., & Goodson, I. (1996). Teachers' professional lives: Aspirations and actualities. In I. Goodson & A. Hargreaves (Eds.), *Teachers' professional lives* (pp. 1–27). London; Washington, DC: Falmer Press.

Helsby, G., & McCulloch, G. (1996). Teacher professionalism and curriculum control. In I. Goodson & A. Hargreaves (Eds.), *Teachers' professional lives* (pp. 56–74). London; Washington, DC: Falmer Press.

Hopkins, D. (1989). *Evaluation for school development*. Milton Keynes, the United Kingdom: Open University Press.

Hopkins, D., Ainscow, M., & West, M. (1994). *School improvement in an era of change*. London: Cassell.

House, E. R. (1979). Technology versus craft: A ten year perspective on innovation. *Journal of Curriculum Studies, 11*(1), pp. 1–15.

Janis, I. (1972). *Victims of groupthink: A psychological study of foreign-policy decisions and fiascoes*. Boston: Houghton Mifflin.

Lewin, K. (1952). Group decision and social change. In G. Swanson, T. Newcomb, & E. Hartley (Eds.), *Readings in social psychology* (rev. ed., pp. 459–473). New York: Holt.

Little, J. W. (1990). The persistence of privacy: Autonomy and initiative in teachers' professional relations. *Teachers College Record, 91*(4), pp. 509–536.

Lortie, D. (1975). *Schoolteacher: A sociological study*. Chicago: University of Chicago Press.

MacBeath, J. (1999). *Schools must speak for themselves: The case for school self-evaluation.* London; New York: Routledge.

McBer, H. (2000). *Research into teacher effectiveness: A model of teacher effectiveness.* Report by Hay McBer to the Department for Education and Employment. London: DfEE.

Nias, J., Southworth, G., & Yeomans, R. (1989). *Staff relationships in the primary school: A study of organizational cultures.* London: Cassell.

OFSTED. (2000). *Handbook for the inspection of secondary schools with guidance on self-evaluation.* London: The Stationery Office.

Parlett, M., & Hamilton, D. (1977). Evaluation as illumination: A new approach to the study of innovatory programmes. In D. Hamilton, D. Jenkins, C. King, B. MacDonald, & M. Parlett (Eds.), *Beyond the numbers game: A reader in educational evaluation* (pp. 6–22). Basingstoke, the United Kingdom: Macmillan.

Rosenholtz, S. (1991). *Teachers' workplace: The social organization of schools.* New York: Teachers College Press.

Schein, E. (1992). *Organizational culture and leadership* (2nd ed.). San Francisco: Jossey-Bass.

Schön, D. (1983). *The reflective practitioner: How professionals think in action.* New York: Basic Books.

Siskin, L. S. (1994). *Realms of knowledge: Academic departments in secondary school.* Washington, DC: Falmer Press.

Sockett, H. (1993). *The moral base for teacher professionalism.* New York: Teachers College Press.

Stanley, R. (1998). *The motivation of teachers and the management of motivation at West Island School: A case study.* Unpublished master's thesis, University of Leicester.

Stoll, L., & Fink, D. (1996). *Changing our schools: Linking school effectiveness and school improvement.* Buckingham; Philadelphia: Open University Press.

Stoll, L., MacBeath, J., & Mortimore, P. (2001). Beyond 2000: Where next for effectiveness and improvement. In J. MacBeath & P. Mortimore (Eds.), *Improving school effectiveness* (pp. 191–207). Buckingham; Philadelphia: Open University Press.

Strauss, A., & Corbin, J. (1998). *Basics of qualitative research: Techniques and procedures for developing grounded theory* (2nd ed.). Thousand Oaks, CA: Sage.

Strivens, J. (1985). School climate: A review of a problematic concept. In D. Reynolds (Ed.), *Studying school effectiveness* (pp. 45–57). London: Falmer Press.

Watzlawick, P., Weakland, J., & Fisch, R. (1974). *Change: Principles of problem formation and problem resolution.* New York: W. W. Norton.

15

Creating Partnership for Architects, Students and Community

Bernard V. Lim

Abstract

This chapter reviews how the process of creative learning and an appreciation of the built environment may afford an insight into future curriculum development and provide a new model for bringing together professionals and the community in the creative learning process.

As "Architecture" represents a vast source of material for observation and for the learning of many subjects, this chapter examines the idea of an integrated curriculum program by means of an innovative discovery project called "Exploring Architecture and Designing the Built Environment Programmes." The effectiveness of a series of creative discovery and interactive workshops and visits, which aimed to provide an integrated project-learning model, are evaluated in this chapter with illustrative model examples. The built environment became the "classroom" for developing and strengthening skills.

Furthermore, under the auspices of the Hong Kong Institute of Architects as an example, a collaboration between professionals, educationalists, teachers, parents, and students from primary and secondary schools, on a scale unprecedented in Hong Kong, was achieved through an educational process of exploring architecture and the built environment. This will not only promote an integrated rather than the traditional disjointed subject curriculum, but will also extend the perspective of the classroom to include the much wider and more stimulating perspectives provided by the built environment, with the involvement of both professionals and the community.

Introduction

This chapter describes the setting up of an integrated curriculum program involving professionals and community through an innovative discovery project called "Exploring Architecture and Designing the Built Environment Programmes." The project formed the first comprehensive summer program of the "World Day of Architecture 2000 — Architecture for Learning," which was organized by the Community Development Committee of the Hong Kong Institute of Architects (HKIA) and funded by the Quality Education Fund. The purpose was to inspire primary and secondary school students to take a closer look at the people, processes, and materials that are involved in the creation of buildings and places. Students got *involved* with voluntary architects, students of architecture, university professors of architecture, their school teachers, and their parents. They learnt to recognize and solve design problems, test engineering principles, weigh environmental issues, and "read" buildings. The built environment became the "classroom" for developing and strengthening skills in critical and creative thinking, problem solving, analysis, evaluation, teamwork, and, above all, in *designing their environment.*

The effectiveness of a series of creative discovery and interactive workshops and visits was also evaluated. These workshops and visits aimed to provide an integrated project-learning model involving subjects such as social studies, geography, history, science, art, mathematics and industrial arts. Over 600 students, teachers and parents participated in the summer of 2000. The outcome of the project benefited the community over a much wider spectrum, however, through public exhibition, publicity and publication, and its possible future adoption into the curriculum by schools pursuing a similar integrated curriculum program.

The project goal was achieved by working with secondary/primary school teachers, students of architecture, and professionals, in order to help the participating students to appreciate their built environment and architecture and to understand that they can make a positive impact on their environment through their decisions and their creativity. Subsequently, products including the design ideas, creative solutions, drawings, models, and so forth, from these workshops and processes were presented and documented for a public exhibition at the Hong Kong Science Museum during the month of October 2000, and this helped to increase other students' and the general public's appreciation of the built environment. An

Architectural Discovery Programmes Source Book was also published to assist schools and teachers to carry out similar activities in the future.

The chapter also reviews how the *process of creative learning* and *appreciation of the built environment* may offer an insight into future curriculum development, and provide a new model of *associating professionals and the community* in the creative learning process. Eventually it may be possible to appreciate all the creative work done by the students in 2000 during the "Architecture for Learning" summer camps, design workshops, visits and competitions: as the former Director of Education, Mr. Matthew Cheung, JP, remarked in his opening address to the above-mentioned public exhibition, the events created "chances for creativity" for all. Indeed, throughout the events, instead of "one single solution," one saw evidence of "all possibilities," toward which our children in Hong Kong worked boldly and freely in an attempt to express their full potential.

The World Day of Architecture 2000 (WDA 2000) program set a meaningful example by encouraging many young "friends of architecture" from numerous secondary and primary schools to become actively involved in the "Architecture for Learning" program. The partnership role of the HKIA was instrumental first in bringing together the schools, their students and the professionals, and secondly in providing the environment and resources for the discovery process.

To involve the wider community in the process, the HKIA invited other collaborating bodies to contribute to the organization of the events. These bodies included: Friends of the Earth (Hong Kong); the Hong Kong Science Museum of the Leisure and Cultural Services Department; and the Architecture/Building Studies Departments and the Students' Associations of The University of Hong Kong (HKU), The Chinese University of Hong Kong (CUHK), City University of Hong Kong (CityU) and the School of Professional and Continuing Education (SPACE) of HKU. Supported further by the Education and Manpower Bureau and various School Councils, this was the first experiment in *cross-discipline partnership* to be carried out in Hong Kong. Individual schools attempting to adopt a similar project-

learning model may consider a similar cross-discipline partnership arrangement, perhaps on a smaller scale.

The important element is "discovery" — an experiential process by the participating students themselves (Bruner, 1961). As part of the process of encouraging creativity, the organizers allowed the participating students to think of, discover, produce, and invent elements of the built environment that were new to them, and to go even further by creating elements new to our culture and current designs (Kneller, 1965, pp. 62–68). The volunteer architects, university professors and students of architecture acted as facilitators by providing the context for the creative and interactive events — a process of exploratory learning by students that was much needed in Hong Kong. Schools, teachers, and activity organizers were subsequently invited to use or modify these games, activities and exercises to inspire our younger generation to appreciate their built environment, as they will have a part to play in shaping a better one in the future. As pointed out by Baniassad (2001), Chair Professor and Head of the Department of Architecture of the CUHK, "It is a valuable complement to the elementary educational programs, most of which generally focus on memory rather than on discovery and observation as the process of education."

Discovery Camps for Secondary School Students

In order to provide a context for discovery learning and to encourage full participation, a summer camp was organized in July 2000 as the first event of WDA 2000. This was a 3-day Discovery Camp for upper secondary school students from various schools which took place on the CUHK campus. It was structured to incorporate games (including appreciation of form, dimensions, texture, and structure, etc.), day-tour site visits, evening sharing visits by numerous professionals, and the final creation of large models by the students' teams which would be combined to form the future Lantau, demonstrating ingenuity in design ideas as well as the students' concern for a more sustainable environment (for further details, see *HKIA*

Table 1   *Objectives and Activities of the Discovery Camp*

OBJECTIVES OF THE CAMP

1. To inspire secondary school students to experience the various aspects of architecture and the built environment, such as scale, materials, colors, building identity, space, and structure.
2. To inspire students to explore and discover our built environment using all our senses of sight, smell, hearing, touch and feeling.
3. To inspire students to appreciate our built environment and architecture and to recognize associated issues and problems.
4. To develop students' understanding so that they might have a positive impact on our environment through their creativity in design.

METHODOLOGY

The camp comprised a series of interactive games and programs designed to stimulate students to explore and discover what elements go to make up architecture and our built environment. The approach was one of experiential learning rather than lecturing. The students were also encouraged to participate fully, to think critically, to interact and express themselves freely, and to be creative in design during the whole process.

ACTIVITIES OF THE CAMP

CAMP	Part One	Basic Principles of Architecture

CAMP	Part Two	Exploration and Discovery of the Built Environment

CAMP	Part Three	Creation of Your Dream City

Newsletter 2000; see also Lim & Ng, 2000, 2001). Table 1 shows the details of the summer camp. Other activity formats, such as a workshop conducted in a multi-purpose hall, may also be suitably adopted for setting up games and projects, so long as they will give the students a break from the traditional classroom setting and the formal lecturing paradigm.

With the important educational goals for participating students to explore a new subject area of interest, organize themselves to react to a challenge task, and perform their creative expression, "the human LEGO" exercise is one of the group games that centered on observation of the features of the built environment (see Table 2).

After each session of an activity or game, the organizers called for immediate sharing of experiences in small groups, facilitated by university architecture students or volunteer architects group leaders, followed by voluntary sharing or personal response from individuals in front of the whole assembly. The sharing/discussion centered around the following questions:

1. Do we pay attention to things or buildings around us in our daily living environment?
2. How do we distinguish one building from another?

At the beginning of the camp, the students tended to have " laid back" or "observer" attitudes, but later the atmosphere became one of active

Table 2   *The Human LEGO Exercise*

OBJECTIVE OF "THE HUMAN LEGO"
To encourage students to observe everything in our daily living environment and to understand that different buildings and things have different features.

BRIEF
Students are to experience the idea that an object or a building has its own features, and are then tested on their observation, creativity and teamwork in this exercise.

TASK
Students are to imitate, as a group, an object or a building.

POSSIBLE OBJECTS
A Sofa, the Merry-Go-Round, a fax machine, the Cultural Centre, the Bank of China, the Convention Centre extension.

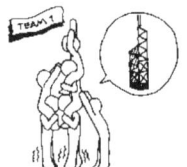  

participation, starting from the game "Feedback against the current Environment," using posters and drama, up to the last game "Human Plot Machine" in the evening, when teams joined hands and moved around a table to create their combined effort paintings. On one such sharing occasion, a participant said that he had not been expecting this sort of camp (He must have had preconceived ideas about the "lecturing type" of education), but then he said, *"It has been — really — quite fascinating!"*

Our daily environment in fact provides the best "classroom" for learning and exploration. Students should be given the maximum opportunity to go outside of their traditional classrooms to learn to experience from their surroundings.

Thus the second day commenced with three teams setting out on different routes to explore the multi-faceted built environment of Hong Kong. It must have been a tiring day even for these energetic youngsters, especially those along the steep Central walking route. Another team with the theme "Discovering Hong Kong Culture" explored the historical and cultural aspects of the Tsim Sha Tsui area, with practicing architects inspiring the students to examine our heritage and explore new possibilities of integrating the old and the new architecture (see Table 3).

The questions asked during the trips related to the concepts that had been covered in the first-day exercises, and which reinforced the concepts and knowledge introduced earlier. The architectural tours were no longer restricted to the professionals, but this time shared with the public — the budding "friends of architecture." After the tours, it was important that all teams concluded with a debriefing together.

There were also moments when students could learn from and work with professionals: Students had moments of warm personal sharing with architects and organizers. What are the answers to: "How do you erect the tower crane?", "How long have you practiced?", "Was it a good decision to pull down the old Railway Station to make way for the Cultural Centre?", and so forth. The young participants had a lot of interesting questions with which to test the professionals for enlightening answers. Having established

Table 3   *Discovering Hong Kong Culture*

OBJECTIVE OF "DISCOVERING HONG KONG CULTURE"

To encourage students to think about the relationship between new and old buildings and the image of a place.

BRIEF

Students are first given background information about the changes in the Tsim Sha Tsui district over time, and then stimulated by the possibilities of a new life or image for the city by visiting newly-renovated and designed buildings and spaces.

THE ITINERARY

1. 60 minutes   Antiques and Monuments Office (AMO) (activity 1 below)
2. 15 minutes   Kowloon Park/Park Lane
3. 15 minutes   Former History Museum
4. 45 minutes   Health Education & Resources Centre (activity 2 below)
5. 15 minutes   Peninsula Hotel (activity 3 below)
6. 10 minutes   Former Marine Police Station
7. 60 minutes   Clock Tower, Cultural Centre, Harbour Front (activity 4 below)

POSSIBLE ACTIVITIES

1. To visit the display and exhibition provided by the AMO as an introduction/ background information input.
2. To highlight the integration of new architecture into old historic buildings.
3. To notice the proportions of the existing hotel and its new extension by means of a simple sketching exercise (making a sketch of the whole building using simple geometrical shapes) so as to experience the harmony of an object.
4. To pay attention to the changes in our well-known harbor front and to think about what qualities go towards composing the image of a city. A sketching exercise to reflect the students' impressions of the district may be carried out.

SHARING/DISCUSSION

- What do you mean by the image/symbol of a city?
- What do you think of when hearing "the Pearl of Orient"?
- What factor(s) do you consider is/are the most critical: heritage, modernism, etc.? Why?
- What do you like and dislike?

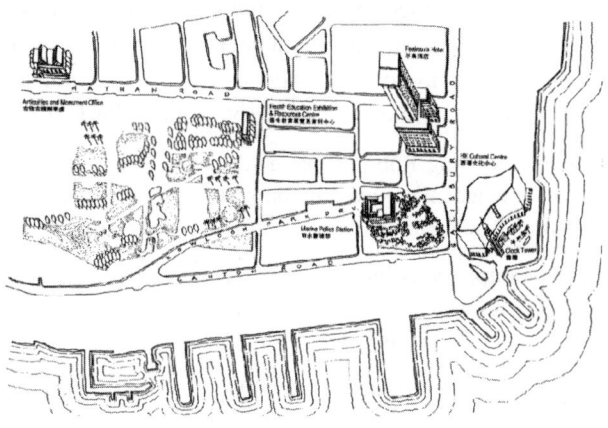

personal familiarity, the architects and the students subsequently worked in teams to construct the longest bridges possible from drinking straws for a competition — an interactive mode of learning for both the students and the professionals:

Everyone learnt from the functions and activities — the "discovery" process applied also to the program leaders, who led the group of over 100 participants through all the excitement and fun, after months of program creation with school teachers, educational psychologists, architecture professors and students, program coordinators and the architecture student group leaders. The high level of collaboration to prepare for the younger students among the professional architects and architecture students and professors was another achievement.

The sharing of experiences by the participants indicated their enjoyment of the functions both as fun and as a way of progressing towards an appreciation of our built environment. This was also reflected in the students' acceptance of an interactive and "discovery" process of learning:

> "People said that Hong Kong people don't have creativity, but now, look at the models we made: We proved by ourselves that we are full of creativity, let's use our gifts to create the future.," a 16 year-old participant said.

> "Before the camp, I was interested in architecture, but now I know that architecture is not only about building, and I will start to care about the environment, appreciate our living environment …"

> "Before the camp, I thought that architects were 'superior,' but now I have met architects who are very friendly and nice, and they deserve to be recognized because they are concerned about our living environment."

> "Before the camp, I thought that it would be a camp full of lectures, but having participated I found out that it was full of excellent games, I can say it is really so COOL! If I had known that before, even if it had cost double, I would still have joined it!"

Creative Workshops for Primary School Students

ACTIVITIES OF WORKSHOP

WORKSHOP Part One   Basic Principles of Architecture

WORKSHOP Part Two   Creation of an Imaginative Project

For younger primary school students, learning through dynamic games and peer group interaction would be particularly effective. At the end of July and August 2000, with the support of the Architectural Students Association of HKU and HKU SPACE students, 2 full-day creative workshops were organized for primary students, and each was joined by over 100 students, with support from over 30 HKIA members and architectural students (for further details, see *HKIA Newsletter 2000*; see also Lim & Ng, 2000, 2001). The morning program consisted of a "treasure hunt" competition, in which participating students were divided into 10 groups, who had to map themselves to different locations on the main campus of the HKU in order to play different games. Fundamental concepts such as texture, form, color and scale were experienced through these dynamic and stimulating interactions. Table 4 shows an example of one of the games: "Material Matching."

In the afternoon, all the children were engaged in a group creativity exercise called "Creation of Your Dream School," using a 60 cm × 60 cm × 60 cm frame or foam board half-cube. The project was immediately charged with creativity, imagination, excitement and fun. In just less than two hours, these half-cubes were totally transformed by the students' joint efforts into models full of energy, creative ideas, interesting forms, and vibrant colors. Representatives from each small group were finally asked

Table 4 *Material Matching Game*

OBJECTIVE OF "MATERIAL MATCHING"
To encourage students to observe the textures of different materials.

BRIEF
Students are to identify the original material from a texture sketch.

TASK
Students are to compare the textures shown on a piece of paper with those of the surroundings, and find out to which material each texture belongs.

SCORING SCHEME
Groups with correct answers to different questions earn corresponding marks [to stimulate interest in the "Treasure Hunt" competition].

MATERIAL PREPARATION:
A piece of white paper with textures from the surroundings (e.g., soil, stone) sketched on it.

to present their combined efforts and ideas, and to describe what had been learnt from the exercise and group efforts:

Table 5   *Creation of Your Dream School*

OBJECTIVE OF "CREATION OF YOUR DREAM SCHOOL"
To stimulate students' creativity and give them a chance to work as a group.

BRIEF
Students are to think of their dream campus and collaborate with each other in groups.

TASK
Students are given a half-cube made of foam board with the dimensions 60 cm x 60 cm x 60 cm. Each group is asked to express their idea of a dream campus using the half-cube and the materials provided.

POSSIBLE OUTCOME
Colorful and fully decorated half-cubes expressing the idea of a dream campus.

SHARING/DISCUSSION
- What is your dream campus?
- What facilities should it have?
- What do people do inside?
- In what way is it different from the school you are studying at?

MATERIAL PREPARATION
- half-cubes made of foam board with dimensions 60 cm x 60 cm x 60 cm
- color papers, poster colors, glue, aluminum foil, cans, paper cups.

Design Competitions/Charrette at the Science Museum

September, 2000 : A Day of Creativity!

The design competitions aimed to exercise imaginative ideas and visionary perspectives in designing a built environment. The primary school section consisted of a 1-day competition at a designated venue. The secondary school section competition, under the theme "i-SCHOOL," involved a presentation by the finalists, whose group works were carried out in the summer.

1. By Secondary School Student Teams — "i-SCHOOL" Design Competition

   Teams of secondary students shortlisted from among the numerous entries made their presentation to the Panel of Adjudicators. The finalist teams had produced such impressive perspectives in designing the school environment that the Panel decided that there should be two winning teams — from Ko Lui Secondary School and Leung Shek Chee College.

2. By Primary School Student Teams — Half-day Competition on "Dream Schools"

   Twenty-four teams of primary students in groups of five students each demonstrated their imaginative ideas, visions and energy using waste materials, colors and an outpouring of craftsmanship in their models for "Dream Schools." Having talked to the team representatives and after a careful viewing of the attractive models, the Panel of Adjudicators made their assessment immediately. Have architects ever imagined that classrooms could be arranged on a flying-wheel? Our winners for the Lower and Upper Primary Sections, from Emmanuel Primary School, Kowloon and the Hong Kong Taoist Association School, had produced such bold models that they attracted the interest of the press and appeared in many newspapers on the following day.

3. By School Principals, Teachers, Parents, HKIA Members and Students of Architecture — School Design Charrette

   While the students were busy with their school design competitions, a full-day School Design Charrette was organized in another wing of the venue, where teams of "potential users" and "architects" discussed the idea of creating a combined primary and secondary school, and presented interesting ideas and concept models at the end of the event/activity . Following the theme of "Architecture for Learning," the objective was to allow the professionals, parents and teachers to explore the possibilities of the learning environment as creatively as the students. The idea that "there can be many varied possibilities, and there need not be one model answer" was confirmed by the variety of solutions and approaches shared by the teams. The "professional" teams seemed to have been rightly inspired by the young students.

Sharing of Learning with the Community Public Exhibition, October, 2000, Science Museum

It was important to allow members of the public appreciate all the creative ideas and models produced by the students during the "Architecture for Learning" educational program, and also the works by HKIA Member Practices on the theme, and the proposals from the School Design Charrette. Students were able to appreciate their own works as well as those produced by professionals. The VIPs were indeed the students of architecture, children, school teachers and principals who participated in the "Architecture for Learning" program.

As the former Director of Education, Mr. Matthew Cheung, JP, said in his speech, the event created "chances for creativity" for all. Indeed throughout the activities, one could observe clearly "all possibilities," rather than "one single solution."

A schoolteacher came forward to the organizers and gave his sincere thanks to the HKIA for having created an opportunity for his students.

A member e-mailed the organizers to the effect that "The event was great. My son and daughters really enjoyed the workshops. I would like to congratulate you and your team for bringing architecture to the hearts of so many."

The Way Forward

In the HKIA's follow-up publication, the *Architectural Discovery Programmes Source Book*, teachers, parents, university lecturers, educationalists, and activity organizers were presented with a concise summary of the "discovery process." This sourcebook was prepared with a view to sharing the experiences of the event. Although the "discovery process" of WDA 2000 was witnessed by many, the Community Development Committee sincerely hopes that more young people of Hong Kong will be able to share a similar experience, with the possibility of an integrated curriculum program created by means of a partnership between the professionals and the community.

WDA 2000 was itself exploratory. As a professional institute, the HKIA collaborated for the first time with educationalists, teachers, parents, and students on a scale unprecedented in Hong Kong, and together they designed an educational process of exploring architecture and the built environment with primary and secondary school students from over 120 schools. Feedback from the participants and the imaginative creations produced and exhibited have provided encouraging signals for the further development of the creative discovery learning process and for the exploration of a new mode of collaboration. The HKIA is committed to continuing this process in the years to come, in order to encourage greater community participation with continuing support from the Quality Education Fund. This is also likely to lead to further examination of the curriculum development and instruction models in education in Hong Kong, and probably elsewhere too.

As mentioned above, architecture provides a vast source of material for observation and for the learning of many subjects, such as history, geography, mathematics, physics, and so forth, both by engaging students in direct observation of the human environment and culture, and by exercising their creativity in design. It is worthwhile in addition considering introducing such an integrated discipline in a creative manner into earlier education, during the current process of education reform and curriculum development in Hong Kong. This will not only promote an integrated rather than the traditional disjointed subject curriculum, but also extend the perspective of the classroom to include the much wider and more stimulating perspective embodied in the built environment (Massialas & Zevin, 1983).

Acknowledgments

The author wholeheartedly thanks all those who contributed to making the program possible: all the co-organizing and sponsoring bodies, in particular the Quality Education Fund Secretariat, the Education and Manpower Bureau and the Schools Councils, for rendering tremendous support, patience and advice; the direct grant from the CUHK; the Science Museum Curators and Administrators, for organizing the major public events and exhibition; the former Director of Education and former Director of Architectural Services, all the guests and jury members who officiated at the various ceremonies and competition judging; the Members/Council Members of the HKIA who contributed their valuable time as volunteer supporters in the WDA events; the Students Associations/student supporters from HKU, CUHK, CityU and HKU SPACE, for contributing their time, efforts and a lot of original, fresh and most creative ideas; the secondary school design competition adjudicator panel; and the primary school design competition adjudicator panel.

The secondary school design competition adjudicator panel included: Mr. Ip Cho-yin (former Quality Education Fund Steering Committee Member), Mr. Ying Yu-hing (former Honorary Treasurer Hong Kong Subsidized Secondary Schools Council), Prof. Patrick S. S. Lau, SBS (Professor of The Department of Architecture, HKU), Mrs. Julie Mo (Head of Division of Building Science & Technology, CityU), and Mr. Lam Wo-hei, JP (Past Chairman of The Architects Registration Board/Past Vice-President HKIA). The primary school design competition adjudicator panel included: Mr. S. H. Pau, JP (former Director of Architectural Services), Mr. S. A. A. Gafoor (former Principal Assistant Secretary for Education and Manpower, Quality Education Fund Secretariat), Mr. Anthony Poon (former Assistant Secretary for Education and Manpower, Quality Education Fund Secretariat), Mr. Fung Man-ching (Quality Education Fund Steering Committee Member), Mr. Lee Siu-hok (Subsidized Primary Schools Council Executive Committee Member), Mr. C. K. Yip (Chief Curator of The Hong Kong Science Museum, Leisure and Cultural Services Department), Mr. Gaylord Chan, MBE (Artist of International Renown), Prof. Essy Baniassad (Chairman and Head of The Department of Architecture, CUHK) and HKIA Past President Mr. Barry Will.

Thanks should also be given to Mr. Barry Will, Past President of HKIA, for his full support of the event and for writing the Forward for the sourcebook; Prof. Patrick S. S. Lau, SBS, Past President of HKIA and Prof. Essy Baniassad, Chairman and Head of The Department of Architecture, CUHK, for their continuing strong support and contribution of the Preface to the sourcebook; the Editorial Team from CUHK — Mr. M. K. Leung, Ms. Irene Wong, Mr. Edward Chung, Ms. Viola Poon, Mr. Jason Tang, Mr. Chan Wing-lung, Ms. Jocelyn Lee, for editing and illustrating the sourcebook; Ms. Rita Cheung and the Secretariat at HKIA; the Organizing Committee of the HKIA Community Development Committee, for turning our vision of sharing into reality with unbelievable commitment and contribution; Mr. Daniel Cheung, Program Leader of WDA 2000, for leading all the program activities; and lastly, to Mr. Stephen Tang, Council Member of HKIA, who initiated the idea of reaching the schools and students, and Mr. Vincent Ng, the Co-Chairman of the Organizing Committee and former Chairman of the HKIA Board of Internal Affairs, whose vision and determination created and successfully led us to the sharing of this most meaningful experience.

References

Baniassad, E. (2001). Preface. In B. V. Lim (Ed.), *Architectural discovery programmes source book* (p. A4). Hong Kong: The Hong Kong Institute of Architects, documented by the Department of Architecture, The Chinese University of Hong Kong.

Bruner, J. S. (1961). The act of discovery. *Harvard Educational Review, 31*(1), 21–32.

Kneller, G. F. (1965). *The art and science of creativity*. New York: Holt, Rinehart & Winston.

Lim, B. V., & Ng, V. (2000). A journey of discovery — Architecture for learning (I). *Space Magazine, 20*(August), 92–96.

Lim, B. V., & Ng, V. (2001). A journey of discovery — Architecture for learning (II). *Space Magazine, 25*(January), 80–84.

Massialas, B. G., & Zevin, J. (1983). *Teaching creatively: Learning through discovery*. Malabar, FL: Robert E. Krieger.

16

Toward Schooling for the 21st Century

Per Dalin

Abstract

Is a "good school" for our temporary society also a good school for those children who will occupy decision-making roles in the year 2020 or 2030? We know that the future is more unpredictable than ever, and one question this chapter is concerned with is: What learning experiences today can best help students to cope with the unfinished and live with uncertainties? The chapter does not present a given future scenario, rather, it selects 10 "revolutions," or major forces in present societies that will continue to have an impact on future living far into this new century. Among these are the knowledge and information revolution, the population growth, globalization, the economic and technology revolutions, the ecological revolution, and the social and cultural revolution, to mention a few. The chapter analyzes the impact on local context, what the learning needs of children are, and what the role of the school could be. It ends up with 10 basic questions for the reader to consider.

It was back in 1987 that IMTEC, the Norwegian-based Educational Foundation, started a project called "School Year 2020." The basic argument for the creation of this international project was the critique felt in many Western industrialized countries that schools did not respond adequately to the rapid changes in society. The schools were not in touch with the realities of daily challenges.

It was, however, an even more basic problem. One important mission that schools have is to prepare for the future when today's children shall be working and providing leadership, perhaps 20 years from now. We discovered that most educators were occupied with yesterday's challenges. Little time was spent in understanding the future. Indeed, the future seemed more uncertain than ever. How could schools respond to a rapidly changing society, where values, norms, cultures, political systems, social relationships, knowledge, technology and ecology are just examples of our living that are constantly challenged by rapid changes that form the global melting pot?

"School Year 2020" made an attempt to create a holistic view of a changing world, and to provide a picture of what a "good school" would be for children who would face the challenges of the new century. If we cannot find a satisfactory answer, we still know that the students as part of their reality have to face the unfinished, and live with the uncertainties of change and new challenges. What are the unique learning opportunities that help children to face changes, and cope with uncertainties?

We are uncertain about the validity of the data of this study beyond the Western industrialized countries; indeed, we also question some of the conclusions in our own systems. We see the value, however, of raising these issues, and begin to tackle the future challenges as the basis for school reform.

The Ten Revolutions

The word "revolution" in this context means a major change in the way realities are thought about and explained, in attitudes, in power relations and structures that have a major influence on the future of societies.

Today the world is moving from the modern industrial era to a new era, the post-modern. The world is in the middle of a social, political, economic and intellectual revolution. In short, the "School Year 2020" project identified 10 "revolutions" that we found particularly powerful in shaping the post-modern world, and which also will have a major impact on the future of schooling. They are: the knowledge and information revolution, the population revolution, globalization, the economic revolution, the technological revolution, the ecological revolution, the social and cultural revolution, the aesthetics revolution, the political revolution, and the values revolution.

The Knowledge and Information Revolution

This revolution emerges out of a new basic understanding of science, out of a large knowledge industry in numerous fields, and out of the development of an electronics and global infrastructure leading to a rapid expansion of knowledge and information. In practical vocational fields 50% of the knowledge today is irrelevant or will be outdated in 2 years (Bildungskommission NRW, 1995). It takes at least 10 years to change a curriculum, print learning materials, upgrade teachers and change schools. If we do not change our strategies of reform, schools will always be left hopelessly behind. The challenge that faces schools is to deal with "key knowledge" that can guide students' learning in the disciplines.

The Population Revolution

Also called a population explosion, it has major consequences for our daily lives and it will be increasingly so as our students become part of the labor force. The food situation, providing food for an additional 85 million new inhabitants each year, for example, is alarming. Access to water and food is increasingly unevenly distributed. The population growth is alarming, since it is a fact that those who have the least resources to pay live in those areas with the highest population growth. Our students are going to face the most difficult re-allocation challenges mankind has ever experienced.

Globalization

The globalization process is already a reality for many people. For some it means losing their job, for others it means better protection. For some regions (mostly North America, Western Europe and Japan) globalization means further economic growth, while others (e.g. Africa) lag behind. This means that the imbalances are maintained or increased. As the globalization process is taking on speed, large population groups are getting worried, and popular resistance movements (e.g. "Attac") are formed. Increasingly new issues that have been dealt with on a national level can no longer be resolved as a national issue (e.g. the fight against drugs). They are seen as global issues. Gradually our students will see themselves as members of a global community. What are the opportunities and what are the dangers, and how can schools prepare for this paradigm shift?

The Economic Revolution

From 1950 until 1980 the OECD countries quadrupled their wealth. In fact today these countries that represent some 17% of the world population control more than 70% of the world income. During the last decade other economies have soared, not the least the Chinese economy. These countries, like all countries with a rapid economic growth, experience "growing pains," including the fact that the differences in economic opportunities are widening. These countries are forced to take giant steps to move further into the "new economy." The rapidly expanding economies have given room and power to individuals who control vast resources enabling them to influence the stock market, and in fact have a major influence on national currencies. An emerging feeling is that economic growth coupled with a liberal globalization policy might undermine vital interests of the state, and ultimately of the individual. How can schools help students to live in the global economic reality?

The Technological Revolution

The century we have behind us, with tremendous breakthroughs in science and technology, provides us with both opportunities and a warning. The opportunities are numerous, as science and technology is changing many aspects of our daily life. The warning is simply to acknowledge that technological changes also come with a bill that needs to be paid. Often the bill is presented two to three generations later. Nevertheless, mankind has just started to use the technological opportunities, for example in information technology and biotechnology. We need to learn how to deal with the many choices that will be available to us. All choices have an ethical dimension. Our students will be faced with the fact that any step forward has a value dimension. What are we doing today to help students to be aware of basic value choices?

The Ecological Revolution

A leading German scientist, Ernst Ulrich von Weizsacher, argues that in the deadlock situation that the world is facing today, the industrialized countries must take the first step (von Weizsacker, 1992). His discussion starts with some fundamental figures: The world population is growing fast, the industrial production is now four times larger than it was in 1950, and through mass media the Western lifestyle has spread to be an ideal in increasingly more countries. Our students will be faced with a nearly impossible dilemma: To argue for less, to sell the argument of moderate consumption, a message that is unpopular today, but that may be the only wise decision looking 50–100 years ahead. How can we develop our democracies to enable them to make unpopular decisions? What learning experiences will help to build the necessary competencies to enable the future generations to think globally, longitudinally and thereby ecologically?

The Social and Cultural Revolution

The Western hemisphere and increasingly other parts of the world are being challenged as far as social relationships and traditional roles are concerned. Definitions of family and home are expanding. The role of youth, especially with regard to its relationship to the adult generation, is changing. One area of great importance in terms of social change is the changing role of women, which also has clear implications for the role of men. Although many will see this social "revolution" more as a careful step-by-step process, nevertheless significant, social changes are taking place. This is also true for the cultural changes that follow from an increasingly multicultural society. Schools have made a significant contribution enabling a changing role for women, and are also in the process of learning what it takes to learn to live in a multicultural society.

The Aesthetics Revolution

An aesthetic revolution is taking place that represents a reaction against the standardized, mass-industrialized consumer society. This movement takes many forms, for example in a rapidly growing interest in music festivals, in visiting museums and attending operas. In Norway over the past 30 years some 250 local communities have created music/art schools, which indicates that daily living is changing. It is vital that each student gets an opportunity to discover and use his/her creativity. We know that the aesthetic dimension in many ways represents the "added value." In fact we may be dependent on it for our living.

The Political Revolution

Modern democracies have a singular characteristic in that they have regularly become mass movements. At least in Europe and North America mass society has begun to de-massify. You will find liberation and self-determination movements, involving ethnic groups, minority groups, neighborhoods, alternative lifestyle groups as well as "single issue" groups. This active engagement in political movements happens at the same time as participation in the political parties is declining, and some of the most important political decisions are taken regionally or internationally because the nation state does not have the necessary power. The rapid changes in alliances in world politics present new challenges and new opportunities, both for the political and economic systems, as well as for the civilian society (e.g. the new "Attac" movement). Shall democracy survive it must renew itself. What do schools do to help our students to become democratic citizens?

The Values Revolution

Plurality and even social fragmentation, above all, have characterized the last century. Increasingly our societies become multicultural, and many ideologies and values are represented in daily settings. Many people are searching for basic values and meaning in their lives, and we see a number of "new age" spiritual values being practiced. Our experience so far is not very encouraging, and a serious dialogue is needed (Küng, 1990). Schools should be in an ideal situation to facilitate this dialogue.

Local Context

To what extent, and in what way have these macro forces influenced the local context of children and youth? Over the past 50 years, and in particular during the last 20 years, major changes have taken place in the life of children and youth in the Western hemisphere. That can be illustrated by looking more closely at the home, the peer group, the religious institutions, the media, and the workplace.

One dimension that is directly related to the rapid change in a number of essential areas of life is the relationship between children and adults. The old hierarchy has been exchanged with what we could call a "horizontal society." The old authority was built on the fact that the adults had relevant experience. That is less and less true. It often leads to unclear adult figures, and the young people are looking for someone and something that can replace the old dependencies.

They turn to the peer group. For the first time in human history, young people have become a powerful force. From the 1960s gradually young people earned their own money, developed their own music and a set of values and norms that were unique to the peer group. We got pop culture and youth power.

The religious institutions were also gradually losing their influence. Influenced by the media, information from the whole world, living in more multicultural settings — all these things made the youth question the traditional values. In many ways children and youth are starting without luggage, facing a tremendous complexity, being bombarded with information. The best example is the Internet.

The media is the new power base in almost all areas of life. Media has vast resources and use young people (most often) as role models. Young people develop their own "language," and use communication technology to influence their network. In Norway 7 out of 10 girls in the 13–15 age group have their own mobile telephone!

Coleman and Hoffer (1987), in a very important study of what they call "social capital" and its impact on learning, give new insight to the relationship of school and the local environment. In a study of public and private schools they discuss the so-called school contract. The researchers studied a large sample of public schools and private schools, and found only small differences in terms of student dropouts and student achievement. The exception was catholic schools, certain other religious schools (i.e. Jewish and Baptist schools), and schools where the majority of students came from Japanese and Chinese homes. The differences between the schools are, first and foremost, explained by different relationships between the school, the homes and the work environment. Coleman (1987) documents that in the last 20 years in the United States there has been a general "erosion" of social capital. He notes, as we have also argued in this chapter, that ego-centered activities, combined with less adult contact, increases the importance of adult participation in particular as far as the weakest students are concerned.

Visions for the New Century

So far we have briefly discussed some major forces contributing to the transformation of society, and we have looked at some implications in the local context. As we mentioned, some elements of the future are reasonably certain, but some elements can develop quite differently from what might be anticipated. We are facing an uncertain future that is holding a number of possibilities. That also means that the future is not a given. Every citizen can help mold our future, however, we need a vision of what we wish to happen.

What is a good school preparing the students for this future? It does not make sense to create a school for the future unless we have a vision for that future. Schools have a unique mission as institutions to prepare us for that vision. As a case in point, the "School Year 2020" project discussed the following vision for the future of society (Dalin & Rust, 1996):

1. An ecological vision: life in harmony with nature;
2. A vision of a fair, democratic society;
3. From dominance to partnership in social relations;
4. From a war to a peace economy;
5. A worthwhile life for the world's poor;
6. From mono-culturalism to multi-culturalism;
7. The vision of work for all;
8. Technology in the service of human growth;
9. Life skills in the service of health; and
10. From standardization to creativity.

"Critical mass" is the phenomenon that occurs when forces pull in the same direction. When this happens, constructive development is more likely. The danger is that the complex world we have outlined may not be capable of a unified movement toward a new future, resulting in catastrophe and chaos in different parts of the world. The world needs a more common vision and a set of ethical norms; otherwise it will be difficult to bring about fundamental change.

Learning Needs of Children and Youth

Dalin and Rust (1996) argue that:

> The starting point of any educational analysis must be the learning needs of children and youth, with the needs of both contemporary and future society being included ... We agree that contemporary issues may be of great importance to the schools. School life is real life. It should give essential

impulses to our lives here and now. It should provide room for students with different talents, as well as emotional and intellectual inclinations. The school must direct its attention to today's needs, but it should also prepare for the future. Therefore, we must meet the challenge: to think through the implications of tomorrow's developments for today's school. (p. 76)

Also, in the future the school will not be alone responsible for the child's learning. Learning takes place in everyday life. Indeed some of the most complex learning tasks take place in the home and the local community (e.g. learning a language). Some of this learning is tied to problem-solving activities where several students work and learn together, or to the introduction of new technologies, new processes, or new standards (Resnick, 1983). What should the role of the school be?

Students Need to Learn Basic Knowledge and Skills

This will include the ability to master their mother tongue. It will include basic knowledge, like basic numerical competence, the ability to understand the natural and social sciences, and the ability to deal with at least one foreign language. It is clear that encyclopedic knowledge, facts and simple data will be important but they certainly will not be sufficient. The fundamentals of science change. What becomes essential is for the students to understand the structure of scientific paradigms, with their attendant facts and concepts, and not to be drawn into peripheral issues. Students must have a wide and stable grasp of basic frameworks and the facts attendant to them (Anderson, 1981).

With such a basic understanding students will be better placed to digest and interpret the large amount of information that is available. It will not be the role of the school to add even more bits of information, but to act as a clearing house and help students to create meaning in what is often experienced as an information chaos.

The Basic Is Also to Learn How to Learn

The deciding factor between successful and unsuccessful students is their ability to connect new information with an existing understanding of the structure of a subject field. They have learned to figure out how things work or under what conditions they function (understanding procedures) and in what context those conditions exist to function successfully (context understanding). They have also learned effective and different ways to reason. They know how to set goals, develop positive relationships in learning and to be self-critical (Dalin, 1991).

Combined with the learning of learning, the learning of the structure of fields of study must constitute a central aspect of schooling, and it is becoming more and more important. Students are being fed so much information that they must have conceptual frameworks in which to place most of this information. If we are correct in our assessment that the social capital of most students is shrinking, then the school must pick up that slack (Dalin & Rust, 1996).

Problem Solving

Challenges do not come with ready-made solutions and connections with fields of study. Often students work with problems for which specialists have only partial solutions or no solutions at all. Their work is devoted, not to solutions, but to gaining a grasp of the problems themselves. However important an understanding of subject fields is, that is not sufficient in today's world, and it will certainly not be sufficient in tomorrow's world.

Communication

It is likely that society will continue to develop horizontal structures that have no clear lines of authority structure. In a horizontal society it becomes important to be able to communicate, to have the ability to handle challenges between people, and to be able to understand and use information effectively. Many students do not have the internal capacity to learn communication skills simply by living in today's world. They fail to meet the challenges of an often-tough peer pressure or of resolving conflicts with parents in the home. They require some guidance in learning how to increase their own insights. Good interpersonal proficiency is an ongoing experiment in how to learn together.

Good communication skills are also linked to the mastery of one or several foreign languages. It is true that in this age of globalization English seems (so far) to be the one "common" language. It could well be that Chinese is the most commonly used language on the Internet within 5–10 years. With the learning of a foreign language, a deeper understanding of the foreign culture is also important. In today's communication it is also of basic importance to learn the "language" of computers and to be able to interpret and to use pictures.

Knowledge and Understanding

School culture is built on the misconception that understanding is synonymous with knowing. In school we learn to describe and explain. Understanding is something more than knowing. We understand something only when it has meaning, when it leads to practical use, when it leads to insight. This does not mean that knowledge is not important. Rather, it is tied together to the intimate understanding (Max-Neef, 1992).

If learners are to have greater understanding, they must internalize the knowledge, the explanations and the insights from formal learning. For example, it is not enough simply to learn how ecological factors affect each other; one must learn how critical ecological understanding is. The young, as well as adults, must become directly involved in ecological preservation by working with conservation organizations (Dalin & Rust, 1996). If the school is to be successful in combining knowledge with understanding, it must help students to become more responsible for their own and other's learning.

Closeness and Belonging

If the young are to grow and to develop understanding, they must experience closeness and belonging. Many students develop low self-esteem and self-confidence, sometimes because they are not as close to their parents and other adults as they need to be. Children and youth have the need for adult role models, and they often only find peers to associate with.

The Consumer and the Producer

One of the characteristics of today's world is that a large amount of time is devoted to consumption. We are all consumers. Because we are at the receiving end, we are not free to decide. But we can learn how to be critical consumers. It is also increasingly important for students to learn how to be producers, not only in producing goods and services, but to be creative in producing ideas, new insights, art, politics, research, in fact in any part of human culture.

In the future society, to an increasing degree, religion, politics and economic interests will compete with one another for people's attention. Each of these spheres has a strong self-serving motive. One of the assignments schools must have is to prepare children and youth to participate critically and actively in making sound choices, to be free and independent people in a complicated society. The school is, perhaps, the one institution that does not have economical, political or ideological interests. Therefore the school is the most reliable institution we know that can prepare students to make active and independent choices (Dalin & Rust, 1996, p. 85).

Summary and Reflection

The changes we have described open up for a variety of practical educational models. Whatever "model of schooling" one decides to implement, the following questions need to be answered:

1. Who is a student?
2. Who is a teacher?
3. What is the curriculum?
4. What is a textbook?
5. What/where is the classroom?
6. What is a productive use of the learning resources?
7. Who pays?
8. Who owns and who controls?
9. Can schools learn?
10. What do we want the school to be in Year 2020?

None of these questions have only one correct answer.

References

Anderson, J. R. (Ed.). (1981). *Cognitive skills and their acquisition.* Hillsdale, NJ: Lawrence Erlbaum Associates.

Bildungskommission NRW. (1995). *Zukunft der Bildung, Schule der Zukunft* [*The future of education — The school is the future*]. Berlin: Luchterhand.

Coleman, J. S. (1987). Families and schools. *Educational Researcher, 16*(6), 32–38.

Coleman, J. S., & Hoffer, T. (1987). *Public and private high schools: The impact of communities.* New York: Basic Books.

Dalin, P. (1991). Å lære å tenke [To learn how to think]. *Norsk skoleblad*, 24–28.
Dalin, P., & Rust, V. D. (1996). *Towards schooling for the twenty-first century.* London: Cassell.
Küng, H. (1990). *Projekt Weltethos* [*World ethics*]. München: R. Piper GmbH & Co. KG.
Max-Neef, M. A. (1992). *From the outside looking in: Experiences in "Barefoot Economic."* London: Atlantic Highlands.
Resnick, L. (1983). Toward a cognitive theory of instruction. In S. Paris, G. M. Olson & H. W. Stevenson (Eds.), *Learning and motivation in the classroom* (pp. 5–38). Hillsdale, NJ: Lawrence Erlbaum Associates.
von Weizsacker, E. U. (1992). *Why the North must act first.* Geneva: International Academy for the Environment.

17

Partnerships for School Development: The Way Ahead

John Chi-kin Lee, Leslie Nai-kwai Lo & Allan Walker

Schools are now encountering the fourth broad phase of educational reform, a movement which emphasizes the enhancement of "the 'capacity' of the school system and its communities [as] the key to reform" (Fullan, 1998, p. 672). There is also clear evidence that successful schools and districts adopt outreach strategies and seek support from external agencies, including universities and state departments (Fullan, 1998, 2001). The chapters in this book have provided different examples and insights into university-school partnerships and changes in school development. These chapters help navigate the way forward for partnerships for school development and illustrate both the conceptual and empirical possibilities therein. From the wide array of issues discussed by the authors, we have selected the following five as being of special interest. These themes, to a certain extent, echo Sanders and Epstein's (1998) analysis on dominant themes of school-family-community partnerships and educational change, which comprise some of the following components: (1) Students need multiple sources of support to succeed in school and in their communities; (2) teachers and administrators are initially resistant to increasing family involvement; (3) policies are important precursors to program development; (4) programs and practices of partnership make a difference in whether, how, and which families are involved in their children's education; (5) the important contribution of international research on partnerships, and that research is needed to understand differences in family involvement across countries.

These key issues are presented as propositions which serve to sketch an initial map of where inquiry and planned action may proceed in future (Walker & Dimmock, 2000).

Proposition 1

In order to help facilitate change in school development, there is a real need to foster various forms of university-school partnership as well as collaboration among occupational groups both within and outside the school and the university locally, nationally, and internationally.

Many different forms of partnerships were evident in the chapters. These ranged from teacher collaboration in the classroom to whole school development programs. Many partnerships discussed in various chapters were built around university-school partnerships, mostly collaboration between teachers and academics. In addition, Butcher and others highlighted the emergence of broader, university-community partnership using the example of an outreach program. The development of alternative, magnet, and charter schools also illustrated examples of partnerships between the school and local community. While explaining charter and alternative school, Parrett and Willison discussed choice for parents and students, whether it was to provide specialist education services or to cater for children with special learning characteristics.

Lim reported on partnership among the professions (architects and educationalists), schools (primary and secondary school students, teachers), and the community (parents, universities, non-governmental bodies, government departments) in a cross-disciplinary experimental partnership in Hong Kong. The example of home-school partnership provided by Dockett, Perry and Howard emphasized the development and implementation of educational partnerships needed different players, ranging from parents, educators, local community members, and the children themselves.

Other than the increasing importance of collaboration among professionals, school staff, and community members in promoting school, teacher and student development, there were calls for partnership and collaboration among teachers within the university and the school organization themselves. For the former, Van Scoy and Ebert suggested: "We must find ways to support on-site work at schools as a regular, and appropriately rewarded, component of university-faculty positions, in order for PDSs [Professional Development Schools] to withstand the test of time. This includes promoting involvement of university faculty, not only within education, but in the arts and sciences as well." For the latter, Berg argued from a multiprofessional perspective that teachers of different specialties and school leaders are expected to have "knowledge of and insights into the school's basic mission ..., and how he/she, in cooperation with fellow teachers as well as other school personnel, can carry out operational tasks that correspond to the mission's content and implications."

Partnership for school development can indeed be established beyond the local community. An example of a university (institute)-school project discussed by Hui and her colleagues highlighted the potential for fostering partnership between institutions from distant places within the same country, such as Shanghai and Hong Kong. Moreover, the experimentation in Hong Kong of the Accelerated Schools Project depicted the possibilities for international collaboration for university-school partnership. These two examples reveal the value held by such connections despite the tyranny of distance.

The above examples echo Caldwell's (1999) remarks on strategic intentions for the new future school in action:

> Schools will establish a richer range of professionals to work with and support teachers. Many of these will be located on site, but increasingly more will be located in other places as the best services are located and made available to meet the needs of all students and students, teachers, and other professionals will increasingly work in teams, reflecting a pattern that is widely evident in workplace arrangements in other fields, with many parallels for professionals in education and medicine. (p. 56)

Proposition 2

Change in school development hinges on various factors including school culture, leadership, time, and whether a common vision and trust can be built between the partners.

This major proposition relates to factors that appear to be conducive to school development. One of the key factors affecting the momentum of school development, as mentioned by Levin, is school culture, which, most importantly, encompasses expectations about student learning. A number of chapters revealed that school culture was often incompatible with proposed school reform. Discussing the Accelerated Schools Project, Levin suggested that differential progress in school development was related to leadership, time, and examination pressure. For example, principals who were less receptive to change and committed to leading the process of change may not support the development of inquiry and powerful learning. The heavy emphasis on performance in public examinations may maintain the status quo, which relies on students' memorization of information as the dominant teaching strategy. Hopkins reinforced the importance of time for teachers to conduct meetings, learn new things, and observe each other, as well as the importance of cultural change to sustain an authentic approach to school improvement. Dyer and Cheung emphasized the influence of school culture and school climate on the development of self-evaluation as a method for school improvement. Pang and Cheung referred to Senge's five disciplines for school's learning capacity, one of which was shared vision. It is "only by reaching a compromise among the individuals and further developing the vision into a common direction can a shared vision be honored with teachers' commitment."

Many scholars (e.g., Goodlad & Sirotnik, 1988; Lee & Lo, 2002) comment that there is a difference in culture between the university and the school, the former being reflection-oriented and the latter being action-oriented. While this dichotomy in culture between the two types of organization may lead to complementary benefits through symbiosis, the transformation in role of a university researcher from an expert to a facilitator is often a challenge to universities. As Day (1999) remarks, "Identifying the strengths and limitations of university researchers and teacher educators in relation to school and teacher development needs will be a key strategic factor in initiating and responding to system needs in the future" (p. 172).

In this respect, Lee as well as Lo and Lai highlighted the importance of a common vision or shared meaning of the partnership between the partners on their strength of collaboration. Butcher and her colleagues echoed that shared agenda in the establishment phase and provision of mutually beneficial environment in the maintenance phase are important principles for the development of the community-university partnership.

In addition to shared vision and meaning, Lamprianou and Boyle suggested that the establishment of trust and cooperation between the partners in the early stages of partnership development is essential. As Hui and her colleagues explained, "A trusting relationship can avoid a lot of misunderstandings resulting from different expectations and cultures. It also means that both partners are willing to think in different perspectives or from different viewpoints."

Proposition 3

Given the increasing examples of working partnerships in different contexts, there is a need to develop systematic and comparative studies on the operation and sustainability of partnership for change in school development.

The development of partnerships with different foci reflects to some extent the issues or needs of particular societies. For example, the partnership project in Australia led by Butcher and others aims to develop a mutual understanding between trainee teachers and the community of the problems of social justice and equity that are endemic in society, and therefore in schools. In contrast, the development of alternative, magnet, and charter schools in the United States supports the argument for responsiveness to market forces in education and democracy at work in education — where consumers of schooling can shape the provision according to their needs and interests.

The partnership in the United Kingdom explained by Lamprianou and Boyle attempted to confound the tendency for schools in these days of examinations and national testing to teach to the test. This is a generic, almost universal, problem which is also prevalent in East Asian societies such as Hong Kong, where "the memorization-examination process is so deeply embedded."

While different partnerships have various emphases, the majority of those described in this book seem to be heavily influenced by some form of "performance-based" reform. As Hopkins explained, "Schools in many countries have been subject to a barrage of legislation and policy that has meant changes in curriculum, assessment, governance, and financing. Both England and Hong Kong have perhaps had more of this than most countries, but the phenomenon of large-scale reform by central governments is worldwide." These developments have brought a new "internationalism," or a genuine willingness on the part of some scholars, policy makers, and practitioners to learn from the experiences of others, if for no other reason than they may come to understand their own context better. However, we must be cautious in making comparisons between systems on superficial grounds with minimal understanding of the deep historical and cultural roots underpinning them (Walker & Dimmock, 2000).

To date, there is a dearth of literature that synthesizes and compares the varied practices and cases of partnerships in education that have been developing around the globe. Two major lines of inquiry are suggested:

1. How the development of partnerships in education responds to the educational agenda in the local and national/societal context? How does the operation of partnerships of a similar nature and interactions between partners differ across societies?
2. How effective on school, teacher and student development respectively are the solutions offered by different partnerships in education in a similar context and what are the constraints?

Proposition 4

More resources, support, and reward structures are needed to sustain partnership endeavors.

As mentioned in the introductory chapter, Fullan (2000) highlights the need for the establishment of external reform infrastructure for large districts through policies focusing on decentralization, local capacity building (investments of training, professional development, and ongoing support), rigorous external accountability, and stimulation of innovation (investments in research, development, and innovative networks).

The successful development of staff development partnerships between Shanghai and Hong Kong highlights the importance of administrative and financial support from both organizations. Lee referred to the survival (or longevity) standard for assessing the success and failure of reforms (Cuban, 1998) and echoed the importance of sustaining educational innovations. Past experiences show that systematic, deep change or institutionalization of any reform initiative takes about 5 to 10 years (Lee et al., 2002; Valdez Perez, Milstein, Wood, & Jacquez, 1999). Various factors, such as principal turnover and lack of support, may destroy the culture and early success of schools engaged in school reform efforts. As Noblit and Patterson (2001) succinctly remark, "A school, once reformed, is not reformed forever" (p. 146). It is therefore suggested that governments and other organizations should explore the establishment of "regular" funding for supporting partnership endeavors beyond the pilot stage.

In the case of Hong Kong, the Quality Education Fund (QEF) has been a major funding agency for school-university partnership projects and school-based projects seeking university assistance. However, the QEF only considers projects on a short-term basis and will not support projects on a recurrent basis. This appears to run counter to experiences in the United States, which shows that private foundations, corporate or government (federal) funding have been responsible for the development and dissemination of the well-known school change models such as the Accelerated Schools, the Success for All, the School Development Program and the Coalition of Essential Schools (Slavin & Madden, 2001).

In addition to the provision of funding and training of university people for developing partnerships, one of the obstacles to successful collaboration is the lack of reward for people either in higher education or in the school (Clark, 1988; Tang & Lee, 2002). The challenge of Professional Development Schools (PDSs) discussed by Van Scoy and Ebert pointed to the concern for the reward structure of the university and "a narrow definition of scholarship that [did] not encompass PDS work." The experience of Unified Professional Development Project (UPDP) suggested that: "If the good work of UPDP is to continue and become institutionalized, it has to be given proper recognition as a formal structure within the Faculty of Education in the University [of Hong Kong]."

In future, there seems to be a need to broaden the portfolio of university researchers from their traditional expertise in research and knowledge generation to new expertise in combining knowledge creation, development, and consultancy organically (Day, 1999). This can only be achieved through a redefinition of scholarship in education toward more emphasis on scholarships of application and teaching (alongside scholarships of discovery and integration) which are exemplified by providing professional consultation to schools as well as the design and development of school-based curricula and instructional materials within and outside school settings (Boyer, 1990; Chan, 1998). As Lieberman (1997) puts it succinctly:

> We must shift our thinking about the knowledge base of teaching and learning
> .... We are hampered from doing so because we typically adopt a paternalistic
> attitude toward schoolpeople and because there is a lack of institutional
> recognition and support for those professors who are actively working in the
> schools. The university must change its view of scholarship so that it recognizes
> and rewards active participation in schools (and the research and writing that
> it generates) as valuable — and time-consuming — scholarly activity.

Proposition 5

Partnerships in education need to meet challenges posed by changes in society in future.

Dalin took a futuristic stance with respect to societal changes and the implications for the learning needs of students in the next 20 or 30 years. One of the visions for the new century is "from dominance to partnership in social relations" (Dalin & Rust, 1996, pp. 63–64). There are possibilities for various partnerships to enhance student learning, for example:

1. To enhance students' knowledge and understanding of ecological matters and their problem-solving capability, "the young, as well as adults, must become directly involved in ecological preservation by working with conservation organizations." Schools can also form partnerships with multicultural groups, environmentalists, and advanced firms to help students get involved in environmental learning and engaged in environmental action in difficult situations (Dalin, 1998; Dalin & Rust, 1996). Likewise, other professionals and specialists connected with the issues in the school curriculum can be involved to provide opportunities for students to resolve real-life problems.

2. With regard to fulfilling the communication needs of children and youth, home-school and university-home partnerships could be developed to help and equip both parents and children to handle and resolve conflicts. To allow children to communicate with people from multicultural backgrounds, schools can foster partnerships with local community organizations or overseas institutions which design and implement activities for interactions among children of different ethnic, linguistic, and cultural backgrounds.

3. With regard to the learning need of closeness and belonging, "children and youth have the need for adult role models, and they often only find peers to associate with." It may be desirable for schools to establish partnerships with alumni associations and professional organizations where "mentors" could be recruited to extend students' exposure and help cultivate their self-esteem and self-confidence.

Conclusion

The five propositions hopefully portray a future-oriented, pluralistic orientation for partnerships in education for school development. In a future "model or vision of schooling," it is probable that everyone including children and adults are partners acting as both co-learners and teachers. They are all partners to provide an everyday life curriculum and construct together authentic learning experiences for meeting the challenges of a rapidly changing world. Dalin (1998, p. 1067) suggests that we may:

1. Help the involved teachers to work in settings with human resources from the local community and industry, to make the task challenging and interesting and to use it as a part of Staff Development;
2. Help the change agents to solicit administrative, funding, and professional support from the educational authority and other constituencies to test the comprehensive reform in a five plus five year test with in-build and ongoing evaluation.

In a nutshell, future schools need home-school, community, school council, and district partnerships too as they can either support or help facilitate school change. Nonetheless, the realization of this vision needs our commitment to act as partners in providing quality schooling for the 21st century.

References

Boyer, E. L. (1990). *Scholarship reconsidered: Priorities of the professoriate.* Princeton, NJ: The Carnegie Foundation for the Advancement of Teaching.

Caldwell, B. (1999). Education for the public good: Strategic intentions for the 21st century. In D. D. Marsh (Ed.), *Preparing our schools for the 21st century* (pp. 45–64). Alexandria, VA: Association for Supervision and Curriculum Development.

Chan, D. W. (1998). Rethinking scholarship in education in Hong Kong: Implications for educational research. *Educational Research Journal, 13*(2), 141–149.

Clark, R. W. (1988). School-university relationships: An interpretive review. In K. A. Sirotnik & J. I. Goodlad (Eds.), *School-university partnerships in action: Concepts, cases, and concerns* (pp. 32–65). New York: Teachers College Press.

Cuban, L. (1998). How schools change reforms: Redefining reform success and failure. *Teachers College Record, 99*(3), 453–477.

Dalin, P. (1998). Developing the twenty-first century school: A challenge to reformers. In A. Hargreaves, A. Lieberman, M. Fullan, & D. Hopkins (Eds.), *International handbook of educational change: Part two* (pp. 1059–1073). Dordrecht; Boston: Kluwer Academic Publishers.

Dalin, P., & Rust, V. D. (1996). *Towards schooling for the twenty-first century.* London: Cassell.

Day, C. (1999). *Developing teachers: The challenges of lifelong learning.* London; Philadelphia: Falmer Press.

Fullan, M. (1998). Introduction: Scaling up the educational change process. In A. Hargreaves, A. Lieberman, M. Fullan, & D. Hopkins (Eds.), *International handbook of educational change: Part two* (pp. 671–672). Dordrecht; Boston: Kluwer Academic Publishers.

Fullan, M. (2000). The three stories of education reform. *Phi Delta Kappan, 81*(8), 581–584.

Fullan, M. (2001). *The new meaning of educational change* (3rd ed.). New York: Teachers College Press.

Goodlad, J. I., & Sirotnik, K. (1988). The future of school-university partnerships. In K. A. Sirotnik & J. I. Goodlad (Eds.), *School-university partnerships in action: Concepts, cases, and concerns* (pp. 205–225). New York: Teachers College Press.

Lee, J. C. K., Chung, S. Y. P., Lo, L. N. K., Wong, H. W., Chiu, C. S., Ho, E. S. C., Leung, A. S. M., Pang, N. S. K., Sze, P. M. M., Walker, A., & Xiao, J. (2002). *The Accelerated Schools for Quality Education Project final report.* Hong Kong: Faculty of Education and the Hong Kong Institute of Educational Research, The Chinese University of Hong Kong.

Lee, J. C. K., & Lo, L. N. K. (2002). School-university partnerships in educational change: View of paradigms. In Lee, J. C. K. (Ed.), *Curriculum, teaching and school reforms: Educational development in a new century* (pp. 213–235) [in Chinese]. Hong Kong: The Chinese University Press.

Lieberman, A. (1997). Navigating the four C's: Building a bridge over troubled waters. In D. J. Flinders & S. J. Thornton (Eds.), *The curriculum studies reader* (pp. 350–354). New York: Routledge.

Noblit, G. W., & Patterson, J. A. (2001). The School Development Program and education reform. In G. W. Noblit, W. W. Malloy, & C. E. Malloy (Eds.), *"The kids got smarter": Case studies of successful Comer schools* (pp. 131–148). Cresskill, NJ: Hampton Press.

Sanders, M. G., & Epstein, J. L. (1998). School-family-community partnerships and educational change: International perspectives. In A. Hargreaves, A. Lieberman, M. Fullan, & D. Hopkins (Eds.), *International handbook of educational change: Part one* (pp. 482–502). Dordrecht; Boston: Kluwer Academic Publishers.

Slavin, R. E., & Madden, N. A. (Eds.). (2001). *Success for all: Research and reform in elementary education*. Mahwah, NJ; London: Lawrence Erlbaum Associates.

Tang, M. S., & Lee, J. C. K. (2002). Curriculum change through university and school partnership — The case study of whole language writing in Hong Kong primary school. In Lee, J. C. K. (Ed.), *Curriculum, teaching and school reforms: Educational development in a new century* (pp. 287–310) [in Chinese]. Hong Kong: The Chinese University Press

Valdez Perez, A. L., Milstein, M. M., Wood, C. J., & Jacquez, D. (1999). *How to turn a school around: What principals can do*. Thousand Oaks, CA: Corwin Press.

Walker, A., & Dimmock, C. (2000). Mapping the way ahead: Leading educational leadership into the globalised world. *School Leadership and Management, 20* (2), 227–234.